WHAT SCIENCE OFFERS THE HUMANITIES

What Science Offers the Humanities examines some of the deep problems facing current approaches to the study of culture. It focuses especially on the excesses of postmodernism but also acknowledges serious problems with postmodernism's harshest critics. In short, Edward Slingerland argues that, in order for the humanities to progress, its scholars need to take seriously contributions from the natural sciences – in particular research on human cognition – which demonstrate that any separation of the mind and body is entirely untenable. The author provides suggestions for how humanists might begin to utilize these scientific discoveries without conceding that science has the last word on morality, religion, art, and literature. Calling into question such deeply entrenched dogmas as the "blank slate" theory of nature, strong social constructivism, and the ideal of disembodied reason, *What Science Offers the Humanities* replaces the humanities-sciences divide with a more integrated approach to the study of culture.

Edward Slingerland taught in the School of Religion and the Department of East Asian Languages and Cultures at the University of Southern California, where he was recipient of the 2002 General Education Teaching Award. He is currently an associate professor of Asian Studies and a Canada Research Chair in Chinese Thought and Embodied Cognition at the University of British Columbia. His previous books include *The Analects of Confucius* and *Effortless Action: Wu-wei as Conceptual Metaphor and Spiritual Ideal in Early China*, which won the American Academy of Religion's 2003 Best First Book in the History of Religions Award.

What Science Offers the Humanities

Integrating Body and Culture

EDWARD SLINGERLAND

University of British Columbia

CAMBRIDGE
UNIVERSITY PRESS

CAMBRIDGE UNIVERSITY PRESS
Cambridge, New York, Melbourne, Madrid, Cape Town, Singapore,
São Paulo, Delhi, Dubai, Tokyo, Mexico City

Cambridge University Press
32 Avenue of the Americas, New York, NY 10013-2473, USA

www.cambridge.org
Information on this title: www.cambridge.org/9780521701518

First published 2008
Reprinted 2010

A catalog record for this publication is available from the British Library.

Library of Congress Cataloging in Publication Data
Slingerland, Edward G. (Edward Gilman)
What science offers the humanities : integrating body and culture / Edward Slingerland.
p. cm.
Includes bibliographical references and index.
ISBN 978-0-521-87770-1 (hardback) – ISBN 978-0-521-70151-8 (pbk.)
1. Philosophy. 2. Science and the humanities. 3. Humanity. 4. Body, Human.
I. Title.
B53.S5355   2008
001.3–dc22   2007016575

ISBN 978-0-521-87770-1 Hardback
ISBN 978-0-521-70151-8 Paperback

Contents

Figures

Preface

The intellectual autobiographies of academic researchers are normally expected to remain invisible as they go about producing their work, which in turn is intended to stand alone and be understood and judged on its own merits. One of the many contributions to intellectual life made by the loose collection of movements I am going to be calling "postmodernism" in the pages that follow is the claim that the author's biography is not intellectually irrelevant. Although this – like many other postmodernist claims – has too often been taken to absurd extremes, explaining how I came to this project will, I think, help to clarify its motivation and the thrust of its argument. This will then also, I hope, make it clearer why someone might want to read this book.

When my colleagues and friends from graduate school see what I am reading these days, their reactions range from puzzled to horrified. When I mention the term "behavioral neuroscience" among a group of religious studies scholars or sinologists, most smile politely and begin slowly backing away, casting about for a safe exit route. As they slip away, I sometimes note wistful expressions of regret: they know that I had a perfectly respectable humanistic upbringing. What went wrong? I was first trained as a sinologist and specialist in early Chinese texts (both my B.A. and M.A. are in the classical Chinese language), and then my interest in comparative thought led me to a doctoral program in religious studies, where I received a firm grounding in my specialty of early Chinese thought, as well as in related areas of Western thought, such as German philosophical hermeneutics and the "virtue ethics" movement in philosophy. My dissertation was a fairly traditional work of intellectual history, from a more or less analytic philosophical angle.

Things began to go awry after graduate school, a few months into my first job, when a student recommended a book that had just come out, George Lakoff and Mark Johnson's *Philosophy in the Flesh* (1999). It immediately became clear to me upon reading this work how conceptual metaphor theory could solve some deep theoretical problems that had been bothering me in my dissertation. Even more, Lakoff and Johnson's work pointed to a way of approaching human thought and culture that seemed to me to avoid the pitfalls of both the traditional objectivism informing the work of my colleagues in philosophy and the postmodern relativism that I saw as paralyzing most other areas of the humanities. The central claim of Lakoff and Johnson's book is that human cognition – the production, communication, and processing of meaning – is not the product of an entirely free and autonomous rational faculty, as the Anglo-American analytic tradition would have it, but is rather heavily dependent on more fundamental, bodily based cognitive processes. These mappings take several forms, but the most dramatic is cross-domain projection, where part of the structure of a more concrete or clearly organized domain (the *source* domain, for instance *darkness*) is used to understand and talk about another, usually more abstract or less clearly structured, domain (the *target* domain, for instance *ignorance*). It is this sort of projective mapping that cognitive linguists refer to as "metaphor," which – understood in this way – encompasses simile and analogy as well as metaphor in the more traditional sense. Conceptual metaphor, Lakoff and Johnson argue, serves as one of our primary tools for reasoning about ourselves and the world – especially about relatively abstract or unstructured domains such as the self, morality, or time. I found their theory to be an extremely powerful tool for approaching Warring States Chinese thought. The theoretical stance of "embodied realism" that Lakoff and Johnson presented also seemed to me to be an ideal path out of the mire of cultural relativism that I continue to see as impeding substantive work in comparative studies.

To invoke the common LIFE AS JOURNEY metaphor, this initial encounter with conceptual metaphor theory turned out to be not a detour, but rather the first step in an entirely new intellectual direction. I hosted a conference at the University of Southern California attended by both Lakoff and Johnson, and also got to know Mark Turner and Gilles Fauconnier, pioneers in the field of mental space theory and conceptual blending. Blending theory encompasses conceptual metaphor theory but goes beyond it to argue that *all* of human cognition – even literal and logical thought – involves the creation of mental spaces and mappings between them. As I explored more widely in the cognitive linguistics literature, I came to see that this work formed just one part of a rich and growing field focused on the imagistic basis of thought and the grounding of abstract human cognition in recurring features of perception and action. This led me to work explaining how these features of perception and action are in turn subserved by an integrated physical system, the body-brain, that evolved gradually from other life-forms. Hence a burgeoning interest in evolutionary psychology, behavioral neuroscience, nonhuman animal cognition, and various branches of psychology. The relatively new field of evolutionary psychology seeks to explain how the human brain and the workings of human cognition can be seen as a response to adaptive pressure in the human "ancestral environment," while the study of nonhuman animal cognition helps to put the achievements of human cognition in their proper phylogenic context. Behavioral neuroscience attempts to provide an account of, among other things, how the structure of the human brain is related to the workings of human cognition and human perception, how neurological events are related to overall behavior, and how analogue schematic structures such as conceptual metaphors might be neurologically instantiated. Cognitive and developmental psychology look for evidence for the emergence of the sorts of mental "organs" or modules that an evolutionarily informed model of the human brain would expect to find – bolstering their universalist claims with cross-cultural studies of prelinguistic infants and children – and recent work in social psychology fundamentally calls into question folk models of human agency and the relationship of conscious processes to actual behavior.

My contact with scholars in these fields eventually led to my current position at the University of British Columbia, where I have been hired not only as a traditionally trained sinologist and scholar of early Chinese thought but also as part of an emerging interdisciplinary field of embodied approaches to the study of human culture. I now find myself surrounded by colleagues trained in social psychology, neuroimaging, cross-cultural psychology, developmental psychology, evolutionary psychology, nonhuman animal cognition, biological anthropology, postrationalist economics, and the neuroscience of perception – all eager to share their knowledge with, learn from, and engage in collaborative projects with scholars from more traditional humanistic disciplines.

This book essentially represents a field report to my fellow humanists concerning the long, strange intellectual journey into the cognitive and natural sciences that I have been on for the past five or six years. I believe that I have come back with something of interest: an outline of what a coherent and empirically responsible alternative to objectivist or postmodernist approaches to the study of culture might look like, and some strong feelings about how we humanists can benefit from establishing collaborative ties with our colleagues in the sciences. The central conviction behind this work is that it would behoove humanists to start paying a lot more attention to what is happening on the other side of campus. Almost any randomly selected issue of *Science* or *Nature* has at least one article that directly addresses some matter of central humanist concern, and journals from the more human-level disciplines, such as *Cognition* or *Behavioral and Brain Sciences*, are invariably rich minefields of relevant material that is, for the most part, entirely unexploited by scholars in the humanities. Cognitive scientists and neuroscientists, for instance, are making extraordinary discoveries concerning the relationship of human thought, language, and perception – a central and venerable issue in philosophy and cultural studies but hitherto explored by humanists primarily by means of armchair speculation. Similarly, recent work on the role of emotions, bodily biases, and "fast and frugal" heuristics in human reasoning processes bears intimately on lively debates in moral philosophy and calls into question rational-actor models that have traditionally dominated economics. Fields on the fringe of the humanities such as economics – more immediately and directly concerned with applications to the real world, and therefore where getting things wrong is more immediately apparent and consequential – have been relatively quick to respond to this sort of work, but little of it has penetrated to the core humanities disciplines.

If we humanists have much to learn from the natural sciences, the reverse is also true: humanists have a great deal to contribute to scientific research. As discoveries in the biological and cognitive sciences have begun to blur traditional disciplinary boundaries, researchers in these fields have found their work bringing them into contact with the sort of high-level issues that traditionally have been the domain of the core humanities disciplines, and often their lack of formal training in these areas leaves them groping in the dark or attempting to reinvent the wheel. This is where humanist expertise can and should play a crucial role in guiding and interpreting the results of scientific exploration – something that can occur only when scholars on *both* sides of the humanities–natural science divide are willing to talk to one another. This book is designed to help my colleagues in the core humanities disciplines see where the points of contact between their own work and the research coming out of the cognitive and biological sciences may lie, as well as how an "embodied" view of the person fundamentally problematizes the dualistic model of the self that informs most of our work. It is becoming increasingly evident that the traditionally sharp divide between the humanities and natural sciences is no longer viable, and this requires that researchers on both sides of the former divide become radically more interdisciplinary. This book is intended as an argument for *why* an integrated approach to human culture is, in fact, necessary, as well as a hint of what such an approach might look like.

∾

This project has consumed the last five years of my academic life, and over the course of those years I have been aided by countless individuals and organizations, so I apologize in advance for any omissions in these acknowledgments.

First I would like to thank my acquisitions editor at Cambridge University Press, Andy Beck. When I approached him years ago with the idea for this rather speculative project he was immediately supportive, and over its development Andy has provided a steady stream of sound editorial advice that has shaped the final product in many ways. I am very grateful to him for having faith in me and in this project.

I also owe a debt of gratitude to Peter Nosco, Darrin Lehman, and Nancy Gallini at the University of British Columbia, who were not at all deterred by this crazy project and made it possible for me to find an institutional home that genuinely values interdisciplinary work. "Interdisciplinarity" has become a fashionable buzzword in recent years, but UBC has turned out to be one of the few places I know of that is genuinely serious about humanities–natural science dialogue and eager to encourage it. In this regard, this project also owes a great deal to the Canada Research Chairs program. My CRC position has provided me not only with the time and resources to complete this manuscript but also with a higher, more broadly appealing research profile that has directly led to a variety of helpful connections and new research collaboration opportunities. This is particularly important for a sinologist, since Chinese studies – especially early Chinese studies – is too often viewed by outsiders as an overly specialized, hermetically sealed discipline.

In the early stages of my research at the University of Southern California I benefited from a Templeton/Metanexus grant for the study of science and religion awarded to USC, which provided me with a wonderful venue for interdisciplinary conversation and facilitated my contact with scholars such as Michael Ruse, Owen Flanagan, and Michael Arbib. A Pew Foundation grant for the study of religion and civic culture awarded to USC similarly gave me an opportunity to meet and to benefit from conversation with one of my intellectual heroes, Charles Taylor, whose work features so prominently in Chapter 6. Thanks also to my former chair at USC, Donald Miller, for having involved me in these grants.

Mohammad Reza Memar-Sadeghi very generously offered to read Chapters 1 and 5, and Brian Boyd heroically slogged through the entire manuscript and provided detailed and extremely helpful feedback. For a variety of reasons, I was unable to make all of the changes they recommended, and if my treatment of the philosophy of science material, in particular, is found by some to be lacking in sophistication or nuance it is entirely my own fault. Substantial and very helpful comments on the manuscript were also provided by Joel Sahleen, Jason Slone, Mark Collard, Joe Henrich, Tim Rohrer, Jon Gottschall, and the anonymous referees who reviewed this manuscript for Cambridge University Press. I have also benefited from feedback from Sharalyn Orbaugh, Jonathan Schooler, Owen Flanagan, Ara Norenzayan, Steve Heine, Mark Turner, Ray Corbey, Todd Handy, Randy Nesse, Coll Thrush, Simon Martin, Barbara Dancygier, Andrew Martindale, Jess Tracy, Liz Dunn, Emma Cohen, and David Anderson. Thanks also to Ian McEwan for a bit of music criticism that helped to smooth out a hastily conceived chapter conclusion.

Monika Dix, Douglas Lanam, and Lang Foo provided research assistance at various stages of the project. I am grateful for the assistance of my production editor Camilla T. Knapp, as well as for the meticulous and sensitive work of my copy editor, Susan Greenberg, who smoothed out the many rough spots in earlier versions of this manuscript. Thanks also to Mark Johnson, Steven Mithen, Marty Smith, *In These Times*, and *The Onion* for permission to use copyrighted images or text.

Most of all I would like to thank my wife, Stefania Burk. She not only has put up with me for the last several years as I feverishly worked on this project but also has been a constant source of conceptual critique, stylistic and editorial advice, and plain good sense. This book would have a very different shape had it not been subjected to the force of her sharp mind, intolerance for jargon, and infallible sense of what is important and what is not. I dedicate this book to her and to my daughter, Sofia Gianna, who was born just as this manuscript was taking its final shape, and who remains a constant source of joy, wonder, and profound sleep deprivation.

WHAT SCIENCE OFFERS THE HUMANITIES

Introduction

*I*T IS SOMETHING OF A COMMONPLACE THESE DAYS THAT THE HUMANITIES are facing a crisis, or at the very least find themselves having, in the words of Bruno Latour, "run out of steam" (2004). In the decades leading up to the end of the millennium, "Theory" triumphantly swept through the core humanities departments – not just literature departments but also anthropology, sociology, religious studies, art history, media and area studies, and large swaths of classics and history departments. It left in its wake a global suspicion of any sort of truth-claim, coupled with a fervent conviction that the distinguishing mark of "sophisticated" scholarship was an ability to engage with a prescribed pantheon of theorists. Now that the headiness of this intellectual revolution has worn off, an intellectual hangover appears to have set in. The application of theory to its object of analysis, for instance, has grown stultifyingly routinized and mechanical, characterized by precisely the kind of rigidity and deference to authority from which Theory was to liberate us. It was quite exciting the first time someone took the tools of analysis that Derrida originally applied to Rousseau or Plato and aimed them at a piece of modern Chinese literature (I am old enough to remember that!). The expansion of deconstruction to encompass media images and packaging – the absorption of *everything* into the world of text – also felt new and deliciously revolutionary in its initial stages.

Decades down the line, though, it is perhaps not unreasonable to ask if the world really needs one more application of Derridean deconstruction to some as yet unexamined corner of popular culture or the traditional canon. More importantly, if we *do* need it, to what end? It is hard to sustain the intellectual momentum of a theoretical playfulness that denies the validity of theory, or an interest in opulent, impenetrable prose that denies the existence of anything beyond luxuriating in language for language's sake. It also rather takes the wind out of one's intellectual sails when, as Latour (2004) notes, one's radically skeptical critique can be so easily coopted by one's enemies – the "Right," corporate culture, and other "bad guys" – for their own nefarious purposes, such as denying the reality of global warming or selling slave labor–produced sneakers to gullible teenagers. It is therefore not hard to see why intelligent undergraduates, often drawn to the study of literature or art or language by the love of the subject material itself, find themselves repelled by the militant theoretical indoctrination with which this material is served up,

1

or wondering what the point of it all might be. Moreover, told that they had better master Irigaray and Kristeva before they can go on to study early modern Chinese literature or Henry David Thoreau at a "serious" level, it is not surprising that accounting or biotechnology might start looking a bit more appealing to a bright and ambitious twenty-two-year-old. Enrollments in the humanities are down, funding levels from external agencies have fallen, and the work of humanists themselves has become increasingly insular and unrelated to normal canons of intelligibility.

The aging vanguard of the Theory revolution are not unaware of the problems currently facing the humanities,[1] but for all their apparent concern they seem perversely determined to block off the one promising route forward. For instance, Brian Boyd (2006) cites a piece by the well-known writer Louis Menand, who recently complained in one of the mouthpieces of the revolution, the Modern Language Association's *Profession 2005*, that the field of literary studies has entered a moribund stage:

The profession is not reproducing itself so much as cloning itself. One sign that this is happening is that there appears to be little change in dissertation topics in the last ten years. Everyone seems to be writing the same dissertation, and with a tool kit that has not altered much since around 1990. (Menand 2005: 13)

Menand argues cogently that the orthodoxy of postmodernist and poststructural-ist theory is intellectually suffocating literature departments across the world, and that what the field needs is some new young Turks unafraid to shake up the status quo and introduce new theoretical directions. What these innovations may look like he, as an old-timer, does not hazard to predict. Despite this apparent intellectual humility in the face of the coming generation, though, Boyd notes that there is at least one innovation with which Menand will explicitly have no truck: the attempt to establish "consilience" between science and the humanities – that is, to integrate science and the humanities into one single, vertical chain of explanation. "Consilience," Menand declares with religious fervor, "is a bargain with the devil" (14). As Boyd observes, for all Menand claims to be looking for someone to tell him and his colleagues that they are wrong, he is "certain that there is at least one thing that just *cannot* be wrong: that the sciences, especially the life sciences, have no place in the study of the human world" (Boyd 2006: 19).

TWO WORLDS: THE GHOST AND THE MACHINE

Menand's attitude is typical of what I think of as the "High Humanist" stance, which holds that the humanities are a sui generis and autonomous field of inquiry,

---

[1] See especially the essays dedicated to the "future of criticism" published in *Critical Theory* 30.2 (Winter 2004).

approachable only by means of a special sensitivity produced by humanistic training itself. Whence this knee-jerk, visceral disdain for the very idea of consilience between science and the humanities? What is so special about the human world, the "cultural dimension" that is constitutive of our "species identity" (Menand 2005: 14–15)? To answer these questions it is necessary to clearly trace the culture-nature distinction back to its roots in a dualistic model of the human being.

The university today is, as we know, divided into two broad magisteria, the humanities and the natural sciences, usually located on opposites sides of campus, served by separate funding agencies, and characterized by radically different methodologies and background theoretical assumptions. Although rarely explicitly acknowledged in our secular age, the primary rationale behind this division is a rather old-fashioned and decidedly metaphysical belief: that there are two utterly different types of substances in the world, mind and matter, which operate according to distinct principles. The humanities study the products of the free and unconstrained spirit or mind – literature, religion, art, history – while the natural sciences concern themselves with the deterministic laws governing the inert kingdom of dumb objects. This relationship of metaphysics to institutional structure is expressed most honestly in German, where the sciences of mechanistic nature (*Naturwissenschaften*) are distinguished from the sciences of the elusive human *Geist* (*Geisteswissenschaften*) – *Geist* being a cognate of the English "ghost," and alternately translatable as "ghost," "mind," or "spirit." German also helpfully provides us with technical terms, always hovering somewhere in the background of contemporary humanistic debate, to distinguish clearly between the two types of knowing appropriate to each domain. The natural world is subject to *Erklären*, or "explanation," which is necessarily reductive, explaining complex physical phenomena in terms of simpler ones. Products of the human mind, however, can be grasped only by means of the mysterious communication that occurs when one *Geist* opens itself up to the presence of another *Geist*. This process is known as *Verstehen*, or "understanding," and it is seen as an *event*, requiring sensitivity, openness, and a kind of commitment on the part of one spirit to another. This is the fundamental intuition motivating the High Humanist conviction that only trained humanists can seriously engage in humanistic inquiry. It is also the framework behind the common charge that any attempt to explain a human-level phenomenon in terms of more basic principles is "reductionistic": the understood spirit must be able to see itself reflected, in terms that it recognizes, in the product of the understanding spirit.

I will be arguing in what follows that mind-body dualism is a universal human intuition, at least as old as *Homo sapiens*, which has much to do with why it is so difficult to get beyond it. When the "dualist West" is contrasted with other, presumably more holistic, cultures, what is really being picked out is the singular intensity with which mind-body dualism has been articulated, the assiduousness with which the boundary between the two has been policed,[2] and the rigidity with which these two different types of knowing about the world – humanistic *Verstehen* versus naturalistic *Erklären* – have been institutionalized in the modern Academy. In the university today, the two are required – at least by humanists – to keep strictly to their own tasks. In disciplines where the boundary between them is particularly problematic, such as anthropology, the field has simply split. Physical or biological anthropologists stick to explaining "bones and stones," while cultural anthropologists explore the more esoteric realm of human social understanding. In a growing number of universities, this division of labor has actually led to separate departments; in others, the two types of anthropology tend to coexist in uneasy separation.

The degree to which the mind versus body – and therefore the understand-ing versus explanation – split has become entrenched in the modern university is reflected by the fact that, in the humanities, "reductionistic" has come to function as an immediately recognizable term of dismissive abuse: a claim that the under-standing *Geist* has crossed the line and inappropriately slipped from *Verstehen* to *Erklären*, treating its subject as an object. People *do* seem fundamentally different to us than objects, which is why this understanding versus explanation distinction is able to gain a foothold in our minds. However, the conviction that the human can never be *explained* – that human-level phenomena can never be reduced to lower-level causal forces – takes this intuition a step further. The result is that the field of human inquiry has proudly wrapped itself in an impenetrable shell of *Verstehen* and violently resists any attempt by the natural sciences to breach this boundary.

BEYOND DUALISM: TAKING THE BODY SERIOUSLY

I will argue in the pages that follow that such rigid dualism is a serious mistake. By enthusiastically embracing the confines of an ontologically divided world – and vigorously opposing and often demonizing anyone who dares to question this divide – it seems to me that humanists have doomed themselves to endlessly and onanistically spinning stories inside of stories. One angle from which to get a sense of how deeply entrenched – but ultimately indefensible – metaphysical dualism hinders the humanities is to consider a couple of pointed satires that I have had taped to my office door for years. The first is a cartoon by Jeff Reid (Figure 1).

Like any good satire this cartoon makes an important conceptual point by placing an absurd idea in a context where its absurdity becomes more salient. No one believes that eating a "Deconstruction Breakfast Food Product" would be enjoyable

---

[2] See Raymond Corbey (2005) for an excellent account of how metaphysical dualism has informed Western treatments of the fraught boundary between humans and animals, particularly with regard to our nearest relatives, the great apes.

1. "Breakfast Theory." From *In These Times*, March 29, 1989 (www.inthesetimes.com), used with permission.

or that an empty bowl of "Foucault Flakes" would satisfy a person's hunger. This is because we never doubt that there is a common structure to human physiology that plays a role in determining things like our preference for corn flakes over, say, shredded cardboard. If, however, there is a common structure to human physiology, there is no reason to think the same is not true for the mind, which means that the extreme relativism of postmodernist theory renders it ultimately as intellectually vacuous as an empty bowl of cereal.

A very similar point – this time taking aim at what we might call the "individualistic constructivism" of French existentialism – is made by a hilarious satire called "The Jean-Paul Sartre Cookbook" that has for years been spreading through the Internet in various iterations, and that I cannot resist quoting at length:[3]

> We have been lucky to discover several previously lost diaries of French philosopher Jean-Paul Sartre stuck in between the cushions of our office sofa. These diaries reveal a young Sartre obsessed not with the void, but with food. Apparently Sartre, before discovering philosophy, had hoped to write "a cookbook that will put to rest all notions of flavor forever." The diaries are excerpted here for your perusal.

> **October 3**
> Spoke with Camus today about my cookbook. Though he has never actually eaten, he gave me much encouragement. I rushed home immediately to begin work. How excited I am! I have begun my formula for a Denver omelet . . .

> **October 6**
> I have realized that the traditional omelet form (eggs and cheese) is bourgeois. Today I tried making one out of cigarette, some coffee, and four tiny stones. I fed it to Malraux, who puked. I am encouraged, but my journey is still long.

> **October 10**
> I find myself trying ever more radical interpretations of traditional dishes, in an effort to somehow express the void I feel so acutely. Today I tried this recipe:
> > **Tuna Casserole**
> > Ingredients: 1 large casserole dish
> > Place the casserole dish in a cold oven. Place a chair facing the oven and sit in it forever. Think about how hungry you are. When night falls, do not turn on the light.
> While a void is expressed in this recipe, I am struck by its inapplicability to the bourgeois lifestyle. How can the eater recognize that the food denied him is a tuna casserole and not some other dish? I am becoming more and more frustrated . . .

> **November 15**
> Today I made a Black Forest cake out of five pounds of cherries and a live beaver, challenging the very definition of the word cake. I was very pleased. Malraux said he admired it greatly, but could not stay for dessert.

In a certain sense, of course, these satires are cheap shots: neither postmodernism nor existentialism would deny human physical commonalities. What both schools of thought *do* deny is human commonalities at the level of meaning – human bodies as inert physical objects may be subject to a common set of laws, but this has little to do with the lived world of human significance. It is this latter world that is culturally constructed (or, for the existentialists, created by the individual ex nihilo), and despite vague animal preferences for cereal over cardboard or cherries over stones, it is this constructed world of culturally or linguistically mediated experience that is all that we are really in touch with.

---

[3] By Marty Smith, originally published in a local Portland paper, *Free Agent*, in March 1987, reprinted in the *Utne Reader* Nov./Dec. 1993 (used with the permission of the author).

Even if only a fraction of the evidence I will review in the pages that follow is reliable, this view is wildly incorrect. French existentialists in their dark Parisian cafés drank espresso with sugar rather than, say, dog urine, because of evolved and universally human preferences for stimulants and sugar, and these physical preferences are not different in kind from our preferences for light over darkness, strength over weakness, or truth over falsity. The humor-producing tension of the Sartre satire, for instance, arises from the conflict between the existentialist assertion of a universe without meaning and the obvious truths of everyday human life: certain things taste good, certain things look good, certain actions make sense, and this ineluctable horizon of significance cannot be erased by a sea of black coffee or a mountain of Galoises. As Charles Taylor has observed in his critique of what he calls the "ethics of authenticity":

It may be important that my life be chosen ... but unless some options are more significant than others, the very idea of self-choice falls into triviality and hence incoherence. Self-choice as an ideal makes sense only because some *issues* are more significant than others. I couldn't claim to be a self-chooser, and deploy a whole Nietzschean vocabulary of self-making, just because I choose steak and fries over poutine for lunch. Which issues are significant, *I* do not determine. If I did, no issue would be significant.... To shut out demands emanating from beyond the self is precisely to suppress the conditions of significance, and hence to court trivialization. (1992: 39–40)[4]

Kurt Vonnegut Jr. makes a similar point in observing that "characters paralyzed by the meaninglessness of modern life still have to drink water from time to time" (1982: 110), as does Terry Eagleton in noting that certain shared and universal human norms, such as the fact that that "people do not throw themselves with a hoarse cry on total strangers and amputate their legs" (2003: 15), are part of an inescapable background of human intelligibility.

This is not to deny the power and poetry of the existentialist position – one would have to be dead not to be moved by the quietly courageous and resolutely lucid stance of Camus' *homme absurde* as portrayed in The *Myth of Sisyphus* or *The Plague* (1942, 1947). But Camus' gift as a writer and rhetorician is what in fact invalidates his basic philosophical point, because – despite his claim that he rejects any "scale of values" (1947: 86) – the very power of his ideal is derived from predetermined and universal human values: being awake is better than being asleep; being clear is better than being muddled; being strong and courageous is better than being weak and cowardly. Camus' creativity consists in recruiting these universal normative reactions and mapping them in a quite novel manner: lucidity consists in knowing nothing for certain, and courage consists in rejecting those transcendent truths that once were perceived as requiring strength to defend

---

4 Taylor tends to view these "demands emanating from beyond the self" as primarily historical and social rather than naturalistic, but the basic critique of individual constructivism is the same.

against unbelief. The mappings are new, but the sources are probably as old as *Homo erectus*.[5] Similarly, despite postmodernist posturing, the motivations and goings-on at any given annual Modern Language Association meeting would, with a little bit of background explanation, be perfectly comprehensible to Pleistocene hunter-gatherers: friendship, intellectual curiosity, coalition recruitment, exchange of adaptive information (including a heavy dose of social gossip), and an overall direct or indirect goal of achieving security, prestige, power, and sexual access.[6]

Unless one is willing to take refuge in strong Platonism or Cartesianism and embrace the existence of an autonomous "Ghost in the Machine," the mind *is* the body, and the body *is* the mind. Despite Camus' anguished claims, then, there is no absurd gap between our need for transparent certainty and a dense world devoid of meaning. The world *is* reasonable – not in the sort of transcendent, absolute sense that Camus rightly dismisses as wishful consolation, but in an eminently embodied, anthropocentric sense. The process of evolution ensures that there is a tight fit between our values and desires and the structure of the world in which we have developed. No appeal to eternal verities is required to assure us that a cigarette and stone omelet would make even Malraux puke, or that an empty bowl of Foucault Flakes would leave us unsatisfied. Of course, as I will argue in Chapter 4, human beings are apparently unique among animals in possessing the cognitive fluidity and cultural technology to effect some substantial changes in what gives us pleasure, what we find worth pursuing, and what we deem as meaningful. But all of this cognitive and cultural innovation is grounded in – and remains ultimately constrained by – the structure of our body-minds.

The fact that these body-minds are, have always been, and will always continue to be part of the world of things also effectively short-circuits the epistemological skepticism that permeates postmodernist thinking. A nondualistic approach to the person promises no privileged access to eternal, objective truths, but is based upon the belief that commonalities of human embodiment in the world can result in a stable body of shared knowledge, verified (at least provisionally) by proofs based on common perceptual access. By breaching the mind-body divide – by bringing the human mind back into contact with a rich and meaningful world of things – this approach to the humanities starts from an embodied mind that is always in touch with the world, as well as a pragmatic model of truth or verification that takes the body and the physical world seriously.

---

[5] Camus himself seems to be pointing in this direction with his observation that "nous prenons l'habitude de vivre avant d'acquérir celle de penser" (We take on the habit of living before acquiring that of thinking) (1942: 23).

[6] A point made with grace, sympathy, and humor by the novelist David Lodge in works such as the trilogy *Changing Places, Small World*, and *Nice Work* (Lodge 1975, 1984, 1988). One of Lodge's more recent works, *Thinks . . .* (2001) takes on issues involving cognitive science, the humanities, and the fear of reductionism, with the usual doses of insight concerning human nature and sexuality thrown in for good measure.

VERTICAL INTEGRATION

In place of what has turned into a jealously guarded division of labor between the humanities and the natural sciences, then, this book will argue for an integrated, "embodied" approach to the study of human culture. While the humanities do concern themselves with human-level structures of meaning characterized by emergent structures irreducible (at least in practice) to the lower-level structures of meaning studied by the natural sciences, they are not completely sui generis. If we are to take the humanities beyond dualistic metaphysics, these human-level structures of meaning need to be seen as grounded in the lower levels of meaning studied by the natural sciences, rather than hovering magically above them. Understood in this way, human-level reality can be seen as eminently *explainable*. Practically speaking, this means that humanists need to start taking seriously discoveries about human cognition being provided by neuroscientists and psychologists, which have a constraining function to play in the formulation of humanistic theories – calling into question, for instance, such deeply entrenched dogmas as the "blank slate" theory of human nature, strong versions of social constructivism and linguistic determinism, and the ideal of disembodied reason. Bringing the humanities and the natural sciences together into a single, integrated chain seems to me the only way to clear up the current miasma of endlessly contingent discourses and representations of representations that currently hampers humanistic inquiry. By the same token, as natural scientists begin poking their noses into areas traditionally studied by the humanities – the nature of ethics, literature, consciousness, emotions, or aesthetics – they are sorely in need of humanistic expertise if they are to effectively decide what sorts of questions to ask, how to frame these questions, and what sorts of stories to tell in interpreting their data.

Of course, calls for breaking down the barriers between the humanities and natural sciences are at least as old as the division itself. In the exciting early days of the scientific revolution, David Hume foresaw the imminent integration of moral philosophy and empirically grounded physiology and psychology:

Men are now cured of their passion for hypotheses and systems in natural philosophy, and will hearken to no arguments but those which are derived from experience. It is full time that they should attempt a like reformation in all moral disquisitions; and reject every system of ethics, however subtle or ingenious, which is not founded on fact and observation. (1777/1976: 174–175)

Hume's prediction was a bit premature. Arguably one of the primary barriers to the sort of integration Hume desired is the fact that human beings seem to be born dualists (Bloom 2004), with a deeply ingrained and universal tendency to see the world as divided into conscious agents exercising free will and dumb, inert objects. Breaking down the humanities–natural science divide thus requires overcoming, or at least bracketing, some very powerful folk intuitions.

As a study of historical paradigm shifts, such as the triumph of Copernicus over Ptolemy, demonstrates, displacing folk intuitions is possible but only with great difficulty, on the strength of overwhelming empirical evidence, and perhaps only partially – I, for one, continue to spend most of my life experiencing a Ptolemaic solar system. What has happened in the last few decades to make Hume's call for integration more feasible is the explosive development of cognitive science. A blanket term for a set of disciplines – artificial intelligence (AI), philosophy of consciousness, and various branches of neuroscience, psychology, and linguistics – concerned with the empirical investigation of the human mind, cognitive science has created an intellectual environment where bracketing our human predisposition toward dualism may finally be a *real*, rather than merely notional, possibility for us.[7] In Hume's time, and indeed up to the last few decades, the cognitive sciences have been in such a primitive state that taking a thoroughly physicalist stance toward the person was no more than a notional possibility, perceived dimly by authors such as Dostoevsky and pioneering empiricists such as William James but patently absurd to most sober thinkers. As Daniel Dennett notes, until the creation of computers and artificial intelligence systems in the 1950s, the idea that dumb matter by itself could ever give rise to consciousness was deemed inconceivable by most philosophers (1995: 26–33), and for good reason: conscious beings have powers that seem so genuinely unique that they *must* have their origin in some ontologically distinct substance. The "intuition pump" needed to get beyond this apparently self-evident fact did not come along until the advent of AI systems such as the IBM supercomputer Deep Blue or the virtual interlocutor named Eliza, which provided fairly concrete evidence that a purely physical, algorithmic system of "myopic, semi-intelligent demons" can produce something that looks and acts very much like consciousness (1995: esp. 200–212, 428–437).

One possible response to the AI revolution is to draw back into what Owen Flanagan refers to as the "mysterian" position: artificial intelligence can produce the *illusion* of consciousness, but we know it can't be real consciousness, because, well, we just *know* it.[8] Other humanists have decided to bite the ontological bullet and explore the consequences of taking seriously what cognitive science seems to be suggesting: consciousness is not a mysterious substance distinct from matter, but rather an emergent property of matter put together in a sufficiently complicated way. The manner in which we engage in the study of consciousness and its products – that is, the traditional domain of the humanities – should therefore be

---

[7] Borrowing terminology from Bernard Williams. As Williams explains, a real possibility for me is one that I could actually embrace without losing my basic sense of reality, while a notional possibility – such as my deciding to lead the lifestyle of a medieval samurai – can be imagined only in the abstract; see Williams 1985: Ch. 9.

[8] See Flanagan's distinction between the "old mysterians" (unabashed dualists) and "new mysterians" – professed naturalists who nonetheless place consciousness outside of the realm of naturalistic explanation (1992: esp. 8–11).

brought into coordination with the manner in which we study less complex (or differently complex) material structures, while never losing sight of the strange and wonderful emergent properties that consciousness brings with it. In other words, we need to see the human mind as *part* of the human body rather than as its ghostly occupant, and therefore the human person as an integrated mind-body system produced – like all of the other body-mind systems running around in the world – by evolution. This is the sentiment behind the arguments for an explanatory continuum extending equally through the natural and human sciences that have recently and prominently been offered by, for instance, the entomologist E. O. Wilson with his call for "consilience" (Wilson 1998), the evolutionary psychologists John Tooby and Leda Cosmides with their argument for the need for "vertical integration" (Tooby & Cosmides 1992), and the neuroscientist and linguist Steven Pinker with his critique of the humanistic dogma of the "Holy Trinity" (the Blank Slate, the Noble Savage, and the Ghost in the Machine) (Pinker 2002). It is also the guiding principle behind the "embodied cognition" approach to the study of human culture that we will be exploring in the pages that follow.[9]

EMBODIED COGNITION AND THE HUMANITIES

When I accepted a new position at the University of British Columbia I was given the luxury of creating my own title. I was to be a "Canada Research Chair . . . ," but chair of *what* was up to me to decide. The formulation I eventually settled on was "Chinese Thought and Embodied Cognition." The first half is fairly straightforward – my specialty is early Chinese thought, and this is my primary claim to expertise – but the second half usually takes some explaining. For instance, at a welcome party soon after my arrival, one of my new colleagues from the Psychology Department expressed amusement at the second half of my new job description, thinking it an oxymoron. "Isn't *all* cognition embodied?" she asked.

This is an unsurprising response from someone working outside of the core humanities disciplines: the fact that human cognition is inextricably grounded in and structured by the body and its sensory-motor systems is an uncontroversial background assumption in the various branches of the cognitive sciences. What my colleague did not realize is that this is not at all the case in the humanities. For instance, in North America most philosophy departments are dominated by a traditional rationalist conception of the body as a simple container for carrying around and supporting a mind with its own independent, formal structure. Many AI researchers, formal linguists, and more traditional cognitive scientists also adhere to a model of the brain as a machine for abstract symbol manipulation, with the body reduced to a simple input-output device. At the other end of the

---

[9] For other introductions to the embodied approach to human cognition and culture, see the Appendix.

ideological spectrum, the forms of postmodernism that dominate most Faculty of Arts departments may talk a lot about the body these days, but for them the body is ultimately nothing more than an inert tabula rasa to be "inscribed" by culture or a passive victim of power structures created by disembodied discourses.

Part of the argument of this book is that – however intuitively appealing – the mind-body dualism upon which both the Enlightenment high-reason model and postmodernism are based is being seriously called into question by recent movements in the study of perception, AI, psychology, cognitive science, linguistics, and behavioral neuroscience. In the science of perception, a tradition going back to William James has been revived by researchers who argue that perception is not simply passive representation of the external world inside the individual's head, but is inextricably bound up with embodied *action* in the world.[10] These insights have been drawn on by AI researchers, who have begun, for instance, to design robots that use pragmatic, embodied heuristics to dramatically outperform more traditional robots relying on passive representation.[11] In neuroscience and psychology there is a growing body of evidence supporting the claim that many, if not most, human concepts and thoughts are imagistic structures grounded in sensory-motor schemas,[12] that human categories are radial structures grounded in prototype images,[13] and that the mind is not a general-purpose computer ready to soak up whatever information is presented to it, but rather a collection of innate, specialized modules designed to handle specific types of information.[14] In the field of behavioral neuroscience, a picture of human reasoning and decision making has emerged that strongly suggests a constitutive role for emotions and other somatic biases,[15] and in economics there has been a shift away from abstract rational-actor theories toward models incorporating inherent cognitive biases and "fast and frugal" heuristics.[16] Linguistics has seen the creation of a new movement called "cognitive linguistics" that argues against an exclusive focus on abstract syntactic rules: semantics inextricably informs syntax, and both semantic forms and abstract concepts can in many cases be seen as being derived from sensory-motor patterns.[17] All of the features of perception and action just described are

---

[10] Gibson 1979, Neisser 1976, Noë 2004; also cf. Varela et al.'s concept of "enacted" cognition (1991: 9).

[11] Ballard 1991 and 2002 and Brooks 1991.

[12] Arbib 1972 and 1985, Johnson 1987, Damasio 1989, Tranel et al. 1997, Barsalou 1999a, Gibbs 2003, Zwaan 2004, Pecher & Zwaan 2005.

[13] Rosch 1973 and 1975, Rosch et al. 1976, Lakoff 1987.

[14] The classic arguments for an at least partially modular model of the mind are found in Chomsky 1965 and Fodor 1983; for a more thoroughgoing modular account, see Tooby & Cosmides 1992 and 2005, Hirschfeld & Gelman 1994, and Carruthers et al. 2005 and 2006.

[15] De Sousa 1987; Damasio 1994, 2000, 2003; LeDoux 1996; Haidt 2001; Solomon 2003, 2004; Prinz 2006.

[16] Kahneman et al. 1982, Gigerenzer 2000, Kahneman & Tversky 2000, Gigerenzer & Selten 2001.

[17] Lakoff & Johnson 1980 and 1999, Johnson 1987, Langacker 1987 and 1991, Sweetser 1990, Talmy 2000; for some recent and concise statements of the position, see Gallese & Lakoff 2005, Gibbs 2005, Langacker 2005, and the essays collected in Hampe 2005.

subserved by an integrated physical system, the body-brain, that to the best of our knowledge did simply not drop out of a spaceship or emerge, like Athena, fully clad in armor from the head of Zeus, but rather evolved gradually from other life-forms – some now lost to us except for spotty fossil records, others alive and well and currently engaged in their own vigorous forms of perception and action. The explanation of the origin of the particular body-brain system we as humans now possess, as well as its relationship to that possessed by other animals around us, has therefore become the focus of the new movement of evolutionary psychology,[18] and has resulted in an increased interest on the part of human psychologists in the cognitive abilities of other animal species.[19] Finally, the recognition that a large part of the environment in which humans find themselves embodied is itself a human creation has focused attention on how cultural differences in embodied experience affect thought,[20] as well as how cultural forms are created and transmitted by cognitively limited organisms.[21]

In a helpful survey article, Margaret Wilson (2002) identifies six different ways in which the claim that cognition is "embodied" can be understood:

1. Cognition is situated
2. Cognition is time pressured
3. Cognitive work is offloaded onto the environment
4. The environment is part of the cognitive system
5. Cognition is designed for action
6. Offline cognition is body based

Wilson argues that it is the last of these claims – the idea that even abstract thinking and imagination is structured by the body and its interactions with the environment – that is the best documented and most important. In the pages that follow I will be arguing at times for all of these claims, but it is claim 6 that will be my focus, since it most directly calls into question traditional objectivist and social constructivist views of the self.[22] What it means, then, to take an embodied approach to culture is to realize that the body does more than merely carry around our brain or serve as a raw material for cultural inscription. As Mark Johnson has

---

[18] See especially the essays in Barkow et al. 1992 and Buss 2005 for an introduction to the massive literature in this field.

[19] E. O. Wilson was one of the pioneers in comparative ethology (see esp. Wilson 1975/2000); see also Premack & Premack 1983 and 2003; Byrne & Whiten 1988; de Waal 1989, 1996, and 2001; Cheney & Seyfarth 1990; Povinelli 2000; and Rumbaugh & Washburn 2003.

[20] Gibbs 1999, Núñez & Freeman 1999, Weiss & Haber 1999, Sinha & Jensen de Lopez 2000, Boroditsky 2001.

[21] Atran 1990, Boyer 1994 and 2005, Sperber 1996, Sperber & Hirschfeld 2004.

[22] Cf. Tim Rohrer 2001: 60–61, who argues that "embodied" with regard to cognition is used at least ten different ways, but that the best overall characterization is as a shorthand for an anti-Cartesian account of mind and language that argues that thought is inextricably tied to bodily sensation, experience, and perspective.

been arguing for decades, we need to "put the body back in the mind" (1987) and acknowledge the degree to which the details of our embodiment help determine the possible structure of meaningful human experience.

The Trouble with Embodiment

Embodied approaches to culture are slowly making inroads into the humanities.[23] In literary studies, a small minority of scholars has been arguing for the relevance of cognitive linguistics, cognitive science, and evolutionary theory, and similar arguments have begun to be advanced in art history, religious studies, and a beleaguered but growing subset of the anthropological community.[24] Even in philosophy, the stronghold of traditional objectivism, there have been signs of movement. One could trace the beginnings of change to W. V. O. Quine and Wilfrid Sellars in the 1960s, when at least a certain subset of the professional philosophical community began to see philosophical inquiry as continuous in many respects with the empirical sciences,[25] and this movement has gathered more steam in the work of philosophers such as Mark Johnson, Paul and Patricia Churchland, Daniel Dennett, Owen Flanagan, and Stephen Stich, whose views we shall examine in the chapters that follow.[26] For the most part, however, these calls for vertical integration seem to have consistently fallen on deaf ears. Almost two hundred and fifty years after Hume's call for an empirically grounded approach to ethics, for instance, the vast majority of academic philosophy is still conducted in blissful ignorance – or active dismissal – of discoveries in the cognitive sciences that bear intimately on central philosophical problematiques. Similarly, the few scholars in religious studies, classics, literature, history, anthropology, and sociology who have even the slightest familiarity with scholarship from a cognitive or evolutionary angle generally react to it with unconcealed hostility. Why is this the case?

Much of the resistance to integrating the humanities and natural sciences arises out of concerns about crude reductionism, or worries about the politically and morally unsavory manner in which essentialist claims about human nature have been employed in the past. These are important concerns, and they will be addressed later. The primary justification and intellectual rallying point for this resistance, however, is theoretical and emerges from a cluster of theories that I have been referring to as "postmodernism." "Postmodernist" is, of course, a notoriously vague

[23] For embodied approaches to aesthetics, literature, morality, and religious studies, see the Appendix.
[24] See especially the work of researchers associated with the Behavior, Evolution, and Culture (BEC) group at UCLA and the Evolution, Mind, Behavior Program at UC Santa Barbara, as well as that of Joseph Henrich and Mark Collard at the University of British Columbia.
[25] See, for instance, Quine's description of epistemology as "a chapter of psychology and hence of natural science" (1969: 82) and Sellars 1963, as well as Patricia Churchland 1986: 2–3 for a short discussion of the "naturalist" movement in philosophy.
[26] This trend, the latest iteration of which was arguably kicked off by Johnson 1987 and 1993 and Flanagan 1991, will be further discussed in the Conclusion, and references are provided in the Appendix.

adjective, being applied nowadays to everything from poststructuralist French literary theory to trendy styles of living room furniture. I think, however, that it has not entirely lost its usefulness as a signifier. What I see as the core of "postmodern relativism" is an approach to the study of culture that assumes that humans are fundamentally linguistic-cultural beings, and that our experience of the world is therefore mediated by language and/or culture *all the way down*. That is, we have no direct cognitive access to reality, and things in the world are meaningful to us only through the filter of linguistically or culturally mediated preconceptions. Inevitable corollaries of this stance are a strong linguistic-cultural relativism, epistemological skepticism, and a "blank slate" view of human nature: we are nothing until inscribed by the discourse into which we are socialized, and therefore nothing significant about the way in which we think or act is a direct result of our biological endowment.[27] As I argued earlier, this approach has served as the background theoretical stance in most fields of the humanities for the past several decades, and even a cursory perusal of the annual conference schedules of the American Academy of Religion, Modern Language Association, or the American Anthropological Association will show that it continues to serve as the default approach in these fields.

From the very beginning postmodernism has inspired backlash, often from an objectivist standpoint. The reception of poststructuralist literary theory in North American philosophy departments, for example, has always been positively frigid, if it even makes sense to describe as "reception" a situation where the received is for the most part contemptuously ignored. Even within the field of literary studies there have always been holdouts. My hero back in the early days of graduate school was Terry Eagleton, whose lucid accounts of the development of poststructuralist literary theory were coupled with what I saw as devastating critiques of its intellectual and motivational bases.[28] These were both godsends to a fledgling scholar trapped in a required graduate seminar on "modern Chinese literature" that involved no Chinese and no literature – merely an endless diet of what seemed to me perversely opaque French theory. More recent critiques of something resembling the postmodern cluster include Tooby and Cosmides 1992 and Pinker 2002, as well as the growing body of counterattacks by defenders of objectivist models of science against social constructivism in "science studies" – the so-called Sokal hoax being perhaps the most notorious.[29]

[27] Cf. Donald Brown's discussion of relativism in anthropology and sociology (1991: esp. 9–38), John Tooby and Leda Cosmides's characterization of the "Standard Social Scientific Model" (SSSM) (1992: esp. 24–32), and Steven Pinker's discussion of the "Holy Trinity" (Blank Slate, Noble Savage, and Ghost in the Machine) that he sees as dominating contemporary humanistic discourse (2002: esp. 5–29).

[28] See, e.g., Eagleton 1983 and 2003. Eagleton's critique, of course, comes yoked to a kind of doctrinaire Marxism that even left-leaning humanists find increasingly difficult to swallow.

[29] See, e.g., Gross & Levitt 1994, Gross et al. 1996, Sokal & Bricmont 1998, Koertge 1998, and The Editors of *Lingua Franca* 2000.

This backlash, however, has not always been carefully aimed, and the proponents and opponents of, say, poststructuralist literary theory or the "strong programme" in the philosophy of science often seem to be talking past each other. Elisabeth Lloyd (1996), for instance, has argued that critiques of feminist approaches to the philosophy of science by the likes of Gross and Levitt are hysterical overreactions, and although she does present what I think are overly tame versions of Sandra Harding and Bruno Latour to support her point, it is hard to argue with the claim that the feminist-insight baby is often thrown out with the bathwater. It probably does not help that both sides of the debate show predilections for straw-man arguments, and that the political and social implications of the controversy have the effect of raising emotions and tempers on both sides (Segerstråle 2000).

Clearing the Way for Embodiment

As should already be quite clear, I do not pretend to be coming from a neutral stance in this debate. Postmodernism seems to me to have outlived its usefulness as a coherent methodological or theoretical position, and the entire point of this book is to make the case that an embodied approach to culture allows us to preserve all of the helpful insights of postmodernism without having to frame them in terms of an empirically false and internally incoherent epistemology and ontology. However, I do think that the proponents of vertical integration bear some of the responsibility for its failure to win wider acceptance among humanists, and this is because its proponents do not fully address the concerns that motivate those who continue to espouse postmodern relativist views. I myself have no formal training in cognitive science. Other recent introductions of the field, written from an expert's perspective, cover more ground and supply more technical detail concerning embodied cognition, and the reader is strongly urged to consult these works as well.[30] What I see as the main contribution of this book is my ability, as a humanistic insider, to speak to the concerns of my colleagues and thereby to help clear the way for the acceptance of embodied approaches to culture. The primary goal in the pages that follow is therefore to work to remove what I see as some important barriers to a more widespread acceptance of an embodied approach to culture – barriers that sometimes appear to be invisible to the champions of vertical integration or consilience.

PROBLEMS WITH OBJECTIVISM. There are real problems with traditional objectivist realism and the representational model of knowledge that together form the "folk" or background assumption of the vast majority of working scientists, and that are implicit in many of the critiques of postmodern relativism. Proponents of the embodied view often take for granted the explanatory precedence of the natural

---

[30] See especially Clark 1997, Pinker 1997, Gallagher 2005, Gibbs 2006, and Thompson 2007.

sciences. To writers such as E. O. Wilson or Steven Pinker, it is self-evident that natural science has a special epistemological status. When they argue that humanists have to take the natural sciences more seriously, they therefore usually end up merely preaching to the converted and irritating the unconverted. To my fellow humanists, it is not at all clear that the natural sciences should be viewed as a more basic level of explanation of the world. "After Kuhn" – a phrase one hears quite a bit when the subject of science comes up among humanists – have we not learned that "science" is simply one discourse among many? Didn't Feyerabend prove this, or Bruno Latour? This attitude that the natural sciences are simply contingent, social constructs needs to be confronted head-on before there can be any talk of vertical integration – the metaphor of verticality makes no sense unless we can make a case for there being "lower" levels of explanation that are, in some important sense, more basic than "higher" levels. Steven Pinker, for instance, is very sensitive to the political sentiments that motivate defenders of the humanistic "Holy Trinity," and he quite rightly points out that yoking these laudable values to an empirically false view of human nature is the best way to assure that they will never be realized. He does not, however, adequately address the fact that resistance to consilience stems from substantive epistemic as well as political concerns. Defenders of the Trinity are not simply wild-eyed liberals with a disdain for rational thought.

Postmodernism is not the only problem. I follow Mark Johnson in feeling that, in order to really put "the body in the mind" (Johnson 1987), it is necessary to get beyond objectivist realism as well as postmodern relativism. Before we can do this, however, we first need to problematize *both* of these dualistic approaches to knowledge and truth that currently dominate inquiry in the core humanities departments, because vertical integration makes no sense if you are a committed dualist. In Chapters 1 through 3, I will therefore explore problems with dualistic epistemologies in general, focusing on both objectivist realism and postmodern relativism. This will involve a particular focus on the philosophy of science.

In Chapter 1, I will sketch out the basic objectivist position and then explore some recent work from the cognitive sciences that call this position into question. For instance, work in the neuroscience of perception in the past few decades has moved away from older, purely representational models and more toward "enacted," embodied ones. Taking an embodied approach to human perception and cognition solves certain venerable objectivist problems – such as the grounding problem, or how symbols "in the head" can connect with things in the world – and helps to clear away some unhelpful and outmoded objectivist theories about how thought and language connect with the world.[31] Other work coming out of cognitive neuroscience and social psychology problematizes the objectivist – and

---

[31] See Hilary Putnam 1999, especially Chapter 2 ("The Importance of Being Austin"), for a lucid explanation of how the contemporary science of perception can help us to immediately cut through long-standing knots in epistemology.

folk – assumption of a fully conscious, unitary "self" that serves as a central clearing house for information and an exclusive initiator of action. Similarly, recent work on the role of mental images and emotional centers of the brain call into question the objectivist view of this little homunculus as guided (at least ideally) by disembodied, algorithmic rationality. Of particular interest will be evidence that human thought consists primarily of manipulating concrete images grounded in value-imbued sensory-motor structures rather than amodal, disembodied symbols. The "somatic marker" hypothesis of Antonion Damasio along with the "perceptual symbol" theory developed by cognitive scientists such as Lawrence Barsalou and Rolf Zwaan represent important correctives to the objectivist model of the self, suggesting as they do that human cognition is embodied through and through.

Turning to critiques of objectivist science, I will attempt to separate the important insights of what I fondly think of as the "good" Kuhn from the rhetorical excesses of the "bad" Kuhn, and will spend some time attempting to pinpoint the moments when philosophers of science such as Kuhn, Feyerabend, and Latour move from offering quite reasonable correctives to traditional objectivist models of science to making entirely unfounded, strongly relativist claims about human knowledge – a move that I have come to think of as the "slide into relativism." Postmodern apologists (and the writers themselves, when pressed on the matter) tend to focus on the preslide comments, whereas their opponents gleefully cite the postslide comments in order to discredit the entire position. My hope is that by disentangling the two we can arrive at a clearer picture of what is right and what is wrong about the postmodern critique of objectivist science, and about critiques of natural science–derived truth claims about things like human nature.

Chapters 2 and 3 will be concerned with the various movements I will be lumping together under the label of "postmodernism." One of the more interesting – and revealing – features of postmodernism in the modern Academy is that virtually every postmodernist denies being one, usually accompanying this denial with the confident assertion that we in the humanities have "moved beyond" postmodern theory. I therefore felt the need to dedicate an entire chapter, Chapter 2, to simply demonstrating that a position quite reasonably described as "postmodern" not only is alive and well but in fact serves as the foundational theoretical dogma in most areas of the humanities. I will also discuss how the rejection of the "postmodern" label itself reveals a growing awareness that something is wrong with this position, while a failure to get beyond a strongly dualist model of the human self makes it impossible for most humanists to formulate a coherent alternative.

Chapter 3 is devoted to the task of philosophical euthanasia: finally putting to rest postmodern epistemology and ontology, with the hope that this will help clear away the intellectual miasma that I spoke of earlier. After reviewing some of the more obvious internal or theoretical problems with the strong postmodernist position, I will spend the bulk of the chapter on a quick tour of the mountain of empirical evidence coming out of the cognitive sciences that suggests that linguistic or cultural constructivism is simply false. This is particularly important because humanists generally do not *know* much about the natural sciences, and I think this is one of the primary reasons why they can continue to hold onto empirically absurd models of, for instance, human nature, or the relationship of thought to language.[32] The current "best-we-can-know" state of the art in the cognitive sciences undermines many venerable humanistic canards. Thought is not language. Perception tells us something about the world besides our own – or our culture's – presuppositions. The basic structures of human thought are not sui generis and share important commonalities with nonhuman animals. Human beings are not blank slates, and the human brain is not an amorphous, general-purpose processor, but rather a collection of specialized modules with specific purposes and structures that were important for human survival in our evolutionary "ancestral environment." This means that the evolved architecture of the human brain imposes a certain structure and set of limitations on human cognition, constraining human conceptions of entities, categories, causation, physics, psychology, biology, and other humanly relevant domains. These commonalities include not only modes of intellectual apprehension but also basic normative reactions: human beings tend to dislike darkness, sickness, and weakness, and tend to like light, health, and strength.

EXPLAINING HUMAN CULTURAL VARIETY. Despite the theoretical and empirical problems with the strong social constructivist position, it continues to appeal to us for at least two reasons. The first is simply the innate plausibility of dualism for creatures like us, an issue that is directly addressed in Chapter 6. The second is the undeniable fact of intercultural variety. Once we feel that we can accept the existence of a set of grounded, human cognitive universals, and have formulated a coherent defense of the empirical data on which claims about such universals are based, more needs to be said about how a shared embodied mind could produce the sort of cultural variety that is the single most salient phenomenon to humanists. This is the purpose of Chapter 4. Cultures are diverse and complicated in ways that are often not immediately apparent to outsiders, and it genuinely raises the hackles of humanists to be told that the elaboration of "thick" cultural description that is their métier is ultimately concerned with trivial epiphenomena. Of course, this is not actually the position of scholars such as Tooby and Cosmides or Pinker, but – especially when they are not read carefully – it certainly *sounds* this way to many humanists.

---

[32] There have been some recent attempts to present aspects of natural science to a humanistic audience (e.g., Varela et al. 1991, Pinker 1997 and 2002, Hogan 2003, and Gallagher 2005), but as yet I do not feel that there exists an accessible, coherent picture of the full range of findings from the natural sciences that are relevant to scholars working in the humanities.

For instance, Pinker notes that adopting a vertically integrated stance toward the study of human culture requires an inversion of the social constructivist position, seeing "culture as a product of human desires rather than a shaper of them" (2002: 69). This is true to an extent, but this claim needs to be qualified by the recognition that human cognitive fluidity, ratcheted up over time by cultural entrenchment, *can* shape human emotions and desires in quite novel and idiosyncratic ways. Any arguments for the existence of human cognitive universals must be accompanied by an account of how the profusion of cultural diversity that humanists see out there in the world could arise from a shared human nature – or at least from a nature that has any kind of significant content. One might concede the fact that all human beings share basic-level categories such as "tree" and generally tend to avoid putrefying meat but still feel that such commonalities pale in comparison to the dizzying diversity of artistic, literary, religious, musical, and culinary practices found across the world and throughout history. For instance, if basic folk conceptions of human agency are shared cross-culturally, what are we to make of the early Theravadan Buddhist doctrine of *anatta*, or "no-self," or of the early Confucian conception of the socially embedded self? When cognitive universalists do acknowledge this sort of cultural variation, it is usually vaguely attributed to human "creativity" and left at that.

In Chapter 4, I will attempt to tell a more convincing story about how diversity can spring from unity by focusing on what the archeologist Steven Mithen refers to as "cognitive fluidity" (1996). One of the more puzzling features of human evolution is the so-called cultural big bang that occurred between 30,000 and 60,000 years ago – at least 40,000 years after the emergence of anatomically modern humans – and that involved the creation of representational art, complex tool technology, long-range trade, the rise of religion, and the rapid spread of *Homo sapiens* across every habitable continent on earth. This cultural revolution was not accompanied by any increase in human brain size or obvious anatomical changes, but it appears that something radical had happened to the manner in which human brains were functioning. Mithen argues that the catalyst for this cultural explosion was a breaking down of the walls between what were previously impermeable cognitive modules, allowing information to flow between these modules in a process that he terms "cognitive fluidity." Once humans began creating art and novel artifacts, the floodgate was opened to an unstoppable wave of continuous cultural innovation leading from multiple-piece spears to complex boats to laptop computers.

The chapter next turns to a discussion of the phenomenon of synaesthesia, which provides us with a hint of how Mithen's cognitive fluidity – portrayed quite schematically by him as chambers in a cathedral or as abstract circles – might actually be instantiated neurologically. Synaesthesia involves the unusual blending of two or more senses, such as experiencing particular musical tones or numbers as tinged with a particular color, particular textures as inducing specific tastes, or specific tastes as inducing textures. Recent research on synaesthesia suggests that it is the result of neurological cross-activation, that it is not as rare as once was thought, and that *all* humans are subject to certain common – and therefore less noticeable – forms of synaesthetic experience. All human beings, for instance, appear to experience "sharp" tastes or "bright" musical notes. There are suggestions that less common forms of synaesthesia are the result of a genetic disorder that leads to incomplete pruning of neural connections during brain development. This gives us some sense of how the "cultural explosion" of the Middle-Upper Paleolithic transition may have occurred despite the lack of obvious anatomical changes in *Homo sapiens*: the *Homo sapiens* who suddenly exploded in geographical range and spread across the globe may have had the same brain as their less creative cousins, but one that – as a result of one or a short series of mutations – was now capable of widespread cross-activation of previously sealed-off cognitive modules. Hominids equipped with these new, "cognitively fluid" brains – as well as with the ability to communicate the culturally novel products of this fluidity – could be expected to radically outcompete their early modern human fellows even without an increase in brain size.

The bulk of Chapter 4 will be devoted to what we might think of as voluntary, temporary, and partial synaesthesia – in other words, metaphor, analogy, and metaphoric blends. The relatively new field of cognitive linguistics provides us with a toolkit of very helpful and concrete methods for tracing the processes of voluntary synaesthesia that pervade human mental life. The focus of this section will be to examine how conceptual metaphors and metaphoric blends are derived from human embodied experience and then recruited for use in practical human problem solving.

Conceptual metaphor theory, originally developed by George Lakoff and Mark Johnson, argues that analogue image schemas – dynamic somato-sensory maps derived from the body and embodied interaction with the world – serve as our primary tools for reasoning about ourselves and the world, especially about relatively abstract or unstructured domains. While abstract concepts such as "time" or "death" may have a skeleton structure that is directly (i.e., nonmetaphorically) represented conceptually, in most cases this structure is not rich or detailed enough to allow us to make useful inferences. Therefore, when we attempt to conceptualize and reason about abstract or relatively unstructured realms, this skeleton structure is fleshed out (usually automatically and unconsciously) by primary metaphors derived from basic bodily experience, often invoked in combination with other primary schema to form complex metaphors. In these cross-domain projections, part of the structure of a more concrete or clearly organized sensory-motor domain (the *source* domain) is used to understand and talk about another, usually more abstract or less clearly structured, domain (the *target* domain). The metaphoric image schema of the source domain brings with it important sets of inferences and normative valuations, which then can be applied to the abstract domain and used to guide decision making. Since conceptual metaphor theory was developed over twenty-five years ago, a large body of evidence from a variety of disciplines has shown conceptual metaphor to be a pervasive and fundamental feature of human cognition.

A more recent development in cognitive linguistics is mental space and conceptual blending theory, developed by Gilles Fauconnier and Mark Turner. Mental space theory encompasses conceptual metaphor theory but goes beyond it to argue that *all* of human cognition – even literal and logical thought – involves the creation of mental spaces and mappings between them. In this way, it serves as a kind of grand unifying theory identifying conceptual metaphor as merely one particularly dramatic cognitive process (a single- or multiple-scope blend) among many processes that are more pedestrian, such as categorization and naming. It also goes beyond linguistic production to describe the manner in which novel motor programs, technological interfaces, and social institutions are created. The power of seeing the process of cross-domain mapping as involving two or more domains projecting into a temporary, "blended" space is that it allows us to deal with situations where structure is coming from more than one input domain, resulting in a novel structure that is identical to none of the inputs. One of Fauconnier and Turner's important insights is that many expressions that seem to be "single-scope" blends – equivalent to Lakoff and Johnson's conceptual metaphors – are, in fact, this sort of double- or multiple-scope blend, where structure from two or more invoked domains are selectively projected to a blended space with its own emergent structure. This gives us a concrete model for how shared image schemas, grounded in common embodied experience, can nonetheless give rise to completely novel structures. Another powerful feature of conceptual blending analysis is that it can go beyond single metaphors to provide an account of how complex metaphorical blends are built up over time in an extended discourse or debate, as well as how multiple-scope blends can recruit what the neuroscientist Antonio Damasio calls "somatic markers" in order to influence the normative reactions of the recipients of the blend. The recursive nature of the blending process also helps to explain how relatively small instances of conceptual innovation can rapidly snowball: blends that have become conceptually entrenched in a given culture can be used as inputs into entirely new blends, leading quickly to quite striking cultural idiosyncrasies. Blocks of discourse from a fourth-century B.C.E. Chinese text, the *Mencius*, will be analyzed to provide a concrete example of various types of conceptual blending in action.

In order to offer a coherent and empirically responsible alternative to objectivist or postmodernist approaches to the study of culture, it is necessary to build a bridge between the cognitive universalism explored in most fields of cognitive science and the mechanisms of creativity explained by cognitive linguistics. There have been vague hints of such a synthesis from both directions – for instance, evolutionary psychologists and cognitive scientists speak of cognitive fluidity and "cross-domain mappings," and many cognitive linguists take seriously the claims of evolutionary psychology and behavioral neuroscience. However, to my knowledge no one has as yet clearly laid out the manner in which the two fields fit together, each compensating for the limitations of the other. For instance, in their discussion of general families of conceptual metaphors, Lakoff and Johnson often make recourse to "folk theories" concerning such things as living beings possessing "essences," but do not explain where these folk theories come from, and elide entirely the issue of why such basic-level structures as paths and containers should appear *as* paths and containers to cognitively normal human beings. These are lacunae that can be filled in by findings in cognitive science and evolutionary psychology. At the same time, the phenomena of cross-domain projection and conceptual blending allow us to be much more specific about the mechanisms of "cognitive fluidity," and to trace out the steps involved in moving from a species-specific set of human cognitive realities and concrete images to highly idiosyncratic and innovative cultural artifacts.

Chapter 4 will conclude with a discussion of more general ways in which culture and language shape the human mind, pointing to work from anthropology and cross-cultural psychology that suggests how diverse cultural training, environmental variety, diversity in modes of production and social organization, and the effects of entrenched cultural forms and metaphoric blends can retune or alter the basic universal perceptual and conceptual structures described in Chapters 1 through 3. The reach of culture is, however, inherently limited by the pregiven structure of human cognition. Unless one is willing to retreat to strong dualism, recognizing that the mind is the body and the body is the mind makes it clear that the humanly knowable world will be cross-culturally comprehensible, and that the process of evolution will ensure that there is a tight fit between our values and desires and the structure of the world in which we have developed. Human beings are apparently unique among animals in possessing the cognitive fluidity and cultural technology to effect some radical changes in what gives us pleasure, what we find worth pursuing, and what we deem as meaningful. But all of this cognitive and cultural innovation has to be seen as ultimately grounded in – and constrained by – the structure of our body-minds.

THE STATUS OF EMPIRICAL INQUIRY. Another problem with recent attempts by natural scientists to sway humanistic thinking is that accepting the empirical arguments against both objectivism and postmodernism requires a minimal commitment to certain epistemological norms: that, for instance, physical evidence should be given greater weight than verbal assertions. The necessity for a coherent defense of empiricism is especially acute considering the fatal problems with objectivism explored in Chapter 1. If we cannot go back to the objectivist longing for God's-eye, timeless certainties, what *is* left other than conversational assertions? The key to answering this question is to get beyond the fundamental dualistic assumptions that underlie both objectivism and postmodernism and to put in their place an embodied, pragmatic model of human cognition and inquiry. In

Chapter 5 I will present the attempts of various philosophers and philosophers of science to formulate just such a pragmatic model of empirical inquiry, based on a knowing subject that is always already in touch with and embedded in the physical world of things because it is *also* a thing, not an otherworldly ghost struggling within the confines of its mortal coil. This sort of pragmatic stance toward human truth-claims can provide us with provisional answers to questions about the limits of our knowledge – less ambrosial, perhaps, than the fruits of objectivism, but also less subject to spoilage. Against postmodern relativism, we can maintain that there *are* structures of cognition common to all human beings regardless of their culture, language, or particular history. Against objectivism, we can argue that these commonalities are not reflections of some a priori order existing independently of humans, and necessarily true for any conceivable rational being, but rather arise out of the interactions of biological systems with a fairly stable physical world over the course of both evolutionary and personal time, which makes the presence of certain cognitive structures inevitable for creatures such as ourselves.

Pragmatic, embodied realism can also provide us with a coherent account of the status of natural scientific claims. Eschewing any sharp demarcation criteria for science, pragmaticist philosophers of science such as Ian Hacking, Susan Haack, and Hilary Putnam argue that what we reward with the approbation "science" merely represents an extension of "commonsense empirical reasoning" – the same sort of reasoning valued in forensics, traditional medicine, manual trades, history, and (at the end of the day) literary criticism. Rather than try to ground this form of reasoning in a priori formalism, I will take a more evolutionary tack in claiming that human beings (and indeed other members of the animal kingdom) have an "empirical prejudice" – that is, they preferentially allow their beliefs and decision-making processes to be influenced by empirical evidence – because such an attitude allows one to move more effectively through the world. Potential ancestors who lacked this preference did not become our ancestors. The sort of embodied pragmatism that I will sketch out in Chapter 5 occupies a middle ground between traditional objectivism and postmodern relativism, allowing us to disengage realism from a representational model of knowledge and thereby preserve some notion of "truth" in our post-Enlightenment world.

Formulating this sort of nondualistic model of truth is crucial if we are to defend the notion of "vertical integration" against postmodern allegations that modern Western natural science is just one discourse among many, with no privileged access to reality. If purportedly accurate accounts of the structure of an organic molecule are nothing more than a product of social negotiation, and supposedly "empirical" results of an fMRI study of moral decision making are no more revealing than the analysis of the free play of signifiers that I perform alone in my office, there is indeed no reason why humanists should pay any attention to results published in *Cognition* or *Trends in Cognitive Science.* In the postmodern world, literary analysis, educational strategies, historical genealogies, organic molecule assays, and neuroimaging studies are all equal and indistinguishable riders on the spinning semiotic merry-go-round. A pragmatic model of human inquiry can validate the natural sciences' claim to have discovered more basic levels of causation – that is, to have *explained* certain aspects of human behavior in the full technical sense of *Erklären*. The fact that previous arguments for integrated or embodied approaches to culture have failed to directly address the more basic status of natural science as a mode of inquiry has much to do, I believe, with why they have been dismissed as "naïve" by the majority of my humanist colleagues.

THE FEAR OF REDUCTIONISM. Although they are not entirely insensitive to the problem, most proponents of vertical integration fail to go far enough in addressing the humanists' worries about reductionism – worries that reflect the core appeal of the dualist model of the person, as well as the distinction between *Verstehen* and *Erklären*. The average modern Westerner is comfortable acknowledging that most of his or her body conforms to the laws of physics and chemistry described by the natural sciences but balks when it comes to one part in particular: the brain. While we are generally perfectly willing to admit that our bodies are, at some level, deterministic, entirely physical mechanisms, there remains a stubborn belief that there is something to us besides the "merely" physical – a special substance or power, variously referred to as the "mind" or the "soul," that is nonmaterial and nondeterministic, and that serves as the locus of free will and human dignity. Human beings are remarkably resistant to the idea that this *Geist* is coterminous with the brain, and that the brain – no less so than the eagle's wing or the starfish or the human spleen – is a deterministic, physical mechanism produced by evolution.

In asking us to give up a dualistic model of the person, the appeal for vertical integration therefore calls into question what seem to be deeply engrained assumptions about consciousness, creativity, the language-thought relationship, and human agency. Accepting this new, "embodied" model of the self has been likened to the Copernican revolution, although striking much closer to home. Daniel Dennett gives perhaps the most cogent expression of this theme in his discussion of what he calls "Darwin's dangerous idea" (1995), and I will examine the positions of Dennett and his physicalist compatriot Richard Dawkins in some detail in Chapter 6. My argument there, however, will be that hardcore physicalists often mischaracterize the "danger" of Darwin's idea by taking the Copernican analogy too literally.

In the view of Dennett and others, belief in the soul will ultimately go the way of belief in an earth-centered solar system, falling away as a more accurate model of reality penetrates popular consciousness.[33] The problem with this view is that it fails to adequately appreciate an important disanalogy between the Copernican

---

[33] Dennett 1995: 19; similar arguments are made by Paul Churchland (1979) and Owen Flanagan (2002: xiii, 19–20).

revolution and the Darwinian one. Adopting a heliocentric view requires overcoming our sense perceptions: it certainly *seems* to us that the earth is stationary, and most of us continue to experience the sun as "rising" and "setting." There does not appear, however, to be any principled barrier to us retraining our sensory schemas in such a way that we come to genuinely *live in* a heliocentric universe, and perhaps professional astronomers have already done so.[34] On the other hand, when it comes to adopting a physicalist stance toward human beings – seeing ourselves and others as determined physical systems fully subject to the laws of nature, rather than as autonomous souls merely inhabiting physical bodies – our own built-in cognitive mechanisms seem to be working against us. There is an increasing body of evidence for the presence in human minds of a "theory of mind" (sometimes abbreviated ToM), which causes us from a very early age to make a sharp distinction between animate agents and inanimate things. The former seem to us to possess volition, beliefs, desires, fears – in short, free will and consciousness – whereas the latter are subject only to the mechanistic causality of physics. It appears that we are born to be dualists (Bloom 2004). Dennett quotes a wonderful comment from the Italian philosopher Giulo Giorello, "Yes, we have a soul, but it is made up of many tiny robots" (Dennett 2003: 1). I fundamentally agree with this observation, but what we need to add is that we are robots designed to be constitutionally incapable of *experiencing* ourselves and other conspecifics as robots – or, for that matter, to really believe that we live in a robotic world – since our theory of mind module seems to be overactive, causing us to project agency into the world at large as well as onto other "agents." Human beings thus cannot help but believe that they inhabit a universe full of other soul-bearing human beings, as well as animals endowed with various degrees of consciousness, anthropomorphic gods, angry seas, and threatening storms.

Another way to put this is that we are evolved in such as way as to be incapable, at some level, of believing in evolution. Human-level conceptions based on folk psychology are thus here to stay, even if shown to be false by contemporary neuroscience. Taking the physicalist stance toward human beings that the embodied approach to culture requires of us, then, involves a strange kind of dual consciousness where what we assert qua scientist-intellectuals has to sit in continuous and unavoidable tension with how we cannot help but behave as human beings. In his critique of naturalism, Charles Taylor (1989) has famously argued that human-level concepts are just as "real" as the entities described by the natural sciences, since they cannot be eliminated from our "Best Account" of who we are and why we do what we do. To the extent that such intuitions are built into human cognition, human-level concepts such as "freedom," "beauty," and "courage" are just as real for creatures like us as neurons or vertebrae. I will not ultimately follow Taylor

---

[34] See Paul Churchland's description of how one might retrain one's perception of the earth in relation to the rest of the solar system (1979: 25–36).

all the way in his dismissal of "sociobiology," but I will argue that his account of the coexistence of mutually autonomous levels of explanation provides a helpful framework for understanding how we can have vertical integration without falling into eliminative reductionism. Taylor's account helps us to see the limits of a thoroughly reductionistic approach to human culture and the need to finesse our understanding of what counts as a "fact" for creatures like us. Hopefully, this will help to alleviate what is perhaps an unarticulated fear in the back of many humanists' minds that natural scientists are determined to put us out of work, and to make it quite clear how we can at some level give up our belief in the *Geist* in the machine without having to give up the *Geisteswissenschaften*.

Why Embodiment Matters

If we are to adopt a pragmatic model of truth, as I argue we should in Chapter 5, it is natural to ask about all of the material just outlined, what does it matter? How would accepting – at least provisionally – these points as "true" concretely change the manner in which we, as humanists, go about analyzing an Elizabethan sonnet or explaining the interaction of patronage and literary forms in medieval Japan? Any proponent of a "new" approach to the humanities has to address the venerable and valuable "so what?" question. In the Conclusion, I will briefly try to suggest how the "embodied realist" approach might impact the way "we" – that is, the general humanist who is the intended audience for this book – study and discuss culture. To begin with, opening up the humanities to the demands of vertical integration simply rules out such deeply entrenched dogmas as the "blank slate" theory of human nature, strong versions of social constructivism and linguistic determinism, and the ideal of disembodied reason, which has immediate and obvious global implications for humanistic inquiry.

Focusing on more specific applications, getting beyond the objectivist model of the self has important implications for ethics and moral philosophy, while jettisoning the basic assumptions of postmodern relativism allows us to realistically confront what seems to me to be the basic humanistic problem: how do we know the insides of other people? The embodied approach to culture allows us to talk in a responsible way about specieswide conceptual, affective, and aesthetic norms, while at the same time enabling us to remain sensitive to differences and focused on cultural nuance. Vertical integration therefore offers, I will suggest, a way for humanists to avoid the excesses of both objection and postmodernism, replacing them with a pragmatic, embodied approach to human-level truth. The manner in which embodied approaches are beginning to impact various humanistic fields will also be briefly discussed, with a selected bibliography in the Appendix designed to point interested readers toward further exploration.

Finally, I will turn to a discussion of the remaining barriers to moving from our current "biversity" – sharply divided between arts and science faculties – to a true university, where researchers on both sides of campus are motivated to exchange expertise and engage in collaborative work. There are few places in the Academy where one does *not* hear the new buzzword "interdisciplinarity" being bandied about with great enthusiasm. In most cases, however, the sort of interdisciplinary interaction that is being encouraged and funded is of a rather tame variety: English professors accustomed to working with texts interacting with musicologists, for instance, or someone in history producing a Web site to go along with a printed monograph. "Interdisciplinary" in these contexts often means not much more than "multimedia." Of course, multimedia work and interdisciplinary interaction within humanities departments is a wonderful thing. It becomes problematic only insofar as it functions as a substitute for breaching the humanities–natural science divide itself, or to the extent that it merely serves to reinforce deeply engrained and empirically implausible theoretical presuppositions. The Appendix will also alert readers to some of the signs of institutional change, focusing on a handful of new programs and centers scattered across Western universities that suggest that, in at least a few places, high-level university administrators are getting serious about facilitating and rewarding genuinely interdisciplinary work that cuts across the humanities-science divide.

Much more can be said about almost every topic that I treat in the pages that follow, and my hope is that the in-text citations, Appendix, and References sections will point readers in useful directions. My goal is to, by the end of this book, have given my colleagues in the humanities at least some sense of the promise represented by an embodied approach to culture, as well as how – far from threatening the existence of the humanities – vertical integration can allow us to escape from traditional dualism and its methodological dead ends.

PART I

❧

EXORCISING THE GHOST
IN THE MACHINE

1

The Disembodied Mind: Problems with Objectivism

*I*N CHAPTER 5 I AM GOING TO TRY TO MAKE THE CASE THAT THERE IS SOME-thing special about science as a discourse – and that it has nothing to do with the socially constructed prestige of men and women in white lab coats. I will also argue that, in an important sense, the type of physicalist explanations advanced in the natural sciences take explanatory priority over human-level explanations. First, though, it is important to recognize the limitations of more traditional models of science and the legitimacy of some of the arguments that have come out of the science studies movement. Because humanists are my target audience for this book, this critique of objectivism will be less detailed than that of postmodernism in Chapters 2 and 3 – in our "post-Kuhnian" age, the limitations of objectivism have become something of a truism. What I am going to call "objectivism-rationalism" (or "objectivism" for short) has, since its heyday among Enlightenment humanists, seen its realm of absolute sway reduced mostly to philosophy departments, although it is still prevalent in history and classics and – in the form of folk realism – functions as a kind of default position for humanists who are not inclined toward "Theory."

The bulk of this chapter is concerned with both theoretical and empirical prob-lems with the objectivist model of the self, the representational model of knowledge, and the objectivist-rationalist model of human decision making and action. The final portion is dedicated to the critiques of objectivist models of science that emerged from the philosophy of science in the 1960s and 1970s – critiques that call into question sharply dualistic, representational models of knowledge and the folk or naïve realism on which they are based – because these critiques are central to the question of what, if anything, is special about natural scientific inquiry. While this short excursion into philosophy of science may seem like a detour, I think it is a crucial step in the overall argument of this book. If humanists are to be convinced that the natural sciences have something to say to them, the deep conceptual prob-lems with traditional models of science have to be explicitly acknowledged and dealt with – a step that is too often overlooked by advocates of "consilience" or "vertical integration."

CHARACTERIZATION OF OBJECTIVISM

Mark Johnson provides a concise summary of the cluster of claims that make up what I will be calling objectivism:

The world consists of objects that have properties and stand in various relationships independent of human understanding. The world is as it is, no matter what any person happens to believe about it, and there is one correct "God's-Eye-View" about what the world is really like. In other words, there is a rational structure to reality, independent of the beliefs of any particular people, and correct reason mirrors this rational structure ... [Concepts] map onto the objects, properties, and relations in a literal, univocal, context-independent fashion ... Words are arbitrary symbols, which, though meaningless in themselves, get their meaning by virtue of their capacity to correspond directly to things in the world. (1987: x; cf. xxii–xxxviii)

The ideal of having a "God's-eye," representational account of the universe falls rather naturally out of objectivism. As Hilary Putnam explains, for objectivism there is "a definite totality of all objects (in a sense of 'object' that was imagined to have been fixed, at least in philosophy, once and for all) and definite totality of all 'properties'" (1999: 21), which means that, at least in principle, there is a "definite totality of all possible knowledge claims, likewise fixed once and for all independently of language users or thinkers" (22). The objectivist model of science, exemplified by Rudolf Carnap and his fellows in the Vienna Circle, had as its goal the creation of a formal theoretical language – free of the ambiguities inherent to natural languages – that could eventually, at least in theory, serve as a comprehensive representation of physical reality.

As Johnson notes, rationalism and a "sentential paradigm" of knowledge also piggyback naturally onto objectivism. The world is conceived of as consisting of a fixed number of discrete objects, with determinate properties that impress themselves upon our senses in a predictable fashion and are then organized into clearly demarcated categories. These categories of things we represent to ourselves with arbitrary, amodal word-symbols, and by putting these words into logical relationship with one another we form sentences that mirror the fixed relationships of categories in the world. Reasoning is thus essentially "a rule-governed manipulation of connections among symbols. It consists of a series of operations in which connections among symbols and rule-governed combinations of symbols are established and traced out according to various logical canons or principles" (Johnson 1987: xxiv).[1]

Of course there exist in the Western tradition older, more pragmatic models of rationality that can be traced back to Aristotle and that involve a mind always already

---

[1] Cf. Núñez & Freeman's (1999) characterization of "cognitivism," the manner in which this basic objectivist framework was elaborated in first-generation cognitive science.

in direct, constant contact with a messy world of tangible things. The strongly dualistic model of a disembodied mind, organizing sense data into symbolically labeled categories with clearly defined criteria for membership and then producing true statements by means of algorithmically manipulating these categories, really takes rigid hold on Western thought in the Enlightenment. As Putnam has noted, part of the impetus for this trend may have been the new mathematization of nature coming out of the fledgling natural sciences:

For the first time "nature" in the modern sense (*that* sense hardly existed before the seventeenth century) became conceived of as the realm of mathematical law, of relations expressible *more geometrico* – soon to become: of relations expressible by means of algebra and calculus. [Interactive qualities such as] color and warmth seemed to have no place in such a conception of nature and were banished to the status of mere subjective affections of the mind. (1999: 23)

Whatever the impetus behind the objectivist-rationalist model's rise to dominance, it has clearly become entrenched as the sole proper model of ontology and episte-mology in most areas of academic philosophy, and – in a somewhat less formalized folk version – functions as the basic background assumption for most historians, classicists, and less militantly theoretical humanists in other fields. In the philos-ophy of science, Larry Laudan (1996) has observed that the objectivist view of knowledge is perhaps the only remaining point of agreement between positivist defenders of scientific realism and their skeptical opponents.[2] The problems with the objectivist model, to be discussed in the next section, thus threaten some fairly bedrock traditional assumptions in both the natural sciences and the humanities.

Mark Johnson identifies objectivism with the Western philosophical tradition, and attributes our difficulty in moving away from it to the fact that its "roots . . . lie deep within our cultural heritage" (1987: xxv). Most other critics of objectivism similarly blame it on the heritage of Plato or Aristotle, or the Judeo-Christian tradition. As I will discuss briefly in Chapter 3, the roots of objectivism – like those of dualism – seem to lie much deeper than the early Greeks. Although it was perhaps most rigorously elaborated in the Western tradition, the idea of objects possessing determinate properties, falling into clear categories, and being represented by words seems to fall quite naturally out of the human perceptual-cognitive system, and constitutes a kind of universal "folk epistemology" that formed the raw material for philosophers such as Plato. Other philosophic traditions, such as that of ancient China, may not in the end have chosen to follow Plato in fetishizing representation and algorithmic reasoning as the royal road to knowledge, but they certainly shared

---

[2] Laudan characterizes this model as holding that the definition of terms is contextual; that interthe-oretic choice involves the translation from one theoretical language to another; that "the only kind of rational rule worth considering as a rule is some sort of algorithm – mechanical in application, unambiguous in sense, and capable of invariably producing a unique outcome" (1996: 18); and that "wholesale retention of explanatory content is precondition for cognitive progress" (1–25).

our basic folk understanding of these processes.[3] Our difficulties in seeing the problems with objectivism-rationalism (to which we turn now), or in formulating clear alternatives to it, thus may have deeper roots than simply being philosophical heirs to the ancient Greeks.

PROBLEMS WITH OBJECTIVISM

The picture of human reasoning and decision making that is emerging from the cognitive sciences calls into question some of the basic assumptions of objectivism-rationalism. Pure, bloodless rationality seems to play little role in ordinary decision making, and indeed an absence of emotion – a hallmark of the ideal moral agent for Plato or Kant – apparently transforms us into ethical incompetents. We are rarely fully conscious or in control of what "we" are doing, and indeed the very idea of a unitary, conscious "I" in control of the dumb, animal-like non-self (the body, the emotions) appears to be an illusion. Even such quotidian achievements as ordinary language comprehension and basic perception of our surroundings rely heavily on tacit know-how and fast and frugal heuristics, guided by embodied and mostly unconscious emotional reactions to our environment. Perception is not concerned primarily with representation, but with action, and the concepts we acquire from interacting with the world seem to be based primarily on imagery and sensory-motor schemas. Concepts are therefore not amodal, abstract, and propositional, but perception- and body-based. Even when dealing with "abstract" concepts or complicated, novel situations, somatic knowledge appears to plays a fundamental role.[4] Next, I will touch on each of these themes, noting both the theoretical and the empirical considerations involved.

Human Knowledge Not Fully Propositional: The Importance of Tacit Know-How

John Searle asks his readers to consider the sentences, "Sally cut the cake," "Bill cut the grass," or "The tailor cut the cloth." None of these sentences is characterized by lexical ambiguity or obvious metaphorical usage,

but in each case the same verb will determine different truth conditions or conditions of satisfaction generally, because what counts as cutting . . . will vary with the context . . . If somebody tells me to cut the cake and I run it over with a lawn mower or they tell me

---

[3] This is an arguable point, and of course it contradicts the mountain of literature that has been accumulating since initial European contact with China dedicated to outlining the sharp dichotomy between Western "analytic" (read: alienated and bad) ways of knowing and the "holistic" (read: healthy and good) ways of the mysterious Orient. Making this argument in detail is the task of my next monograph project (I refer to the reader to Slingerland 200x, or perhaps 20xx!), but it is my opinion that the early Chinese possessed all of the basic folk psychological and philosophical categories I will be discussing in Chapter 3.

[4] For a helpful, recent discussion of the objectivist model of concepts and the embodied alternative, with a wealth of experimental evidence, see Gibbs 2006: Ch. 4.

to cut the grass and I rush and stab it with the knife, there is a very ordinary sense in which I did not do as I was told to do. Yet nothing in the literal meaning of those sentences blocks those wrong interpretations. (1995: 130–131)

What *does* block the wrong interpretation of these sentences is our recourse to what Searle calls "the Background": a reservoir of tacit social and ontological assumptions and skills for coping with the world (129–137). Involving a type of inarticulable "know-how," this Background cannot be translated into a finite set of explicit sentences, which means that the comprehension of human sentences cannot be reduced to simply the algorithmic transformation of strings of symbols.[5]

A similar point is made by Hilary Putnam, who asks us to consider the sentence, "There is a lot of coffee on the table." This string of symbols could equally mean that there are individual cups of coffee on a "contextually definite table" (*help yourself to one*); that liquid coffee has been spilled on the table (*wipe it up*); or that there are physical bags of coffee on the table of a coffee wholesaler (*load it in the truck*) (1999: 87–88). In addition, it could also quite easily mean that a large amount of (as yet unseen and therefore theoretical) coffee is being offered in a particular commodities deal – present only on the metaphorical "bargaining table" (*we need to move fast on this opportunity*). The ease with which we access our background knowledge disguises the potential ambiguity of sentences like this one; it is clear, upon reflection, that we need recourse to "good judgment" in order to figure out what a given string of words means in any given context. Putnam points out that this need for contextual judgment undermines the algorithmic model of sentence processing, for "as Kant long ago said (if not in those terms), there isn't a recursive rule for 'good judgment'" (89). He summarizes a point made by Stanley Cavell in *The Claim of Reason* (1979), that "our 'atunement' to another, our shared sense of what is and what is not a natural projection of our previous uses of a word into a new context, is pervasive and fundamental to the very possibility of language – without being something that can be captured by a system of 'rules'" (89).[6]

It is thus apparent that the understanding of even quite pedestrian human utterances involves reliance on a huge reservoir of tacit, nonalgorithmic knowledge,[7] and

---

[5] Regarding the limitations of Searle's conception of "the Background," Shaun Gallagher observes that it is compatible with the "brain in a vat" picture, it "need not be embodied, and need not even be reflective of the physical or social environment that normally surrounds and interacts with a human body" (2005: 135).

[6] Daniel Dennett (1984a) makes a similar point in the context of the frame problem in AI.

[7] Or at least knowledge that is not *consciously* algorithmic. As Dennett has observed, if the physicalist model of the self is correct (i.e., if we are not to invoke a Ghost in the Machine or something like Searle's "Original Intentionality"), then *all* human cognitive processes must be implemented by some sort of algorithm (Dennett 1995: 428–443). In the case of emotions, intuitions, etc., it is merely that these algorithms are not consciously available to us – they are "black boxes" that provide us with ready-made images of typical scenes or simply spit out an answer to implicit contextual questions. As Dennett remarks, "whenever we say that we solved some problem 'by intuition,' all that really means is *we don't know how* we solved it" (442) – i.e., that the algorithm was phenomenologically invisible to us.

on a pragmatic "feel" for the conversational environment. The sentential paradigm does not seem to capture either how knowledge of the world is stored or how it is processed online, and this fact is not surprising considering what knowledge is supposed to *do* for creatures such as ourselves. As Paul Churchland has observed, there are hordes of different cognitively active species on the planet, and it would seem that for all these creatures, including us, the function of cognition is not the production of true descriptive sentences, but the "ever more finely tuned adminis- tration of the organism's *behavior*" (1985: 45). This fine-tuning is going to involve corrections in response to reality, but there is no reason to think that its purpose is to build a full representational model. "It is far from obvious," Churchland con- cludes, "that sentences or propositions or anything remotely like them constitute the basic elements of cognition in creatures like us" (45).[8] Andy Clark makes a similar point in arguing that AI systems based on explicit data storage and logi- cal manipulation – the "filing cabinet/logic machine" design – are doomed from the start if their goal is to emulate biological minds, since biological "intelligence and understanding are rooted not in the presence and manipulation of explicit, language-like data structures, but in something more earthy: the tuning of basic responses to a real world that enables an embodied organism to sense, act, and survive" (1997: 4). Clark observes that even the most powerful logic-crunching AI systems developed to date cannot come close to the real-world performance of the simple cockroach, which suggests that cockroach cognition – and, by extension, biological cognition in general – is operating on the basis of something other than disembodied, explicit data manipulation.

Philosophers such as Gilbert Ryle and Michael Polanyi have developed theoreti- cal accounts of the function of know-how and the distinction between explicit and tacit knowledge, and the importance of implicit, bodily skills for human flourish- ing can be traced in the West as far back as Aristotle.[9] Here I would like to focus on a growing body of empirical work coming out of social psychology and behavioral neuroscience that bolster these theoretical accounts by highlighting the crucial role that tacit, nonpropositional forms of knowledge play in everyday human cognition. In their review of the social psychology literature on "automaticity," for instance, John Bargh and Tanya Chartrand discuss studies revealing the power of priming to affect modes of behavior, the effect of stereotype priming on social judgments, the unconscious acquisition of goals from external stimulation, and the unconscious mimicry of behavior and its effect on social judgments. For instance, subjects whose movements – crossing their legs, playing with their hair – were subtly mimicked by an interviewer subsequently rated the interviewer as more likable, and the interview process itself as having gone more smoothly, than if the interviewer maintained

---

[8] Cf. Patricia Churchland's criticism of Fodor's "sentential paradigm" (1986: 388–395).
[9] See especially Ryle's famous distinction between "knowing how" and "knowing that" (1949) and Polanyi 1967.

a relaxed, neutral physical posture. Bargh and Chartrand conclude that, in many areas, people "classify their experience as either good or bad and do so immediately, unintentionally, and without awareness that they are doing it" (1999: 474):

Automatic evaluation of the environment is a pervasive and continuous activity that individuals do not intend to engage in and of which they are largely unaware. It appears to have real and functional consequences, creating behavioral readiness within fractions of a second to approach positive and avoid negative objects, and, through its effect on mood, serving [as] a signaling system for the overall safety versus danger of one's current environment. All of these effects tend to keep us in touch with the realities of our world in a way that bypasses the limitations of conscious self-regulation capabilities. (475–476)

In other words, the social psychology literature documents the pervasive importance of unformulizable "good judgment" on human behavior and attitude formation.

It is also apparent that there are separate human cognitive systems that work on the implicit and explicit levels, with "know-how" functioning primarily at the former level. Robert Zajonc and his colleagues have demonstrated that people can have affective responses to stimuli without being able to consciously recognize them,[10] and Antonio Damasio has shown that skin conductance reactions to emotionally charged stimuli *precede* conscious awareness of emotion: emotional states happen first, and conscious feelings follow (2003: 101). Joseph LeDoux has postulated the existence of two systems of memory, an unconscious, implicit "emotional memory," and an explicit "declarative" memory. He reports an early experiment – one that nowadays would never win human-subject approval – performed by a French physician named Edouard Claparede with a subject who had, as a result of neurological damage, lost the ability to form new explicit memories: if Claparede left the room for a few minutes and returned, the patient would have no memory of having seen him before. One day when, as usual, Claparede shook her hand in greeting, he concealed a tack in the palm of his hand, causing the patient to withdraw her hand quickly in pain. The next time he returned to her room, and she refused to shake his hand, although she could not tell him why and continued to insist that she had never met him (LeDoux 1996: 181–182).[11] LeDoux also reviews studies indicating that priming, manual skills, and cognitive skills (such as the ability to solve a particular type of puzzle) are preserved in amnesiac patients, suggesting

---

[10] See Kunst-Wilson & Zajonc 1980 and the literature review in Zajonc 1980. For a very helpful recent review article on the topic of emotional processing and automaticity, see Pessoa 2005, which concludes that emotional processing appears to enjoy a degree of autonomy from conscious "top-down" processes, but not complete automaticity.

[11] Cf. the similar phenomenon observed by Tranel & Damasio 1993 with their amnesiac patient "David," who despite being unable to form conscious memories seemed able to acquire affective preferences and aversions to specific individuals, as well as the selective and long-term preservation of complex, emotion-based learning in the amnesiac patient studied by Turnbull & Evans 2006.

that implicit "know-how" is developed and stored in brain systems separate from those that subserve conscious memory (195–198).

Of course, it is obvious that the brain systems associated with abstract reasoning and cognitive control can, at least sometimes, bring implicit biases and other sorts of emotions into consciousness in order to modify or override them. Indeed, there is evidence that cortical control is necessary for the normal conscious experience and expression of emotion. Animals that have had their cortex removed, for instance, are still capable of having emotional reactions, but they are not entirely normal – such creatures are easily provoked and seem entirely incapable of regulating their emotional reactions, which suggests that cortical areas normally rein in and control emotional reactions (LeDoux 1996: 80). But it is equally clear that conscious self-control is something of a limited resource. The work of Roy Baumeister and his colleagues (Baumeister et al. 1998, Muraven et al. 1998) has shown that when conscious control is exerted in one domain, this depletes the individual's ability to exert it in another unrelated domain. This suggests that conscious self-control must be a relatively rare occurrence, since it seems to require a lion's share of cognitive resources. There is also considerable evidence that conscious intervention in automatic processes can be counterproductive. Baumeister's work has shown that automatic behaviors are disrupted when people analyze and decompose them (Baumeister 1984). Similarly, Timothy Wilson and Jonathan Schooler have shown in a series of studies that, in many domains, people form automatic and apparently quite adaptive evaluations that can then be disrupted when these people are asked to reflect on their reasons for their evaluative feelings. Untrained subjects who were asked to spontaneously rate the taste of a variety of jams, for instance, assigned ratings that best matched their demonstrated future satisfaction, as well as the ratings of food industry expert tasters; when asked to rationalize their rankings by analyzing their reasons as they went along, however, the optimality of their ratings decreased significantly.[12] In summary, evolution seems to have off-loaded the vast bulk of our everyday decision making and judgment formation onto automatic, unconscious systems, because such systems are fast, computationally frugal, and reliable.

No Unitary Subject: The Objectivist Knower Is Not Master of Its Own House

The objectivist model of reasoning and rational decision making assumes the presence of a unitary, conscious self – the locus of rationality and will – whose job is to evaluate incoming sense data, classify it, and enforce appropriate conclusions and behavioral decisions on the dumb, recalcitrant emotions or body. While it is

---

[12] Wilson & Schooler 1991; cf. Wilson et al. 1989 and Wilson 2002.

acknowledged that this rational self is not always successful in exerting control over other portions of the self, it is assumed that the self is at least *aware* of what "it" is doing and why.

The phenomenon of automaticity discussed earlier calls this assumption into question, and the outline of the human neural architecture emerging from neuro-scientific research indeed calls into question the very idea of a unitary ego as the locus of consciousness. One of the main Cartesian "errors" at which Antonio Damasio takes aim in his famous 1994 book *Descartes' Error* is the concept of a Cartesian theater: a central area of consciousness that experiences the world and the self in a unified fashion and serves as a kind of headquarters of knowledge and decision making. As Damasio notes, there is no single region in the human brain equipped to act as such a central theater; although there are various intermediate-level "convergence zones" that coordinate information coming in from more specialized sensory-motor regions, there is no "master" convergence zone that has an overall view of the entire process (Damasio 1994: 94–96; cf. Damasio 1989). As Andy Clark observes, this lack of a central administrator is what one would expect in light of the potential computational difficulties involved, which is why more recently developed and successful AI systems have

reject[ed] the image of a *central planner* that is privy to all the information available anywhere in the system and dedicated to the discovery of possible behavioral sequences that will satisfy particular goals. The trouble with such a central planner is that it is profoundly impractical. It introduces what Rodney Brooks aptly termed a "representational bottleneck" blocking fast, real-time response. The reason is that incoming sensory information must be converted into a single symbolic code so that such a planner can deal with it. And the planner's output will itself have to be converted from its propriety code into the various formats needed to control various types of motor response. The steps of translation are time-consuming and expensive. (1997: 21)

Cutting-edge robot designers such as Rodney Brooks, who runs a robotic and AI lab at MIT, are thus creating systems where executive control is distributed among multiple, quasi-independent subsystems, each with its own self-contained sensory-motor loops that respond selectively to different adaptive and behavioral challenges. Evidence coming out of social psychology and cognitive neuroscience suggests that humans, like other organisms, are designed the same way as these robotic systems. Of course, in our everyday experience we certainly *feel* a strong sense of mental integration – the intuition of a unified self in charge of and informed about everything is very powerful and universal. This is, however, "a trick of timing," Damasio argues, an illusion "created from the concerted action of large-scale systems by synchronizing sets of neural activity in separate brain regions" (1994: 95; cf. Damasio & Damasio 1994). How this sort of "binding" occurs is still not precisely understood, but what is clear is that there is no little homunculus collecting data and running a central command post in the brain.[13] It is also likely that each of the various interconnected subsystems that together make up the mind encode and process information in their own task-specific manner, merely transmitting the results of their processing to other appropriate subsystems, which means that there is probably not even the kind of central, universal representational format that such a homunculus would need to function (Clark 1997: 136–141).

One of the more dramatic illustrations of the decentered nature of the self emerges from a series of experiments with split-brain patients performed by Michael Gazzaniga and his colleagues. In these patients the corpus callosum, which normally connects the left and right hemispheres, has been severed (this has been found to be an effective, if last resort, treatment for certain severe forms of epilepsy). The left brain is the seat of verbal ability and interpretative synthesis – in other words, the locus of our sense of unified self – and Gazzaniga and his colleagues found that the illusion of an in-control, unified self that the left hemisphere weaves persists even when it is most certainly *not* in control. For instance, in one experiment, images were selectively presented to each hemisphere: the left hemisphere was shown a chicken claw, the right a snow scene. Subjects were then presented with an array of objects and asked to choose an object "associated" with the image they were shown. A representative response was that of a patient who chose a snow shovel with his left hand (controlled by the right hemisphere and prompted by the snow scene) and a chicken with the right (controlled by the left hemisphere and prompted by the chicken claw). Asked why he chose these items, "he" (i.e., his left hemisphere "spin doctor") replied, "Oh, that's simple. The chicken claw goes with the chicken, and you need a shovel to clean out the chicken shed" (1998: 25). Gazzaniga and LeDoux found a similar effect with normative judgments: in one particular patient, referred to as "P. S.," the left hemisphere could correctly identify the emotional valence of a stimulus presented to the right hemisphere ("good" or "bad") without any conscious awareness of the nature of the stimulus (reported in LeDoux 1996: 14–15). In other words, the left hemisphere "was making emotional judgments without knowing what was being judged" (15).

As Gazzaniga observes, "The left brain weaves its story in order to convince itself and you that it is in full control" (1998: 25). He argues that, in place of the all-powerful legislator or canny calculator, a more appropriate metaphor for the conscious, verbal self might be a "harried playground monitor, a hapless entity charged with the responsibility of keeping track of multitudinous brain impulses running in all directions at once" (23), and also responsible for concocting an ex post facto story of unified control for the consumption of both itself and others.

---

[13] Much of the vast literature on the neuroscience of consciousness, to be discussed in more detail in Chapter 6, also focuses on deconstructing the folk notion of a unitary self; see especially Dennett 1991 and Flanagan 1992.

One is reminded of Nietzsche's claim that the idea of free will is "the expression for the complex state of delight of the person exercising volition, who commands and at the same time identifies himself with the executor of the order," taking pleasure in the illusion that "L'effet c'est moi"[14] (Nietzsche 1886/1966: 26).

Lest one think this sort of illusion of self-control is confined to people with extreme trauma, such as a severed corpus callosum, a large body of psychological experimental evidence has demonstrated the existence of a rather deluded "spin doctor" in neurologically normal individuals. The classic studies in this field were performed by Richard Nisbett and Timothy Wilson (Nisbett & Wilson 1977, Wilson & Nisbett 1978), who demonstrated in a series of experiments that people often report having thoughts and desires that they could not, in fact, possibly have, and that the verbal reports given by subjects concerning the effects of stimuli on their judgments and behavior in experiments are often highly inaccurate. In a now classic experiment, Nisbett & Wilson presented shoppers at a mall with a display of identical nylon stockings, laid out from left to right. They observed the well-attested phenomenon that, given such a horizontally oriented presentation of otherwise identical items, people display a preference for the items on their right-hand side: in this experiment, the rightmost stocking was preferred almost four to one over the leftmost. What they found most interesting, however, was the confabulated rationales the subjects concocted to justify their choices – swearing, for instance, that their preferred stocking was clearly of better quality than the identical stocking to its left. None of the subjects mentioned the position of the article, and virtually all of the subjects absolutely denied the possible effect of the article's position on their judgment when directly questioned about it by the researchers, "usually with a worried glance at the interviewer suggesting that they had misunderstood the question or were dealing with a madman" (1977: 244).

Studies of subjects given posthypnotic suggestions show a similar effect. For instance, Philip Zimbardo et al. (1993) found that subjects in which both hypnotic arousal and amnesia were induced generated a range of plausible explanations for their mental state that had nothing to do with the actual context of the experiment, and Paul Rozin and Carol Nemeroff (1990) found that subjects justified disgust-based attitudes with rationalizations that proved upon examination to be poor predictors of their actual behavior. Jonathan Haidt and his colleagues have found a similar effect with regard to moral judgments: judgments resulting from emotional reactions or posthypnotic suggestions are invariably given ex post facto – and utterly specious – rational justifications by experimental subjects.[15] Together with the vast literature on the unconscious effects of stereotype, mood, and emotional

---

14 "I am [the cause of] the effect," a play on Louis XIV's famous declaration, "L'État, c'est moi" (I am the state). Nietzsche's wordplay also points to his model of the self as a collection of independent agencies rather than a unified, single entity.

15 See especially Haidt et al. 1993, Haidt 2001, and Wheatley & Haidt 2005.

priming,[16] these results suggest that the objectivist self is not, in fact, master of its own house, or even of "itself."

Embodied Emotions in Human Cognition: The Role
of "Fast and Frugal" Heuristics

As Gerd Gigerenzer and Reinhard Selten (2001) explain in an introductory essay on the concept of "bounded rationality," economists and psychologists have, since the 1950s, been moving away from models of behavior that assumed humans are optimal calculators toward models that assume that, in most situations, human beings rely on domain-specific, "fast and frugal" heuristics.[17] These heuristics generally do not result in rationally optimal results, but they often outperform general-purpose, time-consuming, and "information-greedy" optimizing strategies, especially in the specific situations of partial knowledge and computational limitations for which they are designed. A representative example is the "recognition heuristic" (Gigerenzer & Goldstein 1996, Goldstein & Gigerenzer 2002), whereby an organism presented with a choice between two options – say, two potential food items – simply chooses the one that has been previously encountered over the one that is unknown. Bennett Galef (1987) has shown that Norway rats have evolved to employ this heuristic in feeding decisions, choosing food items they have encountered before (through personal experience or detecting the scent on another rat's breath) over unknown items. It is not hard to imagine how this strategy might be adaptive: items that have been consumed before by you or by a conspecific are more likely to be edible than an item chosen randomly from the environment, and this might very well outweigh any potential advantage derived from discovering a superior new foodstuff. What is perhaps less intuitively obvious is how such crude heuristics can outperform more "rational" strategies even in quite complex and evolutionarily novel situations, such as stock market investment (Borges et al. 1999).

These heuristics and biases often take the form of tacit skills, unformulizable hunches, or – the focus of this section – emotional reactions. In the last decade there has been an explosion of literature on the role of emotions in human reasoning in such fields as behavioral neuroscience, cognitive science, economics, social psychology, and philosophy.[18] Because of space restrictions, I will focus here on

---

[16] For a recent literature survey and an account of the role and power of the "adaptive unconscious," see Wilson 2002.
[17] The term "bounded rationality" was coined by Herbert Simon in 1956. For more on the topic, see Simon 1956 and the essays gathered in Gigerenzer et al. 1999, Gigerenzer & Selten 2001, and Gigerenzer 2000.
[18] For just a sampling, see Rorty 1980; de Sousa 1987; Ortony et al. 1990; Tooby & Cosmides 1990; Damasio 1994, 2000, and 2003; Ekman & Davidson 1994; LeDoux 1996; Nussbaum 2001; and Solomon 2003, 2004.

the work of perhaps the best-known pioneer in this field, Antonio Damasio, and in particular his theory of "somatic marking." In his discussion of the "body-minded brain," Damasio points out that the mind evolved in order to assure the survival of the entire mind-body unit, and argues that the best way to do this is by "*representing the outside world in terms of the modifications it causes in the body proper,* that is, representing the environment by modifying the primordial representations of the body proper whenever an interaction between organism and environment takes place" (1994: 230). The result is a set of "somato-motor maps" that provide a "dynamic map of the overall organism anchored in body schema and body boundary" (1994: 231). So, when we are presented with a situation – or called upon to imagine a situation (neurophysiologically not that different a process) – we rely on the "dispositional representations" (1994: 104–105) that constitute our full repository of knowledge in order to comprehend it, and these representations inevitably include emotional information. As Damasio observes, "When we recall an object . . . we retrieve not just sensory data but also accompanying motor and emotional data. . . . We recall not just sensory characteristics of an actual object but the past reactions of the organism to the object" (2000: 161). In other words, the images that form the basis of our concepts are somatically "marked" with visceral and often unconscious feelings of "goodness" or "badness," urgency or lack of urgency, and so on, and these feelings play a crucial role in everyday, "rational" decision making.[19]

In *Descartes' Error* (1994), Damasio describes his work with patients suffering from damage to the prefrontal cortex, a center of emotion processing in the brain. The accidents or strokes that had caused this damage had spared these patients' "higher" cognitive faculties – their short- and long-term memories, abstract reasoning skills, mathematical aptitude, and performance on standard IQ tests were completely unimpaired. They were also perfectly physically healthy, with no apparent motor or sensory disabilities. Nonetheless, these patients had been brought to Damasio's attention as a physician because, despite their apparent lack of physical or cognitive impairment, they were no longer functional members of society. In real-life decision-making contexts they were appallingly inept, apparently incapable of efficiently choosing between alternate courses of action, taking into account the future consequences of their actions, or accurately prioritizing the relative importance of potential courses of action.

One representative example is the patient Damasio refers to as "Elliot." Formerly a successful businessman and respected husband and father, Elliot's life began to unravel after he was operated on for a brain tumor, a procedure that involved removing parts of his prefrontal cortex. As Damasio describes it, "Elliot's smarts

---

[19] Cf. Gerald Edelman's concept of "value-memory," where "current value-free perceptual categorization interacts with value-dominant memory" (1992: 121) through the online construction of scenes.

and his ability to move about and use language were unscathed. In many ways, however, Elliot was no longer Elliot" (36). Elliot needed to be prompted to get up and prepare to go to work in the morning, and once there seemed incapable of managing his time properly, focusing his attention effectively, or completing even the most routine of tasks.

Imagine a task involving reading and classifying documents of a given client. Elliot would read and fully understand the significance of the material, and he certainly knew how to sort out the documents according to the similarity or disparity of their content. The problem was that he was likely, all of a sudden, to turn from the sorting task he had initiated to reading one of those papers, carefully and intelligently, and to spend an entire day doing so. Or he might spend a whole afternoon deliberating on which principle of categorization should be applied: Should it be date, size of document, pertinence to the case, or another? The flow of work was stopped. (36)

Understandably, Elliot was soon fired. He proved no more successful in negotiating his way through unemployed life. He developed bizarre collecting habits, took up a bewilderingly diverse array of projects (often dropping them almost as quickly as he had picked them up), entered into questionable financial ventures with disreputable individuals, lost his life's savings, divorced, briefly remarried a woman of whom none of his friends or family approved, divorced again, and finally – completely destitute and without any means of support – was reduced to living off social security disability payments.[20] Elliot's behavioral profile is fairly typical of individuals with prefrontal cortex damage. Damasio describes a similar inability to contextualize actions within a larger framework of meaning in an anecdote concerning his attempts to set up an appointment with another prefrontal patient. This individual pulled out his appointment book and launched into a tiresome cost-benefit analysis, spending approximately thirty minutes enumerating the reasons for and against two alternate dates, citing any factor that could conceivably impinge upon the decision – previous engagements, possible meteorological conditions, etc. – until an exasperated Damasio finally intervened and simply decided for him (194–195).

In the view of Damasio and his colleagues, the problem with prefrontal cortex patients such as "Elliot" is that they lack "somatic markers" – the unconscious, visceral normative weights that ordinarily accompany our representations of the world. This prevents them from unconsciously assigning different values to different options, thereby rendering their "decision-making landscape hopelessly flat" (1994: 51). In any given situation, the number of theoretically possible courses of action is effectively infinite, and the human mind is obviously not capable of

[20]   In fact, Elliot was initially denied disability on the grounds that there was nothing medically wrong with him – being reckless, foolish, and irresponsible is not, the government contended, a recognized "disability." This was why Damasio was called in to examine Elliot's case and establish that his most recent pattern of behavior was, indeed, the result of neurological damage.

running simultaneous analyses of all of them at once. Therefore, the body contributes by biasing the reasoning process with somatic markers – often unconsciously – before it even begins. Patients such as Elliot perform well on abstract moral reasoning and utilitarian calculation tasks because such abstract analyses are artificially simplified. Thrown into a real-life situation, but deprived of the biasing function of somatic markers, they seem to attempt to dispassionately consider *all* of the options theoretically open to them, with the result that they become paralyzed by indecision or simply commit themselves to what appear to outside observers as poorly considered and capriciously selected courses of action.[21]

It is not easy to study realistic decision making in the lab. In real life, humans are usually functioning under time pressure, with extremely limited or sometimes inaccurate information, and often without clearly defined decision-making parameters. To try to simulate to some extent realistic decision making, and therefore to get a chance to see somatic markers in action, Damasio and his colleagues developed a game that has come to be known as the Iowa Gambling Task.[22] Subjects are given a pot of play money and told that the goal of the game is to maximize this pot, but they are not told how long the game will last. They are presented with four decks of cards, which they are told contain monetary penalties or rewards in varying amounts, and asked to begin picking from any pile that they wish. Unbeknownst to the subjects, the game has been structured by the experimenters in certain ways. Decks A and B are "risky" decks (they provide large rewards but also large penalties), while decks C and D are "safe" decks (the cards in these decks provide modest rewards and penalties). In addition, the game has been rigged so that the safe decks provide the best payoff overall: the large rewards obtained from the risky decks are more than outweighed by the dramatic penalties, whereas the safe decks provide an overall positive payout. The players are stopped after 20 rounds (and each 10 rounds thereafter) and questioned about their knowledge of the game, which is brought to a halt after 100 rounds. In some versions of the experiments, subjects' skin conductance responses (SCRs) are monitored in order to measure their emotional reactions.

Damasio and his colleagues have run this game with large numbers of both normal control subjects and patients with prefrontal cortex damage, and the results are invariably the same. Both groups begin by randomly sampling from all of the decks; this "trial" period lasts around 10 rounds. After the trial period, normal control subjects begin to generate "anticipatory SCRs" – heightened emotional reactions – before picking from decks A and B and begin to gravitate toward the safe decks, although when stopped and questioned after round 20 they are not consciously aware that they are doing so. Damasio and his colleagues call this

---

[21] Cf. Gigerenzer & Selten's characterization of emotions as "effective stopping rules for search and a means for limiting search spaces" (2001: 9).
[22] See especially Bechara et al. 1994, 1997, and 2000.

the "pre-hunch" stage: here normal individuals seem to be guided entirely by unconscious somatic markers, with little or no "executive" – conscious planning, choosing, and monitoring – control.[23] By about round 50, all normal controls begin expressing a conscious "hunch" that decks A and B are somehow "bad" or "dangerous," and all generate SCRs when contemplating picking from these decks. By about round 80 (the "conceptual" stage), most control subjects can explain logically why decks A and B are bad and decks C and D are good, but even those controls who never reach the conceptual stage continue to make advantageous choices.

The prefrontal cortex patients perform very differently. Despite severe punishments from decks A and B, they continue to sample from them throughout the game, fail to generate anticipatory SCRs before picking from the "bad" decks, and inevitably lose their pots of money – often having to "borrow" additional "money" from the experimenters in order to continue playing. Interestingly, some of the prefrontal cortex patients manage to reach the conceptual stage and can correctly describe which are the advantageous decks and which are the disadvantageous decks and why, but then continue to sample from the bad decks and lose all of their money anyway! Some researchers have compared their situation to that of alcoholics or compulsive gamblers, in that mere conceptual knowledge that something is harmful is not necessarily adequate – in the absence of the appropriate somatic markers – to motivate a person to actually avoid those harmful things. The problem with impulsive behavior thus may not be too much emotion, but rather not *enough* emotion.

Of course, it is important to note that, despite the crucial importance of somatic markers for normal decision making, navigating through the world by means of hunches and know-how does not necessarily lead to advantageous results. The same patient of Damasio's who was infuriatingly incapable of deciding on a date for the next appointment had calmly steered his way through a skid on icy roads earlier that same day, avoiding an accident in one sort of scenario where a person's immediate emotional response to a perceived danger (slamming on the brakes) typically leads to unhelpful behavior. More generally, it is clear that human beings are sometimes quite *bad* – that is, not rationally ideal – decision makers, especially when operating in modern industrial societies, far outside of their ancestral environment. In the field of economics, Daniel Kahneman and the late Amos Tversky have been the best-known proponents of a move away from rational choice theory toward more psychologically realistic models that take into account the role of the

---

[23] A recent study by Turnbull et al. (2005) found that loading by a traditional executive task (random-number generation) does not inhibit learning on the Iowa Gambling Task by normal controls, suggesting that emotion-based learning skills relying on somatic markers do not overlap with rational faculties; cf. the selective preservation of Iowa Gambling Task learning in the otherwise amnesiac patient studied by Turnbull & Evans 2006.

nonrational heuristics and biases that guide everyday decision making.[24] Dispassionate calculation makes it clear that we are likely to achieve a much better payoff from investing twenty dollars weekly in some conservative mutual fund than from using that money to buy lottery tickets, but the reasoning processes of many are (incorrectly, in this case) biased by the powerfully positive somatic marker attached to the image of the multimillion-dollar payoff. Similarly, the powerfully negative image of a jetliner falling in flames from the sky prevents many from making the "rational" decision to fly rather than drive, even though commercial airline travel is demonstrably much safer than automobile travel. George Loewenstein and his colleagues have formulated a "risks as feelings" hypothesis very similar to Damasio's somatic marker theory, finding that human risk assessment of an imagined scenario is driven largely by vividness and not by the probability of that scenario's actually occurring. One study (Loewenstein et al. 2001) found that people are willing to pay more for airline travel insurance covering death from "terrorist acts" than for insurance covering death from "all possible causes"! At the other extreme, people tend to be underinsured against emotionally "pallid" risks like floods. Other studies have found that people are also much more responsive to warnings that are linked to individuals and anecdotes than to warnings put in statistical terms.

Thus, although navigating by means of powerful, reasoning-biasing somatic markers must have been adaptive in our dispersed hunter-gatherer "environment of evolutionary adaptation" (EEA), it sometimes leads us into errors of judgment in the more complex world of settled agricultural societies, especially when modern technology is thrown into the mix. More generally, recognizing the importance of somatic markers in no way requires us to neglect the crucial importance of good old-fashioned "offline," bloodless, rational calculation and algorithmic reasoning – indeed, the fact that humans are even *capable* of such forms of reasoning indicates that they have proven their worth over evolutionary time. The best way to view the work of Damasio and his colleagues is as a corrective to the fetishization of reason in the post-Enlightenment and as an indication that the objectivist-rationalist model as it has been traditionally formulated has some serious and fundamental flaws.

The Purpose of Our Body-Brain Is Not Accurate Representation but "Enacted Perception"

The fact that our senses seem subjectively to be windows onto the world – when we are awake, an accurate impression of the world seems to come spontaneously

---

[24] The locus classicus of this movement is Tversky & Kahneman 1974; see especially the essays gathered in Kahneman et al. 1982 and Kahneman & Tversky 2000. Kahneman & Tversky tend to emphasize the suboptimal nature of ordinary decision making. In contrast, the "bounded rationality" movement discussed earlier contends that, in ecologically realistic situations, the rationally optimal decision (the economist's usual standard for the "right" decision) is not necessarily the best or the most adaptive because of the costs of information gathering and processing or lost opportunities.

flooding in – is the basis for the folk appeal of something like an objectivist, representational model of knowledge. It is, however, no more than an illusion created
by the clever engineering of our perceptual systems. To take our dominant sense,
vision, as an example, our phenomenological experience is that, when we open our
eyes, an accurate picture of the world "as it is" simply floods in. To get a helpful
sense of how this impression is wrong, consider photography. Your average amateur
photographer nowadays is much more sophisticated than amateur photographers
were when I was a child, and contemporary cameras do a much better job of automatically correcting for the basic mistakes people tend to make, but photography
is still a helpful tool for giving us a sense of why our phenomenological sense about
our vision is wrong. When I was young, amateur color photography was still a
relatively novel phenomenon, and there were of course no digital cameras: you
pointed the camera, clicked, and had no idea of what you were getting until a week
or so later when the photos came back from the lab. I don't think that my parents
were any worse than most amateur photographers of the time, but I still recall getting those packs of photos and being immensely disappointed: out of an entire roll
of film, you were usually lucky to get five or six decent pictures, and most simply
had to be discarded. People in shadows were invisible, shots into the sun blotted
everything out, the colors were strange – the pictures rarely came even close to
capturing what you remembered the scenes to be like. The functioning of a camera
essentially models the folk idea of what vision involves: light entering through a
lens and being passively recorded. The difference between the world as seen in a
roll of bad color photographs or a tape from a hand-held camcorder and what we
are used to actually seeing gives us a sense of how much work the brain is doing in
filtering, preprocessing, and editing the information being gathered by our retinas.
I have spent most of the past decade in either Los Angeles or Vancouver, two major
centers of the film industry, and another way to get a sense of how much work
the brain is doing is to observe your average motion picture set, and realize what a
massive collection of expensive equipment and how large a team of specialists are
required to reproduce on film the effect of what we get all the time, for free, just by
opening our eyes and looking around.

   The fact is that we enjoy sharp vision only at the very center of our visual
field – the fovea, the central region of the retina, is much more densely populated
with receptors than are the peripheral regions. If you doubt this, perform a quick
empirical test: remain focused on the word "test" in this sentence and then hold
something up even six inches to the side and attempt to identify it. You will receive a
vague impression of shape and color, but nothing like the sharpness of your image of
the few words at the center of your visual focus. Our impression of uniformly sharp
vision throughout our entire visual field is created by rapid and constant saccades,
small eye movements that move the spotlight of our fovea about quickly to take in
anything that catches our interest (Blackmore et al. 1995). Our peripheral visual

acuity and color perception is actually quite poor; it is best at detecting movement and thereby redirecting the focus of our fovea. Even these motion detectors respond to a fairly narrow range of the potential full spectrum, reacting only to scales that correspond to likely animal locomotion – which is why, for instance, we are not constantly distracted by the movement of growing grass as we walk across a field, but are immediately drawn to the sight of a rabbit darting out from under cover.

This, of course, reflects the evolutionary function of our vision, which is to track things in our environment relevant to survival and reproduction, especially potential predators, prey, or mates. As Patricia Churchland et al. note, our visual system seems designed, not to provide an accurate and objective replica of the world, but rather to provide us with task-relevant information when it is needed, and not a moment before:

What we see at any given moment is a partially elaborated representation of the visual scene; only immediately relevant information is explicitly represented. The eyes saccade every 200 or 300 msec, scanning an area. How much of the visual field, and within that, how much of the foveated area, is represented in detail depends on many factors, including the animal's interests (food, a mate, novelty, etc.), its long- and short-term goals, whether the stimulus is refoveated, whether the stimulus is simple or complex, familiar or unfamiliar, expected to unexpected, and so on. (1994: 25)

One of the more dramatic illustrations of this fact is the phenomenon of "change blindness" or "inattention blindness": our ability to overlook changes in a scene or what one would normally think of as quite salient features of a scene when our attention is focused on a task that does not involve these features. My personal favorite is an experiment performed by Daniel Simons and Christopher Chabris (1999, "Gorillas in Our Midst"). They asked subjects to watch a video of some people playing a basketball game and count the number of times one team took possession of the ball. They found that subjects so engaged tended not to notice a confederate dressed in a gorilla suit wandering into the middle of the frame, facing the viewer and performing a little jig, and then wandering out again.[25] Indeed, basic functioning in the world would seem to *require* that our sensory systems provide us with something other than an accurate picture of the world, as is illustrated by the phenomenon of sensory "adaptation," or reduced responsiveness to continued stimuli. As Mark Rosenzweig et al. observe,

Adaptation means that there is a progressive shift in neural activity *away from accurate portrayal* of maintained physical events. Thus the nervous system may fail to register neural activity even though the stimulus continues. Such a striking discrepancy is no accident; sensory systems emphasize *change* in stimuli because changes are more likely

---

[25] See also Rensink et al. 1997 and Simons & Levin 1997.

to be significant for survival. Sensory adaptation is a form of information suppression that prevents the nervous system from becoming overwhelmed by stimuli that offer very little "news" about the world. (2005: 225)

Even the sensory data that manages to register upon our retinal cells – after the imperceptibly slow movement of growing grass, or infrared or ultraviolet wavelengths of light are ignored – is further filtered as a result of the massive data compression that occurs in the retina, in the early stages of visual processing in the brain, and finally at the level of explicit and implicit visual awareness in accordance with a set of pregiven perceptual "schemas." As Ulric Neisser explains,

A schema is that portion of the entire perceptual cycle which is internal to the perceiver, modifiable by experience, and somehow specific to what is being perceived. The schema accepts information as it becomes available at sensory surfaces and is changed by that information; it directs movements and exploratory activities that make more information available, by which it is further modified. (1976: 54)

An example of a lower-level schema is the system of short-, mid-, and long-frequency color cones in the human retina that, as a result of their distribution, relative sensitivity, and the way their input is processed in the early visual cortices, create the palette of colors that appear to us. An example of a larger-scale schema is the particular physical causality schema that gives rise to the Michotte "launching illusion," whereby a moving dot on a screen coming into "contact" with another dot, which then in turn begins to move, appears irresistibly to both adults and infants to involve physical transmission of momentum.[26] Schemas are necessary for there to be any perception at all – creating perception out of the riot of possible sensory data in the world has been compared to trying to drink from a waterfall – but they inevitably "prepare the perceiver to accept certain kinds of knowledge rather than others and thus control the activity of looking" (Neisser 1976: 54). Patricia Churchland expands on this theme by noting that, since human knowledge of the world is mediated by receptor neurons and the brain processes that deal with this information, this means that our possible ways of knowing are physiologically restricted and species-specific:

Receptors are the interface between world and brain, and our conception of what the universe is like and what we take to be the truth about the universe is inescapably connected to the response characteristics of cells at the periphery . . . The world as perceived by humans is not the world as perceived by any organism. Rather, it is that narrow dimension of the world evolution has permitted our specialized receptors to detect. (1986: 43–47)

---

[26] See Michotte & Thinès 1963 for the original experiment, and Leslie 1988 for a review of evidence with infants.

There are also a variety of theoretical grounds for doubting that the purpose of human cognition is to produce an accurate representation of the world. From an evolutionary perspective, for instance, Paul Churchland has noted that:

Human reason is a hierarchy of heuristics for seeking, recognizing, storing, and exploiting information. But those heuristics were invented at random, and they were selected for within a very narrow evolutionary environment, cosmologically speaking. It would be *miraculous* if human reason were completely free of false strategies and fundamental cognitive limitations, and doubly miraculous if the theories we accept failed to reflect those defects. (1985: 36)

Stephen Stich makes a similar observation regarding the claims of philosophers such as Jerry Fodor and W. V. O. Quine that humans have somehow evolved to have "true" sets of beliefs about the world, because organisms with false beliefs would not survive. He points out that there are typically no infallible danger-detecting strategies, since predators and pathogens are always trying to come up with new ways to avoid detection by their victims. This means that "trade-offs . . . between overall reliability and reliability-when-it-counts-most will often be live options" (1990: 62–63). With regard to many aspects of interacting with the world, then, evolution might therefore favor overly sensitive (though inaccurate) mechanisms when the price of a false positive is not as high as that of a false negative – for instance, when it comes to the detection of poisons or predators. "Natural selection does not care about truth; it cares only about reproductive success," Stich concludes. "It is often better to be safe (and wrong) than sorry" (62). This is further reason to be skeptical that human minds are designed to be perfect representational "mirrors of nature." Our sensory systems are not designed to give us an objective representation of the world – whatever that would look like – but rather the heavily edited and very thin slice of it that has historically proven relevant to the survival and reproduction of creatures like us.

Another theoretical problem with the representation model of knowledge revolves around the so-called grounding problem: how internal representations could correspond to anything real "out there" in the world, or how a set of arbitrary, amodal symbols could map onto the objects of our perception. As Lawrence Barsalou has observed, no one has ever provided a truly satisfactory account of a transduction process whereby perceptual states could be converted to amodal symbols, and there is in fact absolutely no cognitive or neurological evidence that such a system exists in the brain (1999a: 580).[27] As many other critics of objectivism have pointed out, the grounding problem falls quite naturally out of a dualist model of perception whereby a disembodied mind, separated from the world of physical things, is limited to dealing with mental representations that have, in some

---

[27] Also see Varela et al. 1991 and Gibbs 2003 on the grounding problem in objectivist models of language and the embodied alternative to them.

mysterious way, been "caused" by those otherwise unknowable "things in themselves." As Putnam explains:

On the traditional conception, what we are *cognitively* related to in perception is not
people and furniture and landscapes but *representations*. These "inner representations"
are supposed to be related to the people and furniture and landscapes we ordinarily
claim to see and touch and hear, etc., only as inner effects to external causes; and how
they manage to determinately *represent* anything remains mysterious in spite of hun-
dreds of valiant attempts by both "realists" and "antirealists" to clear up the "mystery."
(1999: 102)

In response to these empirical and theoretical considerations, cognitive scientists interested in the phenomenon of human perception have, in recent decades,
been moving away from representational models toward more embodied, "enactive" or "interactive" models. The enactive approach in the modern psychology of
perception can be traced back to James Gibson's (1979) concept of perception as
the experience of the sensory-motor "affordances" of objects in the environment –
the possibilities of physical interaction that objects spontaneously present to the
embodied observer[28] – as well as to Ulric Neisser's campaign for a more embodied and "ecologically valid" model of perception. "Perception and cognition are
usually not just operations in the head," Neisser argues, "but transactions with
the world" (1976: 11). Perception is best understood not as a passive absorption of
information, but as "a kind of doing," a largely implicit skill developed and refined
as the embodied mind interacts with the world (52). More recently, the enactive
perception has been championed by Varela et al. 1991 and Alva Noë, who emphasize
the crucial role played in perception by physical movement in and interaction with
the world:

Perceiving is a way of acting. Perception is not something that happens to us, or in us.
It is something we do. Think of a blind person tap-tapping his way around a cluttered
space, perceiving that space by touch, not all at once, but through time, by skillful
probing and movement. This is, or at least ought to be, our paradigm of what perceiving
is. The world makes itself available to the perceiver through physical movement and
interaction. (2004: 1)[29]

One of the more convincing sources of support for the enactive view of perception and cognition comes out of AI and robotics research, where more traditional,

[28] For some recent experimental work on Gibsonian affordances, see Borghi 2004 and 2005 and Creem-
Regehr & Lee 2005.
[29] See Noë 2004: 17–24 for a helpful review of the enactive perception position and the evidence coming
out of philosophy, psychology, and cognitive science that supports it. Also cf. Michael Arbib's schema
theory of human cognition and action (1989), the evidence provided by Patricia Churchland et al.
(1994) in their critique of the "Theory of Pure Vision" in favor of an "interactive" view, and Andy
Clark's conception of "environmentally embedded cognition" (1997).

objectivist strategies of abstract representation coupled with disengaged algorithmic processing are gradually being supplanted by enactive models because the latter simply *work* better. Noë discusses the "animate vision" program developed by Dana Ballard,[30] asking the reader to consider, for example, two possible strategies for navigating around a strange city in order to reach a castle on a hill. The first strategy – the representation approach – would be to formulate a map of the city, plot one's position, and then use the map as a guide to reach the castle. The second strategy – messier, more prone to errors such as getting caught in a dead end, but certainly faster and less computationally complex – is to simply lock one's eyes on the castle and start walking toward it. The view of robotics and AI experts such as Ballard is that the nature of our environment and our embodiment makes the second strategy much more likely to succeed, and this is the strategy that is being pursued in the creation of more sophisticated robots and AI systems. As Noë observes, the take-home lesson from AI attempts to build machines that can actually interact successfully with the world is that

if your aim is to pick up a coffee cup . . . you don't need first to build up a detailed internal representation of the cup in space . . . You can just lock your gaze on the cup – your gaze is a way of pointing at the cup, a deictic act – and let the cup play a role in guiding your hand to it . . . Instead of having to ground ourselves by sheer cognition . . . we take advantage of the fact that we have more immediate links to the world because we are in the world from the start, and that we have the sort of bodily skills to exploit those linkages. (24)

This calls into question the objectivist model of knowledge as amodal and, to borrow a term from computer programming, platform-independent. "To perceive like us . . . you must have a body like ours," Noë argues. "The point is not that algorithms are constrained by their implementation, although that is true. The point, rather, is that the algorithms are actually, at least in part, formulated in terms of items at the implementational level" (25). For instance, in the case of Ballard's cup-grasping example, "The algorithm says 'reach where I'm looking now' or 'put your hand here now' rather than something like 'the cup is at such and such a point in space; move your hand there'" (25).

A similar point is made by Gigerenzer and Selten in their thought experiment concerning the contrasting strategies of two hypothetical engineering teams trying to build a robot able to catch a baseball. The "optimizing team" attempts to program what we might call a representational robot: able to, at a glance, measure the path of the launched ball, take into account all of the relevant environmental variables, and then run to the point where it has calculated the ball will land. The "bounded rationality" team, in contrast, programs their robot with a small set of heuristics: to wait and look, estimate whether the ball is going to come down behind or in

---

[30]   Ballard 1991, 1996, and 2002 discussed in Noë 2004: 23–24.

front, and then start running in the proper direction while maintaining a fixed angle between its "eye" and the ball, adjusting its running speed as appropriate.

Note that this boundedly rational robot pays attention to only one cue, the angle of gaze, and does not attempt to acquire information concerning wind, spin, or the myriad of other causal variables, nor perform complex computations on their estimates. Note also that the gaze heuristic does not allow the robot to compute the point where the ball will land, run there, and wait for the ball. However, the robot does not need to make this difficult calculation; it will be there when the ball lands. (2001: 7)[31]

It is of course an open empirical issue which of these robotics team would prove more successful, but the fact that actual human players appear to employ the "bounded rationality" strategy suggests that evolution has found this to be the more viable effective strategy. Indeed, it appears that much of human perception may be closely tied to specific motor programs rather than designed to serve as a general-purpose representation device. Andy Clark describes an experiment performed by W. Thomas Thach et al. (1992) concerning the perceptual adaptation of a dart thrower wearing special glasses that systematically shifted the vision image to the right or the left. It has been widely demonstrated that humans and other animals can adapt in time to such shifts in perception, but what Thach et al. found was that this perceptual adaptation was very motor-loop specific, disappearing if the subjects were asked to switch hands or throw the dart underhand as opposed to overhand. As Clark notes, the adaptation was thus apparently "restricted to the specific combination of gaze angle and throwing angle used in the standard throw" (1997: 38), which suggests one way in which perception in general may be tightly linked to specific motor routines rather than designed to provide an accurate, general-purpose image of the world.

It seems to be human intellectual nature to counter one extreme position by swinging to the opposite one, and some have argued that the "perception is action" movement in cognitive science has gone a bit too far in denying any role for abstract, stored representations and disembodied calculation. For instance, it is apparent that there are at least two visual systems running along the ventral and dorsal sides of our cortex, often referred to as the "what" and "where" systems.[32] The former subserves conscious visual awareness, whereas the latter seems capable of guiding fine-tuned motor behaviors in the absence of conscious perceptual awareness. The subject "DF," for instance, who suffered brain damage as the result of carbon monoxide poisoning, reported extremely poor awareness of objects presented in her visual field. Despite her complete inability to correctly characterize the size or orientation of objects presented to her, she was able to precisely calibrate her grip when asked

---

[31] Cf. Andy Clark's description of the "New Robotics Vision" being pursued by Rodney Brooks and others (Clark 1997: 11–33).
[32] Ungerleider & Mishkin 1982 and Milner & Goodale 1995.

to pick up objects and to correctly and fluently insert flattened objects into narrow slots (Goodale et al. 1991). Similarly, Salvatore Aglioti et al. (1995) demonstrated that subjects who were consciously tricked by a visual illusion whereby different-sized disks were made to appear the same size nonetheless formed appropriately calibrated grips when asked to pick the disks up, indicating that only their ventral stream was "fooled."

Margaret Wilson has observed that this distinction between "what" and "where" systems seems to involve a cognitive division of labor, with the "what" system appearing to specialize in the abstract identification of patterns and objects, "apparently engag[ing] in perception for perception's sake" (2002: 632), leaving the "where" stream to guide embodied action. "Our mental concepts," Wilson notes, "often contain rich information about the properties of objects, information that can be drawn on for a variety of uses that almost certainly were not originally encoded for," and this seems to be the evolutionary advantage of the less spatially precise but more flexible ventral stream processing. As Andy Clark has argued (1999), in neurologically normal individuals the two streams no doubt work in concert, interacting with and guiding each other, but in any case it would appear that our perceptions of objects are not always and inextricably bound up with their precise sensory-motor affordances. Thus Clark argues that a set of views that he refers to as "Radical Embodied Cognition" goes too far in denying *any* role to representation and computation in human cognition, and he proposes instead a more moderate model of "action-oriented representation" (1997: 159).

Even with this important caveat in place, it should be clear how the action- and body-bound nature of much of perception challenges objectivist-representational models of knowledge. Shaun Gallagher observes that, in certain respects, the enactive model of perception can be seen as a turn away from more Platonic models of knowledge toward something that looks more Aristotelian:

The Aristotelian idea of the soul as the form of the body . . . offers an important counterpoint to the Platonic, Cartesian, and functionalist-computational traditions. The very shape of the human body, its lived mechanics, its endogenous processes, and its interactions with the environment work in dynamic unity with the human nervous system to define necessary constraints on human experience. (2005: 152)

Gallagher also compares the enactive-perception approach to the phenomenological model of Merleau-Ponty, whereby "physiological processes are not passively produced by incoming stimuli. Rather, my body *meets* stimulation and organizes it within the framework of my own pragmatic schemata" (142).[33] In either case, it appears that in order to place the model of enactive perception in a larger conceptual

---

33 Cf. Varela et al. 1991, who explicitly ground their enactive approach toward cognition in the phenomenology of Husserl and Merleau-Ponty, as well as Mark Johnson 1987.

context, it is necessary to turn to philosophical resources outside of the currently dominant Anglo-American objectivist tradition.

Human Concepts Are Primarily Perceptually Based

One of the most fundamental challenges to the objectivist framework is the growing consensus in the fields of neuroscience and cognitive science that human thought is primarily image-based and modal in character – that is, deriving its structure from sensory-motor patterns. This view follows naturally in many respects from the enactive model of perception. As Noë observes, once one rejects the objectivist "input-output" model of perception and cognition, where thought is seen as a separate activity mediating perception and action, the alternative is a model whereby "all perception is intrinsically thoughtful" and "perception and perceptual consciousness are types of thoughtful, knowledgeable activity" (2004: 3). Damasio has similarly argued that real-time or recalled perceptual images "are the main content of our thought" (1994: 107), and cognitive linguists such as Mark Johnson and George Lakoff have long argued that linguistic representations have an analogue, spatial component rather than being simply amodal, formal symbols.[34]

The image-based view of human concepts has been most systematically developed by Lawrence Barsalou and his colleagues, who argue for a "perceptual symbol" account of human cognition. According to this model, the symbols manipulated in human thought are understood, not as pictures, but as "records of neural activation that arises during perception" (1999a: 583). These records can be abstracted from and combined in various ways in areas of the brain "upstream" from the sensory-motor cortices (what Damasio 1989 refers to as "convergence zones"), but they always remain to some extent grounded in sensory-motor systems. Against the objectivist view of concepts as amodal, arbitrary symbols, Rolf Zwaan and Carol Madden argue that

there are no clear demarcations between perception, action, and cognition. Interactions with the world leave traces of experience in the brain. These traces are (partially) retrieved and used in the mental simulations that make up cognition. Crucially, these traces bear a resemblance to the perceptual/action processes that generated them . . . and are highly malleable. Words and grammars are . . . a set of cues that activate and combine experiential traces in the mental simulation of the described events . . . (2005: 224)

Against Chomskyan models that portray grammar as a purely formal, hermetically sealed, algorithmic process, Michael Spivey and his colleagues offer the view that perception and sensory-motor skills are crucial in guiding syntax processing, with affordances offered by the visual display often determining the processing of

---

[34] On the importance of mental imagery for human cognition, also see Arnheim 1969, Kosslyn 1994 and 2005, and Pinker 1997: 283–293.

syntactically ambiguous sentences. "It is clear that the information flow between language processing and visual perception is substantially greater than was predicted by modular accounts of mind," which is probably due to the fact that "deep down, both language and vision are using formats of representation that already have a substantial amount in common" (Spivey et al. 2005: 249).

There is a huge and constantly growing body of evidence in favor of at least some version of the perceptual symbol account.[35] To begin with, it is clear that offline reasoning and language comprehension is imagery based. In a series of classic experiments on the mental rotation of three-dimensional objects, Roger Shepard, Lynn Cooper, and Jacqueline Metzler showed that reaction times for subjects asked to match objects varied consistently as a function of the angular difference of the objects, suggesting that subjects were mentally simulating physical rotation of the objects in real time.[36] Observation of eye saccades during sentence comprehension reveals that subjects' eyes react to a described situation in an attenuated but similar manner to how they would react if the situation were actually in front of them, suggesting that descriptive sentences are serving as cues for imagistic reconstruction of scenarios (Spivey & Geng 2001). It is also apparent that imagination involves the activation of the appropriate sensory-motor regions. Damasio and his colleagues, for instance, have found that achromatopsia (the loss of color perception) also precludes imaging color in recall (Damasio 1985), and Mark Wexler et al. 1998 found that the premotor cortices utilized in actual physical rotation of objects are also activated in mental rotation.[37] Further, this sort of sensory-motor simulation is necessary in processing even less obviously perceptual concepts. Damage to sensory-motor systems, for instance, results in category-specific deficits in cognition: damage to visual areas selectively disrupts the conceptual processing of categories specified by visual features (e.g., birds), while damage to motor regions selectively disrupts the use of categories specified by motor programs (e.g., tools) (Warrington & Shallice 1984). Work on imitation has similarly found that both the perception and the conceptualization of action and action-related words require the activation of the appropriate sensory-motor regions of the brain (e.g., Rizzolatti et al. 2001).

That sensory-motor activation plays a crucial role in human language comprehension is also suggested by the fact that the affordances derived from sensory-motor simulations have a significant impact on both semantic and syntactic processing. Robert Stanfield and Rolf Zwaan (2001) found that pictures matching the implied spatial coordination of a given test sentence were recognized faster by

---

[35] For reviews see Barsalou 1999a: 579–580, Pulvermüller 1999, Martin & Chao 2001, Glenberg et al. 2005, Spivey et al. 2005, and Zwaan & Madden 2005. For the classic counterargument against the imagistic view of abstract concepts, see Pylyshyn 1980 and 1981.

[36] See the essays collected in Shepard & Cooper 1982.

[37] Cf. the recent study by Winawer et al. (2005) demonstrating that imagined and implied motion appear to recruit the same neural circuits involved in viewing actual motion.

subjects: if the test sentence, for instance, was "The pencil is in the cup," subjects were quicker to verify that a picture of a pencil depicted something mentioned in the sentence if the picture was of a vertically rather than of a horizontally oriented pencil. A series of experiments by Arthur Glenberg and Michael Kaschak (Glenberg & Kaschak 2002, Kaschak & Glenberg 2000) demonstrated that test sentences were comprehended more quickly when the movement required to physically make the response (reaching for a button) matched the implied movement of the sentence, and that novel verb argument constructions were accepted as comprehensible to subjects only if the subject could simulate a perception of them – that is, if they involved a physically possible scenario. Daniel Richardson et al. 2001 found that linguistically naïve subjects produced remarkably consistent image schema diagrams for given sample sentences in both forced-choice and free-choice experiments. For instance, when asked to provide visual representations of sentences such as "X argued with Y" or "X respected Y" using a simple computer drawing program, subjects provided remarkably consistent drawings. In addition, Richardson et al. (2003) showed that image schemas in stimulus verbs interfered with perception in corresponding regions of the visual field, and also facilitated recall and recognition of pictures. As Spivey et al. 2005 note, this second finding is important because it demonstrates that spatial knowledge is not merely being accessed by otherwise amodal representations, but that "spatial representations become active during normal real-time comprehension of language, and can be revealed in a concurrent but unrelated perceptual task" (260). With regard to syntax, Monica Gonzalez-Marquez & Spivey (2004) have demonstrated how an image-schema approach allows one to easily explain problems in linguistics that seem intractable from a formal perspective, in their case example the "*estar/ser*" distinction in Spanish. Ronald Langacker's and Leonard Talmy's work on cognitive grammar and semantics have similarly demonstrated the superior explanatory power of image-schematic over formal analyses of natural language use (Langacker 1987, 1991; Talmy 2000).

Perhaps the strongest argument in favor of something like the perceptual symbol account is that it avoids two fundamental problems that plague amodal symbolic accounts, the transduction problem (how perceptual signals could get "translated" into amodal symbols) and the grounding problem (how arbitrary, abstract symbols could ever come to refer to something in the world). As Spivey and his colleagues note, "True digital symbol manipulation would require a kind of neural architecture that is very different from the analog two-dimensional maps that might implement image-schematic representations (cf. Regier 1996) and that we know populate much of the cortex (e.g., Churchland & Sejnowski 1992; Swindale 2001)" (2005: 272). They argue that Occam's razor therefore favors a view whereby much of perception and cognition "is implemented in two-dimensional spatial formats of representation that we know exist in the brain, without the use of discrete symbolic representations that we have yet to witness." Barsalou sums up this argument against classical amodal theories of meaning by concluding that such theories "are unfalsifiable, they are not parsimonious, they lack direct support, they suffer conceptual problems such as transduction and symbol grounding, and it is not clear how to integrate them with theory in neighboring fields, such as perception and neuroscience" (1999a: 580).[38]

Prototypes and Radial Categories

Objectivist philosophy relies on classic Aristotelian categories, which have sharp boundaries and clearly defined sufficient and necessary conditions for category membership. If something like the perceptual symbol account of concepts is correct, this would entail the need for a different model of categorization, and evidence from cognitive psychology and linguistics has long suggested that the mode of categorization generally relied on by human beings differs significantly from the classical account. Much of the early work in this field was done by Eleanor Rosch and her colleagues,[39] who developed a theory of "radial" categorization based on a "prototype effect." Categories as they are usually active in human minds are based on certain exemplars or prototypes; membership in the category is then based on family resemblance and can be a matter of degree (there can be "better" or "worse" members of a given category). For example, most North Americans have an understanding of the category "bird" that is based on an image of a sparrow, robin, or jay. Most people can switch into a "logical category" mode and acknowledge that chickens, penguins, and ostriches are "birds," but they will continue to insist that these are not particularly "good" examples of birds. The same effect can be seen with social categories such as "bachelor": the pope, for instance, is not a particularly good instance of a "bachelor" (Lakoff 1987).

The dominance in everyday thought of prototype-based categorization is to be expected from the perspective of the perceptual symbol account of cognition. If concepts are a form of sensory-motor simulation, categorization will be based on imagined exemplars and family resemblances. As Barsalou notes, categorization understood from this perspective will also be designed not as a rigid net for exhaustively cataloguing and organizing sets of clearly defined objects in the world, but rather as a dynamic, contextual, and embodied means of gaining access to categorical inferences – that is, suggestions as to how to interact successfully with encountered objects and situations and to reason about absent (future) entities (1999a: 587). Jesse Prinz similarly observes that "we rarely categorize things for categorization's sake. Instead, we categorize things because we want to bring past knowledge to bear on the present, and we want to learn new things about the entities that we encounter in the world" (2005: 95). He argues for an "active tracking" model of conceptual categories, whereby concepts are understood as "tools for

---

[38] For analytic counterresponses, see Pylyshyn 1980, 1981, and 2003, Block 1983, and the replies to Barsalou 1999a.

[39] Rosch 1973 and Rosch et al. 1976; also see Lakoff 1987 and Medin 1989.

negotiating successful interactions with categories . . . allow[ing] us to react appropriately to category instances and to plan future interactions" (95). Experimental
work by W. Kyle Simmons and colleagues found that fMRI images of brain activity
in sensory regions of subjects asked to confirm the property of categories cor-
responded significantly with the predicted sensory profile of the category,[40] and
studies by Diane Pecher et al. 2003 on property verification tasks found significant
temporal costs in shifting from one sensory modality to another – suggesting that
subjects are activating sensory-motor prototype images in processing categories.
As Raymond Gibbs concludes, "prototypes are not summary abstractions based
on a few defining attributes, but are rich, imagistic, sensory, full-bodied mental
events" (2006: 83).

The Crucial Role of Metaphor in Abstract Thought

One central problem for the perceptual symbol account is that it is not yet entirely
clear how well it can handle abstract concepts, which is an especially pressing
problem because of recent evidence that abstract and concrete concepts are han-
dled by different representational systems in the brain (Pulvermüller 1999, Crutch &
Warrington 2005). In his recent work, Barsalou has argued that even abstract concepts are imagistic, understood perceptually by means of scene construction.[41]
Drawing upon work that suggests that words are normally and spontaneously
understood against a situational background, Barsalou and Wiemer-Hastings
(2005) argue that even quite abstract words are comprehended by activating images
of relevant situations. On this account, both *hammer* and *truth* are comprehended
by means of concrete imagery; our sense that *truth* is more "abstract" derives from
the fact that its content is distributed across a multitude of situations and involves
complex events, introspective simulation of internal somato-sensory states, and
multiple modalities of perception.[42]

An alternate – and perhaps more promising – approach to grounding abstract
concepts is by means of conceptual metaphor and conceptual blending theory,
which argue that sensory-motor schemas are inevitably drawn upon when human
beings contemplate or attempt to reason about abstract concepts.[43] Metaphor
and blending theory will be discussed at length in Chapter 4; for now we will
merely observe that there is a large and growing body of empirical evidence that
the inextricably perceptual character of concepts extends beyond more concrete
examples, such as birds, tools, or observable actions, to such abstract realms as
time, causation, and mathematics.

---

[40] Simmons et al. 2003, reviewed and discussed in Simmons & Barsalou 2003.
[41] See especially Barsalou et al. 2003 and Barsalou & Wiemer-Hastings 2005.
[42] For more on the abstract-concrete distinction, see Wiemer-Hastings & Xu 2005.
[43] See Fauconnier 1999, Gibbs & Berg 1999, and Langacker 1999 for concise statements on how Barsalou's
     perceptual symbol account relates to long-standing arguments in cognitive linguistics.

Some advocates of the perceptual symbol account, such as Barsalou himself, have argued for an exclusive role for analogue images as the sole medium of human thought (Barsalou 1999a and 1999b), whereas more moderate voices have argued that abstract concepts must have at least some amodal, "skeleton" structure independent of the image schemas drawn upon to flesh them out, and that human beings must have at least occasional access to an alternate, amodal, and "digital" mode of representation (Pinker 1997: 296–297).[44] In any case, as we will explore in much more detail in Chapter 4, cognitive linguists such as George Lakoff and Mark Johnson have made a strong case that nonpropositional, embodied "image schemas" play a fundamental and inextricable role in human cognition. Granting a substantive role to experiential, analogue image schemas in human cognition highlights the importance of tacit know-how and bodily engagement with the world and serves to undermine the objectivist goal of a purely formal account of reality.

The typical objectivist response to this challenge has been to grant that phenomena such as concrete images or metaphors play an important role in *everyday* language, and this has in fact been one of the main motivations behind the effort to construct an artificial formal language – perfectly literal and purged of sloppy images and metaphors – to express scientific or logical truths. The work of scholars such as Mary Hesse (1966), Earl MacCormac (1976), and Theodore Brown (2003) has called into question, however, the extent to which science has succeeded in freeing itself from metaphor, documenting in detail the foundational role that metaphor has played in both the formulation and the interpretation of scientific theories.[45] Lakoff and Johnson have made similar critiques of the objectivist project in philosophy, arguing that even such supposedly amodal and formal systems as Kant's or Frege's are, in fact, grounded in and motivated by particular sets of foundational metaphors that have their origins in human embodied experience (1999: 415–468).

As noted earlier, the metaphorical nature of our understanding of the world will be a major theme in Chapter 4. For now it is enough to note that, when we are really worried about accessing truth claims, they tend not to be the sorts of claims like "the cat is on the mat" that were the focus of the positivist Vienna Circle. We

---

[44] In their response to Barsalou 1999a, for instance, Fred Adams & Kenneth Campbell (1999) raise the classic Cartesian objection to the thoughts-as-images position: that we understand the concept of a chiliagon (thousand-sided closed figure), and understand how it differs from a myriagon (million-sided closed figure), while remaining completely incapable of forming an accurate mental image of either figure.

[45] Also cf. the work of Kevin Dunbar and his colleagues (see Dunbar 1999 and 2001 for a review) for a series of "in vivo" studies of weekly laboratory sessions documenting the formative role of analogical reasoning in the interpretation of results and formation of hypotheses. As Nancy Cartwright (1999) has noted, this idea that any abstract scientific model "always piggy backs on more concrete descriptions" (45) goes back to Lessing's notion of the "fable" as intuitive basis for scientific theories (37–39).

can look and see whether or not the cat is on the mat, and if so whether or not the mat needs to be dry-cleaned. This is not terribly interesting. What we are generally much more interested in knowing about – and most invested in debating – are claims like that of an American military commander, speaking in the early stages of the second Gulf War, that the United States had passed the "tipping point" in Iraq, or that the Iraqi insurgency "was on the run." The logical positivists believe such metaphorical statements can be reduced to equivalent "literal" ones, but what would it possibly look like to translate either of these claims into formal semantics and then match it against the world to see whether or not it "corresponds"? Or consider a perhaps less politically contentious statement such as the following, made by a political scientist at Istanbul University concerning the role of Turkey in the modern world: "I know it's a cliché, of Turkey being the bridge between East and West, between the modern and the traditional . . . But it's true. We are in between in every sense."[46] One might want to argue that at least in the geographical sense Turkey is "in between," but even this involves a metaphorical organization of our mental map of the world into a homogenous "East" and "West." And of course this geographical sense is not what most interests this political scientist or us, and evaluating his more abstract claims is a much less cleanly algorithmic process than determining whether or not Whiskers is on the mat again. If we take metaphor seriously as a tool of cognition – as an overwhelming amount of empirical evidence suggests we should – this fundamentally calls into question the objectivist correspondence model of truth.

PROBLEMS WITH OBJECTIVIST SCIENCE: WHAT DOES IT MEAN TO LIVE IN A POST-KUHNIAN WORLD?

The epistemological status of natural scientific inquiry is an important component of the overall argument of this book: what is the point of marshalling empirical evidence if the very status of empirical evidence is in doubt? If humanists are to be convinced that the cognitive sciences warrant their attention, the commonplace that natural science is merely one discourse among many has to be addressed. For this reason it is worth reviewing some of the genuine problems with objectivist models of science – problems that have led many in the humanities to the conclusion that science has been effectively stripped of any special epistemological status. Because of space and expertise constraints, this will be no more than a quick overview,[47] but it will, it is hoped, give some sense of the sorts of antiobjectivist critiques to which a viable model of scientific inquiry will have to respond.

---

[46] Fatmagul Berktay, quoted in the *Los Angeles Times*, Oct. 12, 2004.
[47] A very readable, even-handed, and short introduction to the philosophy of science is Chalmers 1999, and Schick 2000 provides a broad selection of primary writings on the subject, including many of the excerpts I will be citing.

Inductionism and Deductivism

The model of scientific inquiry that most closely matches the layperson's folk theory of science is inductionism, the idea that scientific theories arise from simply paying attention to "the facts." In a crude form it goes something like this: if we are interested in how X works, we assemble the appropriate instruments, gather observational data about X, perhaps check these observations by trying to replicate them, and then construct a theory that will account for our observations. Alan Chalmers quotes a typical expression of this commonsense view of science from a 1940s textbook:

It was not so much the observations and experiments which Galileo made that caused the break with tradition as his *attitude* to them. For him, the facts based on them were taken as facts, and not related to some preconceived idea . . . The facts of observation might, or might not, fit into an acknowledged scheme of the universe, but the important thing, in Galileo's opinion, was to accept the facts and build the theory to fit them. (Anthony 1948: 145, quoted in Chalmers 1999: 1–2)

As Chalmers notes, we see here a crystallization of not only a very common model of how science works but also an expression of the widespread view that science's attention to the facts, and only the facts, is what sets it apart from other, more "primitive" and traditional, ways of thought.

Even within traditionalist philosophy of science circles it has long been recognized that strict inductive observation could never by itself result in scientific theories. To begin with, there is Hume's fundamental observation that there is no way to guarantee that the future will resemble the past: no matter how many times we have, for instance, derived nourishment from a physical substance with the color and consistency of bread, the conclusion that this will always be the case does not logically follow – although humans nonetheless seem to have a strong tendency to trust that such inductive generalizations are linked to true and stable properties of objects around them.[48] Beyond this basic logical problem with generalizing from observation, there are more practical problems with a strictly inductivist account of science. What does one choose to observe, at what level of detail, and for how long? When is one done observing? Both defining one's given object of interest, X, and deciding what sorts of observations count as observations about X involve prior theoretical assumptions. Even Carl Hempel, who has defended a positive role for a broader conception of induction in science with his "hypothetico-deductive method," acknowledges that "empirical 'facts' or findings . . . can be qualified as logically relevant or irrelevant only in reference to a given hypothesis, but not in reference to a given problem" (1966: 12), which means that "the transition

---

[48] Hume 1777/1975: 33–34; a related point is made in Nelson Goodman's famous "grue" thought experiment (1954/1983).

from data to theory requires creative imagination. Scientific hypotheses and theories are not *derived* from observed facts, but *invented* in order to account for them" (15).[49]

Other philosophers of science take the stronger stance that there is no causal line from observation to theory. One of the most prominent critics of inductivism is Karl Popper, who argues that there is no consistent "logic of discovery" – that is, there is no consistent principle or method that would allow the derivation of scientific laws from any set of observation data (1934/1959). In Popper's view, the formulation of scientific hypotheses is an irrational (or nonrational) act of insight; he approvingly quotes Einstein's remark that "there is no logical path leading to [universal natural] laws. They can only be reached by intuition, based upon something like an intellectual love (*Einfühlung*) of the objects of experience."[50] While there may be no logic of discovery, there *is*, in Popper's view, a logic of corroboration, and it is this process of corroboration that forms the core of the scientific method. Scientific hypotheses are as much a product of nonrational intuition as works of poetry or mystical religious experiences; what separates scientific claims from nonscientific ones is that the former have been subjected to a rigorous process of attempted falsification. Through deduction, one can make observational predictions that constitute the logical consequences of a given theory. Through observation, one can then attempt to falsify these predictions. To the extent that a given theory resists repeated attempts to falsify it, it becomes more and more "corroborated" – and thereby worthy of our attention and trust – but no hypothesis is ever verified absolutely.

Popper's deductivist model of science has proven enormously influential, and most contemporary popular accounts of science follow him in citing falsifiability as the distinguishing characteristic of the scientific enterprise.[51] The birth of "science studies" in the 1960s was occasioned by the realization that there are some serious problems with both inductivist and deductivist-falsificationist models of science, which we will now sketch out briefly.[52]

---

[49] More sophisticated, formalized inductivist models have been proposed by the Bayesians, a group of philosophers of science inspired by the eighteenth-century mathematician Thomas Bayes. See Chalmers 1999: 174–192 for a basic introduction to Bayesianism, the Bayesians' attempts to get around the problem of induction, and further references. Bas Van Fraassen (1980) is the most prominent contemporary advocate of a nonrealist, instrumentalist Bayesianism.

[50] Quoted in Popper 1934/1959: 32.

[51] Brian Boyd (personal communication) has pointed out to me that many of the features of what I am calling the objectivist model of science are not characteristic of Karl Popper's actual position and that, in his critique of the Vienna Circle, Popper in fact advanced many of the same critiques of objectivism that I will be discussing here. Although it is a common practice to associate with Popper the sort of deductivist-falsificationist model of science that often serves as a default for both laypeople and working scientists, this is arguably a distortion of Popper's work.

[52] For a good overview of post-1960s philosophy of science and the objectivist models it was reacting against, see Shapere 1981.

There Is No Clear Distinction Between Facts and Theories

Both inductivist and deductivist models of science assume that there is a clear distinction between facts – the data that one gathers by means of observation or experiment – and the theories that then emerge out of and explain the data (inductivist model) or are to be falsified or confirmed by the data (deductivist-falsificationist model). One of the central contributions of science studies and pragmatist critiques of objectivism has been to problematize this crucial distinction.

This is of course the central import of Thomas Kuhn's famous concept of a "paradigm": what can count as a fact – what can be "observed" in the context of scientific inquiry – is to a certain extent determined by the scientific theory to which one is committed. The objectivist story of the development of physics, for example, is that Newtonian physics was superceded by Einsteinian physics, which explained everything Newtonian physics could plus more. In this understanding, Newtonian physics should be derivable from Einsteinian physics as a special case – that is, as Einsteinian physics applied at a certain macrophysical scale. Kuhn points out that this simply is not the case (1962/1970: 101–103), that the *physical referents* of the two theoretical paradigms are fundamentally different. "Successive paradigms tell us different things about the population of the universe and about that population's behavior," he observes, which means that each paradigm will have its own unique ontology and its own standards of what counts as a solution to a problem (103–104).

Talk of scientific "discovery" gives the impression that there is some preexisting object out there in the world, with a set of invariant and observer-independent properties, simply waiting to be found the way one finds a lost sock under the bed. Kuhn points out that such talk conceals the fact that, in some cases, "discovering a new sort of phenomenon is . . . a complex event, one which involves recognizing both *that* something is and *what* it is" (55). Hilary Putnam makes a similar point in observing that "particles" as understood in the context of quantum mechanics are not objects in the traditional, Newtonian sense of the word. The fact that quantum mechanics is nonetheless taken seriously as "science" is thus "a wonderful example of how with the development of knowledge our idea of what counts as even a *possible* knowledge claim, our idea of what counts as even a *possible* object, and our idea of what counts as even a *possible* property are all subject to change" (Putnam 1999: 8). In Putnam's view this supports William James's critique of objectivism that holds that "'description' is never a mere copying and that we constantly add to ways in which language can be responsive to reality" (9).

Expectations certainly do seem to play a large role in determining what human beings – including those human beings who pursue science as a career – are capable of noticing. Kuhn cites an early psychological experiment on paradigm-guided perception performed by J. S. Bruner and Leo Postman (1949), where subjects were exposed to decks of playing cards that contained a mixture of normal and anomalous cards – the latter being, for instance, a black ace of hearts or red six of spades – and asked to identify what they had seen. At early stages of exposure the anomalous cards were stubbornly misperceived: a red six of spades, for instance, would be reported to have been a (normal) six of spades or, say, a six of hearts. After repeated exposures, subjects gradually became aware that something was amiss – an awareness accompanied by increasingly intense personal distress – but continued to display a surprising degree of difficulty in identifying precisely *what* was wrong about the cards they had been seeing. In Kuhn's mind, the process undergone by subjects in this experiment parallels what happens in scientific paradigm shifts: inability to perceive anomaly followed by vague unease, then gradual and simultaneous emergence of observational and conceptual recognition, resulting finally in a paradigm shift. "In science, as in the playing card experiment," he observes, "novelty emerges only with difficulty, manifested by resistance, against a background provided by expectation" (1962/1970: 64). This is what leads Kuhn to conclude that "scientific fact and theory are not categorically separable, except perhaps within a single tradition of normal-scientific practice [period of paradigm stability]" (7). Paul Feyerabend makes a similar argument in noting that the "fact" of the perturbation in the orbit of Uranus that led to the discovery of Neptune (discussed in the next section) only counted as a fact for observers with very specific, Newtonian theoretical commitments. "[This supposed 'perturbation'] cannot be discovered by just anyone who has healthy eyes and a good mind. It is only through a certain expectation that it becomes the object of our attention" (1993: 152).

The dependence of observation on theory, and the consequent difficulty of disentangling fact from belief, has been the central theme of science studies critiques of objectivism. At this point in our discussion it should also be clear how this problem with attaining true "objectivity" falls out of the more basic problems with objectivism noted earlier: the enactive, embodied nature of perception, the crucial role of tacit know-how, the inevitable biasing effect of emotion, and the metaphoric nature of abstract reasoning.

Hypotheses Are Not Clearly Falsifiable

The Popperian method involves formulating a hypothesis and then designing a carefully controlled "crucial experiment" that would allow one to selectively falsify this hypothesis. As many philosophers of science have long argued, such "crucial experiments" are in fact impossible in principle, because the hypothesis one wishes to test is always embedded in a vast network of auxiliary hypotheses and background assumptions. If the experiment returns a false result, it is impossible to say for certain *what*, in fact, has been falsified: it may be the hypothesis one intended to test, but it may also be any one or combination of the myriad background assumptions and auxiliary hypotheses. This problem with falsification was first systematically formulated by Pierre Duhem and elaborated by Quine, and has since become known as the Quine-Duhem thesis. As Duhem observes,

The physicist can never subject an isolated hypothesis to experimental test, but only a whole group of hypotheses; when the experiment is in disagreement with his predictions, what he learns is that at least one of the hypotheses constituting this group is unacceptable and ought to be modified; but the experiment does not designate which one should be changed. (1906/1954: 187)

Besides this theoretical problem of determining *what* precisely is falsified when an experiment does not work, there is also the more practical consideration that actual working scientists are not, in fact, strict falsificationists – nor would it be desirable if they were. Perhaps the most famous illustration of this is the story of the discovery of the planet Neptune in 1846. At the time, the outermost known planet was Uranus, which was found to follow an orbit that deviated from what would be predicted by Newtonian mechanics. Strict falsificationism would seem to demand that astronomers and physicists therefore abandon Newtonian mechanics as a falsified theory, but of course this is not how important and deeply entrenched hypotheses are actually treated. Rather than discard Newton, astronomers instead questioned their auxiliary hypotheses, in particular their assumption that there were only seven planets in the solar system. What if there were a hitherto unknown and unobserved eighth planet whose presence was causing the "perturbations" observed in the orbit of Uranus? The Englishman John Couch Adams and the French astronomer Urbain Jean Leverrier both produced calculations that predicted where one might expect to find such a hypothetical planet, and in 1846 the planet that came to be known as Neptune was observed by the German astronomer Johann Gottfried Galle, supposedly within 2.5 degrees of the position predicted by the mathematicians.[53]

This oft-cited example of the triumph of mathematical prediction also incidentally illustrates the scientific productivity that comes from *resisting* the falsification of important hypotheses. In his criticism of Popper, Kuhn has such examples as this in mind when he makes the point that important hypotheses ("paradigms") are in practice *never* falsified – or recognized by scientists working within the paradigm itself as having been falsified – until there arises an alternate hypothesis to fall back upon:

Once it has achieved the status of a paradigm, a scientific theory is declared invalid only if an alternative candidate is available to take its place. No process yet disclosed by the historical study of scientific development at all resembles the methodological stereotype of falsification by direct comparison with nature. (1960/1970: 77)

---

[53] A nice discussion of this example and of the Quine-Duhem thesis in general can be found in Patricia Churchland 1986: 260–265.

When anomalous experimental results arise within a given paradigm, Kuhn argues that the typical response is to devise "numerous articulations and *ad hoc* modifications of [the] theory in order to eliminate any apparent conflict" (78), and this is certainly what one observes in the case of the discovery of Neptune.

Hilary Putnam has therefore argued that, while we can agree with deductivists that there is no logic of discovery, we must also admit that there is no logic of *testing* either:

All the formal algorithms proposed for testing, by Carnap, by Popper, by Chomsky, etc., are, to speak impolitely, *ridiculous*: if you don't believe this, program a computer to employ one of these algorithms and see how well it does at testing theories! There are *maxims* for discovery and maxims for testing: the idea that correct ideas just come from the sky, while the methods for testing them are highly rigid and predetermined, is one of the worst legacies of the Vienna Circle. (1981: 78)

We will explore in Chapter 5 how Putnam believes that a pragmatic conception of truth can get us past some of the logical problems surrounding induction and empirical testing, but the point that concerns us now is that falsification does not seem to provide the algorithmic certainty that objectivism requires of it.

Underdetermination: Facts Consistent with an Infinitude of Hypotheses

Another consequence of the Quine-Duhem thesis is the principle of the underdetermination of theories by evidence, which holds that any set of observational data can be explained by theoretically innumerable rival hypotheses that are all consistent with the evidence. This is a skeptical observation with an ancient pedigree; one of its more prominent early-modern forms is Descartes' famous concern that the entire world of experience may not be what it seems, but rather may be an illusion created by an all-powerful "evil genius." In philosophy of science, the principle of underdetermination is invoked to explain how serious theoretical controversy can continue to exist even when there is broad agreement concerning the empirical evidence.[54] For instance, Feyerabend, in his account of the Copernican revolution, argues that the central issue was not empirical disagreement, but what theoretical framework was to be employed in order to interpret commonly accepted data: "Copernicus thought the Ptolemaic system to be *empirically adequate* – he criticized it for *theoretical reasons*" (1993: 145). What we might see as a weak form of underdetermination was wielded by Cardinal Bellarmine in his case against Galileo in the seventeenth century. In a letter to the monk Foscarini, the cardinal acknowledges that the Copernican system seems to "save appearances" better than the Ptolemaic, in that it resorts to fewer ad hoc devices like eccentrics and epicycles. It

---

[54] See Laudan 1996: 29–54 for a summary of how the principle of underdetermination has been employed by philosophers of science from Quine through Kuhn to Derrida; Laudan's position will be discussed in more detail in Chapter 5.

does not, however, eschew the use of ad hoc adjustments altogether, which means that Galileo was unable to demonstrate absolutely the *truth* of heliocentrism. Since the Copernican and Ptolemaic systems could thus *both* be seen as consistent at some level with the evidence, and taking into consideration all the evidence in the Bible for the Ptolemaic cosmos, Bellarmine concluded that the most reasonable strategy was to stick with scripture (Finocchiaro 1989: 68).

Feyerabend typically takes underdetermination in its strongest sense: choice between competing theories is radically underdetermined, which means that the *only* criteria for theory choice are personal whim or preference. Paradigm shifts, in his view, are brought about solely by "*irrational means* such as propaganda, emotion, *ad hoc* hypotheses, and appeals to prejudices of all kinds" (1993: 114). It is certainly the case that, given a particular set of data concerning, say, global warming, there is no formal, principled algorithm for deciding between theory T_1 and the theory T_1 + "Madonna will put out a Grammy-winning album in 2010." While the latter seems absurd in the context of what we are trying to explain, no amount of observation by itself will allow us to reject it in favor of the former. In Chapter 5 we will discuss pragmatic considerations, including Occam's razor, that appear capable of blocking the slide into strong underdeterminationism, allowing us to dismiss absurdly ad hoc theories. In the meantime it is sufficient here to observe that the principle of underdetermination suggests that theory choice often has as much to do with prior theoretical and ontological commitments as with "the facts themselves."

The Disunity of Science

John Dupré's *The Disorder of Things* (1993) challenges the objectivist model of the physical world as one great mechanism driven by a single, fundamental form of causation, whose workings could eventually be encompassed by one grand theory. His "radical ontological pluralism" or "promiscuous realism" argues that "there are countless kinds of things . . . subject each to its own characteristic behavior and interactions" (1), which means that "there are countless legitimate, objectively grounded ways of classifying objects in the world" (18). Ontologies and principles that allow one to develop a coherent model of, say, oceanic current flows may prove utterly useless when applied to, say, human physiology, and there is no a priori reason to expect there to be some sort of more basic level of ontology that could consistently and systematically unify the various levels of explanation that we see out in the world. Nancy Cartwright makes a similar argument that scientific laws are a "patchwork, not a pyramid." Rather than converging toward a single, grand, unifying theory, the laws of science are most accurately seen as

apportioned into disciplines, apparently arbitrarily grown up; governing different sets of properties at different levels of abstraction; pockets of great precision; large parcels of qualitative maxims resisting precise formulation; erratic overlaps; here and there, once in while, corners that line up, but mostly ragged edges; and always the cover of law just loosely attached to the jumbled world of material things. (1999: 1)

She argues for what she terms "metaphysical nomological pluralism," "the doctrine that nature is governed in different domains by different systems of laws not necessarily related to each other in any systematic or uniform way" (31).

In addition to arguing that the various branches of the natural sciences are not unified as the objectivist tradition would have it, many philosophers of science have also argued that it is unclear what it is, precisely, that distinguishes science from nonscience. Paul Feyerabend has been the most extreme advocate of this position, arguing that the goal of laying down sharp criteria that would clearly demarcate science from nonscience has proven to be a chimera:

> The events, procedures and results that constitute the sciences have no common structure; there are not elements that occur in every scientific investigation but are missing elsewhere... The assumption of a single coherent world-view that underlies all of science is either a metaphysical hypothesis trying to anticipate a future unity, or a pedagogical fake; or it is an attempt to show, by a judicious up- and down-grading of disciplines, that a synthesis has already been achieved. (1993: 1)

Science, therefore, is in Feyerabend's view merely the form of religion that is currently most dominant in the modern West, with no more claim to epistemological priority than faith healing or astrology. In Chapter 5 I will ultimately reject the "anything goes" epistemology that Feyerabend advocates and attempt a broad, pragmatic definition of science. It is, however, clear that when it comes to formulating a strict demarcation between science and nonscience, the usual suspects – particularly the principle of falsifiability – have not lived up to their promise.

Absolute, Disinterested Objectivity Is an Illusory Goal

One of the more prominent themes of the science studies movement has been the locating of natural science investigation within a network of less-than-godlike social and economic concerns. Bruno Latour and Steven Woolgar (1979/1986), for instance, produced one of the early science studies classics by applying anthropological techniques normally reserved for studying non-Western cultures to a "tribe" of scientists at the Salk Institute investigating the structure of a hormone that came to be known as TRF. One of the more reasonable points Latour and Woolgar make is that the scientists they are studying are not godlike, purely disinterested observers of Nature, but human beings driven by a complex mix of motives, partially blinded by a host of unexamined assumptions, and utterly dependent on complex, theory-derived technologies to "observe" the phenomena in which they are interested.

In addition to more obvious personal motives, such as a desire for prestige, more subtle and difficult to detect socially derived prejudices and assumptions play a role in shaping the direction of scientific inquiry. Elisabeth Lloyd cites as an example the revealing case of statistician and primatologist Jeanne Altmann, who questioned male- and dominance-centered assumptions involved in sampling primate behavior and introduced "focal animal sampling," which provided a more accurate and representative cross-section of primate behavior. This methodological shift – which came to be widely viewed in the primatological community as empirically superior – can arguably be credited to the exposing of previously hidden background social and gender assumptions that informed not only theory formation but also the very manner in which data was gathered (1996: 240–241). One of the more laudable goals of the science studies movement is, as Sandra Harding explains, to detect these sorts of "culture-wide presuppositions that shape the dominant conceptual frameworks of disciplines and public discourse. Such presuppositions, if unexamined, function as evidence, 'laundering' sexism or racism or class interests by transporting them from the social order into 'the natural order'" (1996: 18).[55]

The problem of personal and social biases aside, the role of modern instrumentation in mediating scientific knowledge is worth focusing on for both theoretical and practical reasons. Theoretically, the degree to which scientific "observation" has become more and more massively mediated by more and more indirect sorts of instrument technologies calls into question any sort of simplistic objectivist model of an unbiased observer coming directly into contact with reality. This is Elisabeth Lloyd's point when she comments on Robert Boyle's experiments at the dawn of the modern scientific age:

we, and not exclusively the reality independent of us, are "responsible" for what we know. The point is both simple and incontestable: more than the existence of reality is necessary for us to know it; it has been there all along, and yet we have not known it until very recently; in order for us to know it, it must necessarily come within the purview of whatever methods and experimental apparatus we do have, which are, themselves, our own creations. (1996: 232–233)

Besides this theoretical consideration – subsumed under the problems with theory-fact distinction discussed earlier – there is another dimension that is more immediately pragmatic. These complex instruments are expensive, and in order for scientists to do their work someone has to be willing to pay for them, as well as for the construction and upkeep of the complex buildings in which this instrumentation must reside. Foundations, research universities, governments, the military wings of governments, and private corporations are the sorts of social entities that possess the needed capital, but how do these entities decide which projects to fund, and why? What do they expect in return for their investment? A central theme in

---

55 Of course, this "laundering" metaphor assumes that there are valid and invalid sources of knowledge, something that, as we will discuss in Chapter 3, is undermined by Harding's broader position.

the science studies movement is that these sorts of social and economic interests play an important role in moving scientific investigation in certain directions and shaping the sorts of questions scientists are able to ask.

OBJECTIVISM ON THE ROPES

Despite the common refrain that dualism and objectivism are the nefarious creations of the alienated Western tradition, I will make the case in Chapter 3 that a more moderate, folk version of both is probably part of shared human cognitive architecture. The world *does* appear to human beings as made up of discrete objects with clear boundaries and as falling into sharply demarcated ontological classes – living things, objects, agents. Even the basics of algorithmic reasoning seem to come naturally to us: formal operations such as basic arithmetic, geometrical reasoning, *modus ponens* and *modus tollens* are not entirely foreign to any conscious, cognitively active human being. What *is* probably unique to the West is the manner in which, especially since the Enlightenment, the particular cluster of human cognitive abilities encompassed by the label "objectivism-rationalism" has been both obsessively refined and increasingly singled out as the only worthwhile mode of human cognition. It is this fetishizing of what is, in the end, merely one among many ways human beings cope with their world that sets Western epistemology up for the big fall: once objectivist-rationalist models have become entrenched as the sole avenue to truth, perceived problems with objectivism appear to threaten the very foundations of knowledge itself. This is why Larry Laudan has argued that strong postmodern relativism is "positivism's flip side" (1996: 25), and why Richard Bernstein has traced the origin of modern philosophical skepticism back to our "Cartesian anxiety" (1983: 16–25).

Easing this anxiety without provoking a complete philosophical nervous breakdown requires a gentle relaxing of our grip on objectivism. Part of the vehemence and persistence of postmodern relativist movements in the Academy can, I think, be attributed to the refusal of objectivist champions to surrender any ground. Faced with both postmodern and pragmatist critiques of objectivism, the response from traditionalist quarters – particularly Anglo-American philosophy departments – has been to circle the wagons and huddle for protection, taking occasional potshots at the easier targets flashing by. I will argue later that the extremes of postmodernism have driven many intelligent young people away from areas of the humanities that are dominated by obscure, pretentious jargon and empty rhetorical posturing. Philosophy departments might have served as a haven for many of these intellectual refugees, but the methodological rigidity and increasingly irrelevant formal navel-gazing that dominates most Anglo-American philosophy departments has made them less than welcoming – especially to those who have become aware of the real chinks in objectivism's armor. Although analytic philosophers and formal linguists cannot help but be aware of some of the problems already discussed, the fundamental challenge that they present to the analytic framework is rarely confronted. In most circles such issues as conversational expectations or background knowledge are either dismissed outright as matters of "mere pragmatics" or else treated like inconvenient guests: given polite attention and allowed a cursory walk about, but then hurried out the door so that one can get back to work.

A representative example of objectivism's problem with denial is related by Hilary Putnam. Having noted the sorts of problems with a strictly algorithmic, formal model of sentence processing described earlier – the various potential meanings of "There is a lot of coffee on the table" – Putnam describes the response of "a philosopher of language of [his] acquaintance," who suggested that one could still insist that there is a single "standard meaning" of the sentence: there are *many molecules of coffee* on the table. All of the other meanings Putnam discusses are mere derivations of this objective, Gricean meaning. "But if that is right," Putnam observes, "the 'standard' sense is a sense in which the words are never used!" (1999: 88). It is this sort of reaction to critiques of objectivism from analytic philosophers – not at all untypical, in my experience – that Putnam argues has prevented academic philosophy from formulating an effective response to relativist critiques. He observes that

analytic philosophy pretends today not to be just one great movement in the history of philosophy – which it certainly was – but to be philosophy itself. This self-description *forces* analytic philosophy . . . to keep coming up with "new solutions" to the problem of the Furniture of the Universe – solutions which have become more and more bizarre, and which have lost all interest outside of the philosophical community. (1990: 51)

We can recognize the great achievements in the formalization of logic by the Vienna Circle, for instance, while still recognizing that formal logic is an occasionally helpful tool, applicable to particular types of problems, and not the royal road to Truth itself. We turn now to a consideration of the panoply of movements I am gathering together under the rubric "postmodern relativism" – objectivism's evil twin, which draws its strength from objectivism's continued refusal to admit its own limitations.

2

&

They Live Among Us: Characterizing Postmodernism in the Academy

A CASE COULD BE MADE THAT EVERYTHING INTERESTING THAT HAS happened in "thought" – philosophy most broadly understood – in the past hundred years or so is at least foreshadowed, and in many cases clearly laid out, in the writings of Friedrich Nietzsche. Unfortunately, those inspired by Nietzsche's critiques of objectivism did not also follow his lead back to the body and the biological roots of human cognition, but rather seem to have, in the end, fallen into the very sort of idealism and intellectual "Tartuffery" that Nietzsche so despised. The popularity of postmodern and poststructuralist theory in the heady years of the 1970s and 1980s is understandable, and it would be unfair to slight their contributions as an important reaction against the sort of unreflective, culturally myopic, naïve Enlightenment realism that dominated the Academy at that time. Its appeal as part of the post-1960s Zeitgeist is also undeniable, with its questioning of authority, celebration of cultural diversity, and opposition to pervasive racism and sexism. It is also all too easy to caricature postmodern theory, or to present a straw-man version of it, and I will do my best to avoid doing so here. Postmodern theorizing has in innumerable ways changed the landscape of the humanities for the better. It has given us an increasingly nuanced picture of human sexuality and gender identities, exposed widespread cultural myopia and intellectual imperialism, and redirected scholarly attention away from often unrepresentative and moribund high intellectual traditions toward the richness of cultural experience as it is lived on the ground. I will argue, however, that because it never casts off the limitations of dualism, its explanatory and liberatory potential ultimately remains unrealized, undercut by deep internal and external flaws.

DO AS I SAY, NOT AS I DO

Strict Calvinists believe that everything that has ever happened, and that ever will happen, in the world was and is predetermined by God. When asked about their beliefs on questionnaires, they are able to follow the implications of this belief in predestination – for instance, that nothing a person does can affect that person's eventual salvation or damnation – in a quite consistent manner. When given time-pressured, realistic tasks to solve, however, they usually fall back immediately into everyday modes of reasoning, where human actions are freely chosen and individuals have some control over their destiny. The same Calvinists can also often be observed on Sundays fervently and sincerely praying for God to help their favorite football team.[1]

A similar gap between professed theoretical belief and actual practice can be observed throughout the humanities. Over the past decades, militantly strong forms of social constructivism have established themselves as the foundational theoretical assumptions in most of the core humanities disciplines: the various national literatures and comparative literature, religious studies, social anthropology, media studies, history, art history, areas of sociology, and even geography. I will be referring to these various strands of social constructivism as "postmodern" because they are unanimous in rejecting the Enlightenment belief that we can know something about the world beyond disguised social opinions or prejudices. The problem with this sort of position is that its profound skepticism about truth-claims makes it difficult to see how it can continue to function as a viable intellectual position within the Academy. If it is impossible to make substantial truth-claims, and if all that we as humanists (or as any sort of intellectual or scholar) are doing is merely rearranging signifiers in an essentially arbitrary manner, it is hard to see – not to put too fine a point on it – why people should be giving us money to do so. Yet this absolute conviction in the "truth" of social constructivism does not prevent humanists from continuing to engage in responsible, thoughtful scholarship. Humanists go on drawing their salaries and teaching their courses with good consciences because, at some level, they appear to believe that they *are* discovering new things about the world. This everyday comportment – along with the Academy's continued insistence on historical and linguistic accuracy, coherence of argumentation, and textual and material evidence – seems to fly in the face of the belief that, "in fact," all we are really doing is wandering aimlessly down an endless hallway of distorting mirrors.

The fact that humanists ignore their absurd theoretical stances when going about their own work does not make the tension between the two disappear – theoretical stances do matter, as do tensions. To my mind, the ever-present gap between theory and practice causes much of the work being produced these days in the humanities to be enveloped in a kind of intellectual miasma. After decades of their embracing increasingly radical forms of postmodern relativism, this miasma has become so thick that humanists are having more and more trouble explaining the nature of their work to outsiders, and are therefore finding themselves increasingly isolated from both other areas of the Academy and normal canons of intelligibility. Undergraduate and graduate enrollments are down, as is general funding support for humanistic studies from universities and foundations – what right-minded appropriation committee wants to fund a study that claims that its conclusions have

---

[1] This phenomenon of "theological incorrectness" (Slone 2004) will be explored in more detail in Chapter 3.

no special truth status? This, of course, serves only to make humanists more persnickety about the evils of the hegemonic, reductionistic, irredeemably bourgeois natural sciences that are sucking up the lion's share of available resources.

Let me illustrate the frustrating nature of this impasse with a recent, and representative, example. A primary theoretical concern in the academic study of religion these days is the relationship of religious insider to religious outsider: that is, the relationship of the scholar of religion to the believers that he or she studies. What are we to make of an account of a particular cult of Hinduism, for instance, that attributes to its adherents motives and subconscious beliefs that the adherents themselves would find unrecognizable, or even repulsive? An influential answer to this question is that such an account is "reductionistic" and, therefore, invalid. As the early religious studies theorist Wilfred Cantwell Smith expressed it, "no statement of a religion is valid unless it can be acknowledged by that religion's believers" (1959: 42). Under this view, scholars of religion are seen as engaged in a delicate task of sympathetic *Verstehen*, coparticipants with the subjects whom they study in the task of creating meaning.

A recent piece in the flagship journal of North American religious studies (McCutcheon 2006a) challenged this view, arguing that any interesting work of scholarship *has* to involve reductionism of some sort. Whether the goal is to document the historical development of a particular doctrine or practice, or to search for underlying themes across historical periods or faiths, the work of the scholar of religion inevitably involves some sort of explanatory reduction. The only way to entirely avoid reductionism would be to simply report, verbatim, the words of the believers themselves, but this would be journalism, not scholarship – and fairly superficial and uninteresting journalism at that. Reductionism of some sort is central to scholarly analysis in any field of the humanities, and therefore to reject reductionism tout court would involve, the author suggests, "the end of the human sciences as we know them" (736).

I agreed wholeheartedly with this sentiment but found myself at a loss as to how it could be reconciled with the thoroughly social constructivist, relativist framework within which it was formulated. Elsewhere in the essay the same author argues that "all acts of signification . . . are a translation of one set of claims into a language that is itself no closer than any other to some presumed authentic source of the Nile" (742), and echoes Jean Baudrillard's claim that all we ever have is representations, "each competing for the chance to stand in for a Real that never was present to begin with" (743). The manner in which this sort of social constructivism has become the basic background dogma in religious studies is made quite clear in the subsequent response and counterresponse to this article, where both participants prefaced their comments by approvingly citing the words (the Word?) of the influential theorist Jonathan Z. Smith: whatever our differences concerning the relative status of religious insider versus outsider, as scholars of religion we all "follow J. Z. Smith and agree that it is history . . . all the way down" (McCutcheon 2006b: 756). It is, of course, difficult to see how one could defend explanatory reductionism if no statement has a greater claim to validity than any other – the very concept of "explanation" presumes a level of deeper causal insight or accuracy. However odd, this is nonetheless a common spectacle in the humanities: otherwise quite thoughtful and analytically gifted humanities scholars genuflecting before the altar of social constructivism while simultaneously defending arguments that lose all of their bite if we take such constructivism seriously.

I certainly was taught that "history goes all the way down" by J. Z. Smith, and Clifford Geertz, and Judith Butler, and all of the other theorists assigned to me in graduate school theories and methods courses – the idea that "history goes all the way down" is a deeply engrained truism in most of the core humanities departments, with only philosophers and perhaps rogue historians still valiantly trying to pin down the ever-receding "Real" that Baudrillard has assured us never existed. It is also easy to understand why scholars across the humanities have become stuck in this theoretical dead end. Impressed by the postmodern critique of Enlightenment ideals, we no longer see objectivism as a viable option; left without a theoretical basis for establishing certain knowledge, we appear incapable of extracting ourselves from the social constructivist quagmire, where the only standard for debate appears to be winning the title of more-social-constructivist-than-thou.

In this chapter I aim to sketch out what I see as the basic "postmodernist" position,[2] in some of its various flavors, in order to document its continued presence as the default intellectual position in many, if not most, humanistic disciplines. I place this discussion in its own chapter, with a discussion of the problems with postmodernism to follow in Chapter 3, because characterizing postmodernism will take quite a bit longer than was the case with objectivism, and I would like to do it in more detail. Objectivists generally *admit* to being objectivists, and the position that I sketched out in the beginning of Chapter 1 is openly embraced by an identifiable set of analytic philosophers and first-generation cognitive scientists. One of the stranger features of the postmodernist position that I am going to outline in this chapter is that few, if any, humanists would admit to being one, and the common refrain heard nowadays is that the humanities have "moved beyond" postmodernism. As the example I cited previously indicates, I do not believe that this is the case, and I hope to show in what follows how the positions of Foucault, Bourdieu, Geertz, J. Z. Smith, Gadamer, and others whose approaches are still de rigeur in humanistic circles can be understood as postmodernist, at least in my sense of the term. I will turn, in Chapter 3, to exploring in some detail the various theoretical and empirical problems endemic to the postmodern position, in order to make it clear why we in the humanities urgently *do* need to move beyond postmodernism. Chapter 4 will then outline what a genuinely post-postmodern approach to culture and cultural diversity might look like.

---

[2] For a helpful recent glance of the current state of field in postmodernist theory, see the essays collected in Connor 2004.

The label "postmodern relativism" (or simply "postmodernism") as I will be using it throughout this book is a radial category encompassing a variety of movements, including most poststructuralist literary theory, Geertzian sociology, the Boasian school of anthropology, Whorfian linguistics, the "individualist constructivism" of French existentialism,[3] the "science studies" movement in the philosophy of science, the "philosophical hermeneutics" of Heidegger and Gadamer, Rortian "neo-pragmatism,"[4] and the sociology of Bruno Latour and Pierre Bourdieu. Many of the thinkers whom I include under my "postmodern" rubric would themselves reject the label, and I did consider concocting a neologism – along the lines of the "Standard Social Scientific Model" (SSSM) of Tooby and Cosmides – to avoid the inevitable objections I provoke when presenting my critique of "postmodernism": that, for instance, I am conflating postmodernism and poststructuralism, or that I am confusing the later, "amodernist" Latour with the postmodernists he criticizes.

I decided to stick with the label because I think it is the most accurate description of a recognizable intellectual position. The core feature of "postmodernism," in my mind, is a model of humans as fundamentally linguistic-cultural beings, combined with the belief that our experience of the world is therefore mediated by language or culture *all the way down*. On this model, we have no direct cognitive access to reality, and things in the world are meaningful to us only through the filter of linguistically or visually mediated cultural preconceptions. Common corollaries of this stance are strong linguistic-cultural relativism, a suspicion of any sort of universalist truth-claims,[5] and a "blank slate" view of human nature: we are nothing until inscribed by the discourses into which we are socialized, and therefore nothing significant about the way in which we think or act is a direct result of our biological endowment.[6] Despite their apparent diversity and rhetorical posturing, then, I think that it is fair to see these movements as "postmodern" because they unanimously reject the Enlightenment optimism that we can clearly tease apart nature and culture, fact and value – that we can *explain* anything. For postmodernism, the only mode of grasping the world available to human beings is humanistic *Verstehen*. This means that there is no way out of the closed circle of endless human conversation, which – by virtue of being utterly cut off from the world of things – can never achieve even partial or provisional conclusions. I now turn to a consideration of

---

[3] French existentialism is slightly different from the other strands of postmodernism in that meaning is created by an otherwise ungrounded *individual* act of will; in any case, meaning is here still an entirely arbitrary, human creation.
[4] Rorty, Heidegger, and Gadamer are favorites of many humanists looking for a "third way" beyond objectivism and subjectivism (see esp. Bernstein 1983, Varela et al. 1991, and Frisina 2002), but I will argue later that none of these thinkers succeed in really taking us there.
[5] As Jean-François Lyotard puts it, "Simplifying to the extreme, I define *postmodern* as incredulity toward metanarratives" (1984: xxvi).
[6] Cf. Tooby & Cosmides' characterization of the "Standard Social Scientific Model" (SSSM) (1992: 24–32) and Pinker's discussion of the "Holy Trinity" (Blank Slate, Noble Savage, and Ghost in the Machine) that he sees as dominating contemporary humanistic discourse (2002: 1–29, 121–135).

several prominent strands of postmodernism in order to bring out this core feature, which is more obvious in some cases than in others.

POSTSTRUCTURALIST THEORY: WORLD AS TEXT

The denial of extralinguistic knowledge of the world is perhaps most dramatically expressed in the various iterations of poststructuralist literary theory, famously summed up in Derrida's claim that *il n'y a pas de hors-texte* (there is no "outside the text"; 1978: 158). Of course, Derrida is not actually denying the existence of an extralinguistic reality of objects. What he *is* denying is the possibility that we can have any kind of direct access to these objects *an sich*; they are known to us only as discursive objects, strands in the woven text that makes up the humanly knowable world. As Roland Barthes explains in his introduction to semiology,

As for collections of objects (clothes, food), they enjoy the status of systems only in so far as they pass through the relay of language, which extracts their signifiers (in the form of nomenclatures) and names their signified (in the forms of usages or reasons) . . . it appears increasingly more difficult to conceive a system of images and objects whose *signifieds* can exist independently of language: to perceive what a substance signifies is inevitably to fall back on the individuation of a language: there is no meaning which is not designated, and the world of signified is none other than that of language. (1968: 10)

This language is not a system of signifiers directly connected to an extralinguistic reality, but rather a self-enclosed "domain of *articulations*." Meaning is thus reduced to "a cutting-out of shape," and the task of semiology is "far less to establish lexicons of objects than to rediscover the articulations which men impose on reality" (57). The inextricable embeddedness of human beings – and anything resembling human experience – in such semiological networks leads Barthes to conclude that "man does not exist prior to language, either as a species or as an individual" (1972: 135).

Though owing more to Nietzsche than to Saussurian structuralism, the work of Michel Foucault follows a similar path in his denial that language is in any way representational – that words refer to any sort of human-independent reality. What he wishes to do in his analyses of discourse deployment, Foucault declares, is to "dispense with 'things,'"

to substitute for the enigmatic treasure of "things" anterior to discourse, the regular formation of objects that emerge only in discourse. To define these *objects* without reference to the *ground*, the *foundation of things*, but by relating them to the body of rules that enables them to form as objects of a discourse and thus constitute the conditions of their historical appearance. (1972: 47–48)

Foucault's discourses ultimately involve more than simply words, implicating as well institutional structures, bodily practices, sexuality, and the application of power, so it is perhaps unfair to see him as espousing a "world as text" view. Yet even such apparently concrete phenomena are, in Foucault's view, accessible to and knowable by human beings only through the mediation of discourse. For instance, the human body is, for him, ultimately no more than "the inscribed surface of events (traced by language and dissolved by ideas), the locus of a dissociated Self (adopting the illusion of a substantial unity), and a volume in perpetual disintegration" (1977: 148). The choice of the term "discourse" is itself revealing, reflecting a deeply ingrained tendency in postmodern thought to conceive of humans as fundamentally linguistic beings.

When I first began presenting my views of postmodernism to academic audiences, I sometimes heard the objection that I was taking on a target that no longer exists – that the sort of strong linguistic constructivism that one finds in 1970s and 1980s poststructuralist or deconstructionist theorizing is no longer very common in the Academy. Indeed, even such an arch-textualist as Derrida himself has periodically attempted to distance himself from the position that "there is nothing beyond language, that we are imprisoned in language . . . and other stupidities of that sort" (1984: 124), and it is clear that the overt denial of extralinguistic reality is becoming increasingly *depassé* in postmodernist circles. Nonetheless, if you look at what postmodern theorists actually *write* (as opposed to what they *claim* about what they write), strong social constructivist themes coupled with metaphors of "authorship" and "text" as the building blocks of human reality are still quite thick on the ground, which suggests that – rhetorical posturing aside – something like the model of world as text is still very much alive and well, and still functioning as the default theoretical stance in most areas of the humanities.

To take one example from my field, Lydia Liu – a representative contemporary advocate of the "semiotic turn" in Chinese cultural studies – presents the interactions of cultures that occurred in the wake of the European colonialism in China as a struggle at the level of the "super-sign,"

not a word but a hetero-cultural signifying chain that crisscrosses the semantic fields of two or more languages simultaneously and makes an impact on the meaning of recognizable verbal units . . . The super-sign emerges out of the interstices of existing languages across the abyss of phonetic and ideographic differences. As a hetero-cultural signifying chain, it always requires more than one linguistic system to complete the process of signification for any given verbal phenomenon. The super-sign can thus be figured as a manner of metonymical thinking that induces, compels, and orders the migration and dispersion of signs across different languages and different semiotic media. (2004: 13)

Colonialism is here no longer a history of individual human beings interacting on the ground, in a shared world of physical objects and inherently meaningful phenomena, but a contest of disembodied semiological networks. One might expect that at least the military force behind certain of these networks might be afforded extradiscursive status, but Liu closes off this possibility as well. For instance, at one point she discusses a scene in Daniel Defoe's *Robinson Crusoe* that captures the essence of European colonialism: Crusoe, in the midst of his "first contact" with the colonial subject Friday, endeavors to intimidate Friday by demonstrating the power of his gun. He points his gun at a distant bird, fires, and drops it dead to the ground – suitably impressing the terrified Friday. Liu explains that "it should be emphasized that the power of Crusoe's gun lies not in its physical ability to take the other's life but in its very indexicality as a sign of terror and human intention," an instance of both "Louis Althusser's notion of interpellation" and "the concept of deixis in linguistic theory" (16). Friday is indeed intimidated by this demonstration, but we might be forgiven for wondering whether or not the "terror of indexicality" is really to blame – sometimes a gun is just a gun. In the semiological approach, though, even such a basic tool for the projection of deadly force from one body to another cannot be apprehended by the human subject until abstracted into the all-consuming world of signs.

From Liu's realm of super-signs to Judith Butler's continued insistence on gender as "a practice of improvisation with a scene of constraint," the terms of which "are, from the start, outside oneself, beyond oneself in a sociality that has no single author" (2004: 1), the image of world as text or as network of symbolic performances is still a widespread force in humanistic studies. The inclusion of a wider spectrum of discursive expressions in recent decades – photographs, films, clothes, cars, billboards, eBay auctions – creates the impression that we may be getting beyond language to some contact with the physical world, but this impression is a superficial one. Clothing, food, media images, and ceramic tchotchkes have all been swallowed up into semiological networks. This idea of the subject and society as linguistic constructions – as products of the "migration and dispersion of signs" – bears obvious resemblance to the strand of postmodernism we turn to now.

THE STANDARD SOCIAL SCIENTIFIC MODEL: THE SOCIAL CONSTRUCTION OF REALITY

Recent defenders of vertically integrated approaches to the study of culture have directed most of their fire against the various forms of social constructivism in anthropology and sociology characterized by Tooby and Cosmides as the "Standard Social Scientific Model" (SSSM). Tooby and Cosmides 1992 (esp. 24–32) provide a comprehensive, detailed analysis of the basic principles of the SSSM, its internal flaws, and its empirical implausibility,[7] so I will confine myself here to sketching out its basic outlines.

---

[7] See also Derek Freeman 1983 (esp. 19–49), Donald Brown 1991 (esp. 9–38), and Steven Pinker 2002 (esp. 5–29).

The basics of the SSSM fall quite naturally out of a dualistic model of human beings. Society or culture, as the product of the collective human mind, is the sole source of meaning; our bodies, as members of the dumb realm of physics, are inert repositories for the meaning structures produced by the collective mind. Society/culture, like the human spirit, is free in the sense of being subject only to its own internal logic and causality. Innate, biological tendencies are mechanistic and inflexible, suitable at most for guiding only basic, animal needs. Societies and cultures, as products of the free play of the collective human mind, will vary from one another in arbitrary and unpredictable ways; unconstrained by the malleable material upon which they impress themselves, they will also be internally monolithic.

As I will argue in Chapter 3, the dualism that lies at the heart of the SSSM is probably as old as *Homo sapiens*, and – Bruno Latour notwithstanding[8] – the distinction between nature and society that falls out of such dualism appears equally universal. The particularly extreme form of it that has become entrenched as the central dogma of modern social sciences can be traced back to Emile Durkheim, the father of modern academic sociology. "Society is a reality *sui generis*," Durkheim declares (1915/1965: 28–29), and this is because

man is double. There are two beings in him: an individual being which has its foundation in the organism and the circle of whose activities is therefore strictly limited, and a social being which represents the highest reality in the intellectual and moral order that we can know by observation – I mean society. (29)

The lower half of this "double being" is, according to Durkheim, causally unrelated to the upper half. The passive quality of the strictly limited organic part of "man" means that "these individual natures are merely the indeterminate material that the social factor molds and transforms. Their contribution consists exclusively in very general attitudes, in vague and consequently plastic predispositions which, by themselves, if other agents did not intervene, could not take on the definite and complex forms which characterize social phenomena" (1895/1962: 105–106).

As Tooby and Cosmides argue, the Durkheimian model of autonomous society impressing its structure upon the blank slate of human nature became the dominant guiding assumption for most subsequent work in anthropology and sociology, from Franz Boas and his disciples Ruth Benedict and Margaret Mead[9] to the social constructivism exemplified in works such as Peter Berger and Thomas Luckmann's influential *The Social Construction of Reality* (1966). This idea of society as an ontological autonomous realm even penetrated into certain regions of biology. For instance, Richard Lewontin, in his ongoing crusade against sociobiology, sees as his greatest weapon against the bogeyman of genetic determinism the "fact" that

---

[8] See the discussion of the "later" Latour in note 11.
[9] For a thorough debunking of Mead's exoticist account of Samoan culture, see Freeman 1983.

the genes "have been replaced by an entirely new level of causation, that of social interactions, with its own laws and its own nature that can be understood and explored only through that unique form of experience, social action" (1991: 123). Since the 1960s and 1970s, the original modernist thrust of Durkheim's project – to construct a rational science of social phenomena – has gradually fallen away as scholars in anthropology and sociology have combined Durkheim's rigid dualism with the epistemological skepticism coming out of poststructuralist literary theory.

The manner in which the "world as text" and "society as autonomous" strands of postmodernism are now usually found intertwined is perhaps best illustrated in the work of Clifford Geertz. Geertz shares the classic Durkheimian "blank slate" model of human nature, arguing that "there is no such thing as a human nature independent of culture" (1973: 49). Humans require symbolic culture because we lack the innate behavioral programs possessed by "lower" animals, which means that

undirected by culture patterns – organized systems of significant symbols – man's behavior would be virtually ungovernable, a mere chaos of pointless acts and exploding emotions, his experience virtually shapeless. Culture, the accumulated totality of such patterns, is not just an ornament of human existence but – the principal basis of its specificity – an essential condition for it. (46)

Geertz updates this model by integrating it with the textually oriented strand of postmodernism described earlier, arguing that culture is "essentially semiotic" (5), a form of "acted document" (10). The analysis of culture, whether our own or another, is thus "not an experimental science in search of a law but an interpretative one in search of meaning" (5). Geertz has spent most of his career vociferously policing the absolute ontological divide between the *Geisteswissenschaften* (the realm of *Verstehen*, or uniquely human "understanding") and the *Naturwissenschaften* (the realm of *Erklären*, or mechanistic explanation) – or, to use categories that he borrowed from Gilbert Ryle, between "thick description" and "thin description." Ryle had asked us to consider the following scenario:

Two boys fairly swiftly contract the eyelids of their right eyes. In the first boy this is only an involuntary twitch; but the other is winking conspiratorially to an accomplice. At the lowest or the thinnest level of description the two contractions of the eyelids may be exactly alike. From a cinematograph-film of the two faces there might be no telling which contraction, if either, was a wink, or which, if either, were a mere twitch. Yet there remains the immense but unphotographable difference between a twitch and a wink. (1971: 480)

The "immense but unphotographable difference" between a twitch and a wink can only be captured by "thick description," Ryle and Geertz argue, which goes beyond the mere physical to what Geertz refers to as the "semiotic meaning" of the gesture

(1973: 6). This meaning, in turn, can be deciphered only by means of a "socially established code," which means that performing true ethnology – focusing on thick description of human behavior – is "like trying to read (in the sense of 'construct a reading of') a manuscript" (10).

This semiotic approach to the study of human behavior has the effect of systematically denying any possible substantive role to "thin" bodily or physical processes, and thus it inevitably leads to the sort of social constructivism and cultural relativism that are defining features of the SSSM approach. Geertz's semiotic approach toward emotions, for instance – among whose practitioners he also mentions Michelle Rosaldo, Catherine Lutz, Jean Briggs, Richard Shweder, Robert Levy, and Anna Wierzbicka – sees them

in terms of the significant instruments and constructional practices through which they are given shape, sense, and public currency. Words, images, gestures, body-marks, and terminologies, stories, rites, customs, harangues, melodies, and conversations, are not mere vehicles of feelings lodged elsewhere, so many reflections, symptoms, and transpirations. They are the locus and machinery of the thing itself. (2000: 208)

"The case for the cultural construction of emotions," Geertz concludes after reviewing some of this work, "seems, to me at least, fairly well made" (210). It should be noted that Geertz has always gone to great lengths to distance himself from what he refers to as "absurd positions – radical, culture-is-all historicism, or primitive, the-brain-is-a-blackboard empiricism – which no one of any seriousness holds, and quite possibly, a momentary enthusiasm here and there aside, ever has held" (1984/2000: 50). Despite this rhetorical posturing, however, it is clear that – except for a rather thin soup of universals such as the fact that "men can't fly and pigeons can't talk" or that "Papuans envy, Aborigines dream" (1984/2000: 51) – Geertz and his followers see the humanly significant world (or perhaps better "worlds") as, in essence, culturally constructed.

SCIENCE STUDIES AND THE SLIDE INTO RELATIVISM

As an arena of battle between traditional objectivists and their postmodern critics, the field of science studies has generated quite a bit of heat in recent decades, with salvos from both sides giving rise to multiple volumes of essays and special issues of journals.[10] In this regard, science studies is a very helpful lens through which to view both the promise and excesses of postmodernism. Some of the genuine contributions science studies has made toward formulating a more sophisticated picture of science were discussed earlier with regard to problems with objectivist

---

[10] See, e.g., Marglin & Marglin 1990, Elvee 1992, Holton 1993, Gross & Levitt 1994, Gross et al. 1996, *Social Text* (Spring-Summer 1996), Sokal & Bricmont 1999, Koertge 1998, and The Editors of *Lingua Franca* 2000. Also see Segerstråle 2000: 333–347 for a short overview of the debate.

models of science, but I wish to examine here the manner in which – like the poststructuralist theory that inspires much of the science studies literature – these insights are ultimately undermined by an inevitable slide into epistemological relativism.

One of my points here is to justify including science studies under my "postmodernist" rubric, since many of its defenders vehemently deny holding to the sort of strong form of linguistic-cultural relativism that I and others attribute to them. Sandra Harding has declared that "feminist and antiracist science studies have called for more objective natural and social sciences, not less objective ones" (1996: 18), and Donna Haraway has similarly argued that feminist historians of science are simply insisting on a "better account of the world" that would result in "enforceable, reliable accounts of things" (1991: 187–188). Elisabeth Lloyd believes that science studies has been unfairly tarred with the label of relativist because its critics "tend not to distinguish between 'demystifying' science and 'discrediting' it," and fail to see that the science studies movement is actually aimed at helping science to be *more* rather than less objective (1996: 223). In Lloyd's view, the key to this misunderstanding is that critics attribute an "exclusivity doctrine" to science studies, whereby "social and scientific/evidential explanations are seen as strictly mutually exclusive" (229). With regard to studies such as Latour and Woolgar's famous (or infamous) *Laboratory Life*, she argues that "it is a mistake . . . to *assume* that social explanations are posed as *replacements* for all the reasons adopted by individual scientists" (230). This is a common move by defenders of science studies, so it is important to first establish that thinkers in this movement are, in fact, "postmodernist" in my sense of the term.[11]

In their second edition of the book originally entitled *Laboratory Life: The Social Construction of Scientific Facts*, Latour and Woolgar explain that they have dropped the word "social" from the subtitle because, in their view, the triumph of science studies and allied theorizing has caused it to lose its function as a referent. "*All interactions are social*," they explain. "What does the term 'social' convey when it refers equally to a pen's inscription on graph paper, to the construction of a text and to the gradual elaboration of an amino-acid chain? Not a lot. By demonstrating its pervasive applicability, the social study of science has rendered 'social' devoid of any meaning" (1979/1986: 281). The purpose of their book, a seminal and heavily cited text in the science studies movement, is to follow a team of scientists at the Salk Institute who are investigating the chemical structure of the hormone TRF. Latour and Woolgar argue that this substance should be viewed as socially constructed in the strongest possible sense of the word. Concerning the "inscription devices" (e.g., mass spectrometer, cell cultures) that the scientists were employing to – at

---

11 It should be noted that one of the founders and dominant figures in science studies, Bruno Latour later repudiated the strong relativist stance of the "strong programme" in science studies that he initially helped popularize; this "later Latour" will be discussed in a separate section.

least in their naïve view – determine the structure of TRF, Latour and Woolgar
note that

the central importance of this material arrangement is that none of the phenomena
"about which" participants talk could exist without it. Without a bioassay, for example,
a substance cannot be said to exist. The bioassay is not merely a means of obtaining some
objectively given entity; the bioassay constitutes the construction of the substance . . . It
is not simply that the phenomena *depend on* certain material instrumentation; rather,
the phenomena *are thoroughly constituted by* the material setting of the laboratory. The
artificial reality, which participants describe in terms of an objective entity, has in fact
been constructed by the use of inscription devices. (64)

Throughout their work, Latour and Woolgar emphasize their wish to avoid
"the misleading impression that the presence of certain objects was a pregiven
and that such objects merely awaited the timely revelation of their existence by
scientists. . . . Rather, objects (in this case, substances) are constituted through the
artful creativity of scientists" (129). TRF's status as a "new recently discovered substance" is only true "within the confines of networks of endocrinologists"; "outside
these networks TRF simply does not exist" (110).

    How do these undeniably relativist statements coming out of the science studies
movement coexist with recurrent claims that science studies is merely offering a
corrective to overly simplified models of science? Not very easily. My observation
has been that authors in all of the postmodernist traditions we have been considering tend to jump constantly between a more moderate "corrective" stance toward
traditional objectivist models of knowledge and a more radical relativist stance –
sometimes over the course of a single sentence – in a move that I have come to
think of as the "slide into relativism." We might select a few authors from the science studies tradition to serve as representative examples of this phenomenon and
try to pinpoint the moment when quite valid critiques of traditional objectivism
suddenly slip – through stunning non sequiturs or empty rhetorical leaps – into
strong cultural-linguistic relativism.

    The first time I read Thomas Kuhn's landmark *The Structure of Scientific Revo-
lutions* (1962/1970), I could not shake the feeling that there were *two* Kuhns, one a
sober critic of overly naïve views of scientific discovery and progress (the "good"
Kuhn), the other a wild-eyed relativist jumping to unsupported conclusions (the
"bad" Kuhn). Kuhn himself was disturbed by the manner in which his work was
embraced by those with relativist leanings, and he dedicated a large part of the
rest of his career to damage control – arguing that he was not a relativist, that he
believed that scientific progress was possible, and that he was being misinterpreted
by his more radical followers.[12] Yet these followers were clearly seeing *something*

[12] See, for instance, Kuhn 1962/1970: 206–209 and 1970.

inspiringly radical in his work, and there is no doubt that the "bad" Kuhn makes quite relativistic statements – usually, I believe, as a result of allowing the antiobjectivist observations of the "good" Kuhn to slide into an extreme relativist position.

Consider the theory-fact distinction. I described in Chapter 1 Kuhn's view of the active role that theoretical paradigms play in observation: what counts for us as a "fact" – or what can even be noticed by us – is very much influenced by our theoretical presuppositions. Kuhn frequently slips from this more moderate claim into the position that paradigms *entirely* determine the structure of our perception, which means that groups living under the sway of different paradigms literally live "in different worlds" (1962/1970: 192–193). This idea of perception being completely structured by one's theoretical paradigm parallels Whorf's claims concerning the power of language (1956), and – as with most of the "bad" Kuhn's claims – is enthusiastically embraced by Paul Feyerabend. "Observation statements are not just theory-*laden,*" Feyerabend declares, "but *fully theoretical*" (1993: 211). Like Kuhn (but more vocally and with fewer compunctions), Feyerabend is seduced into making the slide from saying that what we notice as facts, or how we notice them, is influenced by theory (labeled [1] in quote) to the claim that facts are completely the products of theory [2]: "on closer analysis we find that science knows no 'bare facts' at all but that *the 'facts' that enter our knowledge are already viewed in a certain way* [1] and are, therefore, *essentially ideational* [2]" (11; emphasis and numbers added).

Consider also the issue of paradigm shifts. We have already discussed the "good" Kuhn's argument that it is not simply logic or experimental evidence alone that causes scientific communities to abandon one framework and embrace another. The fact that paradigms to a certain extent determine what we are able to notice about the world – what counts as "data" and what counts as "noise" – at times causes Kuhn to slide into the claim that disputes between competing paradigms cannot be decided by reference to *any* paradigm-neutral "facts." Sounding a bit like Richard Rorty (still to be considered), Kuhn concludes that conversational agreement is the only standard to which we can have access. "As in political revolutions, so in paradigm choice – there is *no* standard higher than the assent of the relevant community" (1962/1970: 94; italics added). This claim is gleefully amplified by Paul Feyerabend, who explains that paradigm shifts are brought about solely by "irrational means such as propaganda, emotion, *ad hoc* hypotheses, and appeals to prejudices of all kinds" (1993: 144). This means that science is merely a type of religion, an opinion echoed in Sandra Harding's characterization of modern science as the "ethnoscience of the West," one culturally constructed discourse among a multitude of potential "borderland epistemologies" (1996: 22). As in the theory-fact distinction, this position is predicated on a non sequitur: the fact that logic or experimental results are not the *sole* factor motivating theory change in the sciences leads to the claim that they play *no* role whatsoever.

As Larry Laudan has noted, part of what is involved here is what he calls the "fallacy of partial description": a leap from observing that science is a social activity to concluding that it is therefore best understood as an entirely sociological phenomenon (1996: 201–202). These sorts of slides are rife in the science studies literature. For instance, in a paragraph arguing for the inevitable historicity of knowledge, Sandra Harding concludes that "we need to be able to see how gender, race and class interests *shape* the project of laboratory life and the *manufacture* of scientific knowledge" (1992: 19; emphasis added). The shift in metaphors here allows us to trace the slide: "shaping" implies the possibility of direct knowledge of the world, with its own structure, that is then influenced by social processes, whereas "manufacturing" conjures up images of creating something entirely new in a manner unconstrained by the preexisting raw material. The slide from the "weak" to the "strong" program in science studies is encapsulated in this shift in metaphors.

THE ALMOST-PRAGMATIST TURN: PHILOSOPHICAL HERMENEUTICS AND "NEO-PRAGMATISM"

Richard Bernstein, who celebrates the philosophical hermeneutics movement of Martin Heidegger and Hans-Georg Gadamer and the "neo-pragmatism" of Richard Rorty in his *Beyond Objectivism and Relativism* (1983), is right about the fact that these thinkers are clearly struggling to get away from the dualist "Cartesian anxiety," and what he sees as a turn back to Aristotelian *phronesis* or "practical wisdom" would certainly constitute a step in the right direction.[13] But to my mind this return to Aristotle does not go far enough, and all three thinkers – as well as Bernstein himself – fail in the end to extricate themselves from the relativist prison house of language.

Heidegger and Gadamer, the philosophical hermeneuts, share a hostility to a certain type of dualism: the Enlightenment ideal of a knowing subject representing accurately a distinct, objective world. For both thinkers "true" knowledge is possible, but this knowledge has to be understood as a kind of genuine engagement with the world rather than its abstract representation. Heidegger, for instance, emphasizes that we can know things only insofar as we bring them into our circle of concern, and that we can understand them only in terms of our own "fore-structures" or assumptions. This is not, he is careful to note, the same as endorsing extreme subjectivism – the "hermeneutic circle" of an interpreter being able to understand

---

[13] Cf. Varela et al. 1991 (esp. 149–150) for a presentation of Heidegger and Gadamer as "embodied" thinkers representing a helpful alternative to the Anglo-American tradition, as well as Frisina (2002) for the related argument that that a metaphysically articulated form of pragmatism (à la Whitehead or the Chinese neo-Confucian Wang Yang-ming) is necessary to take us toward a "nonrepresentational theory of knowledge."

the interpreted only by bringing to bear his or her own prior assumptions is not, he claims, a vicious one.

In the circle is hidden a positive possibility of the most primordial kind of knowing. To be sure, we genuinely take hold of this possibility only when, in our interpretation, we have understood that our first, last, and constant task is never to allow our fore-having, fore-sight, and fore-conception to be presented to us by fancies and popular conceptions, but rather to make the scientific theme secure by working out these fore-structures in terms of the things themselves (*die Sachen selbst*). (1962: 195)

The sort of "true" grasp of the "the things themselves" that Heidegger is calling for is not accurate representation of an external world, but rather truth as "unconceal-ment" (*alethea*), a kind of ecstatic "exposure to the disclosedness of beings" (1993c: 126). Gadamer similarly sees the goal of hermeneutics as a "fusion of horizons" that results from genuine openness to "the truth of the object" (1975: 340–341).

Gadamer in particular, with his focus on legal pragmatics and nonsubjective models of taste, seems to be pushing for a revival of something very much like Aristotelian practical reason, with its connection to the body, emotions, proper objects, and the particulars of the situation against a reliance on abstract, univer-salist rules.[14] For both thinkers, however, it is important to see that their rejection of Enlightenment subject-object dualism ultimately takes the form of an absorption of the latter by the former: the knowing subject, the known object, and the event of knowing are all swallowed up by the ontologically basic realm of language.

Heideggerian *Dasein* – "there-being" or human existence – is itself constituted by language and finds itself confronted by a world that can be disclosed to it only by language.

Language is the house of Being. In its home man dwells. (1993b: 217)
   Language alone brings beings as beings into the open for the first time . . . Language, by naming being for the first time, first brings beings to word and to appearance. Only this naming nominates being *to* their Being *from out of* their Being." (1993d: 198)

Language plays a similar fundamental and ontological role in Gadamer's hermeneu-tics. The Enlightenment hermeneutic ideal of Schleiermacher or Dilthey was based on critical method, whereby the subject's prejudices or assumptions – viewed as a negative barrier to be overcome in grasping the true object of interpretation – could be isolated and removed. Gadamer gives both a positive and ontological role to *Wirkungsgeschichte* – the "effective history," or net of prejudices that constitute the self and form the inescapable horizon from which the "event" of *Verstehen* will occur. These horizons are given to us by our language, which means that, for Gadamer as for Heidegger, we always possess our world linguistically. "Language

---

[14] Gadamer 1975: esp. 19–39, 278–289. For Aristotle on *phronesis* ("practical reason" or "practical intelligence"), see Irwin 1985: 158–161, as well as Burnyeat 1980 and Wiggins 1980 for helpful short essays on the topic.

is the fundamental mode of operation of our being-in-the-world," Gadamer claims, "and the all-embracing form of the constitution of the world" (1976c: 3). He is dismissive of the commonsense view of language as a simple tool to convey prelinguistic thoughts or observations:

We never find ourselves as consciousness over against the world and, as it were, grasp after a tool of understanding in a wordless condition. Rather, in all our knowledge of ourselves and in all knowledge of the world, we are always already encompassed by the language that is our own. (1976a: 62)[15]

The state of ecstasy that occurs in Gadamerian "play" (*Spiel*), or in the answer to the Heideggerian "call" (*Ruf*) of Being, does indeed involve a surrender to and participation in something greater than the individual self – a triumph over mere subjectivism. Even this "real event" (*Ereignis*) of world engagement, however, does not transcend the linguistic: it is in the end a hermetically sealed confrontation of a linguistically constituted being with the Word of God (Gadamer 1976b: 57–58) or the "resounding word" of Being calling itself to Being (Heidegger 1993e: 418, 423).

Another hero of Bernstein's is the "neo-pragmatist" Richard Rorty, and again there are reasons for seeing Rorty as a genuine alternative to either old-fashioned objectivism or "anything goes" relativism. Rorty himself resists the "relativist" label and observes that it is often promiscuously applied to anyone who feels that there are deep problems with the objectivist-rationalist model of knowledge. He argues that no one is really a relativist in the crude sense of thinking any opinion is just as valid as any other potential opinion, and claims that, in fact, "the philosophers who get *called* 'relativists' are those who say the grounds for choosing between . . . opinions are less algorithmic than had been thought" (1980: 727). Rorty believes that once we are able to give up our false hope in a perfect, God's-eye representation of reality that would give us infallible access to the truth, we will come to see – like the philosophical hermeneuts – that the "fusing of horizons" that occurs in conversational consensus is the only possible source of human objectivity. "The real issue [of relativism versus objectivism] is not between people who think one view is as good as another and people who do not. It is between those who think our culture, or purpose, or intuitions cannot be supported except conversationally, and people who still hope for other sorts of support" (728).

Like the advocates of science studies, Rorty is here falling down the slide into relativism: moving smoothly from the observation that, contrary to what objectivism holds, there is no algorithmic method for assuring truth to the non sequitur conclusion that "there are no constraints on inquiry save conversational ones . . . To accept the contingency of starting-points is to accept our inheritance from, and our conversation with, our fellow-humans as our *only* sources of guidance. To attempt

---

[15] Cf. Heidegger's comment that "Man acts as though *he* were the shaper and master of language, while in fact *language* remains the master of man" (1993a: 348).

to evade this contingency is to hope to become a properly programmed machine" (726; emphasis added). It is, in fact, a false dichotomy to say that knowledge must either be algorithmic *or* completely socially constructed. Rorty declares as invalid any sort of constraints "derived from the nature of the objects, or of the mind, or of language" (726), but – as I will argue at some length in Chapter 5 – these are precisely the kinds of restraints that prove decisive in the achievement of real-life social consensus.

I think that Rorty here follows Heidegger and Gadamer in missing the point that there are *other* types of nonalgorithmic knowledge besides conversational consensus, and that in fact real conversational consensus is almost always achieved by appeal to empirical evidence to which all the conversational participants have some sort of independent, perceptual access. By denying this move – dismissing those who would hope for "other sorts of support" than conversational agreement – Rorty ultimately remains as trapped in language as Heidegger and Gadamer.[16] Although he does not share their mystical, ontogenic view of language, Rorty resembles the philosophical hermeneuts in missing the most crucial dimension of human conversation: its direct connection to a physical world that all human beings share as a result of our embodiment. One sees this quite clearly in Rorty's treatment of scientific approaches to the mind, which echoes Gadamer's more extreme rejections of "method." In his "defense of eliminative materialism," Rorty argues that neurological explanations of introspective phenomena are not prima facie incoherent, and concludes that

we should let a thousand vocabularies bloom and then see which survive. The materialist predicts that the neurological vocabulary will triumph. He may be right, but if he is, it is not because of some special feature of this vocabulary which consists of it having originated in theoretical science. Given different cultural conditions, one can imagine the neurological vocabulary having been the ordinary familiar one and the mentalist one the "scientific" alternative. (1970: 119)

It is this type of claim – the idea that, in the end, cultural conditions alone delineate the possibilities of our knowledge – that causes me to place Rorty firmly in the postmodern camp. Even if we follow him and the philosophical hermeneuts in agreeing that the objectivist dream of "copying reality" is a chimera, we can recognize that there are other ways to be in contact with physical reality than representing it from a distance. The obsession of Heidegger, Gadamer, and Rorty with humans as *linguistic* beings – their inability to follow Aristotle all the way and put the body back in the mind – causes them to remain trapped in the postmodern relativist prison, whatever they themselves might claim.

---

[16] Cf. Ian Hacking's comment that "in my opinion, the right track in Dewey is the attempt to destroy the conception of knowledge and reality as a matter of thought and representation. He should have turned the minds of philosophers to experimental science, but instead his new followers praise talk" (1983b: 63).

THE ALMOST-NONDUALIST APPROACH: THE LATER LATOUR

In *We Have Never Been Modern*,[17] Bruno Latour famously turned on the Edinburgh School "strong programme" and postmodernism in general, voicing many of the criticisms we will explore here – that postmodern relativism is simply the flip side of objectivism, or that social constructivism simply substitutes one sort of reductive dogmatism for another – and presenting a "nonmodernism" that sounds at times like a pragmatic alternative to dualism. For instance, in critiquing the strong social constructivist position of "the Edinburgh daredevils," Latour notes that, according to their position,

Society had to produce everything arbitrarily, including the cosmic order, biology, chemistry, and the laws of physics! The implausibility of this claim was so blatant for the 'hard' parts of nature that we suddenly realized how implausible it was for the 'soft' ones as well. Objects are not the shapeless receptacles of social categories . . . Society is neither that strong nor that weak; objects are neither that weak nor that strong. (1993: 55)

His proposed "quasi-objects" are intended to be more nuanced creatures than anything found in the "strong programme"; they are "much more social, much more fabricated, much more collective than the 'hard' parts of nature, but they are in no way the arbitrary receptacles of a full-fledged society" (55). Latour also dishes out similarly cogent and pragmatic-sounding critiques of the "intellectual immobility" of Lyotard, the semiotic turn in deconstruction, and the idealism of Heideggerian "navel-gazing" (61–67). Predictably, Latour's main bogeyman is the Enlightenment (modernity), which he sees as responsible for bringing into existence – for the first time in human history – a stark human–nature dichotomy that produces such dualist absurdities as the disinterested, Godlike scientific spokesperson for nature or the spectacle of French deconstructionists "deconstructing themselves, autonomous glosses on autonomous glosses, to the point of absurdity" (64).

To begin with, the uniqueness that Latour grants to the modern turn in the West is questionable, based on an ignorance of human cognition coupled with an utter unfamiliarity with non-Western or premodern cultures. For instance, his references to the holistic Achuar people of the Amazon notwithstanding (14–15, 42), the distinction between inert physical objects and interest-bearing human agents seems a universal feature of human cognition (emerging at about the age of four in children from Mumbai to the Amazon to China),[18] and a concern with "hybrid" problems such as deforestation – coupled with vigorous attempts to dis-entangle the human from the natural causalities involved – are a common theme

---

[17] Published as *Nous n'avons jamais été modernes: Essais d'anthropologie symmétrique* in 1991, translated into English in 1993.
[18] Refer to the discussion of "folk psychology" in Chapter 3.

as far back as fourth-century B.C.E. China.[19] Understood plausibly, what Latour is presenting is a critique of naïve objectivism similar to what we discussed in Chapter 1 – for instance, that the selection and interpretation of empirical data is always already enmeshed with theoretical presuppositions and both personal and political interests. He is also surely correct in observing, as we did in Chapter 1, that the Enlightenment *is* characterized by a marked increase in the visibility of the nature-culture divide, as well as the vigilance with which this divide is policed. Latour is not content to rest here, however, and instead alternates between more sober observations and grand promises to be the prophet of a nonmodern "Constitution" that will reveal an entirely new ontological realm, the "field of nonmodern worlds" (48). Some have suggested that the entire book is a sort of elaborate joke, a slap at self-important postmodernists *and* their critics, and certain features – particularly the elaborate but nonsensical figures, presented with a completely straight face despite their resemblance to children's doodlings[20] – support such a reading. In any case, Latour's analysis seems to be either a joke or – if we are to see it as a serious attempt to transcend modernity – a typically postmodern retreat into obscurity rather than a genuine middle way.

The analytic usefulness of his proposed "quasi-objects" or "hybrids," for instance, is irritatingly unclear. His nonmodern analysis, he explains, is one that "deploys instead of unveiling, adds instead of subtracting, fraternizes instead of denouncing, sorts out instead of debunking" (47) – whatever that might mean. Having problematized the task of separating fact from value, data from theory, nature from political interests, Latour seems to see no other path than to simply relax into a mushy intellectual morass where everything is hybrid:

Yes, scientific facts are indeed constructed, but they cannot be reduced to the social dimension because this dimension is occupied by objects mobilized to construct it. Yes, those objects are real but they look so much like social actors that they cannot be reduced to the reality "out there" invented by the philosophers of science. The agent of this double construction – science with society and society with science – emerges out of a set of practices that the notion of deconstruction grasps as badly as possible. The ozone hole is too social and too narrated to be truly natural; the strategy of industrial firms and heads of state is too full of chemical reactions to be reduced to power and interest; the discourse of the ecosphere is too real and too social to boil down to meaning effects. Is it our fault that the networks are *simultaneously real, like nature, narrated like discourse, and collective, like society*? (6)

---

[19] For instance, refer to the analogy of Ox Mountain in *Mencius* 6:A:8 (Lau 1970: 164–165), discussed in Chapter 3, where the original, forested, "natural" state of the mountain is contrasted with the artificial, deforested state brought about by human actions, or the distinction made in the *Zhuangzi* between the natural ox roaming free in nature versus the tamed plow animal with a metal ring in its nose (Watson 2003: 105).

[20] My favorite is on p. 102.

As Oscar Kenshur observes with regard to this new position of Latour's, "to be able to denounce paradoxical extremes . . . is by no means tantamount to providing a coherent alternative, and what one person calls nuance another may call waffling" (1996: 289).[21] A truly viable "nonmodernism" would have to involve more than simply replacing traditional metaphysical dualism with new, vaguely defined, and equally metaphysical entities like "quasi-objects." Really getting beyond dualism requires a clear, empirical account of the structure of the embodied mind and the processes by which this unified body-mind interacts with its environment. Anything short of that represents a mere reshuffling of old categories. Ultimately, then, Latour's "amodernism" remains firmly within the orbit of social constructivism.

THE ALMOST-EMBODIED APPROACH: PIERRE BOURDIEU

Pierre Bourdieu seems to provide a more sophisticated and powerful analytic framework designed to get beyond subjectivism and objectivism, aimed at bringing both the physical body and the material world back into cultural analyses. He is, like Latour, critical of both structuralism and most poststructuralist theory, describing his project as one designed to "reintroduce agents that [the structuralists] tended to abolish, making them into mere epiphenomena of structure" (1990a: 9). In the place of free-floating signifiers or abstract, disembodied discourses, Bourdieu introduces the ideas of *habitus* and "field." *Habitus* is an "embodied history" (1990b: 56), a system of mostly implicit schemas of perception and behavior acquired by the individual over the course of his or her upbringing,[22] and a set of disparate "fields" within which this bearer of *habitus* must make his or her way. Bourdieu's approach certainly represents an advance over the various sorts of overly objectivist approaches he criticizes. His analysis of works of art, for instance, is not socially reductionist in the more crude sense of seeing artistic productions as direct reflections of class interests (à la Georg Lukács or Lucien Goldmann), because for Bourdieu economic class is simply one of many semiautonomous "fields" that both constitute the artistic agent – in the form of the long history of interactions that make up the artist's *habitus* – and make up the multilevel environment that represents the agent's field of play. Unlike many of his predecessors, he also takes seriously the fact that human beings have bodies, that these bodies exist in a real physical world, and that there exist prelinguistic, tacit forms of embodied knowledge that are more basic and pervasive than either abstract reason or explicit social discourse.

However nuanced, though, in the end Bourdieu's analysis still represents a form of social constructivism.[23] Both the field and the agent are ultimately products

---

[21] Alan Sokal makes a similar point in observing that "Latour's main tactic, in presenting his vision of the sociology of science, is to empty it of all its content by retreating into platitudes that no one would question" (Sokal 2000b: 129).

[22] For an extended discussion of *habitus*, see 1990b: 51

[23] A point made by Latour as well (1993: 5, 51–54).

of purely social forces, however disparate in structure these forces might be. For instance, the "code" needed to decipher any work of art is presented as a "historically constituted system, founded on social reality" (1993: 223), and defines the very possibilities of perception in a manner strikingly similar to a Kuhnian paradigm, complete with "ruptures" (paradigm shifts) and "classical periods" (normal science) (225–226).[24] Similarly, works of art cannot be reduced to intertextuality in the simple "texts related to other texts" form of analysis found in structuralism and poststructuralism, which Bourdieu firmly rejects. But his idea of the work of art as the product of a socially constructed (though physically instantiated) agent interacting with a socially constructed (though materially instantiated) set of fields nonetheless leaves the artist and work of art caught in the web of purely social meaning making.

The basic problem is that Bourdieu fails to really take embodiment seriously by allowing the body to play an *active* role in the structuring of human consciousness. For all of his talk of the body, it is for him ultimately nothing more than a passive storehouse for socially constructed *habitus* – a "living memory pad" (1990b: 68), a "repository" for values (68), or a "depository of deferred thought" (69).[25] The "tabula" is now the body-mind embedded in a world of physical objects rather than a free-floating consciousness, but it is still "rasa." As a result, his analysis of cultural phenomena such as the rise of Impressionism or our taste for luxury cars remains ultimately superficial: he is able to analyze the higher-level details of a given agent's *habitus* or of the functioning of a given field of cultural production, but he leaves unanswered the much more basic and important questions of *how* *habitus* is formed, *how* fields are perceived and interacted with by agents, or what constraints there might be on *habitus* and field formation. The particular social fields and socially constructed tastes that remain Bourdieu's sole focus represent merely the tip of the human cognitive iceberg: the rich structure of the embodied human mind that *enables* and *motivates* us to construct these fields and act within them remain completely unanalyzed. As I will briefly argue in the Conclusion, one way of understanding Bourdieu's limitations – and the limitations of the entire social constructivist paradigm within which he is working – is to see him as not going *far enough back* in his conception of history. The deposited layers of history that form our schemas of perception and motivation go much deeper than the reaction against L'École des Beaux-Arts or the rise of the salon: they go back into *evolutionary* time, into the history of interactions between creatures more and more like us trying to make their way through a complex world. So, in an important sense we might say that the problem with Bourdieu's postmodernism

---

[24] Also see Bourdieu's approving quotation of Boas's observation concerning the social construction of thought (1993: 226).
[25] The metaphors involved in his discussion of "bodily hexis" as "political mythology realized, *embodied*" or "inscribed" in bodies are particularly revealing in this regard; see especially 1990: 66–79 ("Belief and the Body").

is not that it is overly historicist, but that it has an overly superficial and myopic conception of what history *is*. Bourdieu certainly mentions human perceptual and motor capacities in his account of *habitus*, but they remain for him mere empty capacities, like the Standard Social Scientific Model's notion of "learning": all of the actual content is still derived from an all-powerful, arbitrary, and disembodied society.

THE LAST GASP OF POSTMODERNISM

Bourdieu and the later Latour seem to me to belong to the twilight years of postmodernism, a stage where postmodern theorists have become aware of inadequacies in the strong postmodernist position but have nowhere else to turn. Unwilling – for good reason – to go back to traditional objectivism, and with a zealot's certainty that universalist claims about human nature – or any other form of "grand metanarrative" – are the devil's work, they remain unable to fully extricate themselves from the mire of social constructivism. As a result, they end up taking refuge in vague but ultimately insubstantial references to "integration," to "hybrids," to the body, or to getting beyond dualism, interspersed with periodic ritual denunciations of their own positions. This seems to me to be the state of the field in large swaths of anthropology, sociology, literature, religious studies, and art history, where social constructivism still reigns supreme but where one would be hard-pressed to find anyone who would admit, without qualification, to being a postmodernist or relativist.

This moribund phase of postmodernism can be illustrated by an article sampled more or less at random from a recent issue of *Social Text*. Here we can observe the failure to really break with social constructivism coupled with a rhetorical distancing from the supposed excesses of poststructuralist theory in favor of more "sophisticated" (or, in this case, more "militant") strands of cultural theory:

The [postmodern] picture was that of an empty cultural milieu . . . a real subsumption of culture under capital that problematized even the notion of a cultural politics as such. Is it possible, in fact, to wage a struggle around culture if all culture has become an industry of signification – incessantly drowning meaning in a sea of semirandom noise? More militant strands of cultural theory have thus deemed it necessary to reject the postmodern analysis [of meaning as simply a network of "floating signifiers" or subjects lost in a world of "hyperreality"] as simply a sign of cynicism and unconditional political surrender to the state of things . . . Much work has thus been dedicated to rescuing the vitality of the social from the grip of simulation (or exchange value gone irreversible and orbital). Empirical work on audiences has shown the persistence of counterhegemonic decodings and the resilience of meaning to all attempts at pinning it down within stable hegemonic formations or a closed logic of simulation. We know that meaning has not simply disappeared in the infosphere but that it has multiplied and proliferated in its interface with social microstratifications and segmentations emerging out of and giving rise to classes, genders, sexualities, ethnicities, and races. (Terranova 2004: 52)

To get beyond the limits of more timid forms of postmodernism, this author calls for an analysis of "communication beyond meaning," which will apparently provide an account of

both the development of forms of knowledge and power that explicitly address not only the field of communications but also the potential of the event as it erupts within the closed circuit of communication or the power of the invention to displace the closed horizon of the communication channel . . . [communication beyond meaning] involves a *physical* operation on metastable material processes that it captures as probabilistic and dynamic states; on the other hand, it mobilizes a *signifying* articulation that inserts such a description into the networks of signification that make it meaningful. (70)

Although far less articulate and playful, we see in this more "militant" strand of cultural theory many of the features found in the later Latour: anti-postmodern and anti–social constructivist rhetoric, an expressed desire to get beyond mere language and deal with the physical world of objects, a fondness for paradoxical language, and a stunning lack of clarity about what all this rhetoric really means. What is the source of the "counterhegemonic decodings" or the "resilience of meaning" of which the author speaks? Where in this web of "social microstratifications and segmentations emerging out of and giving rise to classes, genders, sexualities, ethnicities, and races" does the active, knowing subject reside? Despite the rhetorical gesturing, it is hard to see how these sorts of analyses can break anyone out of the prison house of language-culture.

Colleagues who feel more of an engagement with critical theory have complained to me that it is unfair to say that postmodern theorists deny the existence of an external world, or to pin the label of social constructivist on theorists such as Bourdieu or Latour. It is certainly the case that one of the more noticeable recent trends in postmodernism is an overt rejection of relativism, coupled with calls for a better sort of objectivity – "better" meaning more politically progressive or locally "situated."[26] At the end of the day, though, there clearly remains a core epistemological commitment tying together Harding, Latour, Haraway, Geertz, Bourdieu, and all of the other theorists I am characterizing as postmodern relativists: that whatever the status of human-independent reality, the humanly *knowable* world is culturally constructed through and through, and therefore the only sort of truth-claim available to us is purely socially negotiated. The key claim is that individuals have no direct access to the world – no access to what John Searle calls "brute facts" – and thus no way to independently verify or disprove any element of the socially constructed web of signification into which he or she is born. If we wish to preserve the undeniably important insights that have come out of postmodern theorizing,

---

[26] Ursula Heise (2004) provides a nice recent discussion of how, despite their protests to the contrary, it is not in the end clear how science studies figures such as Harding or Haraway have really extracted themselves from relativism.

we need to undermine this key claim and thereby block the slide into epistemological relativism.

The remainder of this book represents a four-step attempt to do this. First, I think it is important to finally put the postmodern epistemology and ontology to rest by laying out clearly why it is both internally inconsistent and empirically indefensible, and this is what I attempt to do in Chapter 3. Next, in Chapter 4, I try to suggest how we can recognize the reality of human creativity and cultural variety while still seeing it as grounded in and constrained by the embodied human mind. In Chapter 5, I defend the validity of empirical evidence by outlining the possibility of a nondualistic, pragmatic model of knowledge and truth – one that recognizes the situatedness of human knowledge without losing contact with a human-independent world. This step is crucial because it seems to be that the slide into relativism seems to occur *despite* the best wishes of postmodern theorists, who for the most part are simply interested in deconstructing undeniably naïve forms of objectivism but then find themselves with nowhere to turn once this is done – lost in a maze of local narratives, hybrid monsters, and decenterings, and desperately and perpetually running to avoid the bogeyman of closure who is always close upon their heels. Finally, in Chapter 6, I try to respond to the concern of dualists of all stripes – objectivists, postmodernists, adherents of traditional religions – that integrating science and the humanities involves crude "reductionism" or some sort of fundamental denial of human-level reality. Let us now turn to step one, the task of philosophical euthanasia.

Pulling the Plug: Laying to Rest Postmodern Epistemology and Ontology

S OME OF THE OBJECTIONS TO POSTMODERNISM THAT I WILL EXPLORE IN this chapter are more obvious than others, and they have all in one form or another been made before by critics of postmodernism – or by postmodernists themselves, for that matter. It is helpful, however, to gather these critiques together in one place to see how they fit together. I also believe that, theoretical considerations aside, the best way to thoroughly and finally put the strong postmodernist position to rest is to supplement these sorts of abstract critiques with a review of the massive amount of empirical evidence concerning human cognition that flatly contradicts the social constructivist position. Postmodernism makes many claims about human thought, language, and culture that theoretically *could* be true, but that, in the light of the best current evidence, appear to be false. Thought is not language, human beings are not blank slates, and all complex animals – human beings included – inhabit a world permeated by inference-rich, finely textured, and decidedly precultural structures of meaning. I will begin with a discussion of the more purely theoretical or internal problems with postmodernism, and then gradually move to problems that become most apparent in the light of empirical results coming out of the cognitive sciences.

SELF-REFUTATION AND INTERNAL INCOHERENCE

It does not require a particularly powerful analytic mind to see that strong episte-mological relativism is logically problematic: to claim that no claims are true is to involve oneself in a form of the famous Cretan liar paradox ("Everything that I say is a lie"). Certain French poststructuralists seem quite comfortable with the paradox, luxuriating in it as if it were a nice warm bath. "Writing is in no way an instrument of communication," Barthes writes (1967: 19), and contemporary postmodern liter-ature is rife with similarly casual self-contradictory statements. Stephen Melville, for instance, provides us with the following description of the sculptor Richard Serra's piece for the Holocaust Memorial Museum in Washington, DC: "*Gravity* no longer simply testifies to the impossibility of sculpture, although it is important that it continues to do that, but also stands irreducibly as an achievement of it (of sculpture, of its impossibility)" (2004: 94–95). These sorts of deliberately para-doxical statements are perhaps meant as a kind of therapy, designed – like Daoist paradoxes or Zen *koan* practice – to shock one out of ordinary ways of thinking. The problem is that Daoist and Zen practitioners have something to catch them once their ordinary consciousness is deconstructed: deconstruction clears the way for the deeper level insights of the heavenly spirit or Buddha-consciousness to emerge.[1] This move is closed off to postmodernists, contemptuous as they are of any sort of metaphysical commitment, so it is unclear what separates this discursive playfulness from intellectual masturbation.

The incoherence of the basic epistemological position is deepened by the fact that this paradoxical language *is*, in fact, presented as a liberatory practice and is usually framed in terms of quite substantive claims about the world – for instance, that the structure of discourse is determined by power relations, that the discourse of a given novel or film is a reflection of sexism or colonialism, or that the chemical structure of a given enzyme is constructed by social forces. Rorty, for instance, is the simultaneous champion of ironic antirealism *and* liberalism, although it is of course hard to see how a strong antirealist could defend anything at all.[2] Foucault's retellings of the history of sexuality or of the development of the modern penal system is intended to reveal patterns of systematic discursive repression, but if we take seriously his claim that objects do not exist outside of the discourses within which they are defined, we might then be entitled to wonder why we should care about homophobia or prisoners' rights. Jean Baudrillard has argued that, since spin-doctoring by the media and the Bush administration played a large role in public perceptions of the first Gulf War, and since the planning and even execution of the "war" on the American side was mediated from the very beginning by long-range technologies, we can conclude that "the Gulf War did not take place" (1995). Of course, the title of Baudrillard's work is deliberately provocative: he is not denying that events occurred in Kuwait and Iraq that involved weapons and people being killed. He is, though, relentlessly negative about the possibility of actually knowing anything certain about what happened – in our era of "hyperreality" we can have access only to images, or to images of images. The corrective motivation behind this analysis is clear, but it is in the end systematically undermined by its own epistemological relativism.[3] Similar problems of internal coherence plague social constructivist and strong relativist approaches to the philosophy of science.[4]

Liberation – the dissolution of oppressive stereotypes, the recovering of suppressed points of view – is a classic Enlightenment ("modernist," if you wish)

---

[1] See, e.g., Loy 1987 and Berkson 1996.

[2] Rorty is certainly aware of the self-refutation problem, but he maintains that there is a "difference between saying that every community is as good as every other and saying that we have to work out from the networks we are, from the communities with which we presently identify" (1991: 202). It is unclear, however, what this difference could possibly be if we take the second claim in the strong sense in which Rorty seems to intend it.

[3] See Christopher Norris 1992: 164–193 for an analysis of how Baudrillard's corrosive epistemological pessimism undermines both itself and the possibility of genuine political action.

[4] See, for instance, Dudley Shapere on Kuhn and Feyerabend (Shapere 1981: 44).

aspiration, but it is difficult to hold it up as a goal and at the same time deny the possibility of knowledge or the fact that human nature has any specific content. If human desires are constructed by social discourse, and we live in a society dominated by discourses of, say, male domination and racial inequality, why not just embrace these discourses? How do we even come to know or feel that things could be different? The politically liberatory aspirations of most postmodernist theory is in fact predicated on hidden ontological and normative commitments – that oppression is bad, or that the oppressed do not like being oppressed – that do not sit well with the corrosive skepticism they aim in other directions. As Philip Kitcher has put it with regard to the science studies movement, "Convinced by the idea that they can never talk about things 'as they are,' some practitioners effectively demand a response to the global skeptical challenge for entities they don't like (the ontologies of the sciences) and then proceed to talk quite casually and commonsensically about things they do like (people, societies, human motives)" (1998: 40). They thus end up embracing what Ken Hirschkop has termed "inconsistent relativism": "relativism in epistemology finds its counterweight in dogmatism in politics; the best knowledge will be that which advances the politics we just *know* is right" (2000: 232).

Now, some postmodernists confront this problem head-on and attempt to bite the epistemological bullet. In *Laboratory Life*, for instance, Latour and Woolgar observe that "historical accounts are necessarily literary fictions," but then go on to declare that "our concern is to demonstrate how a hard fact can be sociologically constructed" (1979/1986: 107). They are clearly aware that they are involved in a paradox here and attempt to address it directly in the second edition of their *Laboratory Life*:

A more reflexive appreciation of laboratory studies is less dismissive of what might be called "the problem of fallibility": the argument that *all* forms of description, report, observation and so on can always be undermined ... Instead of using this argument ironically ... as a way of characterizing the work of *others* (scientists or other sociologists) while implying that our own recommended alternative is free from such deficiencies, we should accept the universal applicability of fallibility and find ways of coming to terms with it. Instead of utilizing it in a merely critical role, the aim would be to retain and constantly draw attention to the phenomenon in the course of description and analysis. We might as well admit that as a "problem" it is both insoluble and unavoidable, and that even efforts to examine *how* it is avoided are doomed in that they entail efforts to avoid it ...

In the closing section of the original draft we declared that our analysis was "ultimately unconvincing." We asked readers of the text not to take its contents seriously. But our original publishers [Sage] insisted that we remove the sentence because, they said, they were not in the habit of publishing anything that "proclaimed its own worthlessness." (283–284)

Avoiding the publication of something that "proclaims its own worthlessness" seems like a pretty sound editorial policy to me; fortunately for Latour and Woolgar,

Princeton University Press – publisher of the second edition of *Laboratory Life* – apparently had a more liberal attitude toward self-undermining discourse.

Like Baudrillard, Latour and Woolgar are of course playing the postmodern irony game here because they do not really think that their work is worthless. After acknowledging the apparent hopelessness of their project, they go on to declare that in fact they *can* escape from their relativist dilemma – otherwise why would anyone want to read them? – by turning to "forms of literary expressive [*sic*] whereby the monster [of relativism] can be simultaneously kept at bay and allowed a position at the heart of our enterprise" (283). This sounds like a wonderful trick, but what could it possibly mean? Statements like this, quite common in the literature,[5] represent the empty rhetorical gestures of postmodernists trapped by their own discourse, flailing about ineffectually in search of a way out – or as a substitute for actually getting out. For, as Terry Eagleton has noted, there is a kind of epistemological and metaphysical comfort to be found within the prison house of language:

> One advantage of the dogma that we are the prisoners of our own discourse, unable to advance reasonably certain truth-claims because such claims are merely relative to our language, is that it allows you to drive a coach and horses through everyone else's beliefs while not saddling you with the inconvenience of having to adopt any yourself. It is, in effect, an invulnerable position, and the fact that it is also purely empty is simply the price one has to pay for this. (1983: 144)

OPACITY OF REFERENCE, STYLISTIC CONFORMITY, AND POLITICAL POSTURING

One of the first things that a neophyte notices about postmodern theorizing is its perverse density, incomprehensibility, and reliance on unclear neologisms. The turgidity and pretentiousness of postmodern writing was, for several years, celebrated annually by the journal *Philosophy and Literature*'s "Bad Writing Contest." Judith Butler won the award in 1998 with a passage that is not at all unrepresentative of her work or of that of the students she has trained:

> The move from a structuralist account in which capital is understood to structure social relations in relatively homologous ways to a view of hegemony in which power relations are subject to repetition, convergence, and rearticulation brought the question of temporality into the thinking of structure, and marked a shift from a form of Althusserian theory that takes structural totalities as theoretical objects to one in which the

---

[5] Latour is a master of this sort of rhetorical hocus-pocus. In his later "anti-postmodern" phase, he dances around the status of his own critique of modernity ("the tricky move to unveil the modern Constitution without resorting to the modern type of debunking" [1993: 43]) by saying that he is "not unveiling a practice hidden beneath an official reading" (which would be a *terribly* modern thing to do) but merely "adding the bottom half to an upper half" – a rather disingenuous way of saying that he is unveiling something hidden (40–41). Despite his expressed contempt for more openly relativist postmoderns such as Derrida, the later Latour is just as slippery a fish.

insights into the contingent possibility of structure inaugurate a renewed conception of hegemony as bound up with the contingent sites and strategies of the rearticulation of power. (1997: 13)

I always found the opacity of postmodern theory rather ironic, considering the liberatory and supposedly antielitist motivation behind much of this work. This opacity of reference seems, however, to be an inevitable consequence of the kind of internal conceptual incoherence discussed earlier. Once you have given up the idea that discourse can be somehow "true" and have dismissed all organized narration as "a matter for the police" (Derrida 1979: 105),[6] you really have nowhere else to look for standards except to stylistic conformity (whom do you cite? what sort of jargon do you use?) and political correctness (if it is liberatory, it must be good).

Even Clifford Geertz, probably the most lucid and compelling spokesperson for the "anti-antirelativist" position, retreats into obscurity when he turns from breezy observations concerning the intellectual cravenness of the "neo-naturalists" – those who lack the sober courage to "sail out of the sight of the land in an outrigger canoe" (1984/2000: 65), as Geertz and his doughty band of anthropological adventurers apparently do – to the issue of what, for instance, labels for the various emotions might refer to. "These words . . . define a space, not an entity. They overlap, differ, contrast, hang together only in oblique, family-resemblance terms – polythetically, as the phrasing goes [!]; the problem is less to fix their referents . . . than to outline their reach and application" (2000: 207). The fact that it is not at all clear how a "space" is fundamentally different from an "entity," or how precisely "outlining [the] reach and application" of emotional words differs from "fixing their referents," is immaterial. The point is that this magical incantation has the salubrious effect of extricating Geertz from cultural relativism – that "absurd position" that "no one of any seriousness holds" (1984/2000: 50) – without sullying him with the taint of crude realism.

The power of opacity of reference, stylistic conformity, and political posturing to short-circuit intelligent analysis is illustrated in an amusing way by the infamous Sokal hoax. Annoyed by the postmodern science studies he had been reading, where "incomprehensibility becomes a virtue; allusions, metaphors, and puns substitute for evidence and logic" (Sokal 2000a: 52), the New York University physicist Alan Sokal concocted a nonsensical piece entitled "Transgressing the Boundaries: Toward a Transformative Hermeneutics of Quantum Gravity" – full of impressive references to postmodern figures and bold political statements, but deliberately designed to be devoid of actual content – and had it accepted and published in 1996 by the fairly prominent, refereed postmodern theory journal

---

[6] Cf. Foucault's comment, "Do not ask who I am and do not ask me to remain the same: leave it to our bureaucrats and our police to see that our papers are in order. At least spare us their morality when we write" (1972: 17). This sort of adolescent defiance of *les flics* is a common theme in French theory.

Social Text (Sokal 1996). As Katha Pollitt notes in a volume of commentary about the hoax,

The comedy of the Sokal incident is that it suggests that even the postmodernists don't really understand one another's writing and make their way through the text by moving from one familiar name or notion to the next like a frog jumping across a murky pond by way of lily pads. Lacan . . . performativity . . . Judith Butler . . . scandal . . . (en)gendering (w)holeness . . . Lunch! (2000: 98)

Sokal also played the politics card by liberally sprinkling his piece with vague but progressive-sounding political slogans. In their half-embarrassed, half-defiant defense of their actions, *Social Text* editors Bruce Robbins and Andrew Ross rather disingenuously suggested that they knew Sokal's piece was nonsense, but published it anyway because of its laudatory liberatory potential (2000). Paul Boghossian notes that this is, in some ways, even more troubling than the idea that they were simply hoodwinked, suggesting as it does that, "under appropriate circumstances, [the editorial board at *Social Text*] is prepared to let agreement with its ideological orientation trump every other criterion for publication, including something as basic as sheer intelligibility" (2000: 175).

    In the absence of belief in external standards governing human inquiry, polit-ical, racial, or gender identification emerges as the magical key bestowing special access to the truth in postmodern circles. Sandra Harding, for instance, observes that the alienated elites who dominate the natural sciences are apparently rendered incapable by their socialization of participating in the liberatory, fully democratic negotiations concerning the proper uses of science that she calls for: "Many people who are most comfortable with hierarchical decision making and have little expe-rience in negotiating social arrangements except among white, Western, econom-ically privileged, men like themselves will find it difficult to participate effectively in these negotiations. (But it is never too late to learn new skills!)" (1992: 18). At least it is never too late to learn! Scientific realists who are critical of Harding's stance are, apparently by definition, part of the elite, white, male, uncommunica-tive, "antidemocratic right," their race, gender, social class, and politics rendering them incapable of participating in the liberatory discourse to which Harding and her cohorts have special access. As Terry Eagleton notes, this common caricature of natural scientists as naïve, reactionary realists is perhaps more a reflection of humanist elitism than of reality: the average working scientist is actually fairly skeptical about strong objectivist models of science, realizing from his or her own experience that science on the ground proceeds as a kind of rule-of-thumb proce-dure. "It is people in the humanities who still naively think that scientists consider themselves the white-coated custodians of absolute truth, and so waste a lot of time trying to discredit them," he observes. "Humanists have always been sniffy about scientists. It is just that they used to despise them for snobbish reasons, and now do so for skeptical ones" (2003: 18).

Although not as radically relativist as mainstream postmodernists, critics of the evolutionary psychology movement – eager to discredit what they see as bio-logical reductionism from a proudly social constructivist standpoint – are often patronizingly reductionistic themselves in postulating racial or right-wing polit-ical motivations as the driving and exclusive force behind any substantive claim about human nature. Hilary and Steven Rose, two of the most prominent critics of "sociobiology," are particularly egregious in this regard. In their editors' introduc-tion to Rose and Rose 2000, they follow their discussion of the political reasons for rejecting Thornhill and Palmer's (2000) work on rape with praise for the "iconic movement of [the] new resistance" against "unconstrained capital" represented by "the dramatic battle against the World Trade Organization in the final months of the twentieth century" (Rose & Rose 2000: 5). The evolutionary psychology move-ment is then explicitly linked to nineteenth- and twentieth-century race theorists and eugenicists, and then (inevitably) to Nazism – claims about human nature should have been silenced after the creation of UNESCO and the defeat of the Nazis, but apparently the job is not yet done (6–7). Finally, evolutionary psychol-ogy is unveiled as a conspiracy to maintain "elite white male social dominance," "transparently part of a right-wing libertarian attack on collectivity, above all the welfare state [!]" (8–9).[7] This kind of muddle-headed linking of WTO resistance to UNESCO to the defeat of fascism to the defense of the welfare state should be confined to adolescent coffee shop ranting, but it is not untypical of the manner in which social constructivist discourse often encourages the demonizing of one's opponents or the vigorous waving of one's liberal political credentials as a substitute for argument in validating one's own stance.[8]

CULTURAL ESSENTIALISM AND ROMANTICISM

That the strong social constructivist position posits culture as an autonomous, sui generis force raises a variety of concerns. Some of these are purely theoretical. If only culture can produce culture, how, for instance, do cultures ever change – as they demonstrably do? Another a priori difficulty is how one would go about delim-iting the boundaries of these self-created cultures: does a fully bilingual Chinese-Canadian born in Beijing but raised in Vancouver simultaneously inhabit two different discourses? Does having been born and raised in New Jersey mean that I inhabit a different discourse than a native of California? More empirically, the social constructivist model has difficulty dealing with the fact that, within any given

---

[7] Also compare the rhetoric in Lewontin 1991 and in Lewontin et al. 1984, who trace all vertically integrated approaches to human cognition and behavior back to a nefarious bourgeois, right-wing, patriarchal conspiracy.

[8] Steven Pinker does a wonderful job of documenting this phenomenon (2002: 105–120); for an in-depth survey of the "sociobiology debate," see Segerstråle 2000.

culture, individuals behave, think, and desire in obviously diverse ways. We might attribute this variety to the presence of multiple, coexisting "microcultures," but there seems to be limits to the power of culture to influence the everyday reasoning patterns of individuals.

Justin Barrett's and D. Jason Slone's research on the cognitive science of religion provides us with a helpful illustration of this point. Much of their work focuses on the phenomenon of "theological (in)correctness": the way in which religious adherents actually think about the world in everyday, "online" situations – as elicited by means of time-pressured thought experiments and scenario analyses – often diverges from the official theologies that they profess to embrace. For instance, the vast majority of Calvinists who Barrett studied (1999), when questioned in "offline" surveys – abstract, non-time-pressured questionnaires where they were allowed plenty of time to reflect – profess to believing in predestination. When given time-pressured tasks to solve, however, they seem to fall back on common-sense models of agency whereby people have the ability to determine their own fates. As Slone observes, the social constructivist model predicts that people are "merely cultural sponges" and that cultures should be "autonomous, confined, and homogenous." The observed mismatch between cultural doctrines and real-time reasoning patterns suggests that, on the contrary, "people have active minds that are continuously engaged in the construction of novel thoughts and in the transformation of culturally transmitted ideas" (2004: 121). Culture appears to be a conceptual resource that individuals draw on selectively (in a context-sensitive and task-specific manner) and in a filtered form (subject to a vast suite of innate human cognitive constraints).

Another nice illustration of the potential mismatch between cultural norms and individual cognitive filters is the difficulty that children have in fully integrating cultural concepts that clash with their own intuitions about the world. This is particularly salient in the case of scientific education, which – as we will discuss more in Chapter 5 – involves retraining or simply suspending certain commonsense intuitions about the world. Stella Vosniadou (1994) performed a wonderful cross-cultural study concerning children's intuitions about the world. She found that, by a certain age, children are capable of remembering and parroting back the models of the earth dominant in their own particular culture. By guiding the children through certain practical reasoning tasks, however, she also discovered that the cognitive penetration of these cultural models was anything but complete. The interview with "Jamie," an American third grader, is representative:

["E" is the experimenter, "C" is the child]
E: What is the shape of the earth?
C: Round.
E: Can you draw a picture of the earth?
C: (Child draws a circle to depict the earth.)

E: If you walked for many days in a straight line, where would you end up?
C: Probably in another planet.
E: Could you ever reach the end or the edge of the earth?
C: Yes, if you walked long enough.
E: Could you fall off that end?
C: Yes, probably. (416)

Jamie clearly has been subjected to enough cultural indoctrination to assert that the earth is round when prompted, and has apparently been exposed to enough round representations of the earth to reproduce them when asked, but when it comes to everyday reasoning tasks he quickly reverts to the physical principles of his directly experienced world. Pascal Boyer and Dan Sperber have similarly argued that cultural concepts and models are subject to innate human cognitive constraints, which play an important role in determining both the possible structure of human concepts and which concepts tend to be successfully transmitted.[9]

The phenomena of theological incorrectness, conceptual resistance to cultural training, and cognitive filtering of cultural ideals all call into question the sort of monolithic model of culture that follows from postmodernism. Of course, one would be hard-pressed to find a postmodernist who would *admit* to holding this absurd view of cultures as monoliths. Such a position, though, is ultimately at the heart of an ideal that *is* openly and enthusiastically embraced in postmodernist circles: the valuing of cultural diversity and celebration of difference for difference's sake. This ideal is of fairly recent, Western liberal origin – it can arguably be traced back to the Judeo-Christian idea that human beings are made in God's image, which endows every single individual human with dignity and which demands our respect. With the rise of individualism and the growing recognition that cultures around the world display quite a bit of diversity, this respect for God-given dignity of the individual human being morphed into a call to value difference as an end in itself: since individuals have their own irreducible value as members of Kant's "Kingdom of Ends," we should not infringe on the rights of nonconforming individuals or cultural groups whose values are not identical to our own.

As a mutated offspring of the Enlightenment, postmodernist theory inherits this respect for diversity, but with a few interesting twists.[10] To begin with, as movements of protest, most strands of postmodernism embrace a form of the Noble Savage myth that has appealed to elite, alienated Europeans since contact with the "New World" began: our (i.e., Western) culture is dualistic/inauthentic/bad, whereas other cultures are holistic/authentic/good. We see this theme, for instance, in the

---

9 For a short introduction to the idea of cognitive constraints and culture, see Boyer 1994 and Sperber & Hirschfeld 2004.
10 See Charles Taylor's account of the transformation of Kant's Christian-inspired ideal of dignity through the "expressivist" turn into the modern valuation of self-fulfillment and radical individualism (1989).

later Bruno Latour's discussion of the "Great Divide between Them – all the other cultures – and Us – the westerners" (1993: 12), the latter being the historically unique bearers of the "white man's burden" of modernity. It is very revealing in this regard that Latour characterizes the vast new field of "nonmodernity" opened up by his own analysis as a "Middle Kingdom, as vast as China and as little known" [!] (48).[11] As a scholar of early Chinese thought, I can say with some confidence that the sort of distinction between nature and culture that Latour thinks unique to the modern West – and from which he has come to save us – is in fact one of the major problematiques in early Chinese thought,[12] but it is important for Latour's argument that we understand the mysterious inhabitants of the Middle Kingdom as having always dwelled in a timeless, blissful harmony with nature.

Of course, there is no *logical* relation between the Noble Savage doctrine and postmodern relativist epistemology – indeed, they are actively incompatible – but they appear together because both themes appeal to critics of our own alienated, dualistic Western culture.[13] Where postmodernist epistemology *does* intersect fundamentally with the Noble Savage myth is in the second twist on the respect for diversity theme: these "other" cultures, like our own, form monolithic wholes, and as monolithic wholes are fundamentally incommensurable with one another. We can see this illustrated in another wonderfully revealing passage, this time from Paul Feyerabend, where he reflects on his experience teaching at the University of California at Berkeley at a time when "Mexicans, blacks, and Indians" first began entering in large numbers as a result of new admission policies. As a white man, it made him uncomfortable teaching white man's ethnoscience to these virtuous, exotic peoples. His discomfort arose from the fact that "their ancestors had developed cultures of their own, colorful languages [!], harmonious views of the relations between people and between people and nature whose remnants are a living criticism of the tendencies of separation, analysis, and self centeredness inherent in western thought" (1993: 263–264). This sentence encapsulates the postmodern transformation of the Noble Savage myth: cultural essentialism; the ideal of exotic, "colorful," innocent native people in harmony with each other and with nature; and of course the contrast with the alienated, dualistic Westerner.

It is perhaps too easy to make fun of this passage, but it is important to do so because similar – if perhaps less obviously absurd – sentiments lurk in the background of much postmodernist theorizing, especially in anthropology. A common

---

[11] We see a similar orientalist fetishizing of the mysterious "other" in Foucault's use of Borges's imaginary "Chinese encyclopedia" in the opening of *The Order of Things* (1971: xv), or Barthes's use of Japan in *The Empire of Signs* (1982).

[12] It is, for instance, at the center of debates between Confucianism and various "Daoist" thinkers, as well as internal Confucianian debates regarding human nature (*xing*).

[13] See Pinker 2002: 124–126 on the Noble Savage as part of the humanist "Holy Trinity," as well as Robin Horton's trenchant observations concerning the phenomenon of "liberal romanticism" in modern anthropology (1993: 88–97, 133–136).

sentiment in postmodern anthropological writings is the need to protect "authentic" native cultures by isolating them from hegemonic Western practices. The problem with this is that the Noble Savages do not necessarily *want* to be "protected" from Westernization: hunter-horticulturalists in the Brazilian Amazon can see the advantages of having air conditioners, refrigerators, guns, and antibiotics as well as we can, and it is all too easy for the Western anthropologist – immunized, cavity free, and well nourished, with a comfortable lifestyle awaiting his or her return – to say that adopting these technologies would be a violation of this culture's authenticity. The cultural homogenization of the world resulting from globalization is indeed worrisome, as is the political and economic domination by North American and European corporations that comes with it. Recognizing that cultures are internally diverse and subject to change does not mean we must follow Thomas Friedman (1999) in his unapologetic cheerleading for globalization, or see the social upheavals caused by globalization – such as a widespread eviction of self-sufficient rural Chinese farmers and their subsequent rehiring as cheap labor in the internationally owned factories built on their land – as unproblematically positive or inevitable. We *do* need, however, to get beyond the romanticizing of difference and the cultural essentialism that comes out of postmodern theory, which denies the obvious historical fact that cultures are permeable and changeable, populated by *individuals* with different capacities and personal agendas.

Postmodern theorists such as Barry Barnes and David Bloor claim that "faced with a choice between the beliefs of his own tribe and those of the other, each individual would typically prefer those of his own culture" (1982: 27), but understood in a strong way this is simply false. As Aristotle said (perhaps going too far in the other direction), "human beings seek out not the way of their ancestors, but the Good."[14] I have several times had undergraduates report to me as solemn fact the claim that, when European ships first reached the "New World," the natives were literally unable to see them – such objects were not part of the natives' discourse, and we all know that one can see only what one's discourse allows. This is, of course, absurd on a variety of levels. The natives not only saw the European ships but – at least after the initial shock at the strange appearances and advanced technology wore off – recognized the passengers and crews as fellow humans bearing potentially useful trade goods, and did their best to acquire the most useful of them (especially guns, steel, and horses) to improve their lives and further their local political interests. Unfortunately, the Europeans also brought their germs along with their trade goods (Diamond 1997). Had it not been for the biological warfare advantage enjoyed by the germ-ridden, livestock-keeping Westerners, however, it is not at all clear that the sophisticated native societies of the Americas,

---

[14] *Politics* 1268a39, quoted in Nussbaum 1988 in the context of a very helpful discussion of universalism in ethics.

would not have, in the end, been able to turn their acquired weapons against their new enemies with more lasting effect.[15]

Taken in a strong way, Western academic cultural essentialism and the relativism that comes out of it is a bit like the smallpox brought to the New World. It represents, as Meera Nanda argues, a "poisoned gift" to the "other" that postmodernism is so intent to celebrate. Criticizing constructivist views of science that celebrate "alternative ways of knowing" (Harding's "borderland epistemologies"), Nanda observes:

What from the perspective of Western liberal givers looks like a tolerant, non-judgmental, therapeutic "permission to be different" appears to some of us "others" as a condescending act of charity. This epistemic charity dehumanizes us by denying us the capacity for a reasoned modification of our beliefs in the light of better evidence made available by the methods of modern science. This kind of charity, moreover, enjoins us to stop struggling against the limits that our cultural heritage imposes on our knowledge and our freedoms and to accept – and in some Third Worldist and feminist accounts, even celebrate – the cultural bonds as the ultimate source of all "authentic" norms of truth, beauty, and goodness. (1998: 288)[16]

The cultural essentialism that follows from postmodern relativism is thus not only logically absurd and empirically false but also politically rather troubling – undermining the very same liberal principles that are so loudly embraced by most postmodern academics.

THOUGHT IS NOT LANGUAGE

When I was in the early stages of graduate training in religious studies, one of the more influential texts in our theories and methods course was Steven Katz's "Language, Epistemology, and Mysticism" (1978), which argued that there was no such thing as a single, universal mystical state that was identically experienced, but then variously described, by practitioners in different religious traditions. It was important for scholars of religion to realize, Katz argued, that since *all* experience – religious or otherwise – is linguistically and culturally mediated, the religious vocabulary, rituals, and conceptual framework of any given "mystic" essentially and inextricably defines the sort of insight he or she experiences.

---

[15] Mann 2005 provides a readable account of the current scholarly consensus concerning the state of human societies in the Americas before European contact.

[16] In summing up the deleterious effects that uncritical celebration of local practices have had on practitioners, Nanda concludes that "the irony is that the largely academic critics who offer sophisticated theoretical justifications for indigenous sciences have the material resources and the opportunities to escape being grounded in them" (2000: 211). Cf. her critique of the celebration of "Vedic mathematics" in the Indian education system (2000: 205), and Janet Radcliffe Richards's concerns about the helpfulness of "feminist epistemologies" for the women's movement (1996).

This was an exciting idea. One of the things that my young colleagues and I were beginning to understand as we became more linguistically and historically sophisticated was the problematic nature of the common view that "mysticism" was some sort of universally uniform phenomenon. Several of us were led to the study of Chinese thought, in particular, because we were personally inspired by the accounts of mystical experiences in early Daoist texts, and it was a bit of an intellectual awakening to discover that the practices and concerns of these fourth-century B.C.E. texts were not necessarily identical to those of late-twentieth-century C.E. American graduate students in California's Marin County with a penchant for experimenting with LSD on the weekends. This insight led many in my cohort group to embrace the widespread conviction that the sine qua non of intellectual sophistication was the rejection of any and all universalist claims: cultural nuance is everything; language goes all the way down.

It is time for a more balanced approach in the humanities with regard to the relationship between thought and language. We can recognize the importance of culture and history while remaining open to the possibility that, for instance, we are motivated to apply the common word "mysticism" to a variety of experiences from different times and places because they share certain features – a commonality that is both the product of human cognitive universals and recognizable because of those universals. It is important to take this step back into a limited form of realism because the weight of the evidence coming out of linguistics, nonhuman animal cognition studies, and the various branches of the cognitive sciences – as well as from simple common sense – suggests that humans and other animals share a quite rich, prelinguistic thought world.

This said, no one would deny that language has an important effect on thought. Ray Jackendoff has noted that, although thought is clearly a mental function sep-arate from language, the existence of language appears to "provide a scaffolding that makes possible certain varieties of thought that are more complex than are available to nonlinguistic organisms" (1996: 2), both anchoring and focusing our attention.[17] Language also clearly shapes and focuses our perception of the world in important ways. When I was an adolescent I was possessed by a passion for learning about edible wild plants, and much to the embarrassment of my family members would spend long hours in the summertime in vacant lots and neighborhood woodlands "stalking the wild asparagus," as my favorite book by Euell Gibbons (1962) had it. Much of the vegetation in these areas would most likely be referred to by the average person as "weeds," and indeed before I developed my interest I would, like most people, look at an abandoned lot and see nothing but "weeds," if I noticed the vegetation at all. Once I was able to identify and apply names to

---

[17] Cf. Andy Clark 1997 (esp. 207–211) and 2006 for external linguistic signs as "cognitive fixatives" or "anchors" or Daniel Dennett's contention that language may be essential for maintaining long trains of thought (1995: 379–380).

individual species, however, my visual world changed: I now looked at a field and saw a complex, tiny ecosystem comprised of yarrow and burdock, blackberry and sorrel.

This is, of course, the phenomenon that so inspires Whorfians: the fact that, for instance, the Inuit supposedly have twenty-two different words for "snow," or that experienced surfers have dozens of words for "wave." What this reveals, however, is not the power of language to shape our world, but the power of our pragmatic interests in the world to shape our language – the Inuits worry a lot about different types of snow and have an interest in being able to communicate effectively about them. As Ian Hacking has observed, the purported existence of twenty-two words for "snow" in Inuit is not an example of the power of the linguistically molded mind to create a new and distinct life-world, but rather is probably the result of fairly accurate tracking of a crucially important environmental variable:

It in no way follows that there are not twenty-two distinct mind-independent kinds of snow, precisely those distinguished by the Inuit . . . the fact that we cut up the world into various possibly incommensurable categories does not in itself imply that all such categories are mind-dependent. (1983b: 95)

Work on lexical categorization and perception has similarly failed to support any strong version of the Whorfian hypothesis that language determines thought. Paul Kay and Terry Regier's recent review of color perception research (2006) notes that, although some studies have demonstrated that lexical classification of colors affects subjective judgments of similarity, there are also clearly nontrivial universal patterns of color cognition and classification.[18] Studies by Peter Gordon (2004) and Pierre Pica et al. (2004) of Amazonians speaking an innumerate language indicate that, as Rochel Gelman and Randy Gallistel suggest (2004: 441), humans share an imprecise but nonetheless useful nonverbal representation of number.[19] Their findings also support the conjectures of Jackendoff, Clark, and Dennett that language or external notation might serve an important scaffolding function, noting that it appears that "learning to represent numbers by some communicable notation (number words, tally marks, numerals) might facilitate the routine recognition of exact numerical quantities" (441). This in turn would support a weaker and more plausible form of Whorfianism: language *helps* us to think, and can focus our thought and attention in very specific ways, but it by no means is *determinate* or the sole medium of thought.

The theme of "thought without language" has been the subject of many recent volumes of essays in cognitive science, neuroscience, and linguistics – work that

---

[18] See Kay & Kempton 1984 for a more general discussion of the Sapir-Whorf hypothesis, Kay & Regier 2007 for a case study involving color classification and cognition in the Berinmo language of Papau New Guinea, Matsuzawa 1985 for color classification in primates, and Berlin & Kay 1969 for the classic work on universal patterns in human color cognition.

[19] Cf. the later discussion of "folk mathematics."

I will not attempt to comprehensively summarize here.[20] A clear short review of some basic commonsense observations that render the strong Whorfian hypothesis very implausible is provided by Steven Pinker (2002: 210–213). One observation is that nonlinguistic children and nonhuman animals appear to share with adult humans the ability to form abstract concepts, as well as many basic categories of thought.[21] Another is that we appear to remember the "gist" of sentences that have been presented to us rather than the exact words themselves, strongly suggesting that such a prelinguistic gist exists. There is also the phenomenon of what Pinker refers to as the "euphemistic treadmill," whereby originally innocuous neologisms ("bathroom") acquire negative connotations because of their actual referent, and therefore need constantly to be replaced by new euphemisms ("facilities"). This strongly suggests that "concepts, not words, are primary in people's minds" (212–213). Pinker and Bloom also note that various intermediate forms of language – pidgins, contact languages, and the languages of aphasics who have lost particular linguistic abilities – display a "continuum of communicative systems" (1992: 479) that would simply be impossible were there no prelinguistic meaning to communicate.

Merlin Donald reviews a series of cases involving congenitally deaf people raised without the benefit of sign language, as well as adults who had lost their linguistic abilities as a result of neurological damage, that demonstrate that "a great deal of knowledge is nonverbal, or is at least stored outside of the language system in nonsymbolic form" (1991: 87). He also observes that a distinction between thought and language has to be behind the human ability to invent new words, because "it is the extralinguistic knowledge that recognizes the need, and perceives the utility, of new symbols" (236). Pinker similarly notes that the commonly experienced phenomenon of groping for words or being unsatisfied with verbal formulations must be predicated on a language-thought distinction (2002: 212). Various forms of aphasia – an impairment of the ability to use or comprehend words – also point to the separability of linguistic ability and thought. Patients with Williams syndrome, for instance, suffer from profound mental retardation and appear to lack ordinary reasoning skills but are astoundingly fluent producers of perfectly grammatical, and ultimately meaningless, sentences full of advanced vocabulary. As Pinker relates,

Ask a normal child to name some animals, and you will get the standard inventory of pet store and barnyard: dog, cat, horse, cow, pig. Ask a Williams syndrome child, and you get a more interesting managerie: unicorn, pteranodon, yak, ibex, water buffalo,

[20] The reader is referred especially to the essays collected in Weiskrantz 1988, Gumperz & Levinson 1996, and Carruthers & Boucher 1998; the lucid summary of the anti-Whorfian position found in Pinker 1994: 53–82; and the recent review of preverbal infant categorization by Mandler 2004a and 2004b.
[21] Some specific examples will be given in the discussion of mental modules that follows. For good general introductions to nonhuman animal cognition, see Premack & Premack 1983 and 2003, Cheney & Seyfarth 1990, Povinelli 2000, and Rumbaugh & Washburn 2003.

sea lion, saber-tooth tiger, vulture, koala, dragon, and one that should be especially interesting to paleontologists, "brontosaurus rex." (1994: 53)

Similarly, Wernicke's aphasiacs fluently produce long sentences replete with extra or nonsense words, and often with no reference to the real world; Broca's aphasia, on the other hand, is characterized by extremely laborious and crude linguistic output that nonetheless reveals fully intact reasoning capabilities.[22]

The apparent organization of information in the brain also suggests that human knowledge is categorized along universal semantic lines rather than linguistically or culturally specific ones. One of the more immediate and powerful demonstrations of this comes from neuroimaging studies of bilinguals, which have shown that semantic cues activate the same brain regions regardless of the language used: for a bilingual speaker of German and English, for instance, the words "trout" and "Lachs" provoke common neuronal and behavioral effects.[23] Jenny Crinion and her colleagues (2006) postulate that the capacity for multiple language use is mediated by what appears to be a universal mechanism for lexical-semantic control subserved by the left caudate. In monolingual patients damage to this region of the brain impairs the patient's ability to make basic semantic decisions – to "find the right word." In multilinguals the left caudate seems to perform a switching function, monitoring and controlling the language being used and produced in both German-English and Japanese-English bilinguals. In an interesting case of a trilingual patient with lesions in the white matter surrounding the left caudate, language comprehension in all three languages was preserved, while the ability to control language output was lost: the patient spontaneously and unpredictably switched between all three languages in language production tasks.[24] That underlying semantics are more basic than the specifics of a given language is also suggested by the quite striking phenomenon of category-specific semantic deficits as the result of neurological damage, which can selectively impair a subject's access to, for instance, abstract or concrete nouns, proper names, body parts, geographical names, living or nonliving things, animals, vegetables, or musical instruments.[25]

The fact that human thought is not linked in lockstep to individual words should not be surprising when we remind ourselves of the work reviewed in Chapter 1 suggesting that the vast majority of human concepts take the form of image schemas that arise when the innate perceptual expectations structures of our body-minds are exposed to and interact with the world. As Michael Arbib notes, "our linguistic abilities are rooted in our more basic capabilities to perceive and interact with the

[22] See Pinker 1994: 45–53 for accounts of these neurological disorders.
[23] Crinion et al. 2006; see Perani & Abutalebi 2005 for a review.
[24] Abutalebi et al. 2000, reported in Crinion et al. 2006: 1540.
[25] One of the classic early reports on this phenomenon is Warrington & McCarthy 1983. Also see the review of the experimental literature in Caramazza et al. 1994, and more recent neuroimaging studies in Martin et al. 1996 and 2001 and Devlin et al. 2002.

world," which suggests that the "basic functional unit of action and perception" is the sensory-motor schema, not the word (1985: 36). Whatever their additional role as cognitive anchors or scaffolding for long trains of thought, words seem to function primarily as cues for reactivating sensory-motor patterns that are themselves nonlinguistic, mostly tacit, and grounded in universally shared human bodies and environments.[26] Indeed, work on the phenomenon of "verbal overshadowing," for instance, suggests that there is a flip side to the helpful "scaffolding" effect of language: language can, in certain situations and for certain types of skills, impair cognition. Jonathan Schooler and Tanya Engstler-Schooler (1990) found that subjects who described in detail the appearance of previously seen faces are markedly worse at subsequently recognizing those faces than if they were not asked to verbalize what they had seen, and similar effects have been found with regard to music, voices, and taste.[27] As Schooler and Charles Schreiber conclude, the body of evidence from verbal overshadowing studies "is highly suggestive in indicating that analytic introspective processes induced by describing memories can sometimes disrupt holistic non-verbal recognition processes" (2004: 25). The work on tacit know-how, automaticity, and unconscious emotional biasing reviewed in Chapter 1 similarly suggests that explicit, linguistically formulated or formulatable knowledge plays a minor role in much of our everyday perception and behavior. The crucial importance of background knowledge pointed out by Searle and others also shows that even language comprehension itself can occur only against the backdrop of implicit, shared, and nonlinguistically specified knowledge.

PERCEPTUAL PARADIGMS ARE NOT ALL-DETERMINING

The idea that culture determines perception – that human beings are simply unable to perceive something that is not part of their cultural discourse – is one of the central themes of the postmodernist position. As discussed earlier, Thomas Kuhn, for instance, often slips from the claim that theoretical frameworks strongly influence what can count as observational data into declaring that paradigms *completely* determine what scientists are able to perceive – normal science represents a "strenuous and devoted attempt to *force* nature into the conceptual boxes supplied by professional education" (1962/1970: 5), with the result that scientists working in different paradigms come to inhabit "different worlds" (150). Talk of different "lifeworlds" created by different cultural or linguistic systems forms part of the rhetorical bedrock of postmodern theorizing.

[26] As I will discuss in more detail in Chapter 4, these basic sensory-motor patterns are often invoked in order to combine them selectively into novel metaphoric blends, resulting – especially when this is combined with the human ability to transform the environment – in culturally unique life-worlds. Nonetheless, the fact that even novel blends are grounded in the body provides a broad and easily traversed common bridge to the "other."

[27] See Schooler & Schreiber 2004 for a review.

There are at least three problems with this view. The first is more theoretical: if cultural paradigms or discourses completely structure our experience of the world, it is hard to see how these structures could ever change, be revised, or even be *recognized* as structuring our perception. For instance, Kuhn's claim that scientific paradigms are all-determining becomes an a priori incoherent claim when set next to his equally important claim that paradigms shift as a result of "the recognition that nature has somehow violated the paradigm-induced expectations that govern normal science" (53). If paradigms really had the power to completely structure one's perceptions, these supposedly anomalous phenomena being displayed by "nature" could never be perceived. Kuhn's own historical examples also belie the strong paradigm-causes-perception claim. For instance, Kuhn describes how Wilhelm Roentgen discovered X-rays by noticing an anomalous phenomenon, the fact that a screen in his laboratory "glowed when it should not" (57). The fact that this glowing screen – an anomalous phenomenon that should not exist according to the dominant paradigm – could be noticed and perceived as significant by Roentgen shows that humans (even scientists!) have at least some degree of direct perceptual access to the world.[28] Of course, Roentgen's theoretical training had something to do with his seeing this glowing screen as significant – it should *not* have been glowing, a fact that derived much of its salience from Roentgen's theoretical expectations – but the role that these expectations play in everyday or even experimental perception should not be exaggerated. As Alan Chalmers puts it,

Nobody need deny the claim that someone who cannot tell the difference between a magnet and a carrot is not in a position to appreciate what counts as an established fact in electromagnetism. [However,] it is surely injudicious to use the term "theory" in such a general sense that "carrots are not magnets" becomes a theory. (1999: 195)[29]

This leads to the second issue. To supplement Chalmers's observation, it is important to recognize that how creatures like us *do* tell the difference between carrots and magnets is a more difficult feat than one might expect, and one that does involve prior expectations and assumptions. Kuhn is thus not entirely wrong in suggesting that "something like a paradigm is prerequisite to perception itself" (1962/1970: 112–113). In Chapter 1, I focused on the important role that preexisting schemas play in human perception; the goal there was to loosen the hold of the folk intuition that our senses are direct windows onto the world, as well as the objectivist ideal of perception as accurate representation. Now it is important to change tack and focus on the fact that our senses do tell us *something* about the

---

[28] Cf. Kuhn's 1962/1970 account of Lavoisier's "discovery" of oxygen (52–60) or Fresnel's white-spot experiment (154–156).

[29] Cf. Ian Hacking's comment that Feyerabend's claim regarding theory-determining observation is "obviously false, unless one attaches quite attenuated sense to the words, in which case the assertion is true but trivial" (1983b: 174), and his illustration of this point using the example of Herschel's discovery of radiant heat (176–178).

world. This may be an obvious point, but it is worth noting: if perceptual schemas were all-determining, there would be no need for perception at all. Organisms have sense organs because it has apparently been important throughout evolutionary time to find out something about the world that you did not already know, and to adjust your paradigms accordingly. As Ulric Neisser notes, the purpose of perceptual schemas is to pick up information – selectively – from the environment, and schemas are always being corrected and fine-tuned in the act of perception. "Perception is directed by expectations but not controlled by them," he concludes. "It involves the pickup of real information" (1976: 43). Approximately one-third of the human brain – already an extremely expensive organ – is dedicated to vision processing alone. All across the living world, a vast amount of evolutionary R&D investment has gone toward refining sensory organs: from plants turning their leaves toward the sun or eels sensing disturbances in their self-generated electrical fields, to dolphin echolocation and hawk vision, one could argue that a major trend in evolution has been the intensive elaboration of ways of acquiring information about the world. This type of expense has to return a large and constant payoff for the project to have gone on for so long and to have produced such refined results.

The third and final point is that, while we must acknowledge that our knowledge of the world is inevitably filtered through paradigms and biases, the vast majority of these paradigms are built-in and species-universal rather than socially or theoretically constructed. This is an important corrective to, for instance, Feyerabend's use of visual illusions – such as three-dimensional cubes that flip back and forth across the plane of the page as one looks at them – to demonstrate human beings' conceptual fluidity (1993: 166–167). What Feyerabend fails to recognize about visual illusions such as this is that they work precisely by exploiting fixed regularities in the human perceptual system – in this case, the manner in which foreshortening is taken by our eye-brain as an indication of depth. Feyerabend is thus justified in concluding that "covert relationships" subserving human perception undermine old-fashioned objectivism (169), while missing the point that such relationships are similarly instantiated and universally shared by *Homo sapiens*. This brings us to our next topic.

NO BLANK SLATE: THE "EVOLUTIONARY KANTIAN" POSITION AND THE MODULAR VIEW OF THE MIND

The idea that the human being is a tabula rasa waiting to be inscribed by language-culture is at the heart of the postmodernist position – a Latourian minotaur that cannot be kept at bay. Even more sophisticated postmodernist thinkers such as Bourdieu, who recognize the problems with identifying thought with language and ignoring the role of embodied knowledge, continue to cling to what is essentially a blank slate view of human nature. As I argued in Chapter 2, the recognition of the role of the body by thinkers such as Bourdieu has not been accompanied by the idea that this body contributes any sort of meaningful structure to human experience, and this tendency to view the body as a passive receiver of culture – or an otherwise featureless "site" for discursive power struggles – is pervasive in postmodern writings on the subject.[30]

The evolutionary psychologists John Tooby and Leda Cosmides have been in the forefront of a movement arguing against blank slate views in favor of what they term an "evolutionary Kantian" position: that human cognition could simply not get off the ground without the existence of a robust set of evolutionarily designed and species-typical categories of understanding.[31] They argue that many of our categories of understanding and the normative valuations that guide our behavior are built-in, and that this is not only an empirical fact but an a priori necessity: completely blank, general-purpose learning systems would simply not be able to *learn* anything. The theoretical necessity for built-in structure goes by various names in different fields – it is the "frame problem" in AI, the "poverty of stimulus" in linguistics, the problem of "referential ambiguity" in semantics, the need for "constraints on induction" in developmental psychology, or the problem of the underdetermination of "stimulus array" interpretation in the psychology and neuroscience of perception – but all of these fields converge in demonstrating that a blank slate would simply remain blank (1992: 103–107).[32] Tooby and Cosmides summarize the theoretical case in favor of a content-rich, domain-specific embodied mind over a general-purpose learning network by observing that

(1) possibilities are infinite; and (2) desirable outcomes – by any usual human, evolutionary, or problem-solving standard – are a very small subset of all possibilities . . . Accordingly, to be endowed with broad behavioral plasticity unconnected to adaptive targets or environmental conditions is an evolutionary death sentence, guaranteeing that the design that generates it will be removed from the population. (101)

The theoretical and evolutionary doubts about the viability of a general-purpose learning machine have been reinforced by the failure in AI to get genuinely general-purpose association networks to learn anything useful. As Pinker observes, programmers have only been able to get such networks to work by sneaking in so many seemingly minor, built-in assumptions that the resulting network is not really general-purpose anymore (2002: 83).

---

[30] A recent collection of excerpts from works concerning the "body" (Fraser & Greco 2005) provides a helpful – albeit truncated – overview of various postmodernist views on the subject; also cf. the essays in Weiss & Haber 1999, which purport to explore "the intersections of nature and culture" but for the most part tend to subsume the former under the latter.

[31] For a nice summary of this position, see Tooby & Cosmides 1992: 70–72. Kant, of course, would be horrified at the notion of categories of understanding being characterized in such an empirically contingent manner.

[32] For more on the general frame problem with regard to human cognition and perception, see Neisser 1976: 63–64, Gelman 1990: 3–4, Hirschfeld & Gelman 1994a and 1994b, Keil 1994, Gazzaniga 1998: 13–16, and Pinker 2002: 30–102.

Taking the evolutionary Kantian position seriously means that the vague notion of "learning" that plays such a crucial role in social constructivist accounts of cultural acquisition needs to be replaced with more specific accounts of how creatures like us are equipped to acquire various *specific* abilities and attitudes – how we are capable of even recognizing something as something to be learned. As E. O. Wilson observes, "the process of learning is not a basic trait that gradually emerges with the evolution of larger brain size. Rather, it is a diverse array of peculiar behavioral adaptations, many of which have evolved repeatedly and independently in different major animal taxa" (1975/2000: 156). This leads Tooby and Cosmides to conclude that that the term "learning" is "not an explanation for anything, but is rather a phenomenon that itself requires explanation" (1992: 122), and they compare "learning" as used by social constructivists to the concept of "protoplasm" in early biology, "a name given to the unknown agent imagined to cause a large and heterogenous set of functional outcomes" (123):

A psychological architecture that consisted of nothing but equipotential, general-purpose, content-independent, or content-free mechanisms could not successfully perform the tasks that the human mind is known to perform or solve the adaptive problems humans evolved to solve – from seeing, to learning a language, to recognizing an emotional expression, to selecting a mate, to the many disparate activities aggregated under the term "learning culture." (34)

Bolstering theoretical considerations that make the blank slate an unlikely design strategy, work in cognitive science, particularly in developmental psychology, suggests the existence of a wide range of innate human assumptions and learning strategies that are both universal and strongly domain-specific. These findings are motivating a move away from viewing the mind as a general-purpose processor, ready to absorb whatever information is presented to it, toward a view of the mind as a "Swiss Army knife": a bundle of semi-independent "modules" with proprietary and dedicated functions, expecting to receive and process information in particular domains.[33] A "domain," as Hirshfeld and Gelman explain,

is a body of knowledge that identifies and interprets a class of phenomena assumed to share certain properties and to be of a distinct and general type. A domain functions as a stable response to a set of recurring and complex problems faced by the organism. This response involves difficult-to-access perceptual, encoding, retrieval, and inferential processes dedicated to that solution. (1994b: 21)

At its most simple, a domain-specific module takes the form of, for instance, the learning biases exhibited by rats and explored by John Garcia and Robert Koelling

---

[33] For an early and influential statement of modularity theory see Jerry Fodor 1983. Also see Cosmides & Tooby 1994: 90–94 for the evolutionary rationale for domain specificity, and Sperber 1994 and 1996: esp. 122–127 for an argument that Fodor's model of the mind is only superficially modular, as well as a response to Fodor's critiques of "modularity theory gone mad" (Fodor 1987: 27).

(1966). Rats that were given (mild) electric shocks paired with both visual and taste stimuli learned to avoid only the visual stimuli, whereas when a nausea-inducing poison was employed the rats learned to avoid the taste but not the visual stimulus. Clearly something like the domain-specific rules "if you feel an unpleasant external jolt, look for a cause in what you last saw" and "if you feel queasy, look for a cause in what you last ate" are at work. Simple perceptual modules have also been at the heart of vision research for the past few decades, where researchers realized quite early on that what phenomenologically appears to humans as a unitary process of "seeing" in fact involves the coordination of a vast range of specific modules selectively dedicated to detecting edges, motion, horizontally or vertically oriented shapes, textures of surfaces, and so on.[34] The first and perhaps best known application of domain-specific modularity theory to "higher" aspects of human cognition was Chomsky's proposed "Universal Grammar" mechanism for acquiring and understanding human languages, which Chomsky felt needed to be postulated because children clearly go "beyond the data" in becoming proficient comprehenders and producers of grammatical sentences.

I wish to turn now to a brief discussion of some of the more interesting or well-attested learning constraints, domain-specific modules, and "folk theories"[35] – focusing on humans, but also noting parallels in nonhuman animal cognition – to give a sense of how the body-mind can be highly selective in what it notices and cares about while at the same time remaining richly responsive to its evolutionarily relevant environment. Much of the work I will be discussing comes from studies involving infants or very young children,[36] which are obviously quite relevant to the assertion of universalist claims. If assumptions or abilities can be clearly demonstrated in infants or prelinguistic children, we can be fairly confident that we have eliminated the influence of language and – at least in the case of infants – culture. Obviously, the linguistic and cultural assumptions of the experimenters are still relevant, but the fact that the child development results we will be discussing have been replicated across a wide spectrum of cultures increases our confidence

---

[34] See Marr 1982. For some quite impressive recent evidence supporting strong modularity in the fusiform face area of macaques, as measured by fMRI combined with single-unit neuron recordings, see Tsao et al. 2006 and the discussion in Kanwisher 2006.

[35] See Gelman et al. 1994 and Hirshfeld & Gelman 1994b on the concept of "folk theory," which refers to observed human tendencies to consistently make use of domain-specific "unobservable, causal-explanatory constructs" (Gelman et al. 1994: 342). As Hirshfeld & Gelman note, such theories lack the conceptual rigor and empirically derived nature of scientific theories, but are theorylike in their "resistance to counter-evidence, ontological commitments, attention to domain-specific causal principles, and coherence of belief" (13).

[36] Infants obviously cannot communicate effectively, so the basic principle relied on by child develop-ment researchers is a very salient "violation of expectation" indicator: the fact that infants tend to gaze longer at novel or unexpected events than at familiar or expected ones. Measurement of infants' gazing times is thus used as an indicator of whether or not assumptions or expectations are being violated. See Bornstein 1985 and Spelke 1985 for discussions of this methodology.

that we are observing specieswide cognitive defaults. Taken together, and seen against the backdrop of the relatively stable and shared environment that produced them, these modules give us a picture of human beings – in many cases, together with nonhuman animals – as dwelling in a shared, elaborately structured, and inference-rich world of prelinguistic thought.

Basic-Level Categories

When I began studying Mandarin Chinese, the words I learned in my first year were primarily basic ones such as "table" (*juozi*), "chair" (*yizi*), "cat" (*mao*), "dog" (*gou*) – the sort we are used to seeing illustrated in basic language textbooks and children's books. This is one of the many phenomena that humans take for granted when learning another language or interacting with another culture: while we are aware that there are likely a host of culturally specific details that we will only comprehend with time, if ever, it is equally – if not usually consciously – obvious to us that our world and the world of others share a basic set of concepts. There will be a word for "table" as opposed to "chair," "running" as opposed to "walking," "standing" as opposed to "sitting."

One possibility, of course, is that this is a colonialist illusion, created by the European powers that wrote the textbooks and the dictionaries and foisted their linguistic worldview upon the rest of the world, whose alien lexicons are now forced to fit the Procrustean bed of Indo-European semantics. While theoretically possible, this appears not to be the case. A host of child development and cross-cultural studies have demonstrated that there exists a level of categorization of the world – the level of so-called basic-level categories – that is shared by members of the species *Homo sapiens*. Basic-level categories are those first learned by children, are shared cross-culturally, and are experienced as being easier to remember and more conceptually important than more detailed or more general categories.[37] What makes them so irresistibly salient to human beings are the details of our embodiment: basic-level categories are distinguished from one another by virtue of their sensory-motor distinctiveness. As Eleanor Rosch et al. (1976) argue, the basic level is the highest level of categorization that can be represented by a single mental image, and with which an individual uses similar motor actions for interacting – they are, as George Lakoff puts it, "human-sized" (1987: 51). "Chairs" are interacted with in a fundamentally different manner than "tables" for organisms with our general size, shape, and capabilities. More detailed categories lack this distinguishability: we do not interact with "armchairs" in a manner fundamentally different from "kitchen

---

[37] The classic and readable introduction to basic-level categorization, with a host of cross-cultural evidence, is Lakoff 1987. For evidence for basic-level categories from child language-acquisition and cognition studies, see Markman 1989 and Behl-Chadha 1996.

chairs." Superordinate categories, on the other hand, simply lack a coherent image or sensory-motor profile altogether: "furniture" as a concept offers us nothing in the way of affordances.

One of the more striking and well-documented illustrations of basic-level universality are the parallels between folk taxonomies across the world. Some of the earliest work on this phenomenon was done by Brent Berlin et al. (1973), who found that a single level of biological classification – corresponding to the modern taxonomical classification of genus – was psychologically basic for speakers of Tzeltal, a language spoken in the Chiapas region of Mexico. This "folk-generic level" has all the features of a basic-level category. Names at this level (e.g., "oak") are simpler and more easily remembered. Categories at this level are perceived holistically, as a single gestalt – for more focused categories ("white oak") individual details need to be focused upon, and for more general categories ("tree," "plant") there is not a single coherent image that can represent the category.[38]

Of course, domain-specific experience and pragmatic interests have an obvious effect on categorization and the salience of levels of classification, as we have already noted with regard to the snow-related categorization of the Inuits or wave-related categorization of surfers. Jeremy Bailenson et al. (2002), for instance, compared U.S. and Mayan categorization of song birds and found marked differences between experts and novices, as well as quite striking transcultural convergences between U.S. and Mayan experts. Douglas Medin et al. (2006) also found that the differing pragmatic orientations of Native American and American majority–culture fish experts result in somewhat different systems of classification. Such specialized categorization, however, develops only against the backdrop of a shared world made up of basic categories of things. As George Lakoff notes, categories at this basic level will tend to be universal and to appear more basic and useful to us because we "share the same general capacities for gestalt perception and for holistic motor movement" and that basic-level categories hook us up to the world in a special way, providing a "crucial link between cognitive structure and real knowledge of the world" (1987: 38).

Folk Physics

As Hume famously noted, causality is not out there in the world for us to see: all we see is a conjunction of events, and we then leap to the assumption of causality (1777/1975). This leap, though perhaps unjustifiable on the basis of first principles, appears to be inevitable for creatures like us. Work in developmental psychology indicates that infants share a set of assumptions about the behavior of the inanimate,

---

[38] More recent and extensive work on folk classification has been done by Scott Atran and his colleagues; see Atran 1987, 1990, 1995, and 1998, as well as the essays collected in Medin & Atran 1999.

physical world that has come to be referred to as "folk physics."[39] Elizabeth Spelke et al. (1995) provide evidence for three basic principles about the behavior of physical objects that appear to be shared by infants:

1. Principle of cohesion: "objects are connected and bounded bodies that main-tain both their connectedness and their boundaries as they move freely." (45)
2. Principle of continuity: "objects exists and move continuously, such that each object traces exactly one connected path over space and time." (48)
3. Principle of contact: "objects act upon each other if and only if they touch." (49)

Spelke and others have shown that these assumptions appear quite early in infant development and are universal cross-culturally. With regard to the "principle of continuity," for instance, Jean Piaget (1954) famously proposed that infants do not acquire the ability to reach for hidden objects until eight months of age, and that the ability to understand that a perceptually absent object still existed was acquired gradually through experience. Studies employing physical occlusion and violation-of-expectation gazing, however, strongly suggest that assumptions about object permanence are innate, even if the actual ability to reach for hidden objects develops later. It has been shown, for instance, that infants as young as two and a half months expect objects occluded by a screen to continue existing even though the objects are hidden from view, and that the infants are surprised when experiments are manipulated to violate this expectation.[40] Recent studies further suggest that infants distinguish between occlusion (one object hidden behind another), containment (one object hidden *inside* another), and support (one object supported by another), and that learning about each of these types of physical events is self-contained – that is, it is not generalized and applied to other relevant categories, as one would expect from a general-purpose learning process.[41]

With regard to Spelke's "principle of contact," Alan Leslie and his colleague have demonstrated that, by six and a half months, infants are subject to the Michotte launching illusion, whereby apparent contact between animated balls on a screen is irresistibly seen to involve a transfer of force (Leslie & Keeble 1987, Leslie 1994).

---

[39] For a basic introduction to folk physics and a review of the relevant experimental evidence, see Leslie 1994 and 1995, Baillargeon et al. 1995, and Spelke et al. 1995.

[40] See Baillargeon et al. 1985, Baillargeon 1986 and 1991, Aguiar & Baillargeon 1999, and Wang et al. 2005. Also see Ruffman et al. 2005 for a recent experiment that controls for the possibility that infants are responding to mere perceptual novelty or familiarity.

[41] See Casasola et al. 2003 and the experiment and literature review in Hespos & Baillargeon 2006, as well as the study in Baillargeon & Wang (2002) that suggests that infant understanding of occlusion and containment are distinct and come online at different points in development.

Leslie argues that it is our intuitive model of how the physical world works that goes beyond the data – animated circles moving on a screen – to "paint" physical principles and mechanical causality onto the world.[42] These intuitive models, though unjustified from an objectivist standpoint, represent the crucial bedrock of our ability to move through the world successfully. As Leslie notes, "without access to the mechanical interpretation [provided by folk physics] . . . none of the inferences concerning cause or agency can be drawn and we are stuck, like David Hume, with the 'impression of our sense,' namely, meaningless spatiotemporal patterns" (1994: 133).

As we will see with other human cognitive modules, there is considerable evidence that the basics of folk physics are not only precultural but pan-species.[43] Aaron Blaisdell et al. (2006), for instance, show sophisticated reasoning about physical causality in rats in a series of experiments designed to control for the possibility of mere associative learning. Perhaps even more suggestive is the widespread use of tools throughout the animal kingdom – tools whose usefulness is immediately comprehensible to humans – which indicates a shared sense of how the physical world works and how to go about manipulating it.[44] While some nonhuman animal cognition researchers have argued that nonhuman tool use could be based on simple behavioralist associations or physical principles quite different from our own (Povinelli 2000), evidence for the nonhuman use of "stepped" tools (tools that require several steps to construct), the modification of available but nonoptimal tools, and tool planning over spatial and temporal distances is rendering the idea of a shared, pan-species set of physical intuitions more and more plausible.[45]

---

[42]   See Choi & Scholl (2006) for interesting studies suggesting that this "painting" of causality onto the world can occur "postdictively" – i.e., as a result of later events.

[43]   See Dickinson & Shanks 1995 and Kummer 1995 for a discussion of nonhuman perception of causality.

[44]   For recent work on primate tool use, see Moura & Lee (2004), who document the use of tools for digging, cracking, and probing in capuchin monkeys in Northeastern Brazil, or the study by Sanz et al. (2004) of wild chimpanzees in the Congo who use "tool sets," including "puncturing sticks" made of a particular species of tree and modified in particular ways and elaborately modified "fishing probes." Also see Mercader et al. (2007) for recent archeological evidence suggesting that chimpanzees have been using stone tools for over four millennia. For an excellent recent review article on corvid (crows and jays) tool use and manufacture – including the spontaneous modification of hooked tools, the use of "stepped tools," and culturally mediated population differences in tool use – see Emery & Clayton (2004).

[45]   Some nonhuman tool use is apparently "cultural," in the sense that it is discovered or invented by one individual and then spread through local populations through imitation or active teaching. (The famous early example of "cultural traditions" among Japanese macaques is documented in Nishida 1987; for a more recent review, see Whiten 2005a and the experimental evidence in Whiten et al. 2005. Also refer to the short exchange between Abler 2005 and Whiten 2005b for the appropriateness of referring to nonhuman "culture.") However, as Kenward et al. (2005) observe, phenomena such as spontaneous tool manufacture in naïve juvenile crows illustrate that tool use and creation abilities are "at least partially inherited and not dependent on social input" (121).

Folk Biology and Essentialism

From a very early age human beings seem to distinguish between living and non-living things, and to attribute to the former a unique set of properties. As described by Frank Keil, both children and adults seem to spontaneously feel that biological kinds, as opposed to nonliving things,

1. "reproduce, preserving important properties of their kind at both the level of the species and the individual";
2. "have complex, heterogenous internal structure";
3. "grow and undergo canonical, usually irreversible patterns of change," moving toward "an ideal target state for that kind";
4. possess "something intrinsic" that produces "most of their stable phenomenal properties" (i.e., they contain an internal essence);
5. possess "typical phenomenal properties" that are usually diagnostic of this underlying essence;
6. possess properties that have purposes; and
7. possess "parts that work together to support each other in complementary fashion" (i.e., are characterized by homeostasis). (Keil 1994: 236–237)

Let us unpack some of the more important of these features of the folk biological conception. Whereas reasoning about nonbiological kinds and entities tends to rely on the principles of folk physics outlined earlier, children as young as three years old tend to view living things – as opposed to physical objects or artifacts – as having "self-serving properties" (248), which are in turn conceived of as arising from some internal, invisible "essence." Kayoko Inagaki and Giyoo Hatano (1993 and 2004) have proposed a distinct form of "vitalistic causality" – an amorphous energy or force seen as maintaining and enhancing life, to be distinguished from mechanistic causality discussed earlier or intentional causality to be treated later – that is perceived by humans to be at work in the biological world, and they have shown that young Japanese children preferentially refer to vitalistic explanations for biological phenomena, a result that has been demonstrated cross-culturally.[46] This sort of "vitalistic" causation seems to be naturally tied to the idea of teleology, and Deborah Kelemen has performed a series of experiments (1999a, 1999b, 2003, 2004) demonstrating a selective preference in children for teleological explanations for natural phenomena – a preference that can be overridden in educated adults through scientific training, but only with difficulty.

Along with teleology, "essentialism" is often presented by postmodernists as a peculiar sin of the alienated West, and both are frequently blamed on Aristotle. The positing of invisible essences to at least living things seems, however, to be an inevitable human tendency. Ask a child what happens to a coffeepot that has

---

[46] Also see Carey 1995 on "biological" causation.

been cut and sealed and filled with birdseed in such a fashion that it looks and functions like a birdfeeder, and the child will reply that the erstwhile "coffeepot" is now a "birdfeeder" – when it comes to artifacts, contingent function determines identity. Ask a child what we are to make of a tiger that has been bleached and had a mane sewed onto it, so that it now resembles a lion, and the answer is quite different: despite the superficial alterations, the tiger will always be a tiger. Here is a representative exchange between the experimenter (E) and a second grader (C):

C: It looks like a lion, but it's a tiger.
E: Why do you think it's a tiger and not a lion?
C: Because it was made out of a tiger.
E: And why isn't it a lion?
C: It's a lion a little, but not very much . . .
E: Why did you choose tiger instead of lion?
C: Because, even though it looks more like a lion, it's a tiger . . .
E: What is the difference between the problems where you said the thing was changed and where you said the thing wasn't changed . . . ?
C: The animals were alive, so they could have babies . . . so you can tell what it is.
E: Why isn't that true for things like the coffeepot and the tire [which was transformed into a boot]?
C: Because what they're made of isn't alive. (Keil 1989: 190)

As this exchange indicates, this "essence" that determines the nature of a living thing is closely linked to its insides, as opposed to its external appearance: a dog with its insides removed, for instance, is judged by young children to no longer be a dog, even though it looks the same on the outside (Gelman & Wellman 1991).[47]

Such a distinction between outside appearance and internal "essence" – the former superficial and variable, the latter "real" and unchanging – seems to be a central human intuition about the living world.[48] In his work on folk taxonomy, Scott Atran has documented these domain-specific essentialistic beliefs across cultures, observing that "all and only living kinds are conceived as physical sorts whose intrinsic 'natures' are presumed, even if unknown," and that these natures encompass certain necessary properties that reveal themselves under "normal" conditions:

[47] There seem to be developmental changes in children's essentialistic intuitions that may be linked to cultural training. Keil (1989) found that children's tendency to distinguish between natural kinds and artifacts becomes much stronger with age, and that they begin to have a more nuanced conception of what is related to the "essence" of biological kinds. Preschool children also believe that a skunk can be turned into a raccoon through surgery, whereas by age nine or so children begin to believe that the resulting animal is still a skunk merely masquerading as a raccoon – by this age, children appear to believe that only changes resulting from "natural," biological growth can effect internal essences (Keil 1989 and Carey & Spelke 1994: 185–186).

[48] See especially Gelman & Wellman 1991 and the literature reviews in Gelman 2003 and 2004.

We can say that a dog born legless is missing "its" legs because we presume that all dogs are quadrupeds "by nature"; but we cannot justifiably say that a legless beanbag chair is missing "its" legs simply because chairs normally have legs. It is this presumption of underlying nature that underpins the taxonomic stability of organic phenomenal types despite obvious variation among individual exemplars. (Atran 1990: 6)

Even in classical Chinese philosophy – often presented as a haven of "holistic," nonessentialistic thinking – we see this folk belief at work in the distinction made between a living thing's external form or appearance and its "essence" (*qing*) or "nature" (*xing*), the thing that makes it what it is. The Confucian thinker Mencius (3rd c. B.C.E) relies on this distinction in his famous parable of Ox Mountain (Lau 1970: 164–165), mentioned in Chapter 2. Ox Mountain once enjoyed a luxurious cover of trees. Being located on the edge of a major city, however, it was denuded by loggers, and the new shoots growing from the stumps are continuously thwarted by hosts of grazing animals. Looking at it now, Mencius says, we are tempted to think that its "nature" is to be desolate, but of course this is an illusion: the baldness of Ox Mountain is an external accident caused by its environment, but its internal essence remains unchanged. Mencius's main concern was not forestry management but rather moral education, and for him the originally lush nature of Ox Mountain is intended as a metaphor for originally pure human nature. The basic intuition, however, is pure folk biology: no matter what happens to the outside, the internal essence remains the same.

Of course, like folk physics, folk biology appears, from the standpoint of modern biological science, to be inaccurate: for instance, if the theory of evolution is correct, there is no such thing as a species-specific "essence," despite the power of genes to reliably produce a particular phenotypic profile. Indeed, our apparently innate folk biology may be one of the factors that makes it so difficult for people to understand Darwinism, since the idea of species as eternal essences is so deeply engrained in our psyches. Like folk physics, folk biology has to be suppressed or at least partially – and perhaps only temporarily – overcome in the process of scientific education. However, as a first approximation, it seems to be a fairly helpful assumption: tigers *do* tend to act in a certain predictable way, even when covered with mud, obscured by mist, missing an ear, or found roaming in uncharacteristic places. Atran thus speculates that folk biology arose because it has been an adaptively useful assumption, "perhaps partially accounted for in evolutionary terms by the empirical adequacy that presumptions of essence afford to human beings in dealing with local biota" (1990: 63).

Innate Body Schemas

Before turning to one of the more important of innate modules, folk psychology, it would be helpful to consider briefly the human cognitive machinery that allows the understanding of other agents to even get off the ground: the set of innate body schemas that make imitation and action recognition possible.

Within moments of birth, human infants attend selectively to their mother's voice, and to human faces in general. While the draw of their mother's voice might be understandable – by six months or so, fetuses in the womb are capable of hearing, and no doubt are exposed in utero to their mother's voice – the immediate appeal of human faces is something that needs to be explained. Even more surprising, upon reflection, is the neonate's astounding capacity to imitate facial expressions. The early work on neonate imitation was done by Andrew Meltzoff and Keith Moore (1977, 1994), who showed that newborns less than an hour old are strikingly accurate in their imitation of human facial gestures, including quite novel ones – for example, sticking one's tongue out at an odd angle. Human adults spontaneously fall into facial expression games with very young infants, and it strikes us as natural (as well as extremely cute) to see our expressions mirrored by them. The ease and apparent naturalness of this obscures what a massive number of perceptual and motor schemas must be built into an infant for the infant to recognize a human face as a face, to discriminate distinct expressions, to have a robust enough image of its own body to "realize" – although this is no doubt an entirely unconscious realization – that it also has a face that can make these expressions, and then to mobilize the myriad muscles that would allow this mirroring to occur. This is no blank slate. As Shaun Gallagher notes, Meltzoff and Moore's work shows that "some primitive and primary sense of embodied self is operative at least from the very beginning of postnatal life" (2005: 78).

By age twelve to eighteen months infants develop the ability to share joint attention – that is, to note where an interaction partner is attending and direct attention accordingly – and to engage intensively in joint action requiring various forms of motor co-coordination with others, and an ability to anticipate what another is about to do.[49] Research in the field of cognitive neuroscience suggests that, in primates (including humans), observed actions are understood through sensory-motor simulation: a monkey observing a human hand grasping an object, for instance, activates the same premotor regions that would fire if the monkey itself were grasping the object. These so-called mirror neuron systems fire even when the crucial final portion of the action is hidden from view,[50] indicating that, as Umiltà et al. (2001) observe, "the motor representation of an action performed by others can be internally generated in the observer's premotor cortex, even when a visual description of the action is lacking," which in turn suggests that mirror neuron activation is at the basis of action recognition.

---

[49] See Sebanz et al. 2006 for a review of research on joint attention and joint action.

[50] The pioneering work on mirror neuron systems was done by Giacomo Rizzolatti, Michael Arbib, and Vittorio Gallese; see especially Gallese et al. 1996 and Rizzolatti et al. 1996. For a recent work on mirror neuron systems in humans, see Rizzolatti & Craighero 2004 and Fadiga et al. 2005.

This innate ability to understand and anticipate the actions of others through a kind of embodied "resonance" would seem to be a basic prerequisite for interpersonal communication, and is no doubt an important precursor to the more sophisticated comprehension of intentionality that is part of the full-blown "theory of mind" to be discussed next.[51] More generally, the ability to extract humanly relevant action and intention schemas from the buzzing, blooming confusion of the world and accurately reproduce them is a profoundly difficult computational task – far beyond the capacities of any current AI system – and gives some sense of the massive iceberg of shared experience that lies beneath even the most basic sorts of human understanding and learning.

Folk Psychology: "Theory of Mind" and the "Intentional Stance"

On my way to the office this morning I noticed a young man with a backpack on the sidewalk in front of me suddenly break into a run. Glancing ahead to see what he might be running for, I saw that a #17 bus – which does not run very frequently – had just turned the corner and come to a halt at the bus stop. The bus disgorged a few passengers and then, as the traffic light changed, began to close its doors and pull back out into traffic. The bus driver must have spotted the runner, however, since the bus paused for a moment, closing its doors and pulling away only after the young man had climbed on board. I noticed him bobbing his head several times as he showed the driver his pass, presumably thanking him for waiting.

A very simple interaction such as this conceals the massive amount of interpretation that goes into noticing and comprehending it. Besides the more obvious need for extensive background knowledge about the formal and informal rules governing public transportation in the city of Vancouver, making sense of this scenario involved the projection of unobserved but assumed intentionality. I see a young man break into a run: there must be something he is running to or from; if I hadn't seen the bus ahead I would have turned around to see if anyone was chasing him. I see the bus pause with its doors open: the immediate and unquestioned conclusion is that the bus driver must have seen the running person, instantly made the same connections that I had made, and decided to lose a few seconds off his schedule in order to wait for the young man to board. *Wanting, waiting, worrying* about being late – these sorts of mental states, goal-directed activities, and desires are no more directly observable in the world than is physical causality, but because of the manner in which we are constituted we apparently cannot help seeing both physical causes and intentional states in the world.

---

[51] See Rizzolatti & Arbib 1998 for an argument that mirror neuron representations form the basis of communication and that a prelinguistic "grammar" of action in monkeys may represent a precursor to the grammar of human speech. For the link between mirror systems and theory of mind, see and Blakemore & Decety 2001.

This tendency of human beings to project intentionality onto other agents has come to be referred to by cognitive scientists as "theory of mind" (ToM),[52] being "theory"-like because it goes beyond the available data to postulate the existence of unobservable, causal forces or principles.[53] It is apparent that, from a very early age, human beings conceive of intentionality as a distinct kind of causality, and distinguish it from both the kind of physical causation that characterizes folk physics and teleological, "vitalistic" causation. Infants and very young children suspend contact requirement for interpersonal causality, and understand that agents – as opposed to objects – harbor goals and desires and experience emotions (Avis & Harris 1991, Spelke et al. 1995). Intentionality is viewed by children as a special type of "internal" cause that can work at a distance and that invites responses from affected agents (Premack & Premack 1995). Even very young children seem to expect agents to be self-propelled, as opposed to objects, which should move only when contacted by another object (Spelke et al. 1995, Rakison & Poulin-Dubois 2001).This attribution of intentionality and agency apparently appears quite early in development. Ann Phillips and Henry Wellman (2005) demonstrated in twelve-month-olds the understanding of object-directed action – that is, the ability to recognize the movement of a human hand as specifically directed toward a given object[54] – and Hyun-joo Song et al. (2005) report the ability of thirteen and a half-month-olds to attribute to a person the disposition to perform a particular action.

It appears that we cannot help projecting intentionality onto the world in this way, often in a quite promiscuous fashion. Some of the earliest work on over-projection of agency was done by Fritz Heider and Mary-Ann Simmel (1944), who found that adults shown simple animations involving geometric figures were very quick and enthusiastic in projecting a variety of mental states and goals onto these otherwise featureless objects. This robust phenomenon is well-known and frequently exploited by animators and by parents trying to amuse their children, and appears to emerge quite early in development.[55] Even very young children observing simple animations of geometric figures instinctively understand

[52] Perhaps the best recent (and quite readable) introduction to theory of mind is Bloom 2004; also see Humphrey 1986, Wellman 1990, Baron-Cohen 1995, Gergely et al. 1995, Nichols & Stich 2003, and the essays collected in Carruthers & Smith 1996.
[53] Especially with regard to "theory of mind" (ToM), there is a lively debate concerning the appropriateness of the word "theory." Some – such as Gopnik & Wellman 1994 – defend the position that theory of mind *is* a sort of implicit theory. The defenders of the "simulation" position (Gordon 1986 and Gallese & Goldman 1998), on the contrary, argue that the achievements of ToM are the result of sensory-motor simulation, relying on our mirror neuron system. A third position is carved out by Shaun Gallagher with his claim that ToM is the result of perception-based "body-reading" (2005: 227).
[54] Cf. the earlier work of Leslie 1982 on five- to seven-month-olds' perception of hands as agents.
[55] Of course, we also spontaneously project intentionality onto "angry" seas or "threatening" skies; this tendency to project intentionality onto the world at large will be discussed further in Chapter 6.

them as agents and expect them to "act" in ways that are logically related to their "goals." György Gergely et al. (1995) found that twelve-month-olds habituated to expect that a smaller circle "wanted" to be next to a large circle were surprised when the small circle did not take the most direct route. Another interesting study of apparent multistage mental attribution in infants by Valerie Kuhlmeier et al. (2003) presented twelve-month-olds with an animation in which a circle appears to be "trying" to climb up a hill, and is sometimes "helped" by a triangle that gently pushes it up or "thwarted" by a square that pushes it down from the top of the hill. (The fact that adults effortlessly and inevitably perceive the scene this way, incidentally, is a paradigmatic example of theory of mind in action.) When subsequently shown an animation where the circle is placed equidistant between the triangle and square and moves toward one or the other, the infants are surprised when the circle moves toward the square, but not when it moves toward the triangle: they appear to expect that the circle now "likes" the helpful triangle, but not the mean square. In an interesting cross-cultural demonstration of this phenomenon as related to quite complex intentional states, H. Clark Barrett et al. (2005) had subjects create short animations depicting various intentional actions – "chasing," "fighting," "courting," "guarding," and "playing" – using only moving dots on a screen. The animations produced in this manner were then shown to both German and Shuar (from Amazonian Ecuador) adults, who were equally accurate in matching particular movement of dots with the intended intentional acts.[56]

There is a fair amount of debate about when in development humans begin to acquire theory of mind, and whether or not other species may possess it. Certain aspects of the debate might be defused by recognizing that "theory of mind" appears not to be a single, monolithic module, but rather a general term referring to a suite of discrete abilities, some of which clearly appear to come online later than others.[57] The earliest manifestations of theory of mind may be newborns' selective attention to human faces and voices, and especially the attractive force of the human eye. Even quite young babies look at human eyes more than anything else in their environment, especially if the eyes are directed at them, and eye contact causes immediate physiological arousal in humans. Simon Baron-Cohen speculates that this may be a kind of "agent early warning system" – the appearance of another agent on the scene is cause for increased attention and readiness (1995: 98).

---

[56] Quicktime samples of the actual animations used are available at http://www.anthro.ucla.edu/faculty/barrett/motion.htm.

[57] Alan Leslie (1994), for instance, argues for at least two different theory of mind systems. "System 1," developed around six- to eight-month-olds, is characterized by following eye gaze (Butterworth 1991) and the beginning of "requesting," "refusing," and "give and take" behaviors (Leslie 1994: 140–141); "System 2," developed in second year of life, involves the ability to pretend and understand pretense in others, and the ability to construe the behavior of others as related to fictional or counter-factual states of affairs.

Many researchers feel that full-blown theory of mind is not achieved until children acquire the ability to pass the so-called false-belief test – that is, to comprehend that the knowledge of others might differ from one's own – which they do not appear to master until around four or five years of age.[58] One classic false-belief test involves the "Sally-Anne" task (Baron-Cohen et al. 1985), where children are told about a character named Sally who hid a marble in a particular place. When Sally is gone, another character named Anne comes and moves the marble. Children are then asked where Sally will look for the marble when she returns. Three-year-olds, conflating their own knowledge and Sally's beliefs, say that she will look in the new place, whereas four- and five-year-olds recognize that Sally holds the (mistaken) belief that the marble is still in the original hiding place.[59] Similar developmental patterns have been demonstrated cross-culturally, with some minor variations – Nicola Knight et al. (2004), for instance, demonstrated the emergence of the ability to pass the false-belief test in Mayan children between ages four and seven, approximately a year later than American children.

The fact that the ability to pass the false-belief test emerges so late in development is taken by some researchers as evidence that full theory of mind requires language and acculturation. This view is supported by the observation that deaf children raised by hearing parents suffer delays in language acquisition that are mirrored by a relatively late understanding of false beliefs (Perner & Ruffman 2005). Others argue that even young infants possess a rudimentary, implicit representation of beliefs. Eye gaze observations suggest that three-year-olds have an implicit understanding of false belief even though their verbal responses fail to reflect it (Clements & Perner 1994, Ruffman et al. 2001), and Kristine Onishi and Renée Baillargeon (2005) found that fifteen-month-old infants seem able to pass a nonverbal version of the false-belief test. In their discussion of these and other results, Josef Perner and Ted Ruffman (2005) conclude that full-blown theory of mind seems to involve cultural and linguistic training building on universal and innate cognitive abilities and biases.

The innate nature of theory of mind is further suggested by the fact that it can be partially or fully impaired by certain forms of neurological damage or congenital impairment.[60] Some of the earliest work on theory of mind, pioneered by Simon Baron-Cohen, was inspired by the particular cognitive deficits exhibited by autistics. Baron-Cohen and colleagues found that autistic children and adults

---

[58] The use of false belief as a litmus test for theory of mind was first suggested by Daniel Dennett (1978).

[59] There is a great deal of debate about *why* children's performance on false-belief tasks changes, with some attributing it to a theoretical-conceptual shift and others to a simple improvement in competence arising from experience; see Wellman et al. 2001 and Yazdi et al. 2006 for differing views on this topic.

[60] For a review article on the neuroanatomical basis of theory of mind, see Gallagher & Frith 2003.

fail to exhibit most or all of the abilities associated with theory of mind, and that this "mindblindness" appears to explain quite well their particular profile of social and cognitive deficits.[61] Lacking the ability to easily and spontaneously attribute mental states and beliefs to others, autistics have a great deal of difficulty functioning in the social world, and generally find the company of other people to be frightening and disturbing. This is understandable: people move through space in a manner that is not easily comprehensible or predictable from the standpoint of folk physics; partially or fully lacking a theory of mind, autistics must be deeply troubled, even terrified, by the erratic and mysterious behavior of people-things. Oliver Sacks (1995: 244–296) paints a moving portrait of what it might be like to live as an autistic "anthropologist on Mars" – that is, to live in a world of agents without a fully functioning theory of mind. His description of the predicament of the subject of his essay, a high-functioning autistic named Temple Grandin, gives some sense of how theory of mind automatically and pervasively colors nonautistic humans' perception of the world:

Temple had longed for friends at school . . . but there was something about the way she talked, the way she acted, that seemed to alienate others, so that, while they admired her intelligence, they never accepted her as part of their community . . . Something was going on between the other kids, something swift, subtle, constantly changing – an exchange of meanings, a negotiation, a swiftness of understanding so remarkable that sometimes she wondered if they were all telepathic. She is now aware of the existence of these social signals. She can infer them, she says, but she herself cannot *perceive* them, cannot participate in this magical communication directly, or conceive the many-leveled kaleidoscopic states of mind behind it. (272; emphasis added)

Her high intelligence allows Grandin to indirectly infer, by dint of immense intellectual effort, the existence of mental states that are immediately and effortlessly apparent to nonautistics, but the amount of effort involved and the poor results achieved give some sense of what a rich world of intention is given to nonautistics "for free" by the automatic functioning of their theory of mind.

Paul Bloom relates an interaction he had as a teenager, when working as a counselor in a camp for autistic children, that also provides a revealing glimpse of how a social world without theory of mind might function:

One afternoon, a severely impaired seven-year-old boy walked up to me and placed his hands on my shoulders. I was surprised, and touched, by what appeared to be a spontaneous act of affection. But then he tightened his grip, jumped up, pressed his feet on my legs, and started to climb. It turned out that I was standing next to a high shelf, and he was using me as a ladder so that he could get to an attractive toy. (2004: 37–38)

---

[61] See Baron-Cohen 1995 for a review.

Lacking a developed theory of mind, this child simply subsumed the person standing in front of him under his folk physics module. The fact that this is not the
most efficient way to move through a world containing agents – as Bloom notes,
"it would have been simpler if he had just asked me to get him the toy" – gives us a
sense of why theory of mind would have evolved in the first place. The adoption of
the "intentional stance" appears to be a crucial tool for dealing with other complex
organisms and negotiating social situations, in the same way that the projection of
billiard-ball causality onto the world helps us with physical objects. Daniel Dennett
argues that, for organisms with limited processing ability and time, the set of short-
cut assumptions provided by theory of mind provides huge computational leverage.
"Predicting that someone will duck if you throw a brick at him is easy from the
intentional or folk psychological stance; it is and will always be intractable if you
have to trace the photons from brick to eyeball, the neurotransmitters from optic
nerve to motor nerve, and so forth" (1995: 237).[62] Humans are social animals,
and one of the more plausible explanations for the immense size of our brains
is that it is an adaptation to the complexities and challenges of social living and
competition.[63] It is therefore not unlikely that significant portions of our cerebral
cortices are devoted to theory of mind–related functions: reading emotions, detecting social deception, evaluating loyalties, remembering past social interactions and
predicting future ones, and keeping track of the Joneses.

   A nice window into the functioning of our theory of mind in contemporary
social situations is provided by the amusing TV show *Malcolm in the Middle*. The
show follows the adventures of the middle of three sons in a household of all
boys, negotiating his way through a social landscape including a trouble-making
oldest brother (Francis) exiled to military school but still manipulating events long
distance, a brutish but not terribly bright older brother (Reese), various peers,
and – hovering over all – the ever-present threat of wrathful punishment by an
all-powerful mother, whose omniscience and taste for vengence makes the God
of the Old Testament look like a slacker. In one episode,[64] the boys discover that
a long punishment they recently endured was the result of having been ratted
out by Francis and come into possession of a letter that can be used as revenge if
revealed to the mother. Agents are dispatched remotely by Francis to acquire the
letter, which it turns out Malcolm has hidden because he had predicted Francis's

---

[62] Cf. Nicholas Humphrey's observation that behavioralism failed as a research project because trying
    to predict an organism's behavior from the outside – that is, in nonmental terms – is a "mammoth
    and almost hopeless task" (1986: 67).
[63] See Humphrey 1986, Byrne & Whiten 1988, Dunbar 1992 and 1993, Aiello & Dunbar 1993, and
    Aiello & Wheeler 1995. Also see Dunbar 1996 and 2004 for the argument that a primary evolutionary
    function of human language has been the communication of gossip, which serves as a kind of long-
    distance, wide-spectrum "grooming," allowing humans to form larger and more complex coalitions
    than other primate groups.
[64] Season 1, Episode 15, "Smunday."

intentions. As they are being interrogated, Malcolm whispers the location of the letter to Reese; Francis, directing his interrogation team by phone and intimately aware of the psychological strengths and weaknesses of each of his brothers, tells the lead interrogator to stare into Reese's eyes. As Francis anticipates, Reese cracks: he flinches, and his eyes momentarily alight on the letter's hiding place. The letter is then triumphantly whisked off by Francis's agents (who head off for a latte), and Reese is crestfallen:

REESE: I'm really sorry you guys.
MALCOLM: For what? You were *perfect!* You did exactly what I thought you would do.
REESE: What are you talking about?
MALCOLM: *They* have a fake letter. I knew Francis wouldn't leave us alone without getting something, and I knew *you*'d give it away. I knew *exactly* what everyone would do.

Every minute plot turn in this scenario depends crucially on theory of mind, including our astounding ability to predict the actions of others based on our knowledge of their "characters," as well as our ability to mind read – that is, to accurately discern the emotions and thoughts of our conspecifics from facial expressions, tics, and eye movements. Our mind-reading ability in turn has created pressure for the development of countermeasures, such as the ability to assume false expressions, and then, in turn, the ability to see through false expressions. This sort of cognitive arms race is one of the best explanations for our incredibly powerful intentionality detection and processing abilities. Though the environment of Malcolm's household appears brutally – though amusingly – Darwinian to many modern Westerners, it is in fact probably a candle-lit, New Age support group circle compared to the situations we had to deal with in our actual evolutionary history. None of the brothers, for instance, was ever forced to kill for food or access to a mate – although I may have simply missed that episode. The fact that even the extraordinarily dense Reese is a social genius compared to, say, an Old World monkey, gives some sense of the evolutionary pressure that has produced our massive, socially tuned brains.

Given the apparent adaptive advantages to theory of mind, one might expect at least some aspects of it to have evolved in other species, especially ones living in large social groups. There is, however, a great deal of debate about whether theory of mind is shared by nonhumans. Studies of corvid cognition suggest that they may possess some elements of theory of mind. A blue jay that has hidden food while being observed by another jay will later go back and move it when the potential competitor is no longer looking; this well-attested phenomenon of selective recaching of food would seem to require the ability to represent the epistemic states of conspecifics.[65] The case for nonhuman theory of mind is strongest, however,

[65] See Hare et al. 2000 and 2001, Emery & Clayton 2001, Dally et al. 2006, and the survey by Pennisi 2006.

with regard to our closest relative, the chimpanzee.[66] It is clear that chimpanzees are able to employ gaze clues to locate food, engage in acts of social deception, and behave in manners that are sensitive to cues of intentional – rather than accidental – behavior. Some researchers also make the additional argument of biological parsimony: chimps are quite closely related to human beings, so if they engage in behaviors that, for humans, require representation of mental states, the most reasonable explanation is that chimps possess some form of theory of mind. Others, most prominently Daniel Povinelli, argue that there is a significant evolutionary gap between chimps and humans, and that our tendency to interpret chimpanzee behavior in mentalistic terms says more about our own minds – and our ineradicable tendency to promiscuously project mental states onto the world – than the minds of chimps.[67] The weight of evidence in recent years seems to favor the position that chimpanzees must possess at least a limited form of theory of mind. In a recent study by Brian Hare and his colleagues that attempted to create an ecologically realistic scenario, a human competitor pulled food out of reach of a hungry chimp. The researchers found that, given the option, chimps would sneak up behind a barrier in order to acquire the food without the human's knowledge. Hare et al. conclude that this demonstrates that chimpanzees can both judge the epistemic state of a human and take measures to exploit it (2006).[68] In any case, it would seem that at least the precursors of human theory of mind are present in our primate cousins.

Folk Mathematics: The "Number Sense"

Despite the difficulty humans the world over may have with trigonometry, it appears that basic arithmetical skills and even geometrical knowledge are part of our built-in cognitive equipment. The classic study of "baby arithmetic" was performed by Karen Wynn (1992), who used gaze measurements to show that infants with a mean age of five months appear to be able to perform simple arithmetic operations – addition and subtraction – on small numbers. More recent studies that have attempted to control for other possibilities – for example, that babies were

---

[66] One early summary of the evidence for theory of mind in primates can be found in Cheney & Seyfarth 1990: 253–254, who conclude that monkeys appear to lack it, whereas chimpanzees appear to possess a limited form of it – although chimps (like very young human children) seem unable to attribute false beliefs. See de Waal 1983/1998 for a study of "chimpanzee politics" that suggests that chimps possess many, if not all, of the elements of human theory of mind.

[67] A helpful, short presentation of the arguments for and against chimp theory of mind can be found in Tomasello et al. 2003 and Povinelli & Vonk 2003; also see Povinelli 2000 for a body of experimental evidence that purports to show that chimps function in a very different thought-world than humans.

[68] In a recent survey by Elizabeth Pennisi (2006), Povinelli continues to hold that their failure to pass false-belief test shows chimps do not have anything like human's full-blown theory of mind, while Hare points out that theory of mind is not necessarily an all-or-nothing module, and chimps may possess some elements of it while lacking others.

relying on general complexity or familiarity – show that infants seem to recognize basic arithmetical operations across sensory modalities, that this ability is not tied to pattern recognition or object tracking, and that it appears to involve an abstract representation of at least small numbers.[69] Although infants appear to possess discrete conceptions only of small numbers (1, 2, or 3) (Feigenson & Carey 2003, 2005), they are also apparently able to discriminate large numbers if the comparison sets differ by a large ratio – e.g., 8 versus 16 as opposed to 8 versus 12 (Xu & Spelke 2000, Lipton & Spelke 2003). Both adults and young children are capable of performing simple arithmetical calculations on nonsymbolic quantities, suggesting the continued existence of abstract and nonlinguistic mathematical knowledge even after the acquisition of language and culture (Barth et al. 2006).[70] Damage to the angular gyrus in the left hemisphere can also result in a condition known as "acalculia" (Gerstmann 1940, Grewel 1952, Dehaene 1997), which renders a person incapable of performing even simple addition and subtraction. This sort of selective knocking out of specific abilities is a primary hallmark of modularity. As Marc Hauser (2005) concludes, the evidence suggests that human adults and infants possess at least two core intuitive mathematics systems – one working precisely on small numbers of discrete objects and the other working approximately on relative ratios of large numbers – and that these systems have a long evolutionary history, being present in chimpanzees, rats, and pigeons.[71]

Going beyond basic numerosity and arithmetic, Stanislas Dehaene et al. (2006) demonstrated that Euclidian geometry presents itself as true in "self-evident" fashion to children and adults belonging to an Amazonian indigenous group with no formal education, and that this group appears to share with American children and adults a common pattern of "core geometrical knowledge." Daheane and his coauthors note the interesting parallel between this demonstration of shared intuitive knowledge and the dialogue in Plato's *Meno* where Socrates proves that even a slave boy possesses an innate knowledge of geometry. Plato was clearly onto something here, although it is more likely that the origin of our shared human knowledge lies in evolved cognitive schemas rather than the metaphysical world of Forms.[72]

[69]   See Kobayashi et al. 2004 and McCrink & Wynn 2004.

[70]   Cf. the studies mentioned earlier by Gordon (2004) and Pica et al. (2004) of Amazonians speaking an innumerate language that indicate that humans share an imprecise but nonetheless useful nonverbal representation of number. Also see Nieder et al. 2006 for evidence in monkeys that numerosity is initially processed separately depending on the sensory modality with which it is acquired but is then transformed upstream into an abstract format.

[71]   Hauser 2005 provides a short, helpful review of the evidence of a number sense in nonhuman animals. Also see the earlier review by Cheney & Seyfarth (1990: 86–96), and the recent studies by Flombaum et al. 2005 and Orlov et al. 2006 that demonstrate language-independent numerosity in monkeys. For a readable book-length treatment of the "number sense," see Dehaene 1997, and for some relevant neuroimaging evidence, see Dehaene et al. 1999.

[72]   See Lakoff & Núñez 2000 for an account of the sensory-motor roots of even quite abstract mathematical concepts, and Joseph 1991 for a historical survey of the cultural elaborations and refinements of human folk mathematics.

HUMAN METACULTURE: A SUITE OF INNATE MODULES
COMBINED WITH "GOOD TRICKS"

Earlier I offered merely a brief glimpse of a few of the human innate cognitive modules that have been proposed. Of further examples, one of the most obvious is the earliest and best known of proposed modules, Chomskyan "Universal Grammar" (Chomsky 1965), which explains how children can acquire grammatical competency despite the "poverty of stimulus" to which they are exposed, why there are observed deep parallels in the structure of superficially diverse human languages, and why grammatical forms emerge spontaneously in newly created languages.[73] Other proposed modules or innate cognitive mechanisms – all backed by an impressive body of accumulated evidence – range from social cheating detectors[74] to genetically transmitted character traits such as introversion and extroversion,[75] from universal and domain-specific taste preferences (both literal and metaphorical)[76] to navigational strategies.[77] Space restrictions make it impossible to explore these topics in any sort of detail; the reader is referred elsewhere for thorough surveys of these and other proposed innate human cognitive universals.[78]

It is, of course, important to recognize that aspects of some of these innatist claims – and, in many cases, even the claims themselves – are still quite controversial.[79] For instance, the existence of at least a small number of basic emotions – subserved by specific neurological structures, characterized by a particular physiological profile, and shared in some respects by all higher animals – seems incontrovertible.[80] There is still lively debate, however, concerning the relationship

---

[73] See Pinker & Bloom 1992 and Pinker 1994 for readable defenses of an innatist view of language acquisition, somewhat different from Chomsky's initial position, and Senghas et al. 2004, Coppola & Newport 2005, and Sandler et al. 2005 for the spontaneous emergence of grammar in newly created sign languages. Also see Cheney & Seyfarth 1990 for a general discussion of nonhuman animal language, as well as Gentner et al. 2006 and Marcus 2006 on the possible existence of recursive syntactic patterns in songbird communication.

[74] Cosmides 1989 and Cosmides & Tooby 1992, 2000, 2005.

[75] Loehlin & Nichols 1976 and Bouchard 1994 and 1998; also see Harris 1998 for a very readable discussion of the relative effects of genes, peers, and parents on child development, and Figueredo et al. 2005 for a review of the state of the field in evolutionary approaches to personality psychology.

[76] See the references in section 1 of the Appendix.

[77] For a recent review of the literature, see Silverman & Choi 2005.

[78] For arguments for the importance of domain-specific versus domain-general learning processes in humans and other animals, and reviews of the empirical evidence, refer to Atran 1990: 51–52 and Pinker 2002, and the essays in Tooby & Cosmides 1992, Hirshfeld & Gelman 1994a, Carruthers & Chamberlain 2000, and Buss 2005. Premack & Premack 2003 provide a readable review of basic human conceptual modules along with a comparison to nonhuman animal cognition, and other helpful introductions to and discussions of the innate, modular view of the mind include Spelke 1994, Boyer & Barrett 2005, and Carruthers 2005. Carruthers et al. (2005, 2006) are in the process of publishing a three-volume collection of essays on the topic.

[79] See Sperber et al. 1995 for a helpful review of some relevant debates.

[80] The classic work on the universality of the six basic human emotions – anger, fear, happiness, sadness, disgust, and surprise – was done by Paul Ekman (1972/1982, 1980, 1999), and his position

between the physiological correlates of emotion and subjective affect, as well as on the influence of cultural factors in the development of the more complex emotions that tend to be the focus of humanistic inquiry.[81] We should also note that no one who has abandoned the objectivist stance can view any empirical finding as a "finding" in an all-determining, eternal sense: the "results" coming out of the cognitive sciences are as provisional as those of any science, and the state of the field is in constant motion. As I will discuss in Chapter 5, however, there is good reason for the fact that creatures like us are inordinately swayed by empirical evidence, because such susceptibility has allowed us to move through and interact with the world quite successfully. It is extremely unlikely – on both theoretical and empirical grounds – that at least the general outlines of the evolutionary Kantian position outlined earlier are entirely incorrect.

It is the existence and interaction of these shared modules that gives rise to the human "commonsense" view of the world, which remains quite robustly universal despite the vagaries of cultural variation. As Scott Atran notes, despite relatively diverse culture-level structures of meaning,

What is not relative . . . is humankind's evolutionary disposition to distinguish – as Hamlet suggests any normal human would – say, a hawk from a handsaw, an artifact from a living kind. Inter alia, humankind is universally disposed to believe, or know, to be true that the world of everyday experience is composed of artifacts that exist by reason of the functions humans give them, and of natural biological kinds that exist in virtue of their physically given causal natures. These are among the universally perceived facts. (1990: 216)

Recognizing and understanding the constraints imposed on culture by our embodied common sense is a crucial element in developing an empirically responsible approach to the humanities, because the learning "frame problem" discussed earlier is an issue not only in the acquisition of one's own culture but also in understanding the culture of others. As Tooby and Cosmides note regarding the kinds of extreme cultural-relativist positions advanced in anthropological circles,

The best refutation of cultural relativity is the activity of anthropologists themselves, who could not understand or live within other human groups unless the inhabitants of those groups shared the assumptions that were, in fact, very similar to that of the ethnographer. Like fish unaware of the existence of water, interpretavists swim from

___

has been borne out by subsequent work in cross-cultural psychology and cognitive neuroscience; see Ekman 2003 and his afterword in Darwin & Ekman 1998. Modern biological speculation about emotional similarities across species goes back as far as Darwin's *The Expression of Emotions in Man and Animals* (1872); for a recent survey article concerning the evaluation and characterization of emotional processes in animals, see Paul et al. 2005.

[81] There is a massive literature on this subject; the reader is particularly referred to A. Rorty 1980b, Ortony et al. 1990, Tooby & Cosmides 1990, Ekman & Davidson 1994, LeDoux 1996, Lewis & Haviland-Jones 2000, Nussbaum 2001, and Solomon 2003 and 2004, and to de Gelder 2006 for a recent review article.

culture to culture interpreting through a universal human metaculture. Metaculture informs their every thought, but they have not yet noticed its existence. (1992: 92)[82]

Culture, they argue, "is not causeless and disembodied. It is generated in rich and intricate ways by information-processing mechanisms situated in human minds. These mechanisms are, in turn, the elaborately sculpted product of the evolutionary process" (3). Taking seriously the existence of the modules outlined above would allow humanists to become more consciously aware of the massive iceberg of human commonalities that underlies their ability to even begin to understand any human culture, including their own. It would also hopefully refocus humanistic attention away from the endless task of butterfly collecting – documenting difference simply for the sake of documenting difference – and toward more empirically and intellectually interesting avenues of inquiry.[83]

This is not to say that all, or even most, of the proposed universal human "metaculture" is innate in any strong sense, as some evolutionary psychologists seem to imply.[84] As Daniel Dennett has noted, human universals commonly arise because they are "Good Tricks": forced solutions to reoccurring situations. "So far as I know," Dennett observes, "in every culture known to anthropologists, the hunters throw their spears pointy-end-first, but this obviously does not establish that there is a pointy-end-first gene that approaches fixation in our species" (1995: 486).[85] The universality of certain types of stories is also probably of this "Good Trick" sort. The writer Kurt Vonnegut, Jr., defending the ideal of coherent narrative against the postmodern deconstruction of the novel, observes that the narratives that seem to have actually appealed to ordinary people from different cultures and different historical periods follow a certain fairly basic set of plots (e.g., "someone gets into trouble, and then gets out again"; "lover loses beloved and then manages to win him or her back again"), and concludes that "no modern story scheme, even plotlessness, will give a reader genuine satisfaction unless one of those old-fashioned plots is smuggled in somewhere" (1982: 110). No one would defend the idea that there is a "hero-slays-dragon-and-wins-hand-of-beautiful-maiden" gene in the human gene pool. However, given that there is a nontrivial set of innate human desires

---

[82] For instance, see Barkow 1989: 162–164 and Brown 1991: 3–5 for an account of the human metacultural universals underlying Geertz's famous study of Balinese cockfighting (Geertz 1973: 412–453), as well as Tooby and Cosmides's argument that even cross-species universals are involved – Geertz and the Balinese cocks themselves share a massive iceberg of assumptions concerning space, motion, vision, pain, etc. (1992: 108).

[83] As Tooby and Cosmides note, "Mainstream sociocultural anthropology has arrived at a situation resembling some nightmarish short story Borges might have written, where scientists are condemned by their unexamined assumptions to study the nature of mirrors only by cataloguing and investigating everything that mirrors can reflect. It is an endless process that never makes progress" (1992: 42).

[84] This is, for instance, the implication of E. O. Wilson's famous (or infamous) metaphor of the human brain as "an exposed negative waiting to be dipped into developer fluid" (1975/2000: 156).

[85] See Tooby and Cosmides's claim that many human universals are not a priori, but are the result of an evolved "fit" between the human mind and regularities in the world (1992: 69).

and capacities, and the fact that the world in which humans operate has had a fairly stable structure for at least the past several millennia, it is not surprising that tales of evil stepmothers or brave underdog heroes will arise universally and have universal appeal.

Donald Brown suggests that, on the analogy of Chomskyan "Universal Grammar" (UG), anthropologists recognize the existence of a set of deeper "Universal People" (UP) structures underlying the surface variations of diverse human cultures, including (to give just a highly truncated list) such features as age terms, baby talk, beliefs about death, body adornment, child care, containers, fire, gift giving, gossip, hospitality, jokes, medicine, music, numerals, planning for the future, play, marriage, practice to improve skills, prestige inequalities, pronouns, rituals, sanctions, sexuality as focus of interest, taste for sweets, tools, trade, units of time, verbs, weaning, and weapons.[86] Some of these (numerals, verbs) likely arise directly from the innate cognitive modules described earlier, but the majority would appear to be of the "Good Trick" variety. People everywhere seem to have come up with broadly similar sets of solutions to the problems of survival presented by their environment, and it is amazing to consider what level of detailed similarity can be generated by a seemingly quite sparse set of physical similarities interacting with relatively fixed environments.

To give just one example, I recall once reading a passage in the *Xunzi*, a third-century B.C.E. Chinese Confucian text that describes someone who has lost a sewing needle and has been looking for it all day: "when they find it, it is not because their eyesight has gotten any more sharp, it is simply because they bent down to look more carefully for it." The passage concludes, "The mind thinking about something is just like this" (Knoblock 1994: 222), and the point of it (invoking as it does the primary metaphor, KNOWING AS SEEING) is that the Confucian Way is understood through hard work and persistence, not because of any kind of natural talent. What actually struck me at the time, however, was my immediate visceral reaction to the source of the metaphor – I had, in fact, just spent some time that morning trying to recover a dropped needle to repair a rip in my shirt, and had been unsuccessful until I finally got down on my hands and knees and did a systematic, sector-by-sector search of the likely region of my apartment. At first it seemed quite strange to me that some third-century B.C.E. Chinese person had shared such a specific and apparently idiosyncratic experience with me, but on further consideration it seemed much less surprising. Human beings lack fur and thus need to wear artificial outer garments when venturing out of their ancestral environment into temperate climates. In order to be usable, these garments have to have certain properties (flexible, not too heavy, etc.), and the limits imposed by available materials found in nature have caused human beings everywhere to independently hit upon an identical response to these demands: pieces of fabric made out of vegetable fibers

---

[86] See Brown 1991 and 2000 for a full list and discussion.

or animal skins, woven together with some sort of strong, thin, thread by means of a needle.[87] Fabrics demand that needles be small so that they do not leave overly large holes in the material, and the limits of human eyesight and dexterity are such that people are likely to drop needles and then have trouble finding them again. Here we see a very complex, highly structured cultural phenomenon being generated by a relatively thin set of physical constraints. It is similarly revealing that a modern American has no problem solving the riddle posed in another chapter of the *Xunzi*[88] that describes, in elusive verse, the detailed characteristics of a sewing needle. The structures of daily life – which we rarely notice, because we assume them unconsciously whenever we read a text from another period or culture – are seen to be remarkably constant when we actually focus our attention on them.

How such "Good Tricks" can even extend across species is illustrated by the manner, documented by Crickette Sanz et al. 2004, in which wild Congolese chimpanzees prepare their termite "fishing probes" for use. They select a suitably thin and flexible stick, fray one end with their teeth to form a brushlike tip, and then wet this tip with saliva in order to insert it into the narrow termite hole. There is no need to postulate a "wet-frayed-end-with-saliva-to-fit-narrow-opening" gene shared by the chimp-human lineage in order to recognize the parallel with human beings trying to thread a needle, and it is equally obvious that we are not likely to see such behavior in dolphins.[89] We can thus conclude that many human cultural universals, from the invention of sewing needles of very specific physical dimensions to metaphors for time and morality, are probably of this "Good Trick" variety: the inevitable result of regularities in human nature interacting with regularities in the human environment.[90]

FINALLY: THE PRAGMATIC RESPONSE TO EXTREME SKEPTICISM, OR WHAT'S *REALLY* WRONG WITH POSTMODERNISM

Both the theoretical and the empirical problems with the postmodernist position just reviewed require a minimal commitment to certain epistemological norms to

---

[87] Bone needles with eyes for threading appear in the archeological record as early as 26,000 years ago; see Gore 2000: 99.

[88] "Fu on the Needle"; Knoblock 1994: 200–202.

[89] Emery & Clayton 2004 note that the remarkably convergent intelligent behaviors between corvids and primates are not based on convergent brains – the ape neocortex and the cognitively analogous nidopallium region in corvids are structurally very different and seem to represent evolutionarily distinct solutions of the problem of complex intelligence.

[90] This is why more sophisticated evolutionary psychologists such as Tooby and Cosmides argue that genotype-environment interactions render the traditionally sharp distinction between "nature" and "nurture" ultimately incoherent: "There is nothing in the real world that actually corresponds to such concepts as 'genetic determinism' or 'environmental determination' . . . every feature of the phenotype is fully and equally codetermined by the interaction of the organism's genes (embedded in its initial package of zygotic cellular machinery) and its ontogenetic environments – meaning everything else that impinges upon it" (1992: 83).

possess their bite. A position that rejects *all* such norms is ultimately unassailable, and there is therefore no satisfying answer to the extreme skeptic who rejects the validity of any form of evidence or logic. Such a position is also, however, ultimately completely empty, and this gets to the heart of what is wrong with any strong form of the postmodernist position. I will therefore conclude my critique of postmodernism with this most general of pragmatic considerations.

Charles Sanders Peirce once advised, "Let us not pretend to doubt in philosophy what we do not doubt in our hearts" (1868/1992: 29), and David Hume similarly argued for the impossibility, at an everyday human level, of genuinely living with extreme skepticism:

Most fortunately it happens, that since reason is incapable of dispelling these clouds [of philosophical skepticism], nature herself suffices to that purpose, and cures me of this philosophical melancholy and delirium, either by relaxing this bent of mind, or by some avocation, and lively impression of my senses, which obliterate all these chimeras. I dine, I play a game of back-gammon, I converse, and am merry with my friends; and when after three or four hours' amusement, I wou'd return to these speculations, they appear so cold, and strain'd, and ridiculous, that I cannot find in my heart to enter into them any farther. (1739/1978: 269).

Whether or not it is psychologically possible for a human being to genuinely embrace an attitude of extreme skepticism, the self-refuting nature of skepticism makes it difficult to see, at the very least, how it could function as a viable intellectual position within the Academy. If it is impossible to make substantial truth-claims, and if all that we as humanists (or as any sort of intellectual or scholar) are doing is merely rearranging signifiers in an essentially arbitrary manner, it is hard to see why people should be giving us money to do it. I have always felt that, if it is "true" that there is no truth, then perhaps the Academy should not be in the business of funding, for instance, Derrida's daring willingness to run the risk of "not meaning anything."[91] Maybe Derrida should have gotten a real job. If endless slippage is all that can be expected from language, but we academics nonetheless expect to be fed and housed, perhaps we should turn from playing with signifiers to something more undeniably useful like farming or plumbing. Of course, most people – even academics – feel that what they are doing is, at some level, useful; this feeling is probably a psychological prerequisite to dragging oneself out of bed in the morning. The fact, then, that postmodern theorists continue to write books and defend them shows that, at some level, they cannot be taking their own epistemology seriously. *Why* they seem incapable of seriously embracing the void gets to the heart of the pragmatic critique of postmodernism.

---

[91] "Je me risque à ne rien-vouloir-dire"; from a 1967 interview (Derrida 1981: 14), quoted in Megill 1985: 259 and alternately translatable, as Megill notes, as "I am taking the risk of not wishing to say anything," or "I am taking the risk of not meaning anything."

Clifford Geertz does a wonderful job of describing the moral imperative of his brand of anthropological work, designed to force us to question our own cultural assumptions, to "keep the world off balance; pulling out rugs, upsetting tea tables, setting off firecrackers. It has been the office of others to reassure; ours to unsettle" (1984/2000: 64). He also argues that relativism is a nonissue – a bogeyman cooked up by the feverish imagination of frightened foundationalists – because it does not lead to the nihilism and collapse of society predicted by the alarmist critics of postmodernism:

Brute fact, natural law, necessary truth, transcendent beauty, immanent authority, unique revelation, even the in-here self facing the out-there world have all come under such heavy attack as to seem by now lost simplicities of a less strenuous past. But science, law, philosophy, art, political theory, religion, and the stubborn insistences of common sense have contrived nonetheless to continue. It has not proved necessary to revive the simplicities. (64)

Geertz is correct that cultural relativism has not in fact led to nihilist despair or the abandonment of the Academy, but this is really because the "stubborn insistences of common sense" have caused postmodern theorists to selectively ignore their own epistemologies when going about their work. The breeze that keeps Geertz's "merchants of astonishment" (64) aloft is intellectual bad faith, not steely-eyed courage in the face of complete uncertainty.

We see this kind of bad faith quite clearly in the contrast between Foucault qua historian and Foucault qua postmodern theorist. Works like *History of Sexuality* or *Discipline and Punish* are pieces of historical analysis with an important political axe to grind. If Foucault was really taking his own social constructivist epistemology seriously, there is no reason why he could not have simply fabricated his historical sources. But he did not, and despite his later breeziness concerning the subject he clearly took his work qua historian seriously. As J. G. Merquoir notes,

To be sure, over and again Foucault kept denying that he was writing normal history. The last time (I think) was in the introduction to his *L'Usage des plaisirs*, where he once more warned that his studies were "of history," not of "a historian." Historian or not, he constantly worked on the assumption that he was being faithful to each age's outlook on each relevant subject (insanity, knowledge, punishment, sex) and that his documents... could prove him right. The very fact that he used words like "documents"... shows that for all his "Nietzschean" affectation of contempt for objective truth, he liked to have it speak for him as much as any conventional historian. In other words, whatever kind of historiography he was up to – the historians' one, or any other – Foucault was the first to claim that the evidence was on his side. (1985: 144)[92]

---

[92] Whether or not the evidence actually *was* on his side is another issue altogether; Merquior also provides helpful assessments and critical reviews of the historical accuracy of Foucault's genealogies.

This is important to observe because the very power of Foucault's liberatory critique comes from the truth-claims he makes on the basis of his radical histories: our current repressive attitude toward homosexuality, for instance, which seems to us to simply reflect the world-as-it-is, is *in fact* the contingent product of a long history from the Greeks to the Christian "confessional" turn, culminating in the nineteenth-century movement from the sodomite as a minor and temporary aberration to the homosexual as a perverse species (Foucault 1978: 42–43). It is not problematic for us to follow Foucault in thinking that the mainstream contemporary Western attitude about homosexuality is "socially constructed" in all of the senses associated by Ian Hacking with this term: a given "X" is "socially constructed" if:

(1) X need not have existed, or need not be at all as it is. X, or X as it is at present, is not determined by the nature of things; it is not inevitable . . .
[frequently added corollaries:]
(2) X is quite bad as it is.
(3) We would be much better off if X were done away with, or at least radically transformed. (1999: 6)

Central to any coherent adherence to this view is that the X in question is a particular social *attitude* toward homosexuality or particular sexual acts. If X is sexuality itself, as Foucault often seems to declare,[93] the entire liberatory project is robbed of meaning. That Foucault's project was *not* meaningless – to him or to others inspired by it – is because of certain background assumptions about human sexuality, human desires, and the impact of social norms on individual self-conception and behavior.

We can make a similar point with regard to the work of the philosopher of ethics Annette Baier. Although she would probably be horrified to be associated with postmodernism, Baier's groundbreaking critique of the Enlightenment conception of the moral self as an overly narrow reflection of a white, land-owning male's perspective is very much in the postmodern spirit, and the trenchant humor with which she exposes blind spots in traditional conceptions of morality recalls Nietzsche at his best. For instance, concerning the "male fixation on contract," she observes:

The great moral theorists in our tradition not only are all men, they are mostly men who had minimal adult dealings with (and so were then minimally influenced by) women. With a few significant exceptions . . . they are a collection of clerics, misogynists, and puritan bachelors. It should not surprise us, then, that particularly in the modern period they managed to relegate to the mental background the web of trust

---

93   E.g., "sexuality" is "the name that can be given to a historical construct: not a furtive reality that is difficult to grasp, but a great surface network in which the stimulation of bodies, the intensification of pleasures, the incitement to discourse, the formation of special knowledges, the strengthening of controls and resistances, are linked to one another, in accordance with a few major strategies of knowledge and power" (Foucault 1978: 105–106). See also the later discussion of "sex" (154–155).

tying most moral agents to one another and to focus their philosophical attention so single-mindedly on cool, distanced relations between more or less free and equal adult strangers, say, the members of an all-male club, with membership rules and rules for dealing with rule breakers and where the form of cooperation was restricted to ensuring that each member could read his *Times* in peace and have no one step on his gouty toes. (1994: 114)

Baier's primary targets are contractarian and utilitarian models of ethics, dominant in Enlightenment moral discourse and the basis of modern Western liberal economic and legal institutions. Such models portray human beings as autonomous, equal, self-sufficient agents, interacting voluntarily and only at their own discretion in order to maximize their own self-interests. In light of such a model, all that we need from an ethical theory or form of government is the assurance of *negative* freedom: freedom from interference as we go about our self-determined pursuit of happiness. Baier's goal is to point out the aspects of human existence that such a model overlooks: the fact, for instance, that our most important relationships in life – parent-child, individual-community, employer-employee, even friends and lovers – are *not* freely chosen in accordance with the dictates of rational interest. As human beings we find ourselves always already imbedded in, or inevitably drawn into, a whole complex network of relationships characterized by varying power dynamics and unique sets of demands. In addition, all of this plays itself out against a background of unarticulated and mostly unconscious ties of trust, empathy, and affection. These dimensions of human existence are, Baier argues, obvious to women, children, caretakers, the poor, the oppressed, and the discriminated against, but are systematically overlooked in the writings of the elite white males who have dominated Western moral philosophy.

This sort of argument represents the core insight that made postmodern analyses so appealing when they first emerged in the 1960s and 1970s. Claims that had always been portrayed as simply, obviously true were shown to be anything but. Claims that had always been presented as universal were unmasked as self-interested expressions of a dominant social elite. Baier, however, is able to make these points without having to resort to a relativistic epistemology. Indeed, the whole basis of her critique is that the peculiar social identities of the dominant Enlightenment moral philosophers resulted in their developing a skewed vision of human relationships, blinding them to important universal aspects of the human condition, and therefore to important aspects of true morality. This, of course, presumes that there *are* important, enduring regularities in the human condition for us to perceive, and that even elite white males *can* perceive them when their attentions are focused in the right direction.

We can be sympathetic to the political and intellectual goals of postmodernism – which, incidentally, are no more than the classical Enlightenment ones decked out in hipper garb – while still thinking that postmodern theorists are not doing themselves any favors by tightly yoking otherwise quite laudable goals to frankly absurd theories of language and cognition, or by demonizing anyone who disagrees with them. This continued uneasy marriage of important liberal values to a defunct theory of language and cognition is a perfect recipe for political and social irrelevance. And this is, in fact, what we have seen over the course of the past few decades: humanistic scholars increasingly isolating themselves from other areas of the Academy and from normal canons of intelligibility, with the result that they are reduced to merely talking to one another. As Steven Pinker observes,

Acknowledging human nature does not mean overturning our personal worldviews . . . It means only taking intellectual life out of its parallel universe and reuniting it with science and, when it is borne out by science, with commonsense. The alternative is to make intellectual life increasingly irrelevant to human affairs, to turn intellectuals into hypocrites, and to turn everyone else into anti-intellectuals. (2002: 422)

Geertz is right that it is too late to revive the old objectivist "simplicities," if such a thing were even desirable. It is, however, the insistent voice of common sense – not some weak craving for certainty – that urges us to find some other story about how the analysis of culture hooks up to a real, shared world.

I would like to suggest that it is an embodied approach to human culture, based on a sense of pragmatic realism, that represents precisely the alternate story that we in the humanities have been looking for, and one that takes seriously the suite of intuitions that make up human common sense. Pragmatism, common sense, and a pragmatic conception of what constitutes "truth" will be the topic of Chapter 5, especially as it relates to scientific truth-claims. Before turning to this topic, however, it is important to say something about how the sorts of human universals I have argued for could coexist with the undeniable fact of human cultural diversity. Cultures obviously *do* differ from one another across geographical space and through historical time, and recognition of this diversity is the primary intuition driving social constructivism or cultural relativism. In Chapter 4, I will try to provide an outline of what an embodied approach to human creativity and cultural diversity might look like, showing how the tools provided by cognitive linguistics can allow us to trace even quite contingent and idiosyncratic cultural artifacts back to a common ground of embodied human experience.

PART II

EMBODYING CULTURE

4

&

Embodying Culture: Grounding Cultural Variation in the Body

*P*ART OF THE CONTINUING APPEAL OF POSTMODERNISM IS THE UNDE-
niable reality of human cultural variation, both across the world and over
the course of history. People value as delicacies such foodstuffs as the durian fruit,
which smells and tastes unmistakably like human vomit, or the Chinese specialty
of – literally translated – "stinky tofu," which is marinated for months in a brined
mixture of rotten vegetables and putrid shrimp. I argued in the previous chapters
that human beings universally value "strength" and have an aversion to "sickness,"
but how are we to reconcile this with the Daoist *Daodejing*, which advocates the
path of weakness, or Kierkegaard's celebration of the spiritual "sickness unto death"
that leads to salvation? The claim that human beings share a set of cognitive and
normative universals needs to be reconciled with the blooming, buzzing cultural
variety that is the single most salient phenomenon to humanists.

This is particularly important because, as I will discuss, there is considerable
evidence from cross-cultural psychology that these various practices, and the environments that these practices create, can result in distinct schemas at fairly early
stages of perception. There is, after all, something to the claim of Thomas Kuhn
that advocates of different conceptual paradigms inhabit different thought-worlds.
It is thus important to balance the exploration of human universals in our previous
chapters with the recognition that human cognitive fluidity, ratcheted up over time
by cultural entrenchment, can shape human perceptions and desires in quite novel
and idiosyncratic ways, from the subtle Japanese aesthetic sentiment of *mono no
aware* (lit. "the sorrow of things") to the sort of "cultivated needs," such as a taste for
fine wines or luxury automobiles, explored in such depth by Pierre Bourdieu.[1] The
push for acceptance of human cognitive universals is rarely presented along with a
convincing story about how the profusion of cultural diversity that humanists see
out there in the world could arise from a shared human nature – or at least from
a nature that has any kind of significant content. Any successful embodied model
of culture needs to be able to provide such an explanation, and this is a topic not
adequately addressed by much of evolutionary psychology literature, for example.

The cognitive science of human creativity is a burgeoning growth field, and
providing even a basic literature review would involve a book-length project in

---

[1] For Bourdieu on cultivated need, which "increases in proportion as it is satisfied," see 1993: 227.

itself.[2] What I would like to do in this chapter is give a brief sketch of some cognitive mechanisms that seem to me likely suspects in any explanation of why human beings build cathedrals and write poetry while chimpanzees do not, and why some human cultures come to celebrate yielding while others valorize only the naked exercise of brute strength. Such a sketch will hopefully give the reader a sense of what alternatives there are to the current dominant theory of human creativity, which is simply that it involves the free and inexplicable movement of the human *Geist*, or the arbitrary and unpredictable transformations of some reified but disembodied "society," *habitus*, or social "discourse." The mechanisms of cross-domain metaphor and metaphoric blending studied by the relatively new field of cognitive linguistics provide us with a model of how human beings can recruit basic sensory-motor patterns and images to use as templates for interacting with and understanding other, often quite abstract domains.[3] Because these cross-domain projections can be combined selectively into novel metaphoric blends, they can very quickly create culturally unique life-worlds – especially when this cognitive blending is combined with the human ability to transform the environment. Nonetheless, the fact that even novel blends are grounded in the body provides, I will argue, a broad and easily traversed bridge to the cultural "other."

COGNITIVE FLUIDITY

As the primatologists Dorothy Cheney and Robert Seyfarth observe, vervet monkeys display quite puzzling gaps in their knowledge of the world, despite their otherwise impressive cognitive skills. For instance, although they are commonly preyed upon by pythons, and even have a specific call to warn conspecifics of the presence of this dangerous predator, they appear to be unable to connect wide, straight tracks in the sand left by pythons – immediately obvious to humans – with the pythons that created them, even though they have ample opportunity to observe pythons leaving such tracks. Remarking on monkeys approaching a recently laid python track, Cheney and Seyfarth note:

In no case did individuals show vigilance or change their behavior when they approached and crossed the track. Indeed, on several occasions we watched in utter mystification as a vervet calmly followed a python track right into a bush, only to leap away in shocked horror when he encountered the snake there. (1990: 286)

---

[2] See especially Koestler 1975, Johnson-Laird 1989, Boden 1990 and 1994, Holyoak & Thagard 1995, and the essays in Sternberg 1988 and 1999. One of the more recent developments in this area is the hire of Antonio and Hannah Damasio at the University of Southern California to direct the new "USC College Brain and Creativity Institute," dedicated to exploring human creativity from an interdisciplinary perspective.

[3] Cognitive linguistics differs from, for instance, formal linguistics, in treating language as the surface manifestation of deeper cognitive processes. See Fesmire 1994, as well as Fauconnier 1997: 1–5, for a brief discussion of how this treatment of language as mere "signals" connected to a deeper, nonlinguistic structure differs from structural or generative linguistic approaches.

Cheney and Seyfarth postulate that this failure to recognize what seems to humans as quite obvious secondary cues of a direct threat to the monkeys' survival is perhaps a consequence of insufficient communication between different, specialized cognitive modules. "Because it evolved to meet social needs," they argue, "the monkeys' system of visual communication is ill-suited to solving certain problems outside the social domain. In their social interactions, the monkeys may never had *needed* to recognize that a visual clue can denote some absent referent" (289). They also observe that chimpanzees seem to be less domain-specific in this regard, with information flowing more freely between different sensory modules. They cite, for instance, the observation of Jane Goodall et al. (1979) that chimpanzees appear to be able to associate rival neighbors' empty nests with the rivals themselves, making aggressive displays at the nests even when the rivals are not physically present (289). That the mind of apes in general may be more interdomain "accessible" than that of monkeys is further suggested by work done with the chimpanzee Sarah, who appears to be able to perform a variety of analogical reasoning tasks.[4]

As unusual as Sarah's abilities are, they still fall a far measure short of what even a five-year-old human child is capable of. As we noted in Chapter 3, there is evidence that chimpanzees possess some degree of theory of mind and are capable of modeling the mental states of others, inventing tools for specific purposes, formulating intermediate-term plans of action, and passing down adaptively relevant information through teaching and emulation. Nonetheless, chimpanzees do not possess language or invent complex tools, they do not spontaneously create visual art or music, and they do not bury their dead with elaborate ritual or engage in other religious activities. What is it that they are lacking?

The first species in the genus *Homo* emerged approximately 2.5 million years ago, but there is no evidence for such distinctively human activities as ritual burial of dead until the emergence of early modern *Homo sapiens* 100,000 years ago, and the first symbolic art does not appear until approximately 30,000 years ago.[5] One of the puzzling features of hominid evolution is that the lifestyle of early modern humans was barely distinguishable from that of other hominid species, such as the Neanderthals, when *Homo sapiens* first emerged ca. 100,000 years ago. This lifestyle remained essentially unchanged until the Middle-Upper Paleolithic transition – the so-called cultural big bang – that occurred between 30,000 and 60,000 years ago, and that involved the creation of representational art, complex tool technology, long-range trade, the rise of religion, and the rapid spread of *Homo sapiens* across every habitable continent on earth. This cultural revolution was not accompanied by any increase in human brain size or obvious anatomical changes, but it appears

---

[4]   Oden et al. (2001) provide a survey of the literature on Sarah's analogical reasoning skills.
[5]   Mithen 1999: 151; cf. Bar-Yosef 2006. A recent study by Vanhaeren et al. (2006) claims a date of 100,000 to 135,000 years ago for sets of necklace beads found in Israel and Algeria, but others dispute both the dating of the objects and their identification as ornamental beads (see Balter 2006 for a discussion).

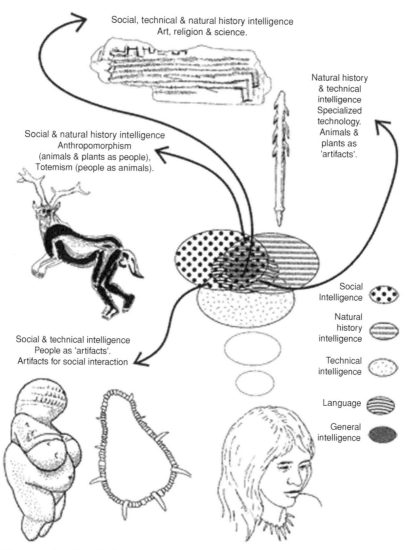

2. Human cultural explosion as the result of cognitive fluidity. From Mithen 1996: 25; copyright by Steven Mithen, used with permission.

that something radical had happened to the manner in which human brains were functioning.

The archeologist Steven Mithen (1996) has argued that the catalyst for this cultural explosion was a breaking down of the walls between what were previously impermeable cognitive modules, allowing information to flow between individual cognitive modules in a process that he terms "cognitive fluidity." Once humans began creating art and novel artifacts, the floodgate was opened to an unstoppable wave of continuous cultural innovation leading from multiple-piece spears to complex boats to the laptop computer on which I am writing this book. Mithen sees the essence of cognitive fluidity to be the conflation of separate realms. He argues that human anthropomorphism, for instance, can be understood as the result of blending social and natural history intelligence – in the terminology of Chapter 3, theory of mind module blended with the folk biology module. Similarly, the sorts of intricate and specialized artifacts that begin to be produced after the "cultural big bang" – such as spears specifically designed for the hunting of particular prey – can be seen as the products of natural history intelligence blending with the sort of technical intelligence that arises out of folk physics (Figure 2).

Chimpanzees appear to be capable of limited feats of cognitive fluidity. Their ability to use tools in acquiring and processing food, for instance, suggests to Mithen a permeability between toolmaking and foraging that is very adaptively advantageous. This ability, however, would appear to be the result of a particular, fixed intermodule conduit rather than a sign of more general cognitive fluidity, as suggested by the fact that the permeability between toolmaking and foraging is not reproduced at the interface of toolmaking and social reasoning. Although chimps employ a variety of social strategies – deception, alliance building, appeasement – to gain social advantage, it apparently never occurs to them to draw on material items for this purpose. "If social status is so important to them, why not use tools to maintain it?" Mithen asks. "Why not display the head of a little monkey that one had killed, or use leaves to exaggerate the size of one's chest?" The failure of chimpanzees to make a connection that seems so obvious to us indicates, in Mithen's view, the existence of "a brick wall between social and tool behaviour – the relationship between these lacks the fluidity that exists between foraging and tool use" (1996: 90). Reviewing work on modern human cognition that points to cross-domain analogy and metaphor as a central driver of creativity, Mithen concludes that the Middle-Upper Paleolithic transition was the result of "a transformation from being constituted by a series of relatively independent cognitive domains to one in which ideas, ways of thinking and knowledge flow freely between such domains" (154). In Mithen's view, this transformation brought into existence the sort of module-free level of metarepresentation described by Jerry Fodor (1983) or Dan Sperber (1994) as the distinguishing characteristic of human intelligence.[6]

Fodor, Mithen, and others portray this "human passion for analogy and metaphor" (Fodor 1983) as a fundamental challenge to the strongly modular view

[6] Cf. Scott Atran's concept of "symbolic representations" whereby "one seeks some empirically intuitable situation that can serve as a model by reference to which the idea can be made more or less comprehensible (e.g., God putting nature in order on the model of a father disciplining his family)" (1990: 215). Dan Sperber portrays this type of cross-module projection – where information from a module's "proper" domain is mimicked in another domain – as one of the primary engines of cognitive fluidity (see esp. 1994: 51–52 and 1996: 136–141).

of the human mind that we reviewed in Chapter 3. As I will argue later, we do not have to follow Mithen and the others to this conclusion. The tools of cognitive linguistics suggest that we are not confronted with a stark choice between a rigidly modular mind and a completely unconstrained general-purpose processor. The mechanisms of conceptual metaphor, metaphoric blending, and mental space creation allow the strongly modular human mind to continue to enjoy the benefits of modular processing while simultaneously transcending the limits of rigid modularity. Before delving into these topics, however, it would behoove us to take a short detour into the phenomenon of synaesthesia, which can, I think, provide us with a hint of how Mithen's cognitive fluidity – portrayed quite schematically by him as chambers in a cathedral or as abstract circles – might actually be instantiated neurologically.

SYNAESTHESIA AND HUMAN CREATIVITY

Synaesthesia involves the unusual blending of two or more senses, such as experiencing particular musical tones or numbers as tinged with a certain color, particular textures as inducing specific tastes, or specific tastes as inducing textures. This phenomenon has been documented for over a hundred years (Galton 1880), but has only recently been documented as a genuine sensory phenomenon – many early studies dismissed it as the result of childhood memories, former drug use, or simple confabulation.[7] Some of the more interesting work on this subject has been performed by V. S. Ramachandran and his former graduate student at the University of California at San Diego, Edward Hubbard. They have shown in a series of experiments that synaesthetes experience perceptual "popping out" and other low-level effects that demonstrate conclusively that synaesthesia is a sensory effect rather than a cognitive or memory-based phenomenon (Hubbard & Ramachandran 2001, Ramachandran & Hubbard 2001a and 2001b), although their more recent work suggests that there may be many different subtypes of synaesthesia functioning on the basis of different mechanisms (Hubbard et al. 2005).

For instance, Ramachandran and Hubbard (2001a) presented synaesthetes and normal controls with matrices of numbers and asked them to decide whether the displays appeared to be grouped horizontally or vertically. The matrices were constructed so that subjects looking solely at the shapes of the numbers would see horizontal groupings (the matrices contained horizontal lines consisting solely of 3s and 8s), whereas induced color-based organization would give the impression of vertical organization (numbers known to induce particular colors in the subject

[7] For relatively recent surveys of synaesthesia (alternately spelled "synesthesia") research, see Hubbard & Ramachandran 2005, Robertson & Sagiv 2005, and the essays collected in Baron-Cohen & Harrison 1997. For lucid popular introductions, see Ramachandran & Hubbard 2003 and Ramachandran 2004.

were lined up vertically in the display). It was found that the synaesthetes grouped on the basis of induced color, whereas control subjects generally grouped on the basis of shape. Similarly, Daniel Smilek et al. (2001) found that synaesthetic subjects had trouble distinguishing a grapheme that evokes a particular color when it was presented against a background of identical color. These and other results suggest that synaesthesia in these subjects was occurring at a very early stage of perceptual processing.[8]

The most common form of synaesthesia is this sort of "grapheme-color synaes-thesia," where letters or numbers are associated with specific colors. The fact that the region of the brain dedicated to identifying the shape of letters and numbers is located adjacent to the early-color-processing region referred to as "V4" suggests to Ramachandran and Hubbard that this type of synaesthesia is the result of either direct cross-wiring between these two regions (2001a, 2001b) or "cross-activation" caused by an imbalance in the neurotransmitters traveling between the two regions (2003). Similarly, less common forms of synaesthesia, such as those involving the "tasting of touch," might be the result of cross-wiring or cross-activation between the taste cortex and an adjacent region involved in the representation of the hand. Since Francis Galton's early work it has also been recognized that synaesthesia tends to run in families, and Ramachandran and Hubbard speculate that it might be caused by a genetic condition that interferes with the "pruning" of redundant neural connections that normally occurs during development (2001b: 9),[9] leaving intact attachments between regions – such as the number shape detection and color cortices – that are normally eliminated.

Interestingly, Ramachandran and Hubbard have also demonstrated the existence of what they term "higher" synaesthesia, where it is not the physical shape of a num-ber that is associated with a given color, but the *concept* of number. This explains the existence of synaesthetes who see months or days of the week as colored: what months and weeks and numerals share is the feature of ordinality. "Lower" synaes-thetes react only to specific Arabic numerals – seeing the grapheme "4" as blue, for instance, but not the same number written "IV" in Roman numerals. "Higher" synaesthetes, however, react to more abstract ordinality, which is processed in a higher region of the brain called the angular gyrus, located in the "TPO" (for the junction of the *t*emporal, *p*arietal, and *o*ccipital lobes) region. Other higher synaes-thetes react to the sound of a letter or number, which is also processed in the TPO. The possibility of cross-activation at such abstract levels begins to give us a hint of how something like synaesthesia may be implicated in human creativity.

---

[8] Cf. other experimental results in Ramachandran & Hubbard 2001a, Hubbard et al. 2005, and the literature survey in Hubbard & Ramachandran 2005.

[9] Original speculation attributed synaesthesia to a single X-linked mutation, but more recent work has called this link into question (Hubbard & Ramanchandran 2005: 509).

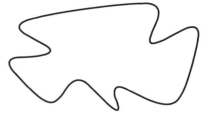

3. "Kiki" and "booba" (after Ramachandran & Hubbard 2001b: 19). Both the shapes and associated words are modified from experiments originally performed by Wolfgang Köhler 1929.

There is a great deal of controversy concerning the prevalence of full-blown, dramatic forms of synaesthesia in the general population, with estimates varying from 1 in 20,000 to 1 in 20, with more recent research narrowing that range down to magnitudes more along the lines of 1 in 200 or 2,000 (Ramachandran & Hubbard 2001b). Given that the phenomenon referred to as "synaesthesia" probably refers to a wide variety of different specific syndromes, such concerns are perhaps meaningless. This is even more the case when one considers that the forms of synaesthesia that have traditionally attracted research attention may represent merely the more dramatic or unusual development of a basic human cognitive tendency. Consider the following experiment run by Ramachandran and Hubbard, which asked subjects to consider the two shapes in Figure 3, and decide which one might be called "kiki," and which one "booba," in an imaginary Martian alphabet.

Ninety-five percent of subjects say that the figure on the left is "kiki" and the other "booba," apparently "seeing" a parallel between the sharp inflections of the tongue against the palate when pronouncing "kiki," the sharp inflections of the word "kiki" as represented in the auditory cortex, and the sharp points of the figure on the left.[10] As Ramachandran observes, that this kind of cross-modal mapping occurs even in "normal" subjects is not surprising considering the presence of sensory convergence zones such as the angular gyrus, which

is strategically located at the crossroads between the parietal lobe (concerned with touch and proprioception), the temporal lobe (concerned with hearing), and the occipital lobe (concerned with vision). So it is strategically placed to allow a convergence of different sense modalities to create abstract, modality-free representations of things around us. Logically, the jagged shape and the sound "kiki" have nothing in common: the shape comprises photons hitting the retina in parallel, the sound is a sharp air disturbance hitting the hair cells of the inner ear sequentially. But the brain abstracts the common denominator – the property of jaggedness. Here in the angular gyrus are

[10] Ramachandran repeated the same result with monolingual Tamil speakers to show that the shape of the English letter "k" was not causing the association (2004: 73).

the rudimentary beginnings of the property we call abstraction that we human beings excel in. (2004: 74)

To this artificial "booba-kiki" example we might add quite pedestrian observations such as our tendency to experience the taste of certain cheeses as "sharp" or certain musical tones as "warm." As Steven Pinker notes, sensations from particular modalities are commonly experienced by human beings as being linked in this way because of the details of our neuroanatomical architecture: for instance, musical notes appear "high" or "low" to us because the mind "treats jumps in pitch like motions in space."[11] Looked at this way, the more dramatic forms of synaesthesia that have served as the subject of neurological study may merely represent less common – and therefore more noticeable – variations of a common human cognitive trait. Lawrence Marks (1975) and Timothy Hubbard (1996), for instance, have demonstrated that even in "normal" subjects variations in brightness are associated with variations in pitch – the basis for our experience of "bright" versus "somber" music – and recent work by Jamie Ward et al. (2006) has replicated these findings and extended them to tone-color associations.

This cross-modal ability may be unique in humans, or at least higher primates. The angular gyrus is certainly larger in primates than in other mammals, and it is proportionally much larger in humans than in other primates, which suggests that at a certain point in our evolution it began to be exapted for metaphor and other sorts of abstraction.[12] Ramachandran speculates that individuals vary with regard to how prevalent such cross-wiring may be in their brains, and that being at the more extreme end of the spectrum, with a brain more prone to cross-wiring, may contribute to artistic and conceptual creativity. Ramachandran and Hubbard (2001b) cite studies that suggest that dramatic synaesthesia is more common among artists, poets, and novelists,[13] and they note the relationship of synaesthesia to metaphor: both involve the linking of otherwise apparently unrelated concepts.

Later I will take this claim a bit further and argue that *all* human beings are constantly and inevitably prone to metaphor. Poets and artists and dramatic synaesthetes – like elite athletes and virtuoso musicians – represent merely the more noticeable upper tail of the bell curve, displaying in heightened relief extraordinary human abilities that most human beings simply take for granted. If Ramachandran and Hubbard are correct that a specific genetic mutation could result in a malfunction in neural connection pruning during brain development – thereby leading to a heightened propensity for intermodular cross-wiring or cross-activation – this gives us some sense of how the "cultural explosion" of the Middle-Upper Palaeolithic transition may have occurred despite the lack of obvious anatomical

---

[11] Pinker 2002: 96; also see Bregman & Pinker 1978.
[12] Significantly, Ramachandran and Hubbard also found that subjects with damage to the angular gyrus no longer experience the "booba-kiki effect" illustrated here (2003: 58).
[13] See Mulvenna et al. 2004 for recent work on synaesthesia and creativity.

changes in *Homo sapiens*. The *Homo sapiens* who suddenly spread over the world may have had the same brain as their less cognitively cousins, but one that – as a result of one mutation or of a short series of mutations – was now capable of widespread cross-activation of previously sealed-off cognitive modules. Hominids equipped with these new, "cognitively fluid" brains could be expected to radically outcompete their early modern human fellows even without an increase in brain size.

Are Synaesthesia and Metaphor the Same?

Although Ramachandran and Hubbard at times seem to treat synaesthesia and metaphor as fundamentally similar cognitive processes, there are also some important disanalogies that we need to keep in mind. To begin with, synaesthesia is not voluntary: it appears to involve relatively fixed cross-wiring or habitual cross-activation, and it irrevocably influences perception: a grapheme-color synaesthete cannot *not* see numbers as having particular colors. Additionally, the cross-activation is simple and complete: the number "5" is purple, and that is that. Metaphor, on the other hand, seems to involve voluntary, partial, and optional synaesthesia. "Juliet is the sun" invites me to see Juliet as radiant, a source of warmth, and so on, but not literally as a glowing orb in the sky. I am also free to reject this metaphor or to switch to an alternate one, and I am at some level aware that even the selected sensory aspects of the sun that I am being asked to project are not "real" attributes of Juliet – not real in the same way that her dress is really purple, or her hair is really yellow.

This is why, although synaesthesia gives us a powerful model for how the ability to create and experience metaphors and analogies might have evolved, we have to recognize that metaphor is infinitely more flexible and powerful than synaesthesia. Grapheme-color synaesthesia, for instance, would appear to be of limited adaptive value: many synaesthetes apparently use it as a mnemonic aid, but its ability to fundamentally change the way in which human beings think or interact is limited by the fact that it is not controllable or communicable to others. Imagine, though, a hominid that acquired the ability to create voluntary instances of synaesthesia, momentarily seeing X simultaneously as Y, and, moreover, to conduct this process in a part of its brain explicitly marked off as an "as-if," or hypothetical, space – giving it the ability both to draw back from the synaesthetic perception and to abandon it if it did not seem helpful. Imagine further that this organism could – through sounds, gestures, or marks on an impressionable surface – cause fellow group members to experience the same instance of voluntary synaesthesia, allowing them to also perceive, for instance, bad behavior as darkness, or members of an out-group as disgusting. Then also imagine this set of instructions for experiencing a very particular instance of synaesthesia becoming publicly available in the social group, widely communicated, passed down from generation to generation and even built into the physical environment – symbolized in cultural artifacts and ritual activities. The behavior and cultural forms of such a group of hominids could quickly become very unpredictable. In the next sections we will examine the phenomena of conceptual metaphor, conceptual metaphor blending, and mental space creation, which provide us with helpful models for tracing the processes of voluntary synaesthesia that pervade human mental life. We will also examine how conceptual metaphors and blends are used in practical human problem solving, including probably the most salient human problem of all: political persuasion, or how to get other people to see and feel about things the way that you do.

CONCEPTUAL METAPHOR: VOLUNTARY, PARTIAL, AND COMMUNICABLE SYNAESTHESIA

The two standard theoretical standpoints that have served as foils for this discussion, postmodern relativism and objectivism, treat metaphor quite differently.[14] Many postmodernists emphasize the important role that metaphor plays in human discourse, but this reliance on metaphor is usually portrayed as yet one more reason that language can never get us in touch with reality. Paul de Man, for instance, moves from the argument that all human language is metaphorical to the conclusion that all linguistic statements are equally fictional and groundless, and therefore "destabilizing" (1978). Paul Ricoeur (1977) sees the pervasive role of metaphor in a more productive light, arguing that it has a kind of revelatory power. By "suspending" and "abolishing" the ordinary literal reference of a word, metaphor "constitutes the primordial reference to the extent that it suggests, reveals, unconceals . . . the deep structure of reality to which we are related as mortals who are born into this world and who *dwell* in it for a while" (1981: 240). As this reference to "unconcealing" suggests, however, the revelatory power of Ricoeurian metaphor does not extend beyond the sort of Heideggerian, existential truth that – as I argued in Chapter 2 – ultimately remains trapped in linguistic idealism. Metaphor as creative, "primordial" reference is connected not to a real world of bodies and things, but only to the free movement of the hermeneutic *Geist* or *Dasein*.

Postmodernists at least *care* about metaphor. Most objectivists, on the other hand, view metaphor – when they view it at all – as simply a poetic or indirect mode of expression that can always be reduced to some literal equivalent. "Juliet is the sun" is thus cognitively identical to "Juliet is like the sun in seeming to the speaker to be bright and warm." This literal paraphrase, in turn, merely serves to draw our attention to a preexisting similarity: Juliet objectively *is* like the sun in certain regards, and the metaphor simply points out this similarity. More sophisticated approaches to metaphor from within the objectivist framework have recognized its importance and its difference in certain respects from literal comparison, but continue to treat

---

[14]   The best introductions to theories of metaphor are Johnson 1981a and Ortony 1979/1993a.

it as picking out preexisting and objectively similar features in the world.[15] If the phenomenon of synaesthesia is any indication, however, metaphor and analogy are doing much more work than simply picking out preexisting similarities.

Some objectivist philosophers have realized that more must be involved in metaphor than similarity highlighting, but their commitment to objectivist theories of meaning make it difficult for them to see how metaphor could possess any sort of substantive meaning. Donald Davidson, for instance, recognizes that literal equivalence explanation cannot account for the function of metaphor, but he sees as the only alternative the idea that metaphor draws our attention to something important in the world while not possessing any "specific cognitive content" (1978/1981: 217). As Mark Johnson characterizes Davidson's position, "a metaphorical utterance is essentially a stick (consisting of a literal sentence) that one uses to hit another person so that they will see or notice something. Davidson has *no account whatever* of how it is that the literal sentence used is in any way connected up with what the hearer comes to notice" (1987: 72). John Searle goes further than Davidson in recognizing that metaphor is telling us *something* about the world, and that understanding this something involves reliance on the nonpropositional, preintentional "Background" that informs all language comprehension (1983: esp. 148–149), but he has no specific account of how this Background is structured or how it might function. To provide such an account, we must turn to the image-schematic, embodied model of concepts and thought that was sketched out in Chapter 1.

Putting the Body in Mind: Concepts as Image Schemas

The growing consensus in the cognitive science community that even quite abstract concepts are based in sensory-motor images was a main component of the critique of objectivism in Chapter 1. The "perceptual symbol theory" developed by Lawrence Barsalou, for instance, argued that perception and cognition should not be viewed as two radically different things. If, as Barsalou claims, "perception is inherently conceptual, sharing systems with perception at both the cognitive and neural levels" (1999a: 577), this means that concepts are not abstract, amodal representations, but rather modal and analogical through and through, fundamentally structured by the sensory-motor systems that produced them. Antonio Damasio has similarly argued that

the experienceable (conscious) component of representations results from an attempt at reconstituting feature-based, topographic or topologically organized fragments of sensory and motor activity; that is, only the feature-based components of a representation assembled in specific patterns can become a content of consciousness. (1989: 45)

---

[15] See, for instance, Tversky 1977, Miller 1979/1993, and Ortony 1979/1993b, as well as Mark Johnson's (1981b) survey of the objectivist position. Literal analogy also serves as the theoretical framework for much of the computer-modeling work on analogy (Kokinov & Petrov 2001 and Wilson et al. 2001).

In other words, there is nothing that is not sensory, and "images are probably the main content of our thoughts" (Damasio 1994: 107). Conscious awareness is fundamentally structured by a set of dynamic "somato-motor" maps anchored in the body (231), which serves as the basic "yardstick" for the various neural processes that we experience as the mind (xvi).[16]

This empirical work coming out of cognitive science and behavioral neuroscience validates the basic argument best laid out in detail by Mark Johnson in his 1987 *The Body in the Mind: The Bodily Basis of Meaning, Imagination and Reason*. Johnson's goal there was to engage in a "descriptive or empirical phenomenology" that would sketch out a "geography of human experience" firmly grounded in the body (xxxviii).[17] His argument is that the fundamental unit of meaning is a nonpropositional, analogue, embodied structure, the *schema*.[18] Schemas are recurring patterns arising from our sensory-motor interactions with the world, similar to what Barsalou (1999a) refers to as "perceptual simulations," and include such fundamental structures as PATH, CONTAINMENT, PART-WHOLE, CONTACT, vertical SCALE, and the recurrent CYCLE.[19] One of Johnson's former students, Tim Rohrer, has recently provided a helpful formal definition of image schemas, which can be said to possess the following characteristics:

- are recurrent patterns of bodily experience;
- are "image"-like in that they preserve the topological structure of the whole perceptual experience;
- operate dynamically in and across time;
- are structures which link sensorimotor experience to conceptualization and language;

[16] Cf. Shaun Gallagher's idea of a "prenoetic" "body schema" that "helps to structure consciousness but does not explicitly show itself in the contents of consciousness" (2005: 32).

[17] One of Johnson's most immediate influences was Merleau-Ponty, and his conception of the image schema is similar in certain ways to Heideggerian *Vorhabe* or Ricoeur's model of metaphor but is grounded in the physical body and embodied experience rather than in linguistic experience. See Wolf 1994: 38–41 for more on the link between European phenomenology and the work of both Johnson and George Lakoff. Johnson is also building on the work of theorists of metaphor such as I. A. Richards (1936), who portrayed metaphor as a fundamental tool for structuring our experienced world, as well as Max Black's (1954–1955) "interaction" theory that proposed that metaphors *create* similarities with irreducible meaning, rather than merely picking out preexisting analogies in the world (Johnson 1987: 68–71). Also see Johnson 2005 for the most recent statement of his views.

[18] The idea that sensory-motor–derived schemas might form the basic units of cognition has also been explored for decades by the neuroscientist Michael Arbib, who argues that sensory-motor schemas serve as "the building blocks of [the] models that guide our interactions with the world around us" (1985: 37). For other early work on image schemas, also see Arbib et al. 1987, Lakoff 1987, Langacker 1987, and Talmy 1988.

[19] Many cognitive linguists have the practice of referring to image schemas and cross-domain schema projects in small caps to remind readers that the word or words in question refer not to some amodal concept or proposition, but rather serve as a label for a bodily based "complex web of connections in our experience and understanding" (Johnson 1987: 7).

– are likely instantiated as activation patterns (or "contours") in topologic and topographic neural maps;
– afford "normal" pattern completions that can serve as a basis for inference. (2005:
173)[20]

As we discussed in Chapter 1, there is a growing body of neuroimaging evidence
for the cognitive reality of perceptual simulations or image schemas, which clearly
play a foundational role in understanding the actions of others and the processing
of language.[21]

The "normal patterns of completion" that schemas bring with them are referred
to by Mark Johnson as the schema's "entailments," a term that Johnson deliberately wishes to divorce from its more narrow technical use in analytic philosophy.
For Johnson, the entailments of a given schema include the "perceptions, discrim-
inations, interests, values, beliefs, practices, and commitments" (1987: 132) that
are tied up with it. Johnson is here inspired by the work of Gibsonian psychologists who argue that perceptions of objects are unavoidably tied to "affordances" –
plans of actions that perceived objects inevitably present to the perceiver. As a
plan for action, a schema is dynamic, possessing its own logic and sets of expectations. As an "irreducible gestalt" (44), a schema also cannot be translated into the
sort of abstract, algorithmic form that the objectivist model of knowledge would
demand. Johnson's argument in this regard is echoed by Barsalou's contention
that the affordances produced by perceptual simulations are fundamentally modal,
and the resulting "inferences" could not be derived from a hypothetical amodal
replacement (1999a: 605).

This discussion so far has itself been rather abstract and amodal, so let us turn
to one of Johnson's concrete examples. Consider the image schema of BALANCE.
BALANCE is something we learn with our bodies as we develop the ability to walk
and interact with the physical world in increasingly complex ways: stacking blocks,
riding bikes, carrying heavy objects in our hands. "It is crucially important," Johnson argues, "to see that balancing is an *activity we learn with our bodies* and not
by grasping a set of rules or concepts . . . the *meaning* of balance begins to emerge
through our *acts* of balancing and through our *experience* of systemic processes
and states within our bodies" (1987: 74–75). Having developed this image schema,
BALANCE, as a result of our embodied experience in the world, we inevitably begin
to project it onto more abstract domains of experience – perceiving, understanding, and feeling these domains through the filter of the BALANCE schema. Our
understanding of what constitutes a "balanced" life, a "balanced" argument, moral

---

[20] Although I will be working with this understanding of image schemas, the issue of precisely how to
characterize them is a rather fundamental and contentious issue in cognitive linguistics; the reader
is referred to the essays collected in Hampe (2005) for the current state of the field and for views of
image schemas that differ somewhat from the Johnson-Rohrer model followed here.
[21] See especially Rizzolatti et al. 2001 and Umiltà et al. 2001.

4. Udo statue from Benin. Drawing by Karen Schmitt, after illustration in Philip J. C. Dark (1982), *An Illustrated Catalogue of Benin Art*. London: G. K. Hall and Co. Copyright Mark Johnson, used by permission.

or legal "balance," and the "balance" we perceive in a pleasing work of art is thus fundamentally structured by our sensory-motor sense of physical BALANCE, and this embodied *feeling* cannot be fully captured in an amodal, formal definition. Consider, for instance, the drawing of a Beninese statue (Figure 4).

The pleasingness of this figure owes nothing to simply formal symmetry. As Johnson observes,

There is a sword in one hand and nothing in the other, for instance. But in spite of this lack of equality, the figure is nicely balanced. Observe the lines formed by the sword in the right hand, the strap across the chest, and the empty left hand and arm. The slight curve of the sword balances off the curve of the left arm, in relations to the angled strap. Part of this balance is the sense of equal lengths of the sword, strap, and arm. The balance here is *visual*; it is not a balance of actual physical weights or masses in the bronze figure. It is a balance of line and of visual forces that can create perceptual motion in an apparently static figure. (81–82)

To supplement Johnson's observations with the work on mirror neuron systems that we discussed in Chapter 3, we might add that the presentation of an image such as this triggers in the perceiver an immediate and unconscious somatic simulation. Processing the visual stimulus of a humanlike shape causes us to activate the necessary sensory-motor regions, allowing us to use our own bodies as a template, to imagine what it would be like to be holding a sword like that, with the sword hanging thus, and our arms positioned and our legs planted so. The resulting feeling of "balance" is thus the verdict of our *body* rather than an amodal, abstract aesthetic judgment. Because bodily simulations are so deeply and fundamentally involved, this judgment of balance also involves not merely a manner of speaking or an intellectual apprehension of similarity, but rather a deep structuring of our experience. Commenting on the concept of psychological "balance," Johnson observes that "when I am emotionally worked up, I feel myself to be out of balance. My world takes on a different character than it normally has. When I feel emotionally 'out of balance' I am not reflecting conceptually on that imbalance . . . I am *feeling* something that I cannot quite articulate propositionally" (89).

Conceptual Metaphor Theory

This idea of bodily based, concrete schemas serving as conceptual templates for our understanding of abstract, or less clearly structured, domains is the basic insight behind "conceptual metaphor theory," which Johnson and the linguist George Lakoff have done the most to develop.[22] Lakoff and Johnson were pioneers in formulating a comprehensive and coherent model of cross-domain projection and – most significantly – in demonstrating the pervasiveness of these projections in all aspects of human conceptual life.[23] Against objectivist theories that portray metaphor as a relatively rare and somewhat "deviant" mode of communication thrown in to add rhetorical spice, Lakoff and Johnson argue in their landmark *Metaphors We Live By* (1980) and *Philosophy in the Flesh* (1999) that "conceptual

[22] The idea that bodily based, analogue schemas play a role in structuring our abstract thought has also been explored recently by other cognitive scientists. As we saw in Chapter 1, Barsalou believes that perceptual simulations of abstract concepts preserves "at least some of the affordances present in actual sensory-motor experiences with category members" (1999a: 587), and Damasio similarly notes that nonpropositional, sensory-motor schemas are constantly "biasing cognitive processes in a covert manner and thus influencing reasoning and decision making" (Damasio 1994: 185). Also cf. Jean Mandler's (1992) claim that nonpropositional, analogue spatial representations related to causation (launching), containment, and agency form the basis of our relevant abstract concepts, as well as the development of these ideas in Alan Leslie 1994.

[23] Lakoff & Johnson 1980 and 1999, Kövecses 2002, Gibbs 2006, and the essays collected in Katz et al. 1998 and Gibbs & Steen 1999 provide helpful introductions to conceptual metaphor theory, and the current state of the field is tracked by the journals *Metaphor and Symbol* and *Cognitive Linguistics*.

metaphor" is in fact a ubiquitous and fundamental aspect of human cognition. Conceptual metaphor, as they understand it, involves the recruitment of structure from a concrete or clearly organized domain (the *source* domain) in order to understand and talk about another, usually more abstract or less clearly structured, domain (the *target* domain). Understood in this way, conceptual metaphors encompass similes and analogies as well as metaphors in the more traditional sense.

The most basic of these projective mappings are a set of "primary metaphors," which are the result of abstract target domains becoming associated with some basic schema source domains – PATH or SCALE, for instance – through experiential correlation.[24] Lakoff and Johnson 1999: 50–54 provide a short list of representative primary metaphors (derived from Grady 1997) such as AFFECTION IS WARMTH, IMPORTANT IS BIG, MORE IS UP, and so on, specifying their sensory-motor source domains and the primary experience correlations that give rise to them. Two examples of primary metaphors that will be referred to again later are:

1. PURPOSES ARE DESTINATIONS
   Subjective judgment: achieving a purpose
   Sensory-motor experience: reaching a destination
   Example: "He'll ultimately be successful, but he isn't *there* yet."
   Primary experience: reaching a destination in everyday life and thereby achieving a purpose (e.g., if you want a drink, you need to go to the water cooler).
2. ACTIONS ARE SELF-PROPELLED MOTIONS
   Subjective judgment: action
   Sensory-motor experience: moving one's body through space
   Example: "I'm *moving* right along on the project"
   Primary experience: common action of moving oneself through space.
   (Lakoff and Johnson 1999: 52–53)

Although Lakoff and Johnson argue that all primary metaphors develop gradually through experiential correlation, it is likely that at least some basic cross-domain associations are the result of fixed synaesthetic cross-wiring, such as the correlation of tones with verticality, or textures such as sharpness with tones or tastes.

However these primary metaphors are developed, all individuals have a huge store of them at their disposal by the time they are able to become productive users of language. These accumulated metaphorical associations then become one of the individual's primary tools for reasoning about himself or herself and the

---

[24] Johnson and Lakoff sometimes present themselves as strict empiricists in the Lockean sense, describing image schemas as something developed anew by each individual purely from experience with the world, and Lakoff in particular has reservations about evolutionary approaches to human cognition (personal communication). It is clear from our discussion in Chapter 3, however, that a schema such as BALANCE, for instance, could be acquired only through the interaction of a highly prestructured body-mind interacting with a world for which it was designed.

world – especially when it comes to relatively abstract or unstructured domains – as well as for communicating thoughts to others. While abstract concepts such as "time" or "death" may have a skeleton structure that is directly (i.e., nonmetaphorically) represented conceptually, in most cases this amodal structure is not rich or detailed enough to allow us to make useful inferences. Therefore, when we attempt to conceptualize and reason about abstract or relatively unstructured realms, this skeletal structure is fleshed out (usually automatically and unconsciously) with additional structure provided by primary metaphors derived from basic bodily experience, often invoked in combination with other primary metaphors to form complex metaphors or conceptual blends. When primary or complex source domains are activated in such cases and mapped onto the target domain, most aspects of the source domain conceptual topology – that is, inference patterns, imagistic reasoning patterns, salient entities, and so forth – are preserved, thereby importing a high degree of structure into the target domain.[25]

To give an illustration of this process, consider the question of how we are to comprehend and reason about something as abstract as "life." Lakoff and Johnson (1999: 60–62) note that, when reasoning or talking about life, English speakers often invoke the complex metaphor, A PURPOSEFUL LIFE IS A JOURNEY, which provides them with a schema drawn from embodied experience. This schema is based on the two primary metaphors mentioned before – PURPOSES ARE DESTINATIONS and ACTIONS ARE SELF-PROPELLED MOTIONS – that have become a part of our conceptual "toolbox" through experiential correlation. When these two primary metaphors are combined with the simple fact (derived from our common knowledge of the world) that a long trip to a series of destinations constitutes a journey, we have the complex metaphor schema, A PURPOSEFUL LIFE IS A JOURNEY, which Lakoff and Johnson map as follows:

Journey	→	Purposeful Life
Traveler	→	Person Living a Life
Destinations	→	Life Goals
Itinerary	→	Life Plan

The PURPOSEFUL LIFE IS A JOURNEY metaphor arises out of our basic embodied experience and gives us a way to think and reason about this abstract "entity," which in itself is unstructured and therefore difficult to reason about. Lakoff and Johnson do not deny that concepts may often be represented literally.[26] For instance, the expression "he achieved his purpose" is not metaphorical in either the traditional

---

[25] "Most" aspects because the skeletal structure of the target domain that is directly represented in consciousness serves to constrain not only what source domains can be mapped onto it but also which aspects of the source domain can be successfully mapped and which ignored as irrelevant (see Lakoff 1990: 67–73 and 1993: 228–235).

[26] In this respect, their position is a less thoroughgoing rejection of the objectivist model of concepts than that of Barsalou.

or conceptual sense. We frequently tend to fall back on formulations such as "he reached his goal," however, because "without metaphor . . . concepts are relatively impoverished and have only a minimal, 'skeletal' structure" (1999: 58). Invoking the Purposes are Destinations metaphor adds crucial "sensorimotor inferential structure" (58) that we appear to find necessary, especially when decisions need to be made or there is some difference of opinion about what to do. As with Johnson's gestalt schemas, the full practical import of a conceptual metaphor thus lies in its entailments: that is, the fact that the metaphoric link between abstract life and a concrete journey allows us to draw on our large stock of commonplace knowledge about journeys and apply this knowledge to "life."

When under the sway of the Purposeful Life as Journey metaphor, for instance, we unconsciously assume that life, like a physical journey, requires planning if one is to *reach* one's *destination*, that difficulties will be *encountered along the way*, that one should avoid being *sidetracked* or *bogged down*, and so on. Having become convinced that I have become *sidetracked*, for instance, I unconsciously import reasoning structures from the source domain and project them on the target domain: exerting more effort (*traveling farther*) in my current endeavor (*direction, path*) will only make things worse (*lead* me *further astray*); if I wish things to improve (get *back* on *track*), it will be necessary to first radically change my current manner of doing things (*backtrack, reverse*) until it resembles the manner in which I used to do things at some particular time in the past (get *back* to the *point* where I went astray), and then begin making effort again (begin *moving forward*) in a very different manner than I am doing now (in a new *direction*). We thus can see how a single complex metaphor can have profound practical implications, influencing decision making and providing us with normative guidance. In addition, the sheer awkwardness of the literal paraphrases just given illustrate how deeply the A Purposeful Life is a Journey schema penetrates our consciousness: it takes a great deal of effort to avoid invoking it in some way when discussing life decisions.

As we can also see from this example, a single complex, conceptual metaphor structure can inform a whole series of specific linguistic expressions. These "families" of specific metaphorical expressions are not random or unrelated but are rather all motivated by a common conceptual schema. This, indeed, is a crucial proposition of cognitive linguistics: that metaphorical expressions are not simply fixed, linguistic conventions but rather represent the surface manifestations of deeper, active, and largely unconscious *conceptual* structures. This means that a metaphoric structure such as A Purposeful Life is a Journey exists independently of any specific metaphoric expression of it and can thus continuously generate new and unforeseen expressions. Anyone familiar with the A Purposeful Life is a Journey schema can instantly grasp the sense of such metaphors as *dead-end job* or *going nowhere* on hearing them for the first time and can also draw on the conceptual schema to create related but entirely novel metaphoric expressions. Were I a country singer, for instance, I might write a song entitled "The Airplane

of Life Is About to Depart the Gate, and I Don't Have a Boarding Pass," which
draws on the A PURPOSEFUL LIFE IS A JOURNEY image schema but employs it in an
entirely novel (albeit somewhat painful) linguistic expression.

Pervasiveness of Conceptual Metaphor

In 1980, Lakoff and Johnson's *Metaphors We Live By* made quite a splash (as it were)
by documenting in detail the pervasiveness of metaphor in everyday conceptual
life, and the subsequent mountain of literature produced by the emergent field
of cognitive linguistics has made it clear that cross-domain metaphorical mappings are a central feature of human language and thought. Image schemas and
conceptual metaphor have been shown to play a foundational structuring role in
human categorization (Lakoff 1987), emotional concepts (Kövecses 1986, 1990),
poetry (Lakoff & Turner 1989), religious discourse (Balaban 1999, Schmid 2002,
Jäkel 2003, Slingerland 2003, 2004a and 2004b), philosophical discourse (Lakoff &
Johnson 1999), mathematics (Lakoff & Núñez 2000), and legal reasoning (Winter
2001), and nothing less than a small cottage industry has sprung up around the
analysis of conceptual metaphors in political reasoning and debate.[27] As mentioned
in Chapter 1, the work of scholars such as Mary Hesse (1966), Earl MacCormac
(1976), and Theodore Brown (2003) – although not explicitly framed in terms of
cognitive linguistics – documents in detail the foundational role that metaphor
has historically played in both the formulation and the interpretation of scientific
theories, while Kevin Dunbar and his colleagues have shown, in a series of "in
vivo" studies of weekly laboratory sessions, that analogical reasoning continues
to play a formative role in the interpretation of scientific results and the formation of hypotheses.[28] Ronald Langacker's "cognitive grammar" approach (1987,
1991) has exhaustively documented the image-schematic basis of basic grammatical categories such as tense and case, and Leonard Talmy's massive two-volume
introduction to "cognitive semantics" (2000) illustrates how basic image schemas
structure concepts and semantics in natural languages.[29]

Much of the early conceptual metaphor theory work was developed through
analysis of contemporary American English and a handful of related languages,

[27] See especially Chilton 1996, Lakoff 1996 and 2004, Rohrer 1995, Coulson 2001, Beer & de Landtsheer
2004, Gibbs 2005, Oakley 2005, and Slingerland et al. 2007. Although not framed in terms of conceptual metaphor theory, the work of Kevin Dunbar (2001) on analogy in political debate is also
relevant in this regard.

[28] See Dunbar 1999 and 2001 for a review. Also cf. Nersessian 1992 on the foundational role that analogy
played in Maxwell's theorizing about electromagnetism.

[29] For instance, Talmy shows how force dynamics – our embodied understanding of physical barriers
and forces – underlies our use of modals such as *may*, *can*, and *ought*. Eve Sweetser (1990) extends
Talmy's original analysis (1988) to the so-called epistemic modals ("You *must* have been home last
night") and applies the tools of cognitive semantics to explain such diverse linguistic phenomena as
conjunctions and conditionals.

such as French and Spanish. The basic claims about the pervasiveness and conceptual centrality of metaphor – as well as the presence of most of the primary and common complex metaphors described by Lakoff and Johnson 1980 and 1999 – have since been confirmed in modern non-Indo-European languages such as Basque (Ibarretxe-Antuñano 1999), Japanese (Hiraga 1995, 1999), Arabic (Abdulmoneim 2006), and the Mandarin dialect of Chinese (Yu 1998, 2003), as well as in ancient non-Indo-European languages. For instance, my first monograph (Slingerland 2003) applied conceptual metaphor theory to a set of fifth-third-century B.C.E. Chinese texts, and found conceptual metaphor to be as pervasive in classical Chinese as in any Indo-European language, and just as foundational for grappling with abstract ideas.[30] The classical Chinese context is perhaps the object of comparison sine qua non for cross-cultural claims: a highly developed literary society completely isolated from other world cultures and functioning in a graph-based language that could not be more different from the Indo-European family. Other recent work has gone beyond linguistic analysis to show how conceptual metaphors have been widely instantiated throughout human history in built physical environments. Julie Gifford (2004), for instance, has argued quite convincingly that the SPIRITUAL PROGRESS AS PHYSICAL JOURNEY metaphor – an offshoot of the basic PURPOSEFUL LIFE AS JOURNEY schema already discussed – served as the basic organizing principle in the architecture of ancient Buddhist stupas in Java.[31]

Experimental Evidence for the Cognitive Reality of Conceptual Metaphor

Simple documentation of the pervasiveness and systematicity of conceptual metaphor in the previously mentioned realms goes a long way toward demonstrating that such schemas play more of a role in human cognition than as mere figures of speech. In addition to the more general experimental evidence for the imagistic basis for concepts discussed in Chapter 1, there is now a veritable mountain of evidence for the pervasiveness of conceptual metaphor cross-linguistically, as well as for the claim that conceptual metaphors in fact represent conceptually active, dynamic, language-independent structures.

Some of the most basic evidence, derived from observations of American English usage, is reviewed by Lakoff and Johnson (1999: 81–89). This includes "novel-case generalization" evidence: the fact that entirely novel linguistic expressions (e.g., "living in the fast lane") are instantly comprehended by a competent speaker because they draw on a preexistent conceptual structure; polysemy (the fact that

---

[30] This will be illustrated in the later detailed case-example. Also see Linda Olds (1991) on foundational metaphors in Hua Yan Buddhism, D. Neil Schmid's (2002) study of metaphors for karma in medieval Chinese Buddhist texts, and James Egge's (2004) analysis of metaphors for emotion in Pali Buddhist texts.

[31] Cf. Scott Ortman's analysis (2000) of the conceptual metaphors behind pottery designs from the Mesa Verde region of the American Southwest.

we find systematically related meanings for single words or expressions such as "dead end" or "lost"); and inference patterns – that is, the fact that reasoning patterns from well-structured source domains (physical travel, for instance) are commonly used to draw conclusions about abstract target domains (e.g., life). On a broader and more historically in-depth scale, Eve Sweetser has demonstrated the existence of systematic semantic shifts in the Indo-European family whereby, for instance, verbs having to do with vision come to refer to knowledge, or verbs having to do with hearing come to refer to more abstract obedience. This strongly suggests that conceptual metaphors such as KNOWING IS SEEING ("I see your point) and HEARING IS OBEYING ("He wouldn't listen to me") have been historically active in the minds of speakers of these languages (Sweetser 1990). The fact that similar sets of conceptual metaphors are present and pervasive – and apparently doing much of the same conceptual work and transforming in predictable ways – in languages as divergent historically and linguistically as modern English, Finnish, and fourth-century B.C.E. classical Chinese strongly suggests that conceptual metaphor is a real and universal human cognitive phenomenon.

In addition to such linguistic evidence, a growing body of psychological exper-iments supports the cognitive reality of metaphor schemas in guiding reasoning, language comprehension, and sensory perception.[32] In Chapter 1 we discussed evidence supporting Barsalou's "perceptual symbol account" of human cognition, which strongly suggests that verbal cues are guiding the construction of specific mental images. Researchers working from a conceptual metaphor perspective also cite such evidence as "bodily priming effects," where subjects asked to perform a physical action (moving their leg as if to kick something) are quicker to comprehend metaphorical statements organized around that act ("kick around the idea"), with a control group showing that the result was not merely the effect of lexical associa-tion.[33] Similarly, a variety of studies have found evidence of "frame-shifting" costs incurred in moving from one metaphorically induced image schema to another. For example, there are two primary schemas for understanding one's relationship to time: the "ego-moving" schema, where time is a fixed landscape through which one moves, and the "time-moving" schema, where time is an object moving in relation to a stationary observer. In a series of experiments, Dedre Gentner et al. (2002) found that time expressions were understood more slowly when they were embedded in a set of expressions that switched between these two schemas, or when they were formulated in terms of a schema that contradicted the one with which the subject was verbally primed.[34]

Another related study looked at different schema primings in English and Mandarin Chinese. One notable difference between English and Mandarin is that,

---

[32] The most comprehensive recent review of the experimental literature is to be found in Gibbs 2006.
[33] Unpublished study, Wilson & Gibbs 2005, cited and described in Gibbs 2006: 183–184.
[34] Cf. the evidence on frame-shifting cost presented in Coulson 2001: 75–83.

although both utilize a horizontal axis to conceptualize time – with events being "before" and "after," "ahead" or "behind" – Mandarin additionally makes reference to a vertical axis, with the past being "above" and the future "below." "Last week," for instance, is "the week above" (*shang ge libai*). Lera Boroditsky (2001) found that response times to questions about temporal reasoning were faster for Mandarin speakers given vertical spatial primes as opposed to horizontal, with the opposite being true for English speakers. Interestingly, she also found that the response times of the two groups became statistically indistinguishable after the English speakers were briefly trained to talk about time using vertical metaphors, which suggests that novel image schemas can quickly become cognitively active.

As a decidedly nonnative speaker of Mandarin, I can attest that, back in the days when I spoke the language on a regular basis, I would find myself occasionally gesturing upward with my thumb for emphasis when talking about the past. David McNeill (1992) provides a mountain of evidence from a decade of spontaneous gesture studies indicating that physical posture and gestures are used along with verbal language to communicate image structures from one person to another.[35] There is also considerable evidence that conceptual metaphors are present in sign language, although the specific mappings found in American Sign Language differ somewhat from spoken English.[36] Reasoning-constraint studies – for instance, the work cited earlier on metaphors in scientific reasoning, or Dedre Gentner and Donald Gentner's (1983) classic study of metaphors guiding subjects' intuitions about electricity – have shown that metaphor and cross-domain analogy play a clear and fundamental role in human problem solving. As Mark Johnson observes, studies like these demonstrate that "metaphors, or analogies, are not merely convenient economies for expressing our knowledge; rather, they *are* our knowledge and understanding of the particular phenomenon in question" (1987: 112).

Finally, more recent work has begun to directly trace cross-domain activation using neuroimaging technologies. Tim Rohrer (2001), for instance, used fMRI imaging to show that there is significant overlap in the brain regions activated by physical hand stroking – which provides an accurate, individualized map of each subject's "hand region" – and both a literal hand comprehension task ("I handed him a beer") and metaphorical hand comprehension task ("I handed him the project"). The overlap was stronger for the literal comprehension task than the metaphorical, but in both cases it was clear that the same cortical regions were being activated. This is strong evidence for the claim that sensory-motor patterns are cognitively active and being directly recruited – albeit perhaps in a "bleached out" form – in the processing of conceptual metaphors.[37] All of this convergent

---

[35] For more recent work on gesture and metaphor, see Cienki 2005.

[36] Taub 2001 and Wilcox 2001, cited and discussed in Gibbs 2006: 190–194.

[37] See Rohrer 2005 for a helpful recent review of neuroimaging research related to image schemas, as well as Burgess & Chiarello 1996.

evidence suggests that conceptual metaphor not only is a real phenomenon, but it also plays an inevitable and fundamental role in embodied human cognition.

Some Limitations of Conceptual Metaphor Theory

All this is not to say that the model of conceptual metaphor as formulated by Lakoff and Johnson is not without its limitations. One of the most basic, and one that Lakoff and Johnson have tried to address, is the question of how the target of a given metaphor serves to constrain possible source domains, as well as to determine what parts of those source domains become conceptually active in the metaphor. As Lakoff and Johnson would have it, the structure of the more concrete source domain is projected onto the target domain, imposing the source domain structure, constrained only by a minimal "skeleton structure" already present in the target. The entailments of the source domain then irresistibly structure our understanding of the target. It is a bit of a mystery, though, how this skeletal structure–constraining function actually works: why some metaphors are felt to be "apt" and others not, for instance, or how source domain structures are filtered as they are projected onto the target.

The idea of complete structuring of the target by the source domain works quite well for many "primary metaphors," such as TIME AS SPACE. It is hard to know how we would think about time except in terms of space, and it is possible that such complete and conceptually inescapable mappings are the result of hard-wired or acquired synaesthesia. Fairly global dominance of the source domain is also clear in even quite complex metaphors. The PURPOSEFUL LIFE AS JOURNEY metaphor, for instance, involves a relatively full and rich projection of source to target domain, where many aspects of the source domain are preserved, and even unmapped elements of the source can usually be perceived as apt, if a bit idiosyncratic. "I'm not getting anywhere with my book project" is a very conventional statement, but there are few limits on what other aspects of the source domain can be drawn on metaphorically – for example, "the argument of Chapter Four is a bit winding and treacherous."

Other metaphors, however, seem to be much more constrained, limited by a target that possesses a great degree of premetaphoric structure. Consider the metaphor "Juliet is the sun." This is an immediately apt and comprehensible metaphor, unlike, say, "Juliet is Jupiter" – which could perhaps work but would need some explanation. We also somehow know to project from the source domain, the sun, only a few specific qualities (such as warmth and radiance) and to ignore others (being an orb of fire up in the sky, being round, etc.). Moreover, which traits can be appropriately mapped seem to be very much dependent on our direct, literal understanding of the target, this human being named Juliet, who in fact has very little in common with the sun. Barsalou makes this point with regard to the common metaphor ANGER IS HEAT, which underlies such expressions as *he blew his top* or *he is getting hot under the collar.* Barsalou argues that it is impossible to understand how such metaphors function without postulating a fairly rich, premetaphorical structure to the target domain:

A direct, nonmetaphorical representation of an abstract domain is essential for two reasons: first, it constitutes the most basic understanding of the domain. Knowing only that *anger* is like *liquid exploding from a container* hardly constitutes an adequate concept. If this is all that people know, they are far from having an adequate understanding of *anger.* Second, a direct representation of an abstract domain is necessary to guide the mapping of a concrete domain onto it. A concrete domain cannot be mapped systematically into an abstract domain that has no content. (Barsalou 1999a: 600)

Naomi Quinn has made a similar point in arguing that preexisting cultural models should be seen as playing a greater role in the construction of metaphors. We often, she argues, have a clear sense in our minds – one derived from cultural beliefs – about what entailments we are looking for, and only then go in search of a metaphor that will provide us with these entailments. She notes that in the online use of metaphor, the conceptual metaphor is often followed by commentary that explains it in more literal language. For instance, one subject, discussing the idea of marriage as a life-long partnership, remarked:

And another thing we've got into problems of, you know, "Who am I? What do I want to be? Who are you? Where are you going? What do you want to be? And how do we both get there?" Being that we're sort of tied together, you know, like a three-legged race, this kind of thing, in terms of, you know, handling an issue of, suppose someone gets offered a job in Alaska or something? (1991: 75–76)

As Quinn observes, "The commentary on the heels of the metaphor shows quite unmistakably that the speaker has adopted the metaphor to make a point already in mind, rather than being led to the point by a previously unrealized entailment of the metaphor" (76). As studies of the use of metaphor in political debate make clear, speakers often have a predetermined conceptual or emotional point that they desire to make, and then choose metaphors that are designed to communicate this point to others.[38]

Perhaps the most important limitation of conceptual metaphor theory is that, if cross-domain mapping involved only the use of one domain to structure another, this would provide an account of human imagination, but not of human creativity. This is a problem shared by Mithen's idea of cognitive fluidity and some of the other models of cross-domain projection we discussed earlier. Seeing A as B certainly provides us with a degree of conceptual flexibility, but what seems really unusual about human beings is their ability to go beyond A and B and create an entirely new structure, C. The most important amendment to conceptual metaphor theory has

---

[38] See, for instance, Slingerland et al. 2007.

thus been the development of an account of how structure from multiple domains can be selectively combined in a separate, "blended" space, resulting in a completely novel structure. Many of the problems with conceptual metaphor as it was originally formulated – as unidirectional mappings from a source to a target domain – are made much more tractable by what we might call "second generation" cognitive linguistics, which portrays conceptual metaphor as merely one form of mapping involving a multiplicity of conceptual spaces.

MENTAL SPACE THEORY AND CONCEPTUAL BLENDING

Mental space and blending theory, originally developed by Gilles Fauconnier and Mark Turner, encompasses conceptual metaphor theory but goes beyond it to argue that *all* of human cognition – even literal and logical thought – involves the creation of mental spaces and mappings between them. In this way, it serves as a kind of unified theory identifying conceptual metaphor as merely one particularly dramatic cognitive process (a single- or multiple-scope blend) among many, more pedestrian processes such as categorization, semantic frame construction, and naming. It also goes beyond linguistic production to describe the manner in which novel motor programs, technological interfaces, and social institutions are created through a process of space blending.

The basic unit of blending theory is the so-called mental space, consisting of a "set of activated neuronal assemblies" (Fauconnier & Turner 2002: 40) that form a coherent structure, often "marked" in some way – as a "past" space or "purported belief" space – and potentially nested inside of other spaces. For instance, as Fauconnier explains,

In saying *Liz thinks Richard is wonderful*, we build a space for Liz's reported beliefs, with minimal explicit structure corresponding to Richard's being wonderful. In saying, *Last year, Richard was wonderful*, we build a space for "last year," and in saying *Liz thinks that last year Richard was wonderful*, we build a space for last year embedded in a belief space. (1997: 11)

Unlike the sort of entrenched cross-domain mappings that are represented by primary conceptual metaphors and stored in long-term memory, mental spaces are momentary constructs that are built up in working memory, prompted by language or other signals, and that draw on more entrenched frames and mappings. As Joseph Grady et al. (1999) observe, mental spaces

are not equivalent to domains, but, rather, they depend upon them: spaces represent particular scenarios which are structured by given domains ... [and where] the recruited structure is only a small subset of knowledge of that domain. In short, a mental space is a short-term construct informed by the more general and more stable knowledge structures associated with a particular domain. (102)

The temporary, schematically structured mental spaces constructed in working memory as we think or talk draw on more stable knowledge and images called up from long-term memory, but then are able to combine, blend, extend, and reframe these domains in quite unexpected and creative ways – often by systematically connecting elements in one space to elements in another space through neural coactivation bindings.

Space considerations prevent anything like a thorough introduction to this field.[39] In the sections that follow, I will flesh out this rather sketchy characterization of mental space and blending theory with a series of examples. These are intended to illustrate how this area of cognitive linguistics can serve as a powerful model for both understanding the general mechanisms of human creativity and tracing out in detail how this creativity arises from, and remains constrained by, embodied and humanly universal cognitive domains.

Double-Scope Blends: Beyond Source to Target Mappings

One of the primary ways in which blending theory emends conceptual metaphor theory is by showing that many expressions that, at first glance, seem to involve simple source to target domain mappings in fact involve the blending of two or more spaces into a novel conceptual structure. A simple source to target domain mapping is understood in blending theory as a "single-scope" blend, where two input spaces (Input$_1$ and Input$_2$) project into a third, "blended" space, but all of the relevant structure comes from only one of the inputs. In such blends, Input$_1$ corresponds to conceptual metaphor's "source" domain, and Input$_2$ corresponds to the "target." The power of seeing this process as a projection of two domains into a third, temporary, "blended" space is that it allows us to deal with situations where structure is coming from more than one input domain, resulting in a novel blend, with its own emergent structure, that is identical to neither of the inputs.

Consider, for instance, Fauconnier and Turner's classic example of a double-scope blend, the expression "digging one's own financial grave" (2002: 131–133), as, for instance, directed by a financially conservative person toward someone speculating on technology stocks. This expression clearly involves at least two domains, GRAVE DIGGING and UNWITTING FINANCIAL FAILURE. Although it might at first glance seem like a simple source to target domain conceptual metaphor (Grave Digging → Financial Decision Making), Fauconnier and Turner observe that this cannot be the case: in the metaphor, finishing the digging of one's own grave actually causes death, which is not at all a feature of the domain of literal

---

[39] For an introduction to mental space theory, see Fauconnier 1997. For recent introductions to blending theory, see Coulson 2001 and Fauconnier & Turner 2002; for a comparison with conceptual metaphor theory, see Grady et al. 1999; and for a very short introduction with some illustrative examples and a helpful bibliography, see Dancygier 2006.

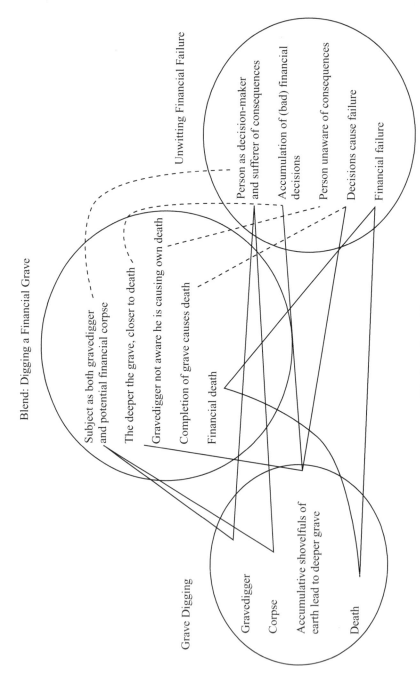

Blend: Digging a Financial Grave

Unwitting Financial Failure

Person as decision-maker
and sufferer of consequences

Accumulation of (bad) financial
decisions

Person unaware of consequences

Decisions cause failure

Financial failure

Subject as both gravedigger
and potential financial corpse

The deeper the grave, closer to death

Gravedigger not aware he is causing own death

Completion of grave causes death

Financial death

Grave Digging

Gravedigger

Corpse

Accumulative shovelfuls of
earth lead to deeper grave

Death

5. Digging a financial grave

178

grave digging. What we have in this example of discourse is in fact a double-scope blend, with elements being projected from both the grave-digging and financial decision-making spaces into a third, blended space. Although Fauconnier and Turner do not map the blend, we might represent it as in Figure 5, with each of the circles representing a mental space, and the lines representing neuronal coactivation binding between elements within each space.[40]

In discussing this double-scope blend, Fauconnier and Turner note that many of its important features, such as agency, causality, and intentionality (indicated by dashed lines in the figure), come from input 2 (UNWITTING FINANCIAL FAILURE). That is, in literal grave digging one does not normally dig one's own grave, one could not be digging a grave without being *aware* that one was doing so, and completing a grave is not generally the direct cause of a person's death. It is, in fact, the financial decision-making space that is giving the blend this structure: in making a series of bad investments one is both the agent and recipient of one's actions, one can be making financial decisions without being aware of the consequences, and so forth. They argue that the point of recruiting input 1 (GRAVE DIGGING) to the blend is to aid apprehension of the situation by "achieving human scale" – that is, by giving the blend tight compression, such as one type of action versus many different types of action, or a short time frame versus an extended time frame. The result is the compression of a situation with diffuse temporality, complex causality, and many potential agents into a single scene that is easy to visualize: the single vivid image of "digging one's own grave" allows one to have a clearer grasp of both what one has been doing in the investment arena and what the consequences of this behavior might be.

Double-scope blends also allow one to account for metaphorical statements where the goal is clearly to set up a contrastive tension rather than impose a source to target domain mapping. Joseph Grady et al. (1999) note that the expression, "This surgeon is a butcher," is meant to convey that the surgeon in question is incompetent, but it is hard to see how this could be the result of direct source to target domain projection: "a butcher, though less prestigious than a surgeon, is typically competent at what he does and may be highly respected. The notion of incompetence is not being projected from source to target" (103). The only way to understand this phrase is to see it as the contrastive blending of two input spaces: the frame of SURGERY, along with its roles (surgeon, patient) and goals (healing), and the frame of BUTCHERY, along with its roles (butcher, animal corpse) and goals (severing flesh). As they explain,

In butchery, the goal of the procedure is to kill the animal and then sever its flesh from its bones. By contrast, the default goal in surgery is to heal the patient. In the blended space, the means of BUTCHERY have been combined with the ends, the individuals and

---

[40] In the interest of space saving, the fourth element (Generic Space) customarily portrayed in blend mappings will be omitted.

the surgical context of the Surgery space. The incongruity of the butcher's means with the surgeon's ends leads to the central inference that the [surgeon] is incompetent. (106)

The Surgeon as Butcher metaphoric blend thus represents a novel, emergent structure, where a person with the goal of a surgeon (healing) employs the means of a butcher, with vividly imaginable results. This novel image is attained through the blended juxtaposition of two incompatible spaces rather than, as conceptual metaphor theory would predict, the unidirectional structuring of one space in terms of another.

BLENDING AND HUMAN CREATIVITY

Single-scope blends – accurately represented by simple source to target domain mappings – remain constrained by the input or source domain: structure is projected to a new domain, but no new structure is created. Many scholars have observed that true human creativity would seem to require selective and novel recombination of conceptual units. As Steven Pinker has noted, the most salient feature of human thought is its potential for infinite expansion, which in turn appears to be related to the human brain's combinatorial power. This is most obvious in natural language use, where a finite vocabulary combined with a fairly modest set of grammatical principles enables even the most prosaic human being on the planet to utter completely novel expressions on a daily basis, and allows a finite system to encompass everything from recipes for black bean chili to beat poetry to vernacular Roman Catholic masses. This combinatorial power of the brain goes beyond language, however, to include nonverbal, analogous schemas. Pinker speculates that sensory-motor systems for spatial or force reasoning could be "copied" and used as scaffolding for more abstract concepts – essentially the conceptual metaphor argument – but potentially in a piecemeal and recursively repeated fashion that sounds very much like the conceptual blending model:

Each part is built out of basic mental models or ways of knowing that are copied, bleached of their original content, connected to other models, and packaged into larger parts without limit. Because human thoughts are combinatorial and recursive, breathtaking expanses of knowledge can be explored with a finite inventory of mental tools. (1997: 360)

Michael Arbib similarly speaks of a "schema assemblage," a temporary "network of interacting schemas pulled together that represents the situation and gives you the knowledge to handle [a] new structure" (1985: 15).[41]

---

[41] Cf. Damasio's discussion of "convergence zones," where information from different modalities is integrated in the mind. "Convergence zones," Damasio observes, "can blend responses, that is, produce retroactivation of fragments that did not originally belong to the same experiential set" (1989: 47).

Blending theory provides us with a general model for how we might represent and trace this sort of selective recruitment and combination of schemas into novel conceptual structures. Indeed, Fauconnier and Turner argue that it is the development of the ability to create double-scope blends that accounts for Mithen's "cultural explosion," as well as for the origin of full-blown human language (2002: 180–187). To return to the "digging a financial grave" example discussed earlier, we can note that, even in a quite prosaic double-scope blend such as this, we have the creation of an entirely novel structure: a world in which one digs one's own grave, the process of digging contributes to one's death, and death itself is caused by completing the grave. There is nothing in our literal experience of the world that would allow us to entertain such a concept. This novel conclusion is the result of blending bits and pieces from distinct domains, and then "running the blend": allowing the inferences and background knowledge attached to these bits and pieces in their original domains to play themselves in this new, imaginary environment. The resulting knowledge obtained from the blend can then be reprojected back into the relevant input space: the purpose of the "digging one's own financial grave" blend, after all, is to draw a conclusion about financial decision making.

The same sort of blending analysis can also be used to trace the development of novel motor skills. Fauconnier and Turner argue that the process of acquiring a new motor skill, such as skiing, involves drawing on existing motor programs and recombining them – blending them – in a completely novel fashion. The primary job of someone trying to instruct another in the acquisition of a new physical skill – learning to ski, roll a kayak, flip an omelet – is, by means of physical modeling and verbal cues, to get the student to draw on the proper pieces of previously existing or easily imaginable motor programs and combine them in a predictable way with the physical environment. Fauconnier and Turner describe a revealing experience involving ski instruction:

One of us had a ski instructor who prompted him to stand properly and face in the right direction as he raced downhill by inviting him to imagine that he was a waiter in a Parisian café carrying a tray with champagne and croissants on it and taking care not to spill them. This might seem like a simple execution of a known pattern of bodily action – carrying a tray – in the context of skiing, but it is . . . not so: When we carry a tray, we create equilibrium by exerting force against the weight of the tray, but in skiing, there is no tray, no glassware, no weight. What counts are direction of gaze, position of the body, and overall motion . . . The instructor is astutely using a hidden analogy between a small aspect of the waiter's motion and the desired skiing position. Independent of the blend, however, this analogy would make little sense. (21)

Learning to successfully and consistently roll a sea kayak similarly draws on preexisting or imagined motor programs and movements that need to be recombined in an entirely counterintuitive manner: punching the paddle through the surface of the water, twisting the body-kayak unit like a corkscrew, letting the head hang back until the body-kayak pulls it up like a slingshot or "snaps" it into place. The role of the teacher is to encourage the creation of the proper motor blend through prompts aimed at a particular student.

This is one of the reasons that it is so hard to learn a new, complex skill like skiing or kayak-rolling from books: written instructions or diagrams on the page represent general blending prompts that have historically worked for large numbers of beginners, but genuinely mastering such complex skills requires real-time, finely calibrated correction. A physically present teacher can, through mirror neuron activation, create an instant model of the motor state of the student, compare this model with the desired end-state as embodied in the teacher's own motor programs, and offer precisely targeted corrective suggestions: "no, you need to keep your head farther back as you come up out of the water; imagine that the paddle has turned into some smelly, disgusting object and you're simultaneously pushing it away from you and throwing your head back to get away from it." Physical demonstrations also allow much more complete and vivid mirror neuron modeling on the student's part than do a series of two-dimensional drawings or photographs in a book. As in the case with conceptual metaphor, the "target" domain – the blended, physical skill that is the goal – also constrains what elements of the input are projected: in the skiing-waiter example, the waiter's gaze, hand-to-body posture, and certain aspects of balance are projected, but the bottle of champagne and the tray are not. The result is a novel, integrated motion that meshes well with the environment, and that draws on the original motor programs involved but is not identical to any one of them.

Seeing "As If"

Another phenomenon that can be easily explained with mental space theory, but is harder to get a handle on with conceptual metaphor theory, is the fact that most metaphors are at least potentially bracketed off from literal experience. To be sure, many primary metaphors like TIME IS SPACE, MORE IS UP, and so on appear to be a form of synaesthetic experience, where the two modalities are irrevocably experienced as linked. With more complex metaphors as well, such as the feeling of being emotionally "unbalanced" discussed earlier, the sensory-motor schema is often projected completely and experienced quite literally: one does not feel "like" one is emotionally unbalanced, one feels that one *is* emotionally unbalanced.

Even with such a basic and powerful metaphor as this, however, it is at least potentially possible to "pull back," as it were, and see the experience as metaphorical in a way that is impossible for someone who is literally, physically loaded down with unequal weights, for instance, or a grapheme-color synaesthetic who cannot help but see "5s" as purple. This is even more the case when it comes to many less common or novel metaphors, such as "Juliet is the sun," where the mappings set up

by the metaphor are from the beginning very clearly bracketed. This sort of bracketing or marking makes perfect sense in terms of blending theory, where single-
and double-scope blends involve not irrevocable "seeing-as," but the creation of a
separate "seeing-as-if" space that is clearly delineated from both the input spaces
and perceptual reality.

As already mentioned, Jerry Fodor, Steven Mithen, and others portray the
"human passion for analogy and metaphor" (Fodor 1983) as a fundamental challenge to the strongly modular view of the human mind that we reviewed in
Chapter 3. For instance, Mithen argues that cross-domain projection is "exactly
what [modularity advocates Cosmides & Tooby] argued should not happen in
evolution, since it can lead to all sorts of behavioral mistakes," such as taking a
plastic, symbolic representation of a banana for the real thing (1996: 60). As we can
see now, though, mental space and blending theory make it clear that we are not
confronted with a stark choice between a rigidly modular mind and a completely
unconstrained general-purpose processor. The ability of the human mind to create
"as-if" spaces explains quite easily why the sort of confusion mentioned by Mithen
does not happen: when we are interacting with a plastic banana, it is not that
we are functioning at a domain-general level of abstract metarepresentation, but
rather that we can allow domain-specific modular processes to play out in spaces
that are clearly marked as not real.[42] The existence of plastic representations of
bananas is no more a challenge to modularity than our ability to imagine things
that are not currently in front of us: no one would deny that color processing is
modular simply because I can imagine what my living room wall might look like
if it were red instead of green. Imagined sensory perception is marked as such by
being segregated into an "as-if" space, and symbolic representations are no different. The mechanisms of mental space creation and single- and double-scope
blending thus allow the strongly modular human mind to continue to enjoy the
benefits of modular processing while simultaneously transcending the limits of
rigid modularity.

The human ability to construct "as-if" spaces also allows us to entertain complex
counterfactuals and conditionals,[43] often to elicit feelings or draw important social
conclusions. Fauconnier and Turner argue that the ability to entertain counterfactual conditionals is the key to causal reasoning, scientific hypothesis formation,
and all forms of everyday and political decision making (2002: 217–247), and this
ability in turn rests on being able to "run" hypothetic blends in a space safely segregated from accepted perceptual or historical reality. This computational advantage

---

[42] This is, incidentally, why children are not troubled by animated cartoons, the surreality of which –
as Mithen observes (1996: 50) – might be expected to terrify them. Children are fully aware that
cartoons are just cartoons, safely segregating them into an "as-if" space. A genuine exploding cat
would not be greeted with the same sort of equanimity and amusement.

[43] See Fauconnier 1997: 99–130 and Coulson 2001: 203–219 on counterfactuals, and Sweetser 1990:
113–131 and Dancygier & Sweetser 2005 on conditionals from a blending perspective.

is subserved by our ability to create mental spaces. As Fauconnier and Turner note, "The great evolutionary change that produced cognitively modern human beings was a matter of evolving an organism that could run offline cognitive simulations so that evolution did not have to undertake the tedious process of natural selection every time a choice has to be made" (2002: 217).[44]

Fauconnier (1996) describes a small but wonderful example of counterfactual reasoning in the form of a dialogue from the movie *The Naked Lie* (1989).

In the movie, a prostitute has been found murdered. Webster, an unpleasant, self-centered character, shows no sympathy, and Victoria disagrees with Webster.

VICTORIA: What if it were your sister?

WEBSTER: I don't have a sister, but if I did, she wouldn't be a hooker.

Later in the movie, Victoria is talking to someone else:

VICTORIA: You know that sister Webster doesn't have? Well, she doesn't know how lucky she is. (76)

The reader is referred to Fauconnier 1996: 76–80 for the complex mapping of individuals and roles from input spaces onto counterfactual spaces that is involved in comprehending even these short snippets of dialogue. It is not difficult to see at a glance, however, both the imaginative power of these blends and the cognitive work being done. Sympathy is elicited, sympathy is blocked, and finally repugnance is expressed with the sort of eloquence and rhetorical power that is produced by a clever cross-space tension: a nonexistent sister portrayed as being lucky by virtue of "her" very nonexistence.

One human activity that crucially involves offline simulation is the phenomenon of "play." Anyone who has spent time around children knows that humans become capable of creating very complex "pretend" worlds at an early age – involving vast worlds of "as-if" social roles, "as-if" locations, and "as-if" objects – and appear to find "running these blends" incredibly appealing.[45] The fact that human children are so driven to spontaneously create and participate in imaginary worlds – the desire to play ranks alongside the desire to eat and sleep – gives some sense of its adaptive advantageousness. Considering its advantages, it is also not surprising that other organisms besides humans appear to have developed at least a limited ability to create "as-if" spaces in their minds. Many mammal species, for instance, engage in play fighting and other forms of "as-if" behavior (Bekoff & Byers 1998), and – as discussed in Chapter 3 – there is evidence that chimpanzees, corvids, and perhaps other species are capable of modeling the belief-spaces of others.

---

[44] Many other scholars have similarly noted the adaptive advantage of being able to work with "as-if" spaces; see Dawkins 1976/2006: 59, Damasio 1994: 156, and Dennett 1995: 374–377.

[45] See Humphrey 1986, Leslie 1987, and Baron-Cohen 1995 on play and pretense as practice for modeling other minds, and Steen & Owens 2001 on "rough and tumble" and "chase" play as a cognitive adaptation allowing mammals to practice dangerous skills in a safe, "as-if" space.

BLENDS AND THE RECRUITMENT AND TRANSFORMATION
OF EMOTION

One of the more important targets of blend-based innovation is arguably the way we feel. If Damasio and others are correct about the crucial role of emotion in human decision making and reasoning, we would expect that the recruitment and selective retargeting of emotions would be a major purpose of blend creation. Although Fauconnier and Turner argue that the primary function of blends is to "achieve human scale" in order to better apprehend an abstract or causally diffuse situation, it would appear that we often construct blends with emotional manipulation rather than dispassionate apprehension in mind.

To illustrate this fact, let us return to the "Digging a Financial Grave" blend example diagrammed in Figure 5, where the GRAVE DIGGING input was presented as a human-scale organizing frame. In considering this blend at more length, one might begin to wonder precisely how urgent the need to achieve human scale is in this situation, or how the GRAVE DIGGING input would be much help in this regard, if abstract apprehension were our main concern. Although not ideally human scale, the process of financial decision making is not terribly abstract or complex, and human beings seem perfectly capable of reasoning about it literally. This concern is heightened by the fact that, in this blend, all of the relevant *intellectual* decision-making information – agency, intentionality, causality – is coming from the UNWITTING FINANCIAL FAILURE space, which makes it puzzling why one would need to involve GRAVE DIGGING at all in one's deliberations. GRAVE DIGGING not only contributes nothing to the abstract structure of the target of the blend (financial decision making), but in many respects it is also actively *incompatible* with it in terms of agency, intentionality, and causality. Drawing on GRAVE DIGGING as an input to the blend, despite its potential usefulness in creating a slightly tighter compression, would thus seem at first glance to be profoundly maladaptive if the point is simply better apprehension of the situation.

This puzzling feature is characteristic, upon analysis, of many single- and double-scope blends. This suggests that, in many cases, the primary purpose of employing a metaphoric blend to achieve human scale is not to help us intellectually *apprehend* a situation, but rather to help us to know how to *feel* about it. This is where Damasio's theory of somatic marking, explored in Chapter 1, can be so helpful for cognitive linguistics. The apparently clumsy choice of GRAVE DIGGING as an input becomes decidedly less so when we think of its recruitment as designed, not to provide tighter structure per se, but rather to invoke the negative, *visceral* reactions (indicated by bold caps in Figure 6) inspired in human beings by graves, corpses, and death, and thereby to project these *somatic markers* (bold lines) onto the blend.[46]

---

[46] Coulson makes a related point in her discussion of this blend by noting that one possible reason for recruiting the grave-digging space is that it "hyperbolically conveys the seriousness of the target domain situation" (2001 : 170) and thus "might plausibly subserve motivational ends" (201).

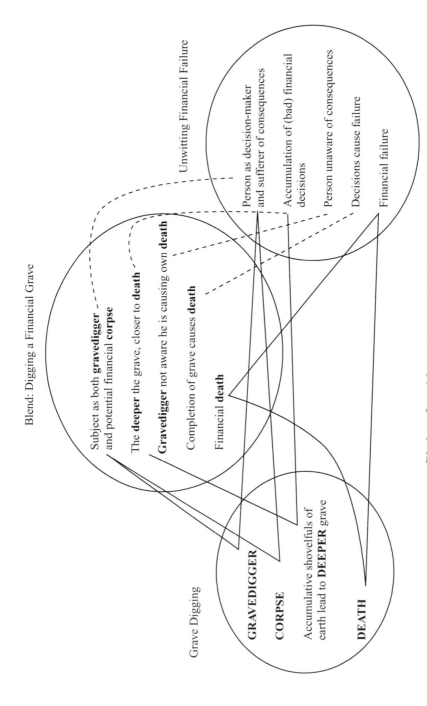

Blend: Digging a Financial Grave

Unwitting Financial Failure

Person as decision-maker
and sufferer of consequences

Accumulation of (bad) financial
decisions

Person unaware of consequences

Decisions cause failure

Financial failure

Subject as both **gravedigger**
and potential financial **corpse**

The **deeper** the grave, closer to **death**

Gravedigger not aware he is causing own **death**

Completion of grave causes **death**

Financial **death**

Grave Digging

GRAVEDIGGER

CORPSE

Accumulative shovelfuls of
earth lead to **DEEPER** grave

DEATH

6. Digging a financial grave (emotional implications)

186

For instance, consider the projection of "accumulated shovelfuls of earth lead to deeper grave" (from input 1) into the blend: each financial decision is now a shovelful of earth, making the financial grave that much deeper, bringing the subject that much closer to financial death. The point is to get listeners to "live in the blend" by associating the unpleasant visceral connotations of a frightening grave being dug deeper and deeper into the earth with, for instance, each additional purchase they make of Cisco Systems stock. The purpose here is not necessarily to help the recipient of the blend to better apprehend the situation intellectually – they presumably already know that they have lost a lot of money on Cisco, and that the stock price is not likely to recover anytime soon – but rather to help them know how to *feel* about it, to convey a sense of impending doom and thereby goad them into making the decision to immediately cease their current activities. The author of the blend has a very particular normative position to communicate (continued investment in Cisco is *bad*), and attempts to communicate this judgment through the exploitation of powerful, negative somatic marking. If the blend is accepted by the recipient, the choice is clear – no one wants to end up in the grave. This highlights a feature of blends that is not sufficiently emphasized: they are not simply normatively neutral devices for accurately apprehending situations, but are in fact often created and communicated in order to advance particular normative agendas, which they accomplish through the stimulation of predictable visceral reactions.[47]

We can see this even more clearly in another blend discussed by Fauconnier and Turner, that of a senator accused of "snatching food out of the mouths of hungry children" by vetoing an aid bill (2002: 313). They argue that the point of this particular blend is to achieve human scale and help the listener apprehend the situation: the vetoing of the bill and its causal implications are somewhat abstract, long-term, and indirect – not at all at a human scale – whereas snatching food from children is an immediately comprehensible scene. Again, though, the point seems to be not so much to allow listeners to understand more clearly, but rather to inspire them to *feel* a certain way: to feel anger, revulsion, and a righteous desire to stop or remedy the situation. The blend thus serves a polemic purpose, communicating a particular normative orientation by recruiting the fairly invariable effects of somatic markers: *any* undamaged human agent will be gripped by revulsion and anger at the sight (or imagined sight) of food being snatched by a powerful, well-fed adult from the mouth of a hungry, helpless child. If we accept the blend, we are then committed to feeling anger and revulsion concerning the senator's vote. By the same token, supporters of the senator's policy will dispute the accuracy of the blend, no doubt suggesting alternate framings of the situation – for instance, by vetoing the aid bill, the senator is in fact helping dependent Third World peoples learn how to "stand on their own feet."

---

[47] The role of affect has not been entirely neglected in the literature on blending; see Fauconnier & Turner (2002: 66–67, 82–83) and especially Seana Coulson (2001).

Blends *do* guide reasoning, and in very particular directions chosen by the creators of the blend, but often by means of inspiring normativity-bestowing emotional reactions. This is why metaphoric blends are arguably *the* primary tool
in political and religious-moral debate, where human scale inputs are recruited
polemically to inspire somatic-emotional normative reactions in the listeners.
Acceptance of the validity of such blends inevitably commits the listener to a
certain course of action (or, at least, a *potential* course of action), and this effect
can be reliably predicted by the blend author because of the relatively fixed nature
of human emotional-somatic reactions. Recast in terms of blending theory, the
goal of recruiting somatic markers can also be seen as the primary motivating force
behind the centrality – noted earlier – of conceptual metaphor (i.e., single-scope
blends) in political debate.

An Example from Ancient China

Another advantage that blending analysis possesses compared to conceptual
metaphor analysis is that it allows us to trace the construction of complex blended
spaces that are built up over the course of a discourse or conversation. Following
this process of blend creation "on the fly," as it were, gives us a sense of how the
recruitment of normativity is a dynamic affair, involving not merely the selection
of appropriate input spaces but also the creative and finely targeted invocation
of "counterinputs" in response to blends created by an argumentative opponent.
I would like to illustrate this process by considering two rather simple examples
drawn from a text in my field of specialty, the fourth-century B.C.E. Chinese Confucian work called the *Mencius*. This will not only provide a concrete example of
the dynamic creation and alteration of blends during argumentation, but it will
also help support the claim that these cognitive processes are universal for human
beings by showing them at work in a text written in classical Chinese approximately
twenty-five hundred years ago.

Book Six of the *Mencius* opens with a famous set of debates between Mencius and
a figure named Gaozi on the topic of human nature, which has obvious relevance to
the issue of how to teach people to be moral. Gaozi has traditionally been viewed
as a follower of Mozi, an early Chinese thinker who believed that much of the
suffering in the world was caused by human beings' selfish, partial tendencies –
for instance, their inclination to favor themselves over others, or their family and
friends above other people's families and friends. Although Mozi believed these
selfish tendencies to be inborn, he also thought that it was possible for humans
to be shown logically the value of caring for everyone equally (his doctrine of
"impartial caring"), which would then persuade them to abandon their natural
selfishness and to force themselves to begin acting impartially. In contrast to the
Mohist position, preferential treatment for family members (especially parents)
was one of the hallmarks of Confucian culture, which Mencius was very much

interested in defending. In the Confucian view, preferential love for one's family is not only a part of human beings' natural inclinations, but also normatively positive – the basis, for instance, of filial piety, the most fundamental of Confucian virtues. Moreover, the Confucians were skeptical about the strong "voluntaristic" aspect of Mohist education. That is, they believed that any sort of sustainable ethical action had to arise from emotional dispositions, and that mere cognitive assent was insufficient motivation for human beings to radically go against their natural tendencies.

The first of these passages begins with Gaozi's opening claim that "Human nature is like the *qi* willow. Morality is like cups and bowls. To make morality out of human nature is like making cups and bowls out of the willow tree." This statement sets up a double-scope blend that can be mapped as in Figure 7.

Here, human beings' partial caring for their parents is portrayed as a raw material that is fundamentally reshaped by the "tool" of the doctrine of impartial caring. The result is a beautiful artifact bearing little resemblance to the original, crude material, and the shape this artifact is determined by the doctrine-tool. While most of the structure of this blend is imported from the CRAFT PRODUCTION space, it is double-scope because one important aspect of the causality (indicated by the heavy dashed line) is derived from the MORAL EDUCATION space: although in craft production it is the artisan who determines the shape of the product (wielding the tool in accordance with his or her design), the behavior-determining importance of the doctrine of impartial caring prevails in the blend, resulting in a situation where it is the tool, rather than the artisan, that determines the shape of the "moral artifact." Gaozi's primary purpose in constructing this blend is to get his listener to take the positive feelings that one has toward beautiful, finely carved artifacts – as well as the corresponding negative feelings toward crude, unshaped raw material – and project these onto the project of neo-Mohist moral education. The inborn human feeling of partial love for one's parents is ugly and crude, whereas impartial caring toward all is beautiful and refined.

Mencius's response is as follows:

Can you follow (lit. "flow with") the nature of the willow in making your cups and bowls? Or is it in fact the case that you will have to mutilate[48] the willow before you can make it into cups and bowls? If you have to mutilate the willow to make it into cups and bowls, must you then also mutilate people to make them moral? Misleading the people of the world into bringing disaster upon morality – surely this describes the effects of your doctrine!

This is a wonderful example of conceptual blending jujitsu: Mencius takes Gaozi's blend and then sets up two new spaces to counteract it, those of LIVING THING and of WATER. We can map this modified blend as in Figure 8.

---

[48] *Qiang'zei*; lit. to "steal" or "rob" the nature of willow tree.

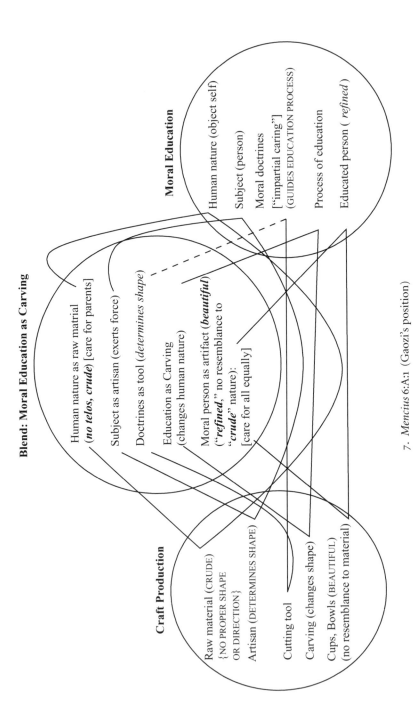

Blend: Moral Education as Carving

Moral Education

Human nature (object self)

Subject (person)

Moral doctrines
["impartial caring"]
(GUIDES EDUCATION PROCESS)

Process of education

Educated person (*refined*)

Human nature as raw matrial
(*no telos, crude*) [care for parents]

Subject as artisan (exerts force)

Doctrines as tool (*determines shape*)

Education as Carving
(changes human nature)

Moral person as artifact (*beautiful*)
("*refined*," no resemblance to
"*crude*" nature):
[care for all equally]

Craft Production

Raw material (CRUDE)
{NO PROPER SHAPE
OR DIRECTION}

Artisan (DETERMINES SHAPE)

Cutting tool

Carving (changes shape)

Cups, Bowls (BEAUTIFUL)
(no resemblance to material)

7. *Mencius* 6:A:1 (Gaozi's position)

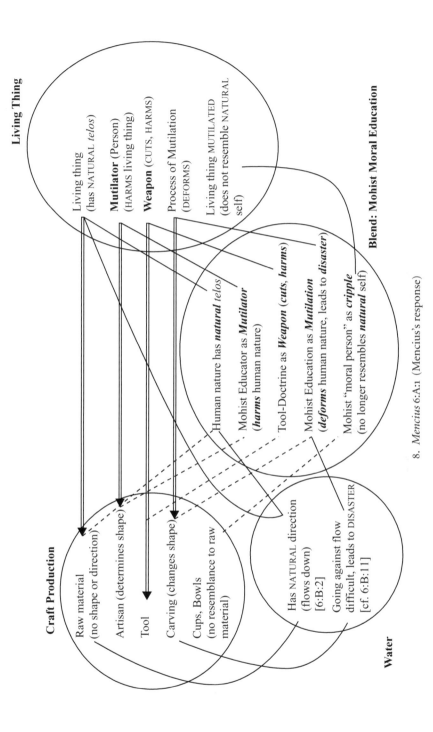

Living Thing

Living thing (has NATURAL *telos*)

Mutilator (Person) (HARMS living thing)

Weapon (CUTS, HARMS)

Process of Mutilation (DEFORMS)

Living thing MUTILATED (does not resemble NATURAL self)

Blend: Mohist Moral Education

Human nature has *natural telos*

Mohist Educator as *Mutilator* (*harms* human nature)

Tool-Doctrine as *Weapon* (*cuts*, *harms*)

Mohist Education as *Mutilation* (*deforms* human nature, leads to *disaster*)

Mohist "moral person" as *cripple* (no longer resembles *natural* self)

Craft Production

Raw material (no shape or direction)

Artisan (determines shape)

Tool

Carving (changes shape)

Cups, Bowls (no resemblance to raw material)

Has NATURAL direction (flows down) [6:B:2]

Going against flow difficult, leads to DISASTER [cf. 6:B:11]

Water

8. *Mencius* 6:A:1 (Mencius's response)

191

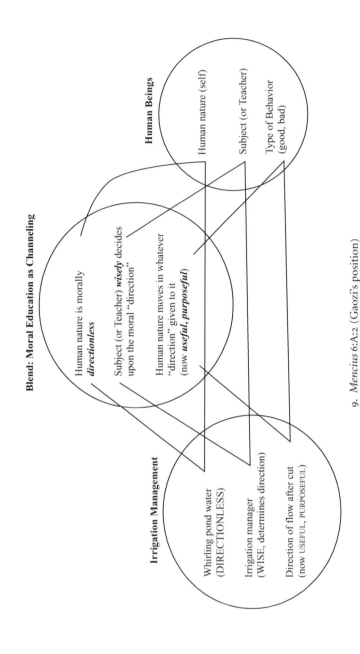

Blend: Moral Education as Channeling

Human Beings

Human nature (self)

Subject (or Teacher)

Type of Behavior (good, bad)

Human nature is morally *directionless*

Subject (or Teacher) *wisely* decides upon the moral "direction"

Human nature moves in whatever "direction" given to it (now *useful, purposeful*)

Irrigation Management

Whirling pond water (DIRECTIONLESS)

Irrigation manager (WISE, determines direction)

Direction of flow after cut (now USEFUL, PURPOSEFUL)

9. *Mencius* 6:A:2 (Gaozi's position)

192

The introduction of these two new spaces has a dramatic effect on the blend. The Living Thing space as Mencius constructs it maps quite nicely onto the Craft Production space, but in an entirely *disanalogous* fashion (represented by the large arrows). The shapeless raw material is now compared to a living thing with an innate *telos*, which, in turn, transforms the skillful artisan of Gaozi's blend into a cruel mutilator, his useful tool into a harmful weapon, and the process of carving into a act of unnatural deformation. Mencius is no doubt counting on the negative visceral reactions inspired by these images of cutting into a living being, causing it pain, and inflicting mutilation. In this way, he effectively subverts Gaozi's blend by transforming the original projections from the Craft Production to the blend space (dashed lines) into normatively strongly negative ones: the product of the neo-Mohist process of education is now portrayed as a tortured moral cripple rather than a skillfully formed artifact.[49] For good measure, he adds the Water space to the blend, which both reinforces the negative connotations of going against the natural "flow" and sets up the transition to 6:A:2.

Mencius 6:A:2 finds Gaozi picking up on Mencius's water imagery and attempting to turn it to his own rhetorical advantage, switching to the domain of irrigation management to make the Mohist point: "Human nature is like a whirlpool. Cut a channel to the east and it will flow east; cut a channel to the west and it will flow west. The lack of a tendency toward good or bad in human nature is just like water's lack of a preference for east or west." If we assume the entrenched metaphor, Type of Behavior as Direction, Gaozi's statement here can be mapped as a rather straightforward single-scope blend, as in Figure 9.

With his craft metaphor of 6:A:1 foiled by Mencius's introduction of the Living Thing and Water spaces, Gaozi attempts to make his point by switching to a different domain, that of Water Management. The normative point here is also the same as in 6:A:1: just as crude raw material needs to be shaped by a craftsperson to become beautiful, directionless whirling water in an irrigation pond needs to be directed by a wise manager if the water is to be brought to the proper place.

The fact that the book is called the *Mencius*, and not the *Gaozi*, should prepare us to see Gaozi's efforts to turn the rhetorical tables on Mencius be thwarted. As in 6:A:1, Mencius responds by subverting Gaozi's metaphor:

Water certainly does not distinguish between East or West, but does it fail to distinguish between up and down? The goodness of human nature is like the downhill movement of water – there is no person who is not good, just as there is no water that does not flow downward.

---

[49] Cf. Seana Coulson's analysis of the "Menendez Brothers" computer virus joke – which "eliminates your files, takes the disk space they previously occupied, and then claims it was a victim of physical and sexual abuse on the part of the files it erased" – (2001:179–185), where the point of the construct is to take an emergent inference derived from the blend and project it back onto one of the input spaces.

Now, as for water, if you strike it with your hand and cause it to splash up, you can make it go above your forehead; if you apply force and pump it, you can make it go uphill. Is this really the nature of water, though? No, it is merely the result of environmental influences. That a person can be made bad shows that his nature can also be altered like this.

Here Mencius subverts Gaozi's blend not by adding new spaces, but by mapping elements of an existing input that Gaozi "missed": water has no preference for east or west, but it certainly has a natural preference for traveling downhill. We can map Mencius's response as in Figure 10.[50]

Mencius's response here nicely shows how deciding the relevant features of an input is a very arguable process – focusing on new elements can give an entirely different quality to the blend. Instead of focusing on a whirling pool's potential to be channeled in whatever direction is determined by the irrigation manager, Mencius uses the WATER space to introduce teleological and normatively charged features: the natural, "internal" tendency of water is to flow downhill, and to go against this tendency requires the application of external force. Although it is possible under certain circumstances to make water flow uphill, this requires a huge expenditure of force and is ultimately unsustainable – going "against the flow" of nature-heaven is bound to lead to failure. This image is reinforced by another passage later in the book, 6:B:11, where Mencius extols the achievements of the great sage-king Yu, who tamed the Yellow River and made China habitable by wisely following the tendencies of nature – gently guiding the rivers into new channels and helping them along to the sea – as opposed to the evil and stupid flood-control managers of Mencius's own day, who go "against the flow," attempting to crudely block and radically redirect the natural flows of China's rivers and thus bringing disaster to everyone. The harm caused by Yu's counterparts in Mencius's age is analogous to the injury caused by the Mohists and their educational strategy that fails to "flow along with" human nature.

Antonio Damasio has observed that, although human emotional reactions are fixed, the stimuli that can trigger them are not necessarily fixed: "the range of stimuli that can potentially induce emotions is infinite" (2000: 58). Blending analysis provides us with a specific tool for tracing the manner in which basic emotional reactions can be harnessed and attached to novel stimuli. Somatic marking works by attaching emotional-normative weight to particular images. These attachments in their original form are probably relatively fixed for organisms such as ourselves – darkness, pollution, and physical debility are always marked with negative emotions and therefore felt as "bad" – and this is what one would expect from evolution:

---

[50] This mapping is simplified by not including the entrenched CONTAINER and ESSENCE metaphors, triggered by the mention of "environmental influences" whereby external, environmental causes are understood as "unnatural," and natural behavior (behavior in accordance with the ESSENCE) is the result of inner causality.

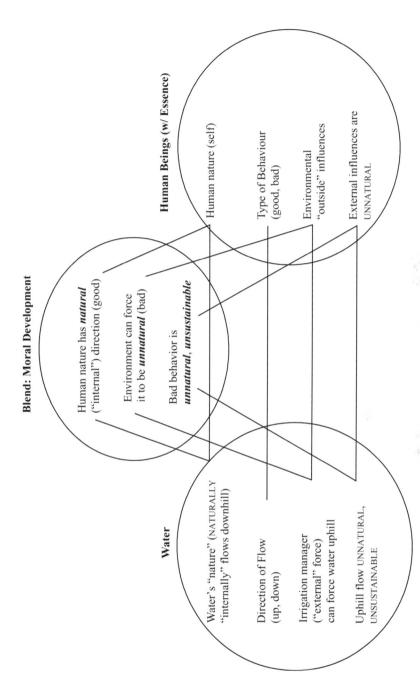

10. *Mencius* 6:A:2 (Mencius's response)

195

potential ancestors infused with warm, fuzzy feelings at the sight of putrefying meat were quickly taken out of the gene pool. The ability of the human-mind to perform conceptual blending, however, means that these relatively fixed "human scale" visceral reactions can be recruited for a potentially infinite variety of purposes, including the conscious exploitation of somatic markers by skilled rhetoricians in order to advance their own agendas.

MULTIPLE-SCOPE BLENDS AND THE ACCUMULATION OF
DIFFERENCE: *MENCIUS* 2:A:2

Certain blends, like the "Digging a Financial Grave" blend discussed earlier, are formed for momentary rhetorical purposes and then abandoned. In other cases, incredibly elaborate multiple-scope blends – blends that acquire structure from a number of independent and partially overlapping input domains – can be built up over the course of even quite short discourses. These blended spaces can quickly grow staggeringly complex, with multiple input spaces selectively projecting structure into an increasingly nuanced target, giving us a sense of how much variety can be created in a short space of time.

I would like to return to the *Mencius* in order to provide an illustration of this phenomenon, focusing on a famous passage, 2:A:2. In this passage Mencius is defending Confucianism not only against Mohists such as Gaozi but also against the so-called Primitivist school, which believed that moral self-cultivation and society should be entirely abandoned so that people might return to some primordial, "natural" way of life. Mencius's goal in this passage is to demonstrate the superiority of what he saw as an intermediate model of moral self-cultivation, involving some effort to become moral, but not "unnatural" effort that would involve going against our inborn natures. We will analyze 2:A:2 in a series of three stages, showing the manner in which a blend is gradually expanded, because it serves as a nice illustration of how complex, multiscope blends are built up over the course of a conversation, resulting in quite novel and idiosyncratic structures.

Stage 1

Mencius 2:A:2 begins with a disciple asking Mencius whether or not the prospect of being given a high official position, and thus being able to put the Confucian Way into action, would cause any "stirring" in his heart/mind. Mencius replies that since the age of forty he has possessed a "heart/mind that does not stir," which in itself is not a terribly difficult achievement, since (he says) Gaozi achieved such a heart/mind even before he did. A discussion of various types of courage follows. Eventually – and more to the point of this discussion – the disciple asks, "I wonder if I could get to hear something about the master's heart/mind that does not stir as compared to that of Gaozi?" Mencius then explains the difference between his own and Gaozi's views about "where one gets it" – that is, where one derives one's sense of what is morally right. The basic background model of the self that is assumed by all participants in this discussion involves both the "heart/mind" (*xin*) and the *qi*.[51] *Xin* refers literally to the organ of the heart, which was understood by the Chinese of Mencius's time as being the seat of thought, language use, and conscious will (hence "mind"), as well as certain normatively positive emotions (hence "heart"). *Qi* refers to a kind of vital energy that was thought to animate all living beings. The influence of doctrines on the individual was understood to be mediated by the heart/mind, which in the Mohist view was able to receive direction from doctrine and then impose this direction on the irrational *qi*. As we will see shortly, although he agrees with Gaozi that one cannot find moral guidance in the animalistic *qi*, Mencius also thinks it is mistake to look to "external" doctrines.

Mencius's initial response to the disciple is as follows:

"Gaozi says, 'If you fail to get it from doctrine, do not look for it in your heart/mind; if you fail to get it from your heart/mind, do not look for it in your *qi*.' It is acceptable to say that one should not look for it in the *qi* after failing to get it from the heart/mind, but it is not acceptable to say that one should not look for it in the heart/mind when one fails to get it from doctrine. As for the intention, it is the commander of the *qi*, whereas the *qi* is that which fills the body. The intention is of utmost importance, whereas the *qi* is secondary. Hence it is said, 'Grasp firmly to your intention and do not do violence to your *qi*.'"

"You just said that the intention is of utmost importance, while the *qi* is secondary. What, then, is the point of going on to say, 'Grasp firmly to your intention and do not do violence to your *qi*?'"

"When the intention is unified it moves the *qi*, and yet when the *qi* is unified it can also move the intention. For instance, stress and hurry move the *qi* [here: lit. breath], and yet this in turn moves the heart/mind [here: lit. organ]."

We might map the blend at this point of the conversation as in Figure 11.

Mencius begins by invoking a MILITARY LEADERSHIP metaphor to conceptualize the relationship of the heart/mind to the *qi*. The heart/mind – in the form of the "intention," a word that refers to the heart/mind when it has a particular orientation – is likened to a general, the *qi* to troops. This sets up a clear hierarchy: a general is obviously more important than the troops, because the job of the commander is to give guidance to his troops, who, left to their own devices, would simply mill about in confusion. Indeed, in several other passages Mencius notes the dangers of letting the *qi* run uncontrolled, in which case it will fixate on external things. It is necessary, then, for the heart/mind to guide and restrain the *qi*, and this accords with Mencius's approval of the maxim, "if one does not get it in the heart/mind, do not look for it in the *qi*." On the other hand, an entailment of the INTENTION AS GENERAL metaphor is that the intention/heart/mind is also

---

[51]   More familiar to some readers in the older Romanization style as "ch'i."

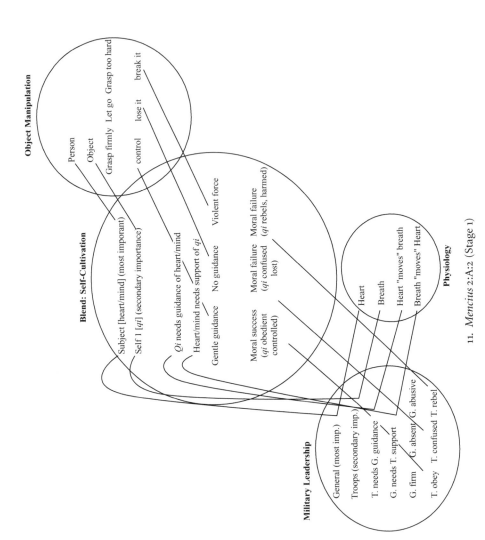

Object Manipulation

Person
Object
Grasp firmly Let go Grasp too hard
control lose it break it

Blend: Self-Cultivation

Subject [heart/mind] (most important)
Self 1 [*qi*] (secondary importance)
Qi needs guidance of heart/mind
Heart/mind needs support of *qi*
Gentle guidance No guidance Violent force

Moral success
(*qi* obedient
controlled)

Moral failure Moral failure
(*qi* confused (*qi* rebels, harmed)
lost)

Physiology

Heart
Breath
Heart "moves" breath
Breath "moves" Heart

Military Leadership

General (most imp.)
Troops (secondary imp.)
T. needs G. guidance
G. needs T. support
G. firm G. absent G. abusive
T. obey T. confused T. rebel

11. *Mencius* 2:A:2 (Stage 1)

198

somewhat dependent on the *qi*, because a general cannot fight a battle without his troops. This means he must guide them firmly but gently – excessive force or abuse will cause the troops to rebel. This INTENTION AS GENERAL metaphor also possesses entailments that reinforce the idea that Mencian self-cultivation, in contrast to Mohist education, cannot result in the kind of forcible reshaping described by Gaozi's metaphor of carving bowls in 6:A:1. Just as a spring arises gradually and spontaneously from a source, a general – no matter how convinced he may be personally that it is imperative to move from point A to point B – still needs to marshal his troops and gradually get them moving in the direction that he orders.

This theme is then clarified and reinforced in Mencius's response by the addition of the OBJECT MANIPULATION space: in order to properly hold an object (= troops = *qi*), a person (= general = heart/mind) must grasp it firmly (= general's "firm" control of troops = heart/mind's control of the *qi*), without letting it go (= general's not commanding troops = heart/mind not directing the *qi*), but also without gripping it so tightly as to damage it (= general's abuse of troops = heart/mind forcing *qi*). Finally, this mutual dependence of the heart/mind and *qi* is reinforced by the concrete, physiological observation that "stumbling and hurrying impact the *qi*, yet this in turn moves the heart/mind" – with both terms meant in the very literal senses of the "breath" (*qi*) and the physical organ of the heart. This literal dependence of the heart/mind on the *qi* thus serves as a physiological or medical metaphor for a more profound, metaphysical dependence.

Stage 2

It is clear from the blend at this point why Mencius agrees with Gaozi that one cannot obtain moral guidance from the *qi*, for this would be like allowing the troops to run the battle or trying to hold onto an object without grasping it firmly enough with the hand. At the same time, Mencius also has begun to make his point that Gaozi is wrong about getting moral guidance from doctrines: trying to impose an external doctrine on the heart/mind would be as counterproductive as applying excessive force with the hand or abusing one's troops. The metaphorical reasoning behind Mencius's position is then further clarified in the next step in the argument:

The disciple asked, "May I ask about the master's strong points?"

"I understand doctrines, and I am good at cultivating my flood-like *qi*."

"May I ask what the 'flood-like *qi*' is?"

"It is difficult to explain in words. As a form of *qi*, it is the most expansive and unyielding. If it is cultivated with uprightness and not harmed, it will fill the space between Heaven and Earth. It is the form of *qi* that accompanies rightness and the Way. Without these it will starve. It is something produced only by an accumulation of rightness; it is not something that can be acquired through a sporadic attempt at [lit. ambush of] rightness. The minute one's actions fail to please one's heart/mind, it will starve. This is why I said that Gaozi never understood rightness: because he looked upon it as something external.

We might update our rapidly growing blend as indicated in Figure 12.

A number of spaces are simultaneously introduced here, in a somewhat piece-meal fashion – a conceptual luxury that Mencius is allowed because some of these spaces have been invoked before and can therefore be assumed by his audience. I will treat them individually.

To begin with, the mention of a "flood-like" *qi* that can "accumulate" until it will "fill the space between Heaven and Earth" invokes the WATER MANAGEMENT space that we already saw in our discussion of 6:A:2. Mencius explains that there is a certain form of *qi* – the "flood-like" *qi* – that, when properly "cultivated," expands to fill the world and to "accompany rightness and accompany the Way." The manner in which this floodlike *qi* supports rightness and the Way is analogous to the manner in which *qi* in the more literal sense infuses the self with motive force – that is, conceptualized as a kind of hydraulic force, it provides the psychological and physical motivation to undertake acts that are right or are in accordance with the Way. This hydraulic image is not ad hoc. Throughout 2:A:2 Mencius is relying on a QI AS WATER metaphor derived from contemporary medical theories – whereby this vital force was thought to be a literal, though invisible, liquid that flowed through and energized the body – and this metaphor of *qi* as a vast hydraulic power source for moral behavior is, in fact, invoked throughout the text of the *Mencius*. In 4:B:14 it is combined with both ESSENTIAL SELF and "effortless action" metaphors:[52]

The gentleman is able to deeply immerse himself in the Way because he desires to get it himself. Getting it himself, he is able to dwell in it with ease; dwelling in it with ease, he can draw upon it deeply; drawing upon it deeply, he finds its source everywhere he turns. Thus the gentleman desires to get it himself.

Although 4:B:14 does not specifically mention the *qi*, the use of water imagery supplies the conceptual link, and the image of an innate resource upon which one can "draw deeply" ties in nicely with the concept of the flood-like *qi* mentioned here in 2:A:2. A similar idea is expressed in passages such as 7:A:21, where the Confucian virtues "rooted" in the heart/mind are described as being so perfectly developed in the gentleman that, "manifesting themselves in his countenance as a vigorous flush, they appear in his face, filling up his back and spreading through his four limbs, thus physically revealing their presence without the need for words." Additionally, the legendary king Shun's attainment of sagehood in 7:A:16 provides us with an image of what it might be like for one's "flood-like *qi*" to spontaneously,

[52] For more on the "effortless action" (*wuwei*) and ESSENTIAL SELF metaphors in early Chinese thought, see Slingerland 2003.

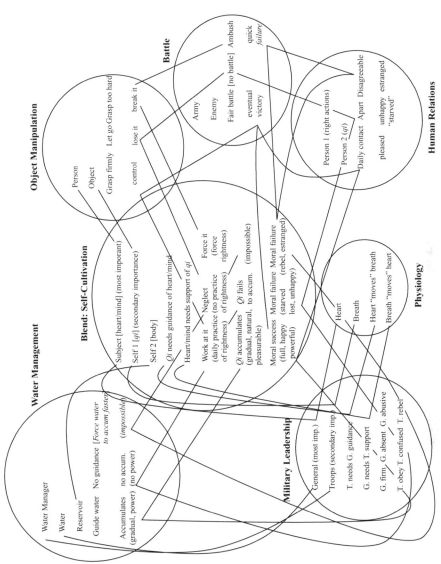

Water Management

Object Manipulation

Battle

Blend: Self-Cultivation

Physiology

Human Relations

Military Leadership

Water Manager
Water
Reservoir
Guide water   No guidance   [*Force water*
                              to accum faster]   (*impossible*)
Accumulates   no accum.
(gradual, power)   (no power)

Subject [heart/mind] (most important)
Self 1 [*qi*] (secondary importance)
Self 2 [body]
Qi needs guidance of heart/mind
Heart/mind needs support of *qi*
Work at it   Force it
(daily practice   (force
of rightness)   rightness)
Neglect
(no practice
of rightness)
Qi accumulates   *Qi* fails   (impossible)
(gradual, natural,   to accum.
pleasurable)
Moral success   Moral failure   Moral failure
(full, happy   (starved   (rebel, estranged)
powerful)   lost, unhappy)

Person
Object
Grasp firmly   Let go   Grasp too hard
control   lose it   break it

Army
Enemy
Fair battle   [no battle]   Ambush
eventual   *quick*
victory   *failure*

General (most imp.)
Troops (secondary imp.)
T. needs G. guidance
G. needs T. support
G. firm   G. absent   G. abusive
T. obey   T. confused   T. rebel

Heart
Breath
Heart "moves" breath
Breath "moves" heart

Person 1 (right actions)
Person 2 (*qi*)
Daily contact   Apart   Disagreeable
pleased   unhappy   estranged
                        "starved"

12. *Mencius* 2:A:2 (Stage 2)

effortlessly, and inexorably flow forth from the reservoir of the self: "When Shun lived in the depths of the mountains, he dwelled among the trees and stones, and roamed together with the deer and wild pigs. At that time, there was very little to distinguish him from the other uncouth hillbillies. But as soon as he heard his first good word and witnessed his first good deed, it was like opening a breach in the dyke of the Yangzi or the Yellow River – nothing could restrain the torrential force."

Although the exceptional sage-king Shun is here portrayed as having been born with a vast store of "flood-like *qi*" simply waiting to be unleashed, in 2:A:2 Mencius portrays the floodlike *qi* as a sort of reservoir of moral energy accumulated gradually over a period of time by a patient water manager. Some effort is required to create such a reservoir (by, for instance, damming a river), but there is nothing one can do to rush the accumulation of water. An interesting feature of complex space construction is that spaces set up early in a discourse often have a strong effect on the topology of spaces subsequently introduced. In this regard, we should observe that, in 2:A:2, the topology of the MILITARY LEADERSHIP and OBJECT MANIPULATION spaces guide the construction of the WATER MANAGEMENT space, encouraging the audience to imagine a similar set of three options and outcomes:

1.   Build a reservoir and wait for the water to accumulate gradually and naturally (result: overwhelming power source)
2.   Do nothing (result: no power accrued)
3.   [Force water to flow faster] (result: impossible)

Option 3 is not a feature of literal water management – it is hard to imagine an actual water manager expecting water to flow faster than it naturally does – but is instead a quality imposed on the input space by the topology of the previously constructed spaces, as manifested in the blend. Nonetheless, its presence in the network (however implicitly) has an effect: the absurdity of water flowing and accumulating at anything other than its natural rate now gets projected into the blend, joining the list of negative normative markers attached to the idea of trying to force morality.

We see a similar example of alien features being forced on a space in the invocation of the BATTLE SPACE. In literal battles, ambushes are actually quite effective, and often lead to victory. At this point in the conversation, however, the idea of a sudden "ambush" – which, because of the pressure of the blend network, now brings with it images of forcing something or trying to achieve a goal unusually quickly (in implicit contrast with an open, more gradual battle) – acquires the negative qualities already associated with its analogous topological slots in the blend, *speed* now being associated with failure and *gradualness* with success. What is gained in the blend by invoking the battle space is all of the normatively negative feelings associated with ambushes, where an inferior force can, through trickery, prevail over a superior force. In attempting to force people to be instantly good, then, the Mohists are trying to "ambush" rightness – certainly something no proper person could countenance.

The mention of "accompanying," "pleasing," and "starving" (for affection)[53] invoke the HUMAN RELATIONS space, with *qi* and "rightness" (here presumably referring to right actions, done in accordance with the moral "Way") conceptualized as metaphoric persons developing a sort of potentially close, affectionate relationship. The organization of this space is similarly forced by the preexisting topology of the network into a structure that possesses three options and outcomes:

1.   Regular, welcome contact (result: pleased, stay together)
2.   Lack of contact (result: unhappy, "starved")
3.   Forced contact (result: displeased, estranged, "starved")

This space recruits our knowledge of human relations to reinforce the desirability of gradualness and lack of force. Rightness cannot be forcibly imposed upon the *qi* (presumably by the heart/mind) any more than friendship or love can be forced. Any type of affectionate human relationship has to develop over time, through regular and welcome contact, in the same way – at least for those of us dwelling in the blend as it has been developed so far – that water in a reservoir must accumulate gradually, that a general must gently guide his troops, and that physical objects must be grasped firmly but not *too* firmly. All of the spaces invoked up to this point involve distinct image schemas and slightly different entailments, but they work together in reinforcing the central themes of the blend.

Stage 3

The entailments of the metaphors introduced up to this point in the conversation strongly support Mencius's argument that self-cultivation cannot be rushed in the Mohist fashion – that rightness cannot be "ambushed." To make the relationship between the intention and *qi* entirely clear, Mencius finally switches to the SELF-CULTIVATION AS AGRICULTURE metaphor in the final stage of the conversation, closing with the famous story of the foolish farmer from Song.

You must put some work into it, but you must not force it. Do not forget about the heart/mind entirely, but do not try to help it to grow either. Do not be like the man from Song. In Song there was a man who – worried because his sprouts of grain were not growing – decided to pull on them. Without any idea of what he had done he returned home and announced to his family, "I am terribly worn out today – I've been out helping the sprouts to grow!" His sons rushed out to the fields to take a look and saw that all the sprouts had shriveled and died. Rare are those in the world who can refrain from trying to help their sprouts to grow. Then there are those who think that there is nothing they can do to help and therefore abandon all effort entirely. They

---

[53]   There is, of course, another metaphor packed in here: that of AFFECTION AS NOURISHMENT.

are the people who fail to weed their sprouts. Those who try to help along the growth are the "sprout-pullers." Not only do their efforts fail to help, they actually do positive harm.

The blend at this point has become fantastically complex. In order to simplify matters, Figure 13 drops all of the spaces considered so far except the two most relevant ones, WATER MANAGEMENT and AGRICULTURE?

The reader is already prepared to understand the literal "sprouts" killed by the farmer of Song in metaphorical terms because the substance of Mencius's claim that "human nature is good" is his belief that all human beings are born with "sprouts" (*duan*) of the Confucian virtues already present in their heart/minds. The addition of the AGRICULTURE space reinforces the "three strategies" structure already developed by adding some powerful normative reactions – probably more vivid for Mencius's audience, who could be expected to be intimately familiar with the growing of crops, than for modern Westerners. Failure to engage in self-cultivation at all is compared to neglecting to water, fertilize, and weed, the consequences of which are obvious: one's sprouts will either starve or be choked by weeds. This "bad" or "lazy" farming strategy is probably meant to refer to the Daoists/Primitivists, whose naïve faith in unimproved nature leads them to reject culture and learning altogether. While this is clearly a poor strategy, it pales in comparison to the monumental stupidity displayed by the neo-Mohist "farmers," whose attempts to force human beings to practice impartial caring through the imposition of external doctrines are as likely to succeed as externally pulling on sprouts of grain will succeed in getting them to grow faster.

The SELF-CULTIVATION AS AGRICULTURE metaphor dominates the *Mencius*, and – as in 2:A:2 – is often used in conjunction with WATER or WATER MANAGEMENT metaphors. The two schemas blend together so easily because they share a generic causal schema and possess all of the qualities that Mencius wants to attribute to moral self-cultivation:

1. It is natural, in accordance with the heaven-endowed *telos*
2. It derives from the inside (the essence), rather than the outside (the incidental)
3. It is necessarily gradual and step-wise
4. It is noncoercive
5. It works along with natural tendencies and derives power from them
6. It is still hierarchical and requires *some* effort: the general, the water manager, and the farmer are required to guide and help the process along – an important entailment targeted at the Primitivists or Daoists

The two metaphors fit together so seamlessly that they are often blended together in single utterances, as in 1:A:6, where the moral virtues of a Confucian sage are compared to formerly dry sprouts after a torrential spring rain that "rise up out of the ground with the force of pouring water . . . who could stop them?" In 4:B:18, the

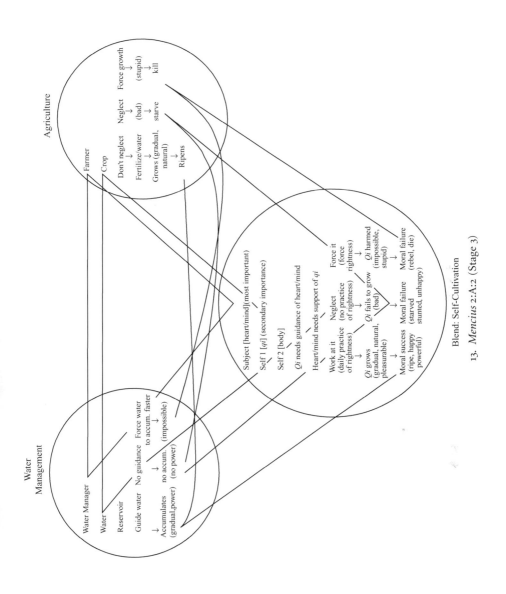

Water Management

Water Manager
Water
Reservoir

Guide water → Accumulates (gradual, power)
No guidance → no accum. (no power)
Force water to accum. faster (impossible)

Agriculture

Farmer
Crop

Don't neglect → Fertilize/water
Grows (gradual, natural) → Ripens
Neglect → (bad) → starve
Force growth → (stupid) → kill

Blend: Self-Cultivation

Subject [heart/mind] (most important)
Self 1 [*qi*] (secondary importance)
Self 2 [body]
Qi needs guidance of heart/mind
Heart/mind needs support of *qi*

Work at it (daily practice of rightness) → *Qi* grows (gradual, natural, pleasurable) → Moral success (ripe, happy powerful)
Neglect (no practice of rightness) → *Qi* fails to grow (bad) → Moral failure (starved stunted, unhappy)
Force it (force rightness) → *Qi* harmed (impossible, stupid) → Moral failure (rebel, die)

13. *Mencius* 2:A:2 (Stage 3)

205

two schemas are blended in response to a disciple's question about a very cryptic utterance attributed to Confucius:

Xuzi said, "Several times Confucius praised water, saying, 'Water! Oh, water!' What was it he saw in water?"

Mencius replied, "Water from an ample spring flows day and night without ceasing, proceeding on its way only after filling all of the hollows in its path, and then eventually draining into the Four Seas. All things that have a root are so, and what Confucius saw in water is simply this and nothing more. If a thing lacks a root, it is like rain water that accumulates after a late summer storm. Although all the gutters and ditches may be filled, you can just stand for a moment and watch it all dry up."

Here the image of water flowing from an ample spring is conceptually blended with the image of a plant growing up from its roots. Because of the commonly accepted Qi as Water metaphor, the juxtaposition of the two schemas reinforces the dual flowing/growing model of *qi* development presented in 2:A:2. In 4:B:18, then, Mencius is able to transform Confucius's famously cryptic expression of admiration for water into an endorsement of Mencius's own model of self-cultivation.

EMBODYING CULTURAL VARIETY

I apologize for having taken the reader on this extensive detour (Argument as Journey...) into early Chinese philosophical debate, but I think that a set of extended, concrete examples such as these allows us to get a firmer grasp on some important points about blending and cultural innovation.

Ratcheted Innovation

To begin with, the debate in *Mencius* 6:A:1 and 6:A:2 draws on conceptual images and somatic markers that, for both fourth-century b.c.e. Chinese-speakers and twenty-first-century c.e. English-speakers, appear to be immediately accessible and predictably structured. Each of the rhetoricians involved, however, draws on these images and normative responses for his own specific and unpredictable purposes. With a subtle blending jujitsu flip, for instance, Mencius turns a quite reasonable claim – unshaped human nature is as useless and ugly as a crude raw material prior to being worked – into a rather counterintuitive image of Crafting as Mutilation. This is an excellent illustration of how shared, species-typical normative reactions can be redirected onto entirely novel targets.

Perhaps more important, the recursive nature of blending can go beyond recruiting source domains in a creative manner to actually creating novel, culturally specific structures. In *Mencius* 2:A:2 we are witnessing the early stages of the creation of a new entity in Chinese thought, the morally activated *qi*, which blends the characteristics of water, growing things, and social subordinates in an entirely unique way. From the WATER input, we get the idea that the *qi* fills the body like liquid in a container, has natural tendencies as water tends to flow downhill, and accumulates slowly like water behind a reservoir dam. From the LIVING THING input, we get the idea that *qi* requires nourishment and will "starve" without it; that it is fragile and easily harmed, especially when young; that it possesses an inner *telos*; and that it grows at its own pace and cannot be rushed. From the MILITARY domain, we get the idea that it can be gently led but not coerced, and that the "leader" (the heart/mind) is powerless without the led (the *qi*). The entailments of these various domains overlap and reinforce each other to a certain extent, but the resulting blend has its own unique emergent structure, and this emergent structure then serves to constrain what sorts of projections from new input domains are allowed. As in the "Digging a Financial Grave" blend, we have here a novel structure derived from, but also distinct from, the input domains that were drawn on in its creation.

Unlike this other blend, however, the Mencian conception of the "flood-like *qi*" became an important cultural concept, adopted by others and acquiring the status of a new metaphysical entity. In subsequent Chinese thought and cultural practice, this new entity began to serve as an input domain in its own right, being drawn on in order to understand other domains such as the movement of humors in the body or the psyche of a calligrapher. This sort of ratcheted innovation is quite common and is a powerful engine for cultural creativity. In Chapter 5 we will briefly look at certain novel blends, such as the mathematical concept of zero or the idea of weight as an extensive property of mass, that provide the cultures that possess them with new tools for reasoning about and even looking at the world. Running these blends leads one to conclusions that are completely counterintuitive from the perspective of the most relevant input domains, which has much to do with why such blends are difficult to create, hard to learn, and easily lost if cultural transmission is interrupted by social chaos or political fragmentation.

Reification of Blends in Material Culture

The power of blends to ratchet conceptual innovation becomes even more clear when we recognize that they cannot only be deposited as formal concepts in long-term memory, but are also physically symbolized in the material world. The human ability to entrench metaphors and metaphoric blends in the world allows us to infuse our immediate surroundings with novel conceptual forms, which means that even quite idiosyncratic cultural products have to be seen as part and parcel of human embodiment – embodied cognition involves more than merely the biological body and the prehuman physical environment.

To take a trivial but representative example, during a recent holiday family visit that was combined with a wedding, I was saddled with the job of logistics director. We had three vehicles at our disposal for twenty-some people, and approximately six different locations that these people needed to get to and stay at for varying amounts of time. I found it impossible to figure out how to make this work "in my head," so I off-loaded the problem onto the world: on the living room floor I laid out a collection of objects that represented the six locations, three pieces of paper that represented the cars, and a variety of coins that represented the people who needed to be moved around in those cars. In other words, I created a physically instantiated blend. The physical objects served as one input, and people, places, and vehicles as the other. In the blended space, physical objects *became* people, places, or vehicles, sharing some of the input space characteristics ("people" could not get from one "place" to another without riding in a "vehicle") but not others (the "vehicles" were moved by my hand, not internal combustion engines; "people" were placed on top of the "vehicles" rather than inside). I also found myself to a certain extent living in the blend during the process of running it: at one point I admonished my sister not to "step on the cars" as she made her way through the living room, and at another point I told my brother, who was helping me run the blend, that "you can't put that many people in the Honda" when he piled too many coins on the triangular piece of paper.

This may seem like a trivial example, but it gets to the heart of the power of blending, and in that sense to the heart of what makes humans so smart. Even a quite simple and ad hoc blend such as this one immediately allows me to draw on something that I am quite good at (manipulating and immediately perceiving the spatial configuration of small objects) to solve a problem in a realm that I am not so good at (thinking about timing of movements of people and large objects over long spatial distances).[54] A structurally identical function is played by all human physical symbols, whether Arabic numerals to symbolize mathematical quantities or clocks to make the TIME AS SPACE metaphor powerfully visualizable. I find that I have trouble pacing talks if all that I have to rely on is a digital clock: the TIME AS NUMBER blend does not give me enough affordances to be helpful in deciding whether or not to skip an example or pick up my pace, although in other contexts it allows me to more precisely and quickly judge the lapse of temporal intervals. When I want an accurate sense of how much time I have left to talk, the analog clock does a much better job, because – in the TIME AS SPACE blend set up by this physical artifact – I can immediately *see* how much time I have left, and as I draw nearer to the end of my allotted time the slowly moving minute hand gives me a helpful and entirely visceral sense of urgency.

The ability to analyze the role played by the culturally transformed physical environment in human cognition is one of the great innovations of blending theory. From analog and digital gauges to money and tombs, and to the very graphemes

---

[54] Cf. Raymond Gibbs's remark that "cultural representations of metaphor enable people to 'offload' some aspects of conceptual metaphor out into the cultural world such that people need not rely exclusively on internal mental representations when solving problems, making decisions, using language, and so forth" (1999: 153), as well as Andy Clark's observation that what is special about humans is our ability to overcome the limits of our working memory by off-loading cognition onto external props such as language or social institutions (1997: 179–180).

that make up written language (Fauconnier & Turner 2002), physical objects and other concrete symbols in our environment serve as "material anchors" that reify blends and make them available to be used as inputs in further blend construction. To return to our example of the Chinese concept of *qi*, archeological evidence makes it clear that by Mencius's time (or shortly thereafter) this blend not only was playing an important conceptual role in the philosophical-religious and medical texts of the time, but was also being reified in artistic portrayals. Paintings on silk and brocade found in tombs of the period portray a strange, water-air-like substance flowing through the cosmos, a bit like water, a bit like smoke, intermingling with numinous snakelike dragons and other spiritual beings. These sorts of visual representations of novel cultural blends help to reinforce them in the mind, and no doubt artistic renderings of a *qi*-infused spiritual cosmos encouraged the Chinese of Mencius's time to see the ephemeral and invisible *qi* at work all around them, descending from heaven, flowing through the landscape, and pulsating down the energy pathways of their own bodies.

Perceptual and Motor Plasticity

We have already discussed how blends can be used to create novel motor programs by recruiting fragments of existing programs and then recombining them in a calculated manner. Our Pleistocene ancestors did not downhill ski or roll kayaks, drive cars or interact with computer screens by means of a mouse, and by the same token a modern Western human would require a great deal of blend-guided instruction to learn the basic survival and recreation skills characteristic of another culture. One aspect of the development of new motor programs is a reorganization of one's body schema to incorporate the specific tools involved: downhill skiing or rolling a kayak can be mastered only when the artificial bodily extensions involved – skis and poles, paddle and boat – have been fully integrated into one's bodily self-representation. As Michael Arbib notes, the proper use of tool to extend our natural capacities involves a fundamental, if only temporary, reorganization of our body schemas: "When we use a screwdriver our body ends at the end of the screwdriver, not at the end of the hand; when we drive a car, our body ends at the rear bumper, not at our buttocks" (1985: 75–76).

This sort of reorganization of our perceptual and motor schemas can occur on a variety of time scales. The screwdriver extension of my hand disappears as soon as the tools is put down, but other manual extensions can apparently be deposited in long-term, know-how memory and become very difficult to alter. I learned racket sports through a rather odd game played in Venice Beach, California, called "paddle tennis," which is played with short, solid paddles, on a half-size tennis court, and with a partially deflated tennis ball. Once I left Southern California and was forced to take up "real" tennis, it took me several extremely frustrating weeks to retrain my implicit body schemas: I kept hitting the ball on the handle of the tennis racket, expecting this extension of my hand to be shorter, and although the swing motion in the two sports is very similar, I had a devil of a time recalibrating the power and angle of my swing to match the size of the court and the spring of the fully inflated ball.

There is a great deal of literature on the sort of cortical plasticity that allows such reformation and transformation of even quite basic body schemas. As a result of congenital or acquired loss of a limb or sensory modality, for instance, humans and other primates can eventually reorganize their sensory-motor maps, although within certain constraints. For instance, in individuals who have been blind since an early age, areas normally devoted to visual processing are taken over by auditory functions, which apparently enables enhanced auditory discrimination (Rauschecker 1995, Röder et al. 1999).[55] More to the point with regard to cultural artifacts, it is also clear that interactions with culturally specific symbols and tools can effect changes in the brain-body's organization. A well-known study by Alvaro Pascual-Leone and Fernando Torres (1993) showed that the cortical area devoted to the right-index (reading) finger in Braille-readers was significantly larger than in control subjects, and a study by Thomas Elbert et al. (1995) found that, in the brains of professional string-instrument players, the cortical representation of the relevant fingers had expanded greatly as compared to that of nonplayers.

Cultural practices and the built human environment also appear to have an effect on perceptual schemas with regard to basic features of the surroundings. Studies on cross-cultural psychology by Richard Nisbett and his collaborators, for instance, have argued for certain fundamental differences between American and Japanese in the perception of space. Takahiko Masuda and Nisbett (2001), for instance, presented American and Japanese subjects with underwater scenes containing some largish fish swimming around against an aquarium background and found that Americans paid more attention to the focal items (the fish), whereas the Japanese recalled a more holistic, contextually accurate version of the scene. Similarly, Yuri Miyamoto et al. (2006) found that, when presented with a variety of street scenes, American subjects attended more to the foreground while Japanese subjects recalled more of the contextual information of the scene. They speculate that a tendency to attend to foreground as opposed to context may be the result of priming by the quite distinct affordances of Japanese as opposed to American physical urban environments, concluding that "culturally characteristic environments may afford distinctive patterns of perception" (113; cf. Kitayama et al. 2003).

Putting the Culture in Body

The fact that reading Braille, playing a string instrument, or living in a particular type of urban environment can reorganize cortical maps and conceptual schemas in a significant way suggests that the acquisition and maintenance of schemas, including one's own body schema, is influenced by cultural practices. Some voices within

[55] See Buonomano & Merzenich 1998 for a review of the literature on cortical plasticity.

the cognitive linguistics community have accordingly begun to argue that more attention needs to be paid to cultural context in understanding the development of the embodied mind.[56] As Raymond Gibbs has argued with regard to the kind of "material anchors" discussed earlier, the human ability to use external symbols as placeholders for and reminders of particular images or blends is why cognitive linguists need to "think about metaphor and its relation to thought as cognitive webs that extend beyond individual minds and are spread out into the cultural world" (1999: 146). This is an important corrective to some earlier versions of cognitive linguistics that focused exclusively on the individual body and the generic physical environment, without taking into account the extent that, especially for modern human beings, the physical environment is pervaded with cultural information.

As a response to this shortcoming, Tim Rohrer observes that more recent work on metaphor and blending acknowledges that "the developing body exists no more in isolation from people and culture than it exists in isolation from interacting in space. In this sense, the embodiment hypothesis is broadened 'upward,' away from the small scale of neurons and neural circuitry and into the larger scale of cultural phenomena of people interacting with one another" (2001: 58). Anthropologists and cognitive scientists interested in the methodologies of cognitive linguistics, but with experience in cross-cultural analysis, have begun to provide a more nuanced picture of how image schemas are developed in contexts that take cultural practices seriously as part of the lived environment. To cite just a few examples, Chris Sinha and Kristine Jensen de Lopez (2000) have, for instance, argued that differences in the specific types of containers available in Zapotec and Danish societies, as well as the manner in which they are employed, impact how children in these cultures develop schemas for understanding such concepts as *under* and *in*. Kathryn Geurts (2003) has similarly argued that, among the Anlo-Ewe people of Ghana, the practice of carrying heavy loads on the head, coupled with a very intensive cultural and ritual focus on physical balance, results in a more nuanced experience of the basic BALANCE schema discussed earlier, as well as a more central and pervasive metaphoric role for this schema within this culture. In a comparison of early Chinese and modern Western metaphors for morality, I have attempted to show (Slingerland 2004b) how different conceptions of the individual's relationship to others, and to his or her social role, results in different schemas for morality being emphasized: MORALITY AS BEING CENTERED predominating in early Chinese ethical theory, as opposed to the more modern Western emphasis on MORALITY AS ACCOUNTING.

In light of this sort of evidence, Michael Kimmel has argued that it is imperative for cognitive linguistics to "overcome a tendency to unidirectionally theorize how image schemas shape discourse, while neglecting how discourse, ritual, and material culture shape image schemas" (2005: 299). The neglect of culture is by no means an inherent part of the cognitive linguistic model of thought and language,

[56]   See especially Gibbs 1999 and Kimmel 2005, as well as the essays collected in Fernandez 1991.

however. Cognitive linguistics is an extremely young field, and it is not surprising that its early stages have been marked by a certain degree of cultural myopia. This shortcoming is quickly being remedied, however, and it is the very tools of cognitive linguistics itself that are proving to be invaluable aids in this process. Metaphor and blending analysis allow us to trace with precision how hybrid cultural-biological environments are built, how they are experienced and integrated by the developing body-mind, and how they are recruited to structure abstract thought. Such analysis thereby gives us the means of both evaluating the "blends we live by" and thinking our way into the thought-worlds of initially alien cultures.

AN EPIDEMIOLOGICAL MODEL OF CULTURE

One interesting finding of the Miyamoto et al. (2006) study was that, when Japanese and American subjects were primed with "Japanese" scenes, both groups attended more to contextual information than when primed with "American" scenes. We can also recall how quickly the otherwise quite strange schema of TIME AS VERTICAL LINE can become cognitively active in non-Mandarin speakers to whom Mandarin time words have been explained. This suggests two conclusions about cultural variety. First of all, the range of possible cultural options seems to be quite limited. Depending upon environmental or linguistic priming, people from different cultures may attend more to focal objects than to the holistic scene, or may conceive of time as running along a vertical rather than a horizontal line, but it appears that no human seeing a rabbit darting across a field would cry out *gavagai* and mean by this "there is a rabbit-event" or "there is an undetached rabbit part."[57] Time may run horizontally or vertically, but human beings perceive TIME AS SPACE, not TIME AS TAPIOCA PUDDING. Considering the logically infinite possible ways an organism might cut up the world, people throughout time and across space seem to cluster around a quite tightly constrained set of alternatives. Second, culturally specific tweakings of the perceptual or conceptual world seem relatively shallow: they appear to be quite easily picked up by outsiders and just as easily dropped when the cultural environment is changed.

The culturally specific component of a given individual's worldview would thus seem to be a rather thin and malleable wafer riding on a deep, massive, and mostly invariant set of cognitive universals. Scott Atran comes to a similar conclusion with his distinction between cultural variety and what he refers to as the human "common sense core":

By nature, human minds everywhere are endowed with common sense. They possess universal cognitive dispositions that determine a core of spontaneously formulated representations about the world. The world is basically represented in the same way in

---

[57] For Quine's famous (or notorious) *gavagai* example and arguments concerning the indeterminacy of translation, see Quine 1960.

every culture. Core concepts and beliefs about the world are easily acquired and tend to be adequate for ordinary dealings with the social and natural environment; yet they are restricted to certain cognitive domains and are rather fixed. (1990: 263–264)

Atran notes that "cultures develop and diversify beyond the common sense core with practical and speculative systems of representation that are not sponta-neously elaborated" (264) – in other words, through the development of con-ceptual metaphors and metaphoric blends – but that such counter intuitive ideas are understandable only because they are rooted in a stable core of "common-sense intuitions" (265).[58]

One increasingly popular way to conceptualize (metaphorically, of course!) the relationship of culture to core cognition is on the model of epidemiology. Epidemi-ology as a structuring input space was suggested by Tooby and Cosmides (1992) as a way of understanding the existence and spread of culture, preferable to the metaphor of "transmission," with its implications of consciously, physically passing an object from one person to another. As they note, the image of epidemiological "spread" is preferable to the image of transmission because cultural acquisition is often the result of entirely unintentional modeling and imitation (118). Another, perhaps more important, reason why epidemiology is a good metaphor is that cul-tural forms, by virtue of their public representation in language, ritual, and material objects, become a force in the environment somewhat independent of individuals. Also, like a literal pathogen, the spread of culture is strongly limited by the make-up of the host: preexisting cognitive structures, many of them innate, strongly con-strain the form that cultural ideas can take and play an important role in filtering and altering them as they move through individual minds.[59] As Pascal Boyer notes, "given the general properties of human minds, certain types of representations are more likely than others to be acquired and transmitted, thereby constituting those stable sets of representations that anthropologists call 'cultures'" (1994: 391).

---

[58] Cf. Daniel Sperber's (1985) distinction between "first-order" cognition (universal common sense) and "second-order" cognition, the latter being more flexible and the result of cultural elaborations and modifications of the first. Also see Sperber & Hirshfeld 2004.

[59] This is also, incidentally, why the idea of "memes" as completely independent genelike parasites inhabiting human brains – initially developed by Richard Dawkins (1976/2006: Ch. 11) and enthusi-astically defended by Daniel Dennett (1995: Ch. 12) – is problematic. Unlike literal genes or viruses, "memes" are pathogens created by the hosts themselves, without any independent substrate of their own. They do not exist in discrete units that could be selected for, and their replication fidelity is simply awful – as the game of "telephone" illustrates, ideas repeated from individual to individual degrade rapidly over time, being quickly invaded by noise, blended with other ideas, and altered to fit preexisting assumptions. Perhaps most importantly, as Stephen Jay Gould observes (2000), cultural change is Lamarckian, not Darwinian: the powerful directionality of cultural evolution entirely swamps any sort of Darwinian selection-driven change. Robert Boyd and Peter Richerson make a similar point in noting that the sort of "guided variation" that one finds in cultural evolution "has no good analog in genetic evolution" (2005: 116). The reader is referred to Aunger 2006 and the essays in Aunger 2000 for good recent summaries of the problems with meme theory as formulated by Dawkins and Dennett, and to Boyd & Richerson 2005: Ch. 3 for an evolutionary model of culture that avoids some of the problems of meme theory.

Boyer is one of a growing number of cultural anthropologists that are trying to take their field beyond Durkheimian "culture as autonomous entity" thinking to see cultural transmission as a selective process, where a large and powerful suite of innate human cognitive biases assure that certain mental representations are more likely to be entertained and transmitted than others.[60]

Fine-Tuning and Minor Violations

A sixteenth- or seventeeth-century commentary on the *Analects* of Confucius remarks, with regard to a situation where a supposedly subordinate political clan has grown more powerful and influential than is proper, that (lit.) "the tail has become too big to wag."[61] To translate this into modern colloquial English we have to tweak it slightly – "the tail is wagging the dog" – but we should be astounded by the convergence of two utterly unrelated cultures on such a presumably idiosyncratic image. It is precisely this sort of convergence that makes cross-cultural communication and translation possible, and oddly striking parallels such as this one are helpful reminders to us of how classicists, anthropologists, explorers, and traders move through a medium of human cognitive commonality so ever-present, pervasive, and vital that – like the air we breath – it is rarely noticed.

Through metaphor and metaphoric blends, this universal common sense can be extended, altered, and transformed in certain ways, but only within fairly strict constraints.[62] Although this still awaits empirical study, my guess is that the sort of ratcheted innovation that can be performed by blends and then entrenched in the linguistic and material environment is probably limited to a maximum of two or three "ratchet turns." That is, once blends become too far removed from their original, domain-specific inputs, they either lose their emotional punch or become simply unintelligible. This means that there is a limit to human creativity as well: an infinite amount of shuffling may be possible, but there is a limit on the number of new cards – or, more accurately, on how different these new cards can get.

Consider human morality. It has become clear that, as a result of the forces of kin selection, most mammals have evolved so as to possess a degree of empathy for

---

[60] See Boyer 1994 for a good introduction to this position; also cf. Barrett 2000, Barrett & Nyhof 2001, Norenzayan & Atran 2004, and Norenzayan et al. 2006.

[61] Jiao Hong *Analects* 3.19 (Cheng Shude 1990: 197).

[62] In this respect, the model of culture that I am defending here differs somewhat from Robert Boyd and Peter Richerson's recent and influential model (2005), which sees culture as an independent, "ultimate" causation factor alongside natural selection. For instance, they contrast species-universal instincts with novel "social instincts" such as shame and guilt, whereas I am arguing that social instincts should be seen as metaphoric extensions of "ancient" ones, never far removed and always less vivid. As they note, the "crucial questions hang on the relative value of biased transmission and natural selection. If the psychological forces are more important, then the causes of cultural evolution will ultimately trace back to innate primary values . . . and culture will have only a proximate role" (80). This is more or less the view that I am defending here.

their fellows.[63] For most of human history, however, what constituted a "fellow" worthy of receiving such empathy was mostly restricted to one's tribe or village members, all of whom were to some degree related to oneself; non–tribe members, as nonhumans, were generally treated accordingly to an entirely different and far less pleasant set of rules. This system worked fine in our ancestral environment – it would not have evolved otherwise – but arguably the huge upheaval in human social organization represented by the invention of agriculture and creation of large towns and cities was made possible only by recruiting this kin-based empathy and, through metaphoric blends, extending it beyond its original domain. Fellow citizens and coreligionists, for instance, become metaphorical brothers and sisters, all united in a new, metaphorical family under a great, supernatural "Mother" or "Father."

For instance, one of the main goals of Mencius, the early Chinese thinker we have discussed so much already, was to get the rulers of his age to metaphorically "extend" (*tui*) their innate moral intuitions – including compassion and an inchoate sense of moral shame – to encompass a broader range of objects, thereby transforming themselves from tribal bullies to true kings. In Mencius's time newly developed political structures were being developed to cope with the demands of administering larger and more complex states. A major theme of a set of recently discovered archeological texts from the time[64] is how to get potential public servants to feel the same sort of love and devotion toward their political superiors as they naturally do toward their own family and clan members. This suggests that making the metaphoric leap from family love to socially extended loyalty is one of the major tricks that protostates had to pull off in order to replace smaller-scale tribal systems. Arguably, a characteristic feature of modern morality is an ever-progressing attempt to continue this expansion of the moral circle, bringing different classes, races, genders, and – as in the case of the animal rights movement – even other species under the empathy umbrella. Yet none of this cultural innovation involves fundamentally replacing or changing our innate empathetic impulses: innate primate empathy is merely being extended to new targets.

Consider another innate moral emotion, the instinct to inflict altruistic punishment – that is, punishment of social cheaters – even at a cost to oneself. There is strong evidence, both theoretical and empirical, for the existence of cheater-detection mechanisms and altruistic punishment motivations in humans and, possibly, in our primate relatives.[65] Yet, as Joseph Henrich and his colleagues (2006)

---

[63] See Preston & de Waal 2002 for a review of the huge body of experiment and behavioral observations with mammals ranging from rats to humans that indicate that "individuals of many species are distressed by the distress of a conspecific and will act to terminate the object's distress, even incurring risk to themselves" (1).

[64] The so-called Guodian find, discovered in 1993 and published in 1998 (Jinmenshi: bowuguan 1998).

[65] For the theoretical need for mechanisms for punishing free riders, see Trivers 1971, Axelrod 1984, Boyd & Richerson 1992, Gintis 2000, Henrich & Boyd 2001, Fehr et al. 2002, and Fehr & Gächter

have found, although the willingness to engage in costly punishment is universal, the degree to which this willingness is translated into action varies widely across cultures. Henrich et al. argue that this reflects the cultural "fine-tuning" of an innate tendency, with the result that "local learning dynamics generate between-group variation as different groups arrive at different 'cultural equilibria'" (1770). They hypothesize that the resulting between-group differences in levels of cooperation might produce a group-selection effect – societies with more robust cheater punishment practices outcompeting those with weaker ones.

We should also mention a cultural phenomenon that, at first blush, seems supremely arbitrary and culturally specific: religious belief and practice. Even here there is a great deal of human commonality lurking beneath the veneer of difference. For instance, religious injunctions and practices revolve around things that are inherently important to people, even if it is to deny or prohibit these things. Many religious traditions throughout history and across the world have independently hit upon asceticism as a practice, denying their serious adherents normal human goods such as sex, food, or physical comfort. Yet the conceptual power of such ascetic practices derives precisely from the deeply innate nature of the things they deny: celibacy is salient and impressive, and therefore likely to be recruited as religious practice, because it involves the denial of something that is supremely important to us for noncultural reasons. As far as I am aware, no culture in history has developed a religion centered on sleeping in late or taking nice strolls on the beach.

This reliance on shared human values and common sense to produce impressive violations also extends to religious concepts, which often initially strike cultural outsiders as strange and unique. A large literature has developed around the theory that religious concepts, despite their apparent strangeness, are memorable and easily transmittable only if they involve "minimal violations" of commonsense intuitions (for instance, beings that are like normal human agents but can also fly or move about invisibly) or simple cross-domain projection of particular traits, such as objects that "behave" like agents (statues that can produce tears, rocks that can hear).[66] The Christian Trinity is an impressive mystery because it involves a violation of the sort of innate numerosity explored in Chapter 3, and the early Buddhist doctrine of no-self is salient because it violates our theory of mind. In all of these cases, cultural variety manifests itself only against the background of deep and mostly unconscious commonalities.

2002; on evidence for the existence of specialized cheater-detection modules in the human brain, see Cosmides 1989, Cosmides & Tooby 2000 and 2005, and Sugiyama et al. 2002; for experimental studies documenting the presence of a distinct cheater-punishment sentiment in humans, see Kahneman et al. 1998, de Quervain et al. 2004, O'Gorman et al. 2005, and Price 2005; and for studies indicating that capuchin monkeys appear willing to incur significant costs to themselves in order to express displeasure with unfair food-distribution reward systems, see Brosnan & de Waal 2003.

[66]   Boyer 1994 and 2001 and Barrett 2000.

THE HUMAN BODY-MIND AS UNIVERSAL DECODING KEY

I assign the portions of the *Mencius* discussed earlier (in English translation, of course) to students in my undergraduate survey course on Chinese thought, and they all find it a powerful and amusing piece of discourse, coming away convinced that the Mohists were misguided and confident in the wisdom of the Mencian approach to self-cultivation. The commonality of this sort of phenomenon – an ancient text from a completely alien culture speaking to a modern person with a clear and powerful voice – is similar to the ease with which we reach out and grasp a moving object, or gauge the emotions of a person with whom we are speaking and adjust our tone and body language accordingly: effortlessness in all these cases obscures the staggering complexity of the actual processes involved. Of course the idea of pulling on a sprout to make it grow is ridiculous. Of course modern college students react predictably to the image of someone foolishly trying to oppose the inexorable downward flow of water. This sense of cognitive transparency makes it easy for us to overlook how astounding it is that a text assembled in archaic Chinese in the fourth century B.C.E. by some wizened Confucian scholars could survive the millennia, be translated into modern English, and trigger the construction of spaces in the minds of twenty-first-century C.E., baggy-pants-clad, MTV-watching college students in a manner more or less predictable to its original author. In other words, a millennia-long chain of copied marks on bamboo strips and pieces of paper has allowed the reproduction of a state of voluntary, partial synaesthesia that occurred in the brain of some person in fourth-century B.C.E. China to be retriggered in the brains of a classroom full of twenty-first-century C.E. twenty-year-olds. This should amaze and astound us.

Of course, my translations of the stories and metaphors, as well as my interpretation of their meaning, play a role in shaping how my students understand the text. I may in fact have misconstrued some of these passages in a variety of ways: perhaps I am mistaken about the "whirling pool" in 6:A:2 having to do with irrigation management (this is a rather new take on it), or I may be ignorant of some important, relevant features of early Chinese irrigation management that in turn has led to a misunderstanding of Mencius's position. It is equally possible that I have missed or improperly interpreted some of the entailments of the metaphors invoked, similarly resulting in misfiring of the intended blend construction. This sort of miscommunication is not uncommon with texts from another culture or time – the primary job of linguists and historians is to help prevent us from making such mistakes – and in fact happens all the time even in quite mundane situations. Having grown up in New Jersey, I discovered upon moving to California at age twenty that many there failed to properly understand sarcasm and other forms of verbal abuse as expressions of friendly affection. Similarly, we all sometimes drop things, stumble on paths, and misread the facial expressions or body language of others. For the most part, however, we move through our world with consummate ease, and the meaning of the vast majority of even quite culturally alien texts such as the *Mencius* is entirely and immediately transparent to people provided with a decent translation. Occasional failures in comprehension and performance are merely superficial and obvious exceptions that prove the deeply buried rule: human bodies (including the brain part) are built to do certain things, and to do them largely unconsciously and quite well.

The fact that the blends constructed by the author of the *Mencius* are re-created by our own brains as we read the translated text supports the argument of cognitive linguists that thought is triggered and communicated by language, but not *constituted* by it. Moreover, the fact that even the specifics of most of the mappings considered – including the somatic-emotional reactions they are intended to trigger – are very similar cross-linguistically, and thus are immediately comprehensible across the millennia, supports the argument advanced in Chapter 3 that human emotional-visceral reactions are fairly invariant and predictable across cultures and times, although the process of conceptual blending allows these reactions to be recruited for a potentially infinite variety of rhetorical purposes. Human beings are apparently unique among animals in possessing the cognitive fluidity and cultural technology to effect some radical changes in what gives us pleasure, what we find worth pursuing, and what we deem as meaningful. But all of this cognitive and cultural innovation is grounded in – and remains ultimately constrained by – the nature of our embodiment. This means that, even when confronted by the most alien of cultural practices or artifacts, our own body-minds can serve as a universal decoding key. The tools provided by cognitive linguistics for uncovering and tracing the embodied origins of the products of the human mind across cultures and across time allow us, then, a clear way out of the postmodern prison house of language without committing us to a rightly discredited form of Enlightenment realism.

PART III

DEFENDING VERTICAL INTEGRATION

5

Defending the Empirical: Commonsense Realism
and Pragmatic Truth

*I*N CHAPTERS 1 THROUGH 4, I HAVE PRESENTED A FAIR AMOUNT OF EMPIR-
ical evidence for various positions, observing that X and X (2003) "found" that Y
was the case, or that the results of X (2001) "suggest" that Z is true. There are several
ways you can take statements like this. You may follow me in taking such evidence
as constituting a fairly convincing case in support of position Y or Z. Alternately,
you may be committed to empirical inquiry, but see these particular cases as flawed
studies that – because of poor experimental design or variables not considered by
the experimenters – fail to demonstrate what they are intended to demonstrate.
Finally, you may be a social constructivist and feel that *any* reference to empirical
evidence is merely a bit of rhetorical handwaving: supposedly "empirical" studies
reveal nothing outside of the presuppositions and expectations of the experimenters
involved, and thus they are not in any way epistemologically superior to other forms
of rhetorical assertion. In our modern Western culture, however, "science" has been
accorded a privileged status as the new official religion, so dressing up assertions
in a sciencelike garb is a very effective strategy. To a committed postmodernist,
my push for vertical integration is best seen as a rhetorical gambit designed to
advance my personal opinions by borrowing some of the prestige of science, and
by throwing in a bunch of impressively scientific-sounding references to give my
arguments a specious appearance of gravitas.

Most cognitive scientists, even when writing for humanists, fail to address this
basic postmodern skepticism concerning empirical inquiry. This is a shame, since
it is a valid concern, and by failing to address it directly researchers in the sciences
simply write off a very important audience – and, as I have argued, an audience
that very much needs to hear what these scientists have to say. The necessity for
a coherent defense of empiricism is especially acute considering the fatal problems with objectivism that we explored in Chapter 1. If we cannot go back to the
objectivist longing for God's-eye, timeless certainties, what *is* left other than conversational assertions? The key to answering this question is, as I suggested in the
Introduction, to get beyond the fundamentally dualistic assumptions that underlie both objectivism and postmodernism and to put in their place an embodied,

pragmatic model of human cognition and inquiry.[1] In this chapter I will present the attempts of various philosophers and philosophers of science to formulate just such a pragmatic model of empirical inquiry, based on a knowing subject that is always already in touch with and embedded in the physical world of things because it is *also* a thing, not an otherworldly ghost struggling within the confines of its mortal coil. Such a model of inquiry can provide us with provisional answers to questions about the limits of our knowledge – less ambrosial, perhaps, than the fruits of objectivism, but also less subject to spoilage.

PRAGMATISM: THE "MOTHER TONGUE" OF THOUGHT

One of the great contributions of the pragmatist movement – and perhaps the most direct reflection of its American origins – was its attempt to restore to philosophical standing the concept of common sense by tying it to an evolutionary account of human cognition. William James dubbed common sense the "mother tongue" of thought, observing that

our fundamental ways of thinking about things are discoveries of exceedingly remote ancestors, which have been able to preserve themselves throughout the experience of all subsequent time. They form one great stage of equilibrium in the human mind's development, the stage of common sense. Other stages have grafted themselves upon this stage, but have never succeeded in displacing it. (1907/1995: 65)

James observed that specialized training, such as that provided by the natural sciences, can modify our initial intuitions and habits of processing information, reshaping them or refocusing them in ways that can lead us to conclusions that seem to contradict untrained common sense – such as the idea that the earth is not standing still, but is hurtling through space in an orbit around the sun. Nonetheless, the thought processes involved in reaching such counterintuitive conclusions are merely extensions of thought habits that are *themselves* quite intuitive.

Understood in this manner, "common sense" is granted genuine epistemological power by virtue of its status as a motley collection of heuristics, ontological assumptions, and prejudices that have proven their worth for our species over evolutionary time – not by virtue of being a formal, a priori algorithm delivering

---

[1] As mentioned earlier, Larry Laudan has made a strong case for seeing strong postmodern relativism as "positivism's flip side" (1996: 25) and for tracing its many slips from reasonable critiques of naïve objectivism into non sequitur relativist conclusions back to shared positivist-relativist assumptions. Laudan's point is that the demise of objectivism does not in any way invalidate a looser, more pragmatic definition of scientific method or rationality. Richard Bernstein makes a similar point in his discussion of the "Cartesian anxiety" that he sees at the heart of modern relativism – an anxiety that he believes can be cured by moving toward a more pragmatic model of knowledge along the lines of Aristotelian *phronesis* (1983: 23).

guaranteed results, or by providing special access to timeless truths. As Scott Atran puts it, common sense

includes statements pertaining to what is plausibly an innately grounded, and species-specific, apprehension of the spatio-temporal, geometrical, chromatic, chemical and organic world in which we, and all other human beings, live our usual lives . . . Common-sense beliefs are beyond dispute not because they happen to accurately describe the facts, but because that is just the way that humans are constitutionally disposed to think of things. (1990: 1–2)

In previous chapters I provided a sketch of the broad outlines of human common sense, as constituted by a suite of innate categories of perception, action, and understanding combined with a massive set of "Good Tricks" created independently by groups of human beings throughout space and time. In this chapter I want to examine some broader features of common sense with an eye toward how they might support a pragmatic conception of empirical inquiry – one that can take us beyond dualism and its attendant epistemological problems.

THE EMPIRICAL PREJUDICE: KNOWING AS SEEING

> Villain, be sure thou prove my love a whore,
> Be sure of it; give me the ocular proof:
> Or by the worth of man's eternal soul,
> Thou hadst been better have been born a dog
> Than answer my waked wrath!
>
> – Othello

The three dominant metaphors for knowledge in all of the languages with which I am familiar are KNOWING AS SEEING (*I see what you mean, don't keep me in the dark*), KNOWING AS HEARING (*I hear you, he was deaf to my argument*), and KNOWING AS TOUCHING (*I get your point, I grasp the concept*). A good case could be made that they are universal.[2] The reason that they are so prevalent is that these three senses are the main avenues through which human beings secure their knowledge of the world. Presumably if we were dogs, for instance, our dominant knowledge metaphor would be KNOWING AS SMELLING. We do sometimes use this metaphor (*something smells rotten about this*), but it is overshadowed by KNOWING AS SEEING to the same degree that our sense of sight dominates our relatively weak and imprecise sense of smell. This is why Othello demands from Iago the ultimate

---

[2] See Sweetser 1990: 28–48 for a historical treatment of perception as knowledge metaphors in the Indo-European language family, as well as Ibarretxe-Antuñano 1999, Lakoff & Johnson 1999: 238–240, Slingerland 2003, and Yu Ning 2003. For the early developmental linking of physical seeing with the epistemic state of knowing in three- to four-year-old children, refer to Pratt & Bryant 1990.

confirmation provided by the "ocular proof" – and also why the devious Iago is able to manipulate that proof to such powerful and tragic effect.

The more general linking of knowledge to sensory perception is, I would argue, a reflection of an "empirical prejudice": human beings, like other cognitively active and mobile animals, preferentially make decisions and adopt beliefs based on what they can see, hear, touch, and smell. The case of Othello being tricked by misinterpreted "evidence" – his beloved's handkerchief being craftily planted on another man by Iago to create the suspicion of an affair – seems to suggest that this is an unhelpful prejudice, but this instance of a misfiring empirical bias merely supports the more basic point.[3] Generally speaking there is a very good evolutionary warrant for the empirical prejudice: any successful animal is successful precisely because its senses have managed to put it in pretty good touch with the world. As Mark Johnson argues, evolution assures that we are "plugged into" reality, at least at the level of basic concepts, in a fairly accurate way. Our basic-level perceptual and conceptual schemas are "motivated by interactions with our environment. The concepts that result from these interactions have been, and continue to be, *tested* constantly, instant by instant, by billions of people over our history as a species. They work pretty well, or we wouldn't be here to talk about them" (1987: 203; emphasis added). Robin Dunbar has for this reason argued that the empirical prejudice, based on the fundamental processes of classification and causal inference, is

not merely typical of all humans, but is also a key feature in the lives of most birds and mammals. Science as we know it in the Western world is the product of a highly formalized version of something very basic to life, namely the business of learning about regularities in the world. Being able to predict what is going to happen in order to be able to act in an appropriate way at the right moment is fundamental to survival. (1995: 58)

Research on nonhuman animal cognition makes it clear that human beings share with other higher animals the ability to classify, make generalizations, and form and test simple causal hypotheses.[4]

In any case there is considerable evidence that – postmodernist claims of extreme cultural variability notwithstanding – people around the world and throughout history have relied on the evidence of their senses in order to discover and exploit causal regularities in the world around them. Moreover, the conclusions that they have come to concerning human-level phenomena in most cases match up quite well with current scientific knowledge.[5] As Steven Pinker has noted, the

---

[3] Othello's misinterpretation of such physical evidence as Desdemona's handkerchief is, incidentally, an excellent example of the sort of interdependence of theory and observation discussed in Chapter 1.
[4] Refer to the work on nonhuman animal cognition reviewed in Chapter 3.
[5] See Dunbar 1995: Ch. 3 for a helpful survey of examples of inductive and deductive empirical reasoning among preindustrial societies; also cf. the discussion of folk biology and folk physics in Chapter 3.

human brain appears to have evolved "fallible yet intelligent mechanisms that work to keep us in touch with aspects of reality that were relevant to the survival and reproduction of our ancestors" (2002: 198), and the importance of these mechanisms to us is made evident by a universal human desire to get beyond visual illusions (blinking the eyes or squinting, for instance, when confronted with suspicious visual evidence) and false impressions (dreamt or imagined events as opposed to actual ones). "People in all cultures distinguish truth from falsity and inner mental life from overt reality," he argues, "and try to deduce the presence of unobservable objects from the perceptible clues they leave behind" (201). This is why would-be deceivers – whether the treacherous Iago or a camouflaged insect trying its best to look like a stick – have to work so hard to achieve their deceptions, as well as why these deceptions are so effective when pulled off convincingly.

In human beings, our ability to communicate about objects and events that are not perceptually available – because they are far away, happened in the past, are going to happen in the future – puts an unusual amount of pressure on the functioning of our empirical prejudice, because sensory illusions and our inner mental life are not the only potentially misleading sources of information. Faced by the prospect of potential social deception – the production and detection of which appears to have been a major focus of the physiologically expensive evolutionary R&D experiment represented by our big brains[6] – successful human beings are going to be those who value physical evidence over verbal assertions, direct evidence over hearsay. This "show-me" attitude forms the basis of human legal systems, which themselves are arguably merely the extension of ancient species-typical conflict-resolution strategies.[7] When faced with disagreement or potential deception, we want evidence – and, as Susan Haack argues, "both in law and in everyday life, there is a usage in which 'evidence' means 'physical evidence,' and refers to the actual fingerprints, bitemarks, documents, etc.," to "objects of experiential evidence" (2003: 61). It is this ability to make reference to a perceptually shared world that breaks us out of both objectivist formal logic and the web of signifiers or endless rounds of conversation to which the social constructivists would condemn us. "Experiential evidence," Haack observes, "consists, not of propositions, but of perceptual interactions; and it contributes to warrant, not in virtue of logical relations among propositions, but in virtue of connections between words and world set up in language learning" (63).

---

[6] For the "Machiavellian intelligence" hypothesis that our large brains have evolved to deal with problems of social deception and political coalition formation, see especially Humphrey 1976 and 1984, Alexander 1979, and Byrne & Whiten 1988; for a recent review article, see Flinn et al. 2005, and for an account of the roots of social intelligence in our primate cousins, the chimpanzees, see de Waal 1989.

[7] For a fascinating account of ancient Chinese legal practices as reflected in recently discovered archeological materials, see Weld 1999.

For instance, we probably could not wish for a better illustration of Baudrillardian hyperreality than the case put forward by the Bush administration for the Gulf War, part II, concerning Saddam Hussein's supposed possession of weapons of mass destruction (WMDs). This was one of the administration's primary rationales for invading Iraq, and they had what they considered to be fairly convincing, though indirect, evidence for the existence of WMDs on the ground: suggestive spy satellite photos, secondhand reports from refugees, and so on. Once the United States invaded Iraq, massive amounts of resources were dedicated to locating these supposed WMDs, and the people directing and participating in this search were highly motivated to find them, to the point that virtually any warehouse containing a few empty canisters was trumpeted as a potential chemical warfare factory. Yet the empty canisters turned out, upon examination, to be merely canisters, and despite the Bush administration's best attempts at spin doctoring, it eventually became clear that no "smoking gun" – itself quite a revealing metaphor! – was going to be found. If ever there was a situation where control of information, control of the evidence-gathering process, and sheer political and economic interest could determine what counted as truth, this should have been it. The fact that the concerted effort of the most powerful nation on earth was not enough to have its version of reality substantiated as fact by the global community gives us a nice contemporary example of how the world as revealed to our senses can, even in an era of hyperreality, still have its say.

Possible Counterexample 1: The Humanities

One common but crude way of distinguishing between the natural sciences and the humanities is to see natural science as concerned with testing and evidence, and the humanities as concerned with *Verstehen*, or "interpretative understanding" – the mysterious process by which one human mind grasps the product of another human mind. According to certain understandings of the process of interpretation, evidence plays little or no role: interpretation is the result of the free apprehension of spirit by spirit, unfettered by the sort of appeal to concrete evidence or proof that we require in our more mundane interactions with the physical world.[8]

While this model of *Verstehen* as free apprehension may accurately describe how individuals approach the arts qua individuals, it does not seem to fit how the humanities as an academic profession now operates. Depending on one's view, this may be a bad thing, but despite how one feels about it, the growing reliance in the humanities on evidential scholarship is an undeniably dominant trend. To take one example from my field, a radical new interpretation of and dating scheme for a classical Chinese text was published several years ago and made quite a stir in the

---

[8] A classic exposition of this position is Hans-Georg Gadamer's (1975) argument against "method" as a route to humanistic truth.

sinological community.[9] The study was meticulously researched and supported by very impressive, vaguely scientific-looking apparati, but what caused many scholars – including myself – to remain unconvinced was the circularity of the argument. There were only two dates that could be independently corroborated by the historical record or archeological evidence, and both of these dates lay firmly within the boundaries of the traditional chronology. The rest of the argument consisted of "evidence" that was dependent on one already accepting the theory: for instance, taking as axiomatic the claim that each chapter of the text was written by a new generation of disciples, or seeing mentions of actual historical figures within the traditional chronology as metaphorical references to later figures. Because of this lack of independent support, the theory ultimately failed to win widespread acceptance in the field – although if tomorrow an archeological version of this text were discovered in a tomb sealed at a known date and matching what their theory would predict, this would go a long way toward converting me and the rest of the sinological community. Another example that hits a bit closer to home concerns what I like to think was a very elegant and convincing argument advanced in my Ph.D. dissertation about the development of an early Chinese religious concept, based on received texts and an archeological text discovered in 1976. Unfortunately for my argument, *another* archeological text found in a tomb sealed at a known date and published in 1998 unambiguously proved my theory wrong, and there was no getting around it:[10] I had to simply drop the argument from my later work.

Now, one might quite reasonably object that the rise of evidence-based "method" in the humanities is a relatively recent phenomenon, becoming dominant in the West only in the Renaissance, and in East Asia only with rise of the "examining evidence" (*kaozheng*) movement of the Qing Dynasty (1644–1911). I would reply that premodern humanistic scholars were not, in fact, indifferent to the appeal of evidence, they simply did not have what we would now consider particularly helpful tools for separating good evidence from bad. For instance, in the traditional Chinese interpretive community, "this is what I think" was typically taken to be quite good evidence in support of the claim that "this is what Confucius could plausibly have thought." Contentious issues were still settled by debate and appeal to evidence; there was just a rather different idea of what constituted convincing evidence or how competing evidence should be evaluated. We would be right in seeing this traditional approach – not by any means confined to China – as a different way of approaching the classics, more akin to the manner in which individuals today approach art or literature in their private lives. We would also be justified in resisting the objectivist view that precise enough methods can give us access to a single, ahistorically "true" meaning of any given text. Nonetheless, there

---

[9] Brooks & Brooks 1998; see Slingerland 2000 for a discussion and critique.

[10] Note the metaphor: we often think of arguments as journeys, as trains of thought, and in this metaphor bits of evidence become features of the landscape that we must navigate around.

is a reason for the rise of "method" in humanistic studies, and we can feel justified in calling it "better" for purely pragmatic reasons: once it develops, it drives other methods out. Very crudely, people find it more convincing. Despite the efforts of Heidegger and Gadamer, the evidential-based approach has only strengthened its hold on the humanities, and the result is arguably a more accurate, nuanced, and rewarding picture of the human past and present.

Despite his disingenuous claims to the contrary, if Foucault had fabricated his sources he would have been tossed out of the Collège de France, and the sinological community rightly rejects the claims by certain "translators" of fashionable Chinese classics to be able to understand these texts – without any knowledge of the language – because they have mystical access to the minds of the ancient authors. As to the question of why the evidential approach appears so late in the cultures of the world, and has such difficulty penetrating into popular culture, anyone who doubts the difficulty of developing source-historical critical tools should spend a few years trying to teach university undergraduates how to formulate and evaluate interpretative judgments!

Possible Counterexample 2: Religion

Perhaps the mother of all counterexamples one might raise in questioning the existence of an empirical prejudice in humans is religion, whose very raison d'être would appear to be the realm of the unseen and unseeable. If, however, we understand the motivations for dealing with the unseen and unseeable as coextensive with more concrete concerns – explaining, predicting, and thereby acquiring a measure of control over life – religion does not appear to be such a stark counterexample.

The "intellectualist-pragmatist" model of religion (Horton 1993: 13), which sees myth, ritual, and magic as practical technologies for understanding and manipulating the causal structure of the world, is most closely identified with the nineteenth-century theorists Sir James Frazer and Edward B. Tylor. Robin Horton, in defending his own form of "neo-Tylorianism," provides a helpful account of the gradual demise of Frazer and Tylor's model, which dominated anthropological theorizing through Malinowski and as late as Lévi-Strauss in the 1970s. With the rise of Durkheimian sociology and the idea of culture as a sui generis reality, this view of myth and religion as a form of protoscience came to be seen as rather naïve, intellectually imperialistic, and passé. Today in anthropology and religious studies it has been almost entirely replaced by the social-symbolic model, whereby myth and religion are viewed as entirely distinct modes of discourse, reflecting disguised social relations, "alternate" modes of thinking completely foreign to scientific reasoning, or discourse concerned with the ontologically unique realm of the "sacred."

Horton argues that this has been an unfortunate development, and that we can salvage what was insightful in Frazer and Tylor while jettisoning their often condescending and culturally myopic attitudes. This, however, requires swallowing what, for Western liberals, is a bitter pill. Consider even one of the less offensive observations of Frazer concerning the supernatural beliefs of "primitive" peoples: "Their errors are not willful extravagances or the ravings of insanity, but simply hypotheses, justifiable at the time they were propounded, but which a fuller experience has proved inadequate" (Frazer 1922/1963: 307). This confident, triumphalist talk of "errors" and "inadequacy" – as well as the title of the section from which the quotation comes, "Our Debt to the Savage" [!] – came quite easily to a Victorian scholar, but strikes a jarring note in a modern context. One of the great appeals of the symbolic account of religion is that it avoids any sort of direct comparison of traditional and modern beliefs – the two are simply different. This allows us to avoid the unfashionable conclusion that, for instance, ancient Chinese diviners were "wrong" when they thought that a particular sacrifice brought about rain, and that modern Chinese methods of bringing about rain over Beijing by firing silver iodide into the clouds is in any way "better."

The modern version of the intellectualist-pragmatist view of religion inevitably involves itself in evaluations of at least certain types of claims, because it argues that religious beliefs, like any sort of belief, are attempts to explain the world around us. The beliefs that we, as modern Westerners, would tend to mark off as "religious" are generally attempts to explain things that are not readily amenable to empirical study, usually by means of projection of more ordinary and readily verifiable intuitions concerning agency, physical causality, and so forth. What we would tend to characterize as religion thus fills the explanatory gap left by phenomena that cannot be grasped according to ordinary physical principles (Lupfer et al. 1996). A nice contemporary example of this sort of filling in of explanatory gaps can be found in a study of children's intuitions about the behavior of various artifacts – stuffed animals, wind-up toys, transparent pepper grinders – performed by Susan Gelman and Gail Gottfried (1996). The experimenters caused these items to move apparently under their own power, and while the children found this completely understandable in the case of the "animals," they seemed to be baffled by the sight of a pepper grinder moving on its own accord. When asked to speculate on what might be behind this, some simply confessed ignorance, but many were moved to postulate the agency of some supernatural being, the intervention of an "invisible person," or the existence of "invisible batteries."

There *are* several aspects of religion that seem hard to bring in under the umbrella of protoscience. One main reason that the social-symbolic account of religion seems plausible is that, in traditional societies, we do find a strong tendency to simply accept traditional religious explanations at face value, without it even occurring to individuals to subject them to empirical testing. As Robert Boyd and Peter Richerson have argued, however, this sort of "conformist transmission" of cultural ideas tends to happen only in two types of situations. The first is when conformity itself is the point: religious beliefs, rituals, and myths are often – like regional dialects, clothing styles, and culinary traditions – used as arbitrary tribal markers, simply to mark off an in-group from others. Conformist transmission also predominates in situations where "individuals have difficulty evaluating the costs and benefits of alternative cultural variants" (2005: 206). Boyd and Richerson point out that when it comes to issues such as child-raising techniques, medical treatments, or the efficacy of praying to the gods for good weather, the empirical support for any traditional cultural model is extremely difficult for a single individual in a preindustrial culture to evaluate. In such cases, cultural conformity is likely the best strategy.[11] I myself – with access to a wealth of information (print media, the internet, a global network of informants) unimaginable to a preindustrial individual – am frankly still unclear about the relative efficacy of modern Western allergy shot therapy versus traditional Chinese medicine for treating my sinus problems, whether rain forecasts from the official Environment Canada meteorologists are any more reliable than the off-the-cuff predictions made by my retired fisherman neighbor, or what the best way to deal with my infant daughter's colic might be.

Among the main areas of human activity in which religious explanations have traditionally dominated – and where, in many cases, they continue to dominate – are therefore precisely those characterized by complex, opaque causality that makes empirical evaluation difficult or impossible. As branches of the modern sciences make inroads into these areas, we would expect that religious and cultural conformist explanations will fade away. The "intellectualist-pragmatist" theory of religion thus makes a crucial prediction: as areas of the world become explainable in ways that are clearly and immediately verifiable by the senses, the scope of phenomena explained by religion will shrink. As many scholars of religion and science have argued, this is in fact what one observes. Robin Horton notes, for instance, that the rise of scientific explanation seems to be squeezing out the more immediately applicable "magical" aspects of traditional religions, while leaving the conceptual frameworks concerned with more abstract questions relatively untouched – suggesting that in areas where the two are in direct competition, the more successful explanatory framework will prevail (1993: 122–123). In a similar vein, Michael Ruse notes that, for most people, religious beliefs and ordinary rationality do not exist in as much tension as one might predict: people have a fairly clear, if implicit, sense of where religious explanations are appropriate. "It is one thing to believe in the miraculous nature of Noah's flood," Ruse notes. "It is quite another to think that a miracle caused the water in your basement. People know when to use the appropriate epigenetic rules" (1998: 178). What I would add to this observation is that the epigenetic rules of natural science have been gradually and inexorably replacing religious explanations in most areas of life. Michael Lupfer et al. (1996) note that even people who describe themselves as devoutly religious seem to prefer naturalistic over religious explanations for most everyday events – and although we

---

[11]   Cf. Steven Mithen's comment that religious beliefs may be "the solution *par excellence* to the problems of decision-making in highly uncertain environments" (1999: 157).

lack firm, long-term longitudinal data on this, one would expect to see a difference in this regard between, say, contemporary and colonial-era inhabitants of Boston.

Of course, if we take underdetermination seriously, we cannot claim for physicalist explanations some sort of a priori superiority over religious ones: if we wish to explain why, for instance, Hurricane Katrina slammed into New Orleans in 2005, there is no formal means for distinguishing between the theory that God caused it to happen to punish the residents of New Orleans for their sinful ways and the explanation that would be offered by a meteorologist. In this respect Feyerabend is correct in saying that modern Western science enjoys no formal epistemological advantage over traditional religion. What he fails to recognize is that, in pragmatic terms, the various branches of modern science have gained and held onto prominence because they do a much better job of facilitating prediction and control of their areas of explanation. As W. V. O. Quine observes,

I do, qua lay physicist, believe in physical objects and not in Homer's gods; and I consider it a scientific error to believe otherwise. But in point of epistemological footage the physical objects and the gods differ only in degree and not kind. Both sorts of entities enter our conception only as cultural posits. The myth of physical objects is epistemologically superior to most in that it has proved more efficacious than other myths as a device for working a manageable structure into the flux of experience. (1951: 41)

The ultimate defense of physicalist over religious explanations, at least at the macro level of everyday, observable objects, is thus a pragmatic one: physicalist explanations so far seem to work better. The Chinese government shifted from sacrifice-based attempts to break droughts to silver-iodine-based ones because the latter has proven to be more effective.

There is, however, one aspect of religion that does not seem to involve explanation, prediction, or control in any strictly practical sense: religion's ability to answer questions of "ultimate concern" (Tillich 1957). This now strikes both laypeople and scholars of religion as a defining quality of what separates religion from, say, science or economics. This idea that the essence of religion is to explain the big "why" questions is relatively recent, and – if the intellectualist-pragmatist model is correct – incomplete: religion used to explain a much wider range of phenomena, and it continues to do so in cultures less penetrated by modern science. Religion seems to us now to be concerned solely with ultimate concerns because this is its last stronghold, to which it has systematically been forced to retreat. As I will argue in Chapter 6, though, religion is unlikely to ever be dislodged from this mountain redoubt. Even as the "universal acid" (Dennett 1995: 63) of Darwinism threatens to render the big "why" questions meaningless – there is, according to Darwinism, no answer why – human psychological architecture appears to be incapable of fully embracing scientific explanation when it comes to questions of origins and meaning. This also points to an aspect in which the social-symbolic account appears to be accurate: because the big "why" questions are not amenable to empirical testing, we should not expect any sort of convergence in the answers to these questions, and evaluative comparisons will be difficult at best. We will return to this issue later.

SCIENCE AS AN EXTENSION OF COMMONSENSE EMPIRICISM

Having secured epistemological standing for ordinary commonsense empiricism, we can now relate this to the status of scientific knowledge. One contemporary philosopher of science who has done a particularly clear job of relating scientific knowledge to common sense is Susan Haack, who has defended a model of science based on what she refers to as "critical common-sensism" (2003: 23) – situated somewhere between the "Old Deferentialism" (objectivism) and the "New Cynicism" (social constructivism) – which sees science as one specific example of a more general human activity of empirical inquiry, common to detectives, historians, journalists, and cooks.

As far as it is a method, it is what historians, detectives or investigative journalists or the rest of us do when we really want to find something out: make an informed conjecture about the possible explanation of a puzzling phenomenon, check out how it stands up to the best evidence we can get, and then use our judgment whether to accept it, more or less tentatively. (24)

People perform informal, loosely controlled experiments all the time. This afternoon, for instance, I noticed a faint, irregular line near the edge of my favorite water glass. I quickly formulated a pair of hypotheses: H_1 (it is a very fine hair) and H_2 (it is a crack). I then generated sets of predictions from these hypotheses: I will run the tip of my finger over the line, and if it moves, it is a hair (H_1 is corroborated); if it does not move, it is a crack (H_2 is corroborated). I performed a crucial experiment that seemed to vindicate H_2 – the "hair" did not move when I ran my finger over it – but then the irrational resistance to the falsification of favored hypotheses kicked in: I am very fond of this glass, and did not want to believe H_2, so I immediately began to question my auxiliary hypotheses. The test assumed the hair was on the outside of the glass; maybe it was on the inside? I performed a new experiment, this time running my finger along the inside of the glass, and still the line did not move; moreover, I could now feel that the line formed a slightly raised, sharp ridge. I reluctantly conceded that H_2 seemed to be the case, and I threw the glass out. This demonstrates another important phenomenon: even unpleasant hypotheses are accepted once the weight of available evidence is overwhelming.

Of course I am unlikely to have thought about my glass exploration in terms of hypotheses and testing had I not spent the entire morning reading philosophy of science, but the comparison is a helpful and important one: there is no difference in *kind* between ordinary exploration of the causal structure of the world and what goes on in the natural sciences. As Larry Laudan notes, as human beings we all "seek to make sense of our world and our experience . . . there is apparently no epistemic feature or set of such features which all and only the 'sciences' exhibit. Our aim should be, rather, to distinguish reliable and well-tested claims to knowledge from bogus ones" (1996: 86) – what Laudan refers to as the principle of "epistemic naturalism" (155).[12]

Extension Through "Helps"

One of the things that *is* different about modern Western science – and that accounts for its startling success in explaining the world – is the manner in which it extends ordinary human empirical exploration by means of what Francis Bacon called "instruments and helps" (1620/1999: 89): instrumentation to expand the senses, experimental technique for isolating causation, and social networks and communication technologies for sharing information. As Haack observes, "Scientific evidence . . . is like evidence with respect to empirical claims generally – only more so: more complex, and more dependent on instruments of observation and on the pooling of evidential resources" (2003: 57), and the modern sciences have achieved their remarkable successes only because of "special devices and techniques by means of which they have amplified the methods of everyday empirical inquiry" (94). Many important scientific advances can be attributed to technological advances that have systematically extended the reach of the human sense, from Galileo's telescope to Hooke's microscope to space probes that send human vision and touch to the edges of the solar system. This explains why such vast amounts of energy and money are spent trying to see and measure things – from the state of the art of lens grinding in Newton's time to the billions of dollars spent by NASA on space probes.

The crucial importance of such "helps" becomes clear when we compare the relative successes of modern and premodern natural scientific inquiry. For instance, Robin Dunbar combed through Aristotle's biological works looking for specific empirical claims and compared them to the current consensus opinion in modern biology:

What is especially interesting about the things that Aristotle got right and those he got wrong is that they partition rather neatly into those things that were easy for him to see and those that were not . . . Essentially, if Aristotle could see the thing and dissect it, he usually got it more or less right; but if he could not, he invariably got it wrong. One reason why he got it wrong in these cases is that he often resorted to the conventional wisdom of his day. As often as not, this was the product of idle speculation rather than careful observation. (1995: 39)

---

[12] Cf. John Dupré's "family resemblance" concept of science (1993: 10 and 242–243) and Chalmers's description of a "common sense" model of the scientific method (1999: 171).

Dunbar's conclusions about Aristotle are also true of most pre–scientific-revolution cultures: they do a very good job on tangible things that they can easily see and manipulate, and not so great a job when it comes to the intangible. What counts as tangible or intangible, in turn, is to a great extent dependent on one's level of technological expertise.

Novel Cross-Domain Mappings

No doubt the development of modern instrumentation has radically expanded the circle of the tangible, but there seems to be more to the scientific revolution than simply a gradual extension and sharpening of human powers of observation. A quite reasonable objection in this regard is, if the empirical, scientific exploration of nature involves merely the extension of human common sense, why is modern science so hard to teach? And why was it only fully developed in the West after the Renaissance? Certainly non-European cultures developed impressive systems for understanding, predicting, and manipulating nature, but there seems to be something qualitatively different about the modern Western method of scientific inquiry.[13]

The really crucial step in the development of modern science seems to have been a ratcheted series of cognitive innovations, involving initially counterintuitive cross-domain mappings, that occurred to the ancient Greeks, were lost to Europe in the medieval period but preserved in Arabic, and then were rediscovered and further developed in the Renaissance. In Chapter 4 we looked at how cross-domain mappings, achieved through conceptual metaphor and metaphoric blending, can transform the intuitive input domains on which they are based. An excellent review article by Susan Carey and Elizabeth Spelke (1994) argues that the ability to grasp modern scientific and mathematic concepts emerges only after human beings' domain-specific intuitions about the world are transformed by means of cultural training in novel cross-domain mappings.[14] The work of Rochel Gelman and colleagues, for instance, argues that preschool children's innate – or "folk mathematical" – conception of number is transformed once they begin school and are socialized into cross-domain mappings "between number and physical objects (as the child learns measurement)" and "between number and geometry (via devices such as the number line)."[15] To use our terminology from Chapter 4, it

---

[13]   See Robin Dunbar's discussion of "cookbook" vs. formal science (1995: 12–33).

[14]   Carey and Spelke are inspired by Pierre Duhem's (1906/1954) argument that scientific physics is a result of a mapping between our ordinary understanding of the physical world – what I refer to as "folk physics" in Chapter 3 – and the domain of math, as well as Nancy Nersessian's (1992) work on physical analogy in Maxwell's conception of electromagnetism. Although not formulated in terms of cognitive linguistics, their idea of projections from "source domains" to "target domains" has obvious parallels to conceptual metaphor theory, and can similarly be integrated into the conceptual blending model.

[15]   From Gelman (1991), described in Carey & Spelke 1994: 184–185.

is only within the space of these new conceptual blends that such concepts as *zero* or *infinity* become comprehensible.

Similarly, with regard to physics, Carey (1991) has found that preschool children distinguish between material and immaterial entities (e.g., objects vs. ideas), but appear to have a slightly different conception of matter than do adults who have been socialized into scientific physics. Weight, for instance, is viewed by preschoolers as an accidental property of matter, which means that preschoolers judge that a pea-sized piece of Styrofoam will have no mass. Similarly, preschool children and roughly half of a sample of six- to ten-year-old children seem to view matter as discontinuous and nonhomogeneous, judging that, if one were to repeatedly cut a piece of steel in half, "one finally will arrive at a piece of steel so small that it no longer occupies space, and also that one will arrive at a piece of steel in which one could (in principle) see all the steel: There would be no more steel inside" (Carey & Spelke 1994: 191). A continuous model of matter does not consistently appear in children until around age twelve, and it appears to be the result of socialization into a novel cross-domain mapping between physics and number. Carey and Spelke draw upon the work of Carol Smith and her colleagues (Smith et al. 1992) for concrete examples of how visual models and physical analogies can drive reconceptualizations of matter in eleven- to thirteen-year-olds, prompting them to create novel conceptual blends.

One wonderful example, as recounted by Carey and Spelke, provides an "online" glimpse of the construction of the idea of weight as an extensive property. Students lacking such a conception argue that a single grain of rice should weigh nothing at all. Carol Smith and her colleagues ran a classroom experiment with such students in which varying numbers of grains of rice were piled on one side of a playing card, which in turn was balanced on a fulcrum whose thickness was gradually decreased. Students observed that, although fifty grains of rice are necessary to topple the card when balanced on a thick fulcrum, only a single grain is necessary when the fulcrum is sufficiently thin.

Students were asked to reconsider whether a single grain of rice weighs a tiny amount or nothing at all. Seven-year-olds are unmoved by this experience; they insist that the single grain of rice weighs nothing. A classroom of 10- or 11-year-olds presents a completely different picture. First, they are very interested in the experiment, and a lively discussion ensues, pitting those who now think that a grain of rice weighs a tiny amount against those who still maintain it weighs nothing. In every class observed so far, the proponents of the former view have spontaneously produced two arguments: (1) a sensitivity of the monitoring device argument and (2) the argument that a single grain of rice must weigh something, because if it weighed zero grams, then 50 grains of rice would weigh zero grams as well.

Note that these two arguments depend on the mapping from physical objects to number: It is only in the realm of mathematics that repeated division of a positive quantity always yields a positive quantity, and that repeated additions of zero always yields zero. In the realm of physics, in contrast, every physical interaction has a threshold. Repeated division of an object always results, eventually, in objects that are too small to be detected by any given physical device. Moreover, a collection of objects, each of which falls below the threshold of a given device, may well be detectable by the device. Like the Aristotelian physicists discussed by Jammer [1961], 7-year-old children who resist Smith's limiting case analysis and continue to insist that a single grain of rice weighs nothing are not necessarily irrational. Rather, they may be reasoning consistently within the domain of perceivable objects and outside the domain of number. (192–193)

Again, to put this in the terms of Chapter 4, the children who continue to insist that a single grain of rice weighs nothing have failed to construct the blend between physical objects and math that this exercise is intended to create. Those children who "get it" *are* able to construct the desired blend, and are now capable of, as Fauconnier and Turner put it, "running the blend" in order to arrive at conclusions that are counterintuitive from the perspective of the most relevant input domain.

This example illuminates several important points. First of all, the sorts of blends involved in modern science – or in any sort of cultural concept – can build recursively on themselves, with the result that the input domains for certain blends may themselves already represent culturally specific blends. In the rice-weighing exercise just discussed, the concept of number being drawn on is not derived from raw folk mathematics, but rather from an already culturally articulated blend between number and geometry whereby such concepts as *zero* and *infinity* are comprehensible. This kind of ratcheted innovation made possible by blending – where novel blends are used as inputs for other blends – allows us to get a sense of how highly articulated cultural models, such as those found in modern science, can simultaneously be grounded in and yet several steps removed from universal "common sense."

Second, as is shown by the age-sensitive nature of the process, the sorts of novel blends employed in science or any other cultural concept system need to be learned. This learning process requires time and effort and may not be mastered by all people. Furthermore, our ability to think in terms of the culturally specific blends acquired through such a process of learning – especially if the blends are multiple-stage ones – will probably never be as great as our ability to handle domains for which we have innate modules, except perhaps in the case of experts who have undergone extensive and long-term conceptual retraining. As Steven Pinker observes with regard to modern-world blended domains such as physics, economics, and math, "It's not just that we have to go to school or read books to learn these subjects. It's that we have no mental tools to grasp them intuitively. We depend on analogies that press an old mental faculty into service, or on jerry-built mental contraptions that wire together bits and pieces of other faculties. Understanding in these domains is likely to be uneven, shallow, and contaminated by primitive intuitions" (2002: 221).

Finally, like the blends examined in Chapter 4, scientific conceptual blends – no matter how elaborated – at some point draw on innate cognitive domains as their inputs. This accounts for Scott Atran's observation that different sciences draw on different innate cognitive domains – such as folk physics, folk biology, folk mathematics – even in the course of transforming our understandings of these domains. This means that "theories and analogies that allow us to speculate beyond commonsense domains must originally be formulated in terms of them, that is, with pointed reference to the cognitive 'givens' of our species" (Atran 1990: xi). As counterintuitive as the cross-domain mappings and blends employed in science may become – quantum mechanics and string theory come immediately to mind – it is important to recognize that the sole reason such apparently counterintuitive methods and claims can be learned at all by humans is that they draw on common sense as their raw material, and then are required to throw themselves at the mercy of common sense as their final court of appeal. The skeptical ten-year-old Aristotelians in Smith et al.'s fulcrum experiment are finally won over by a demonstration that they can *see*: contrary to expectation, a single grain of rice *does* cause the playing card to tip over. Understanding why this should be so requires a transformation of intuitive category understandings, but the impetus for such conceptual reorganization is something that is immediately and physically comprehensible. However counterintuitive, then, the entities involved in modern science can never be accepted by human beings unless they can ultimately show themselves to be efficacious in "the mother tongue of thought."

This may result in some strange cognitive disconnects. Modern physics, for instance, can be shown to "work" in terms that are intuitively convincing and comprehensible, and this is why Newtonian physics has been displaced by quantum physics – and also why Newtonian physics originally displaced the even more intuitively appealing system of Aristotle. Modern physics, however, involves assumptions and claims about reality that, in the end, make no sense to us: extended training can allow us to grasp the mathematical blends involved, but an intuitively satisfying picture of how a quark could have "color" or reality could consist of multidimensional "strings" remains elusive. As Pinker notes, "we have every reason to believe that the best theories in physics are true, but they present us with a picture of reality that makes no sense to the intuitions about space, time, and matter that evolved in the brains of middle-sized primates" (2002: 239). There is a whole host of questions, such as what was there "before" the big bang, or what lies "beyond" the edge of the expanding universe, that are simply unanswerable: there was no such "thing" as time before the big bang, and there is no such thing as space beyond the universe, but middle-sized primates such as ourselves cannot help feeling like such questions are meaningful.

A PRAGMATIC CONCEPTION OF TRUTH

Even if we recognize science as an extension of a deeply engrained and species-specific common sense – or, perhaps more accurately, "common senses" – skeptics might still argue that this type of common sense does not reveal anything "true" about the world. The human retina, for instance, responds only to certain wave-lengths of radiant energy. It is even worse than that: as we discussed in Chapter 1, seeing the world is not simply a matter of the retina passively taking in all of the images that impinge on it and passing them on to the brain, but is rather an active, highly selective process, systematically biased by innate or trained schemas that selectively pick up information about the world. It thus seems as though a truly objective, God's-eye view of reality is out of our reach. As long as we are willing to let go of objectivism, however, this should not trouble us.

Truth as Successful Achievement of Goals

Perhaps the greatest contribution of classical American pragmatism is its formu-lation of a viable alternative to objectivist models of truth based on observable practical *consequences*. Peirce famously argued that "a *conception*, that is, the ratio-nal purport of a word or other expression, lies exclusively in its conceivable bearing upon the conduct of life" (1905/1992: 332). Truth, on this model, is about practical success or verification, potential or actual. As William James argues, "*True ideas are those that we can assimilate, validate, corroborate and verify. False ideas are those that we cannot*" (1907/1995: 77).[16] The possession of truth is not an end in itself, but only "a preliminary means toward other vital satisfactions," and "the practical value of true ideas is thus primarily derived from the practical importance of their objects to us" (78). James sometimes referred to his as an "instrumental" conception of truth, whereby "ideas (which themselves are but parts of our experience) become true just in so far as they help us to get into satisfactory relation with other parts of our experience" (23).[17] This pragmatic conception of truth does not deny the existence of reality, only that formulating a complete and accurate picture of it is a desirable or obtainable goal. For pragmatists, the representation model of correspondence must be replaced with a sense whereby "to 'agree' in the widest sense with a reality *can only mean to be guided either straight up to it or into its surroundings, or to be put into such a working touch with it as to handle it or something connected to it better than if we disagreed*" (212–213).

From Representation to Engagement

Ian Hacking observes that the whole realism versus antirealism problem originates in the objectivist correspondence theory of truth (1983b: 25, 31). The "problem" can

---

[16] James also notes that, necessarily, most of the framework of our belief system is never verified by us personally but becomes part of our framework through some original work of verification that is at least potentially verifiable by us – "truth lives for the most part on the credit system" (1907/1995: 80).

[17] Cf. Putnam's defense of Dewey's concept of warranted assertability (1990: 21 ff.).

thus be circumvented by adopting a pragmatic, "causalist" account of what should count as real, or what should be at least provisionally accorded the status of "truth." By taking the mind out of its mysterious driver's seat – perched somewhere in our cerebral cortex, madly striving to construct an accurate picture of the world from bits of sense data trickling through the pineal gland – and dispersing "it" back into the various control systems of the brain-body where it belongs, we neatly sidestep many of the epistemological pseudoproblems on which the objectivist-relativist debate is based. As Donald Davidson notes, "In giving up the dualism of scheme and world, we do not give up the world, but reestablish unmediated touch with the familiar objects whose antics make our sentences and opinions true or false" (1974: 20).

This sort of embodied, practical, problem-solving approach to truth and under-playing of representational language is reflected in the work of modern pragmatists such as Hilary Putnam, with his defense of "direct" or "commonsense" realism, or George Lakoff and Mark Johnson's conception of "embodied realism." As Johnson argues, "'Accurately describing reality' is not a single, homogenous purpose on par with a purpose like making one's bed. 'Describing accurately how things are' is short-hand for 'finding descriptions of reality that work more or less well given our purposes in framing descriptions of reality'" (1987: 211). Richard Rorty makes a similar point in arguing that the objectivist model of science as a mirror of nature should be replaced by a conception of science as "a set of working diagrams for coping with nature" (1979: 298):

It is the vocabulary of practise rather than of theory, of action rather than contemplation, in which one can say something useful about the truth. Nobody engages in epistemology or semantics because he wants to know how "This is red" pictures the world. Rather, we want to know in what sense Pasteur's views of disease picture the world accurately, or what exactly it is that Marx pictured more accurately than Machiavelli. But just here the vocabulary of "picturing" fails us. When we turn from individual sentences to vocabularies and theories, critical terminology naturally shifts from metaphors of isomorphism, symbolism, and mapping to talk of utility, convenience, and likelihood of getting what we want. (1980: 722)

Even some philosophers of science who have been seen as staunch antirealists are best understood as critics of objectivist metaphysical realism, rather than the more modest sort of realism being defended here. Nancy Cartwright is one prominent example. Some of Cartwright's earlier work, such as her 1983 *How the Laws of Physics Lie*, were seen as targeting all forms of realism, but in her later work she explains that this was a mistaken impression. In arguing for the "disunity of science," Cartwright explains that her aim was to take on a "fundamentalist," objectivist model of science as converging on a unified God's-eye view of reality. A more accurate, situated model of scientific knowledge does not, however, rule out a limited form of what Cartwright calls "local realism." The possibility of "planning, prediction, manipulation, control and policy setting," she notes, is proof of the "objectivity of local knowledge"

I know that I can get an oak tree from an acorn, but not from a pine cone; that nurturing will make my child more secure; that feeding the hungry and housing the homeless will make for less misery; and that giving more smear tests will lessen the incidence of cervical cancer. Getting closer to physics . . . I also know that I can drop a pound coin from the upstairs window into the hands of my daughter below, but probably not a paper tissue; [and] that I can head north by following my compass needle (so long as I am on foot and not in my car) . . .

I know these facts even though they are vague and imprecise, and I have no reason to assume that that can be improved on. Nor, in many cases, am I sure of the strength or frequency of the link between cause and effect, nor of the range of its reliability. And I certainly do not know in any of the cases which plans or policies would constitute an optimal strategy. But I want to insist that these are items of knowledge. (1999: 23–24)

A pragmatic recognition of reality's ability to force itself on us can account for the brutishness of Searlian facts without committing us to a God's-eye ideal of objective knowledge.

PRAGMATIC RESPONSE TO THE PROBLEMS WITH SCIENCE

Adopting the sort of engaged, practical model of truth outlined earlier also allows us to extricate the natural sciences from certain problems that seem unavoidable from within either the objectivist or relativist framework. Here I would like to briefly outline a pragmatist response to some of the problems with science discussed in Chapter 1.

Underdetermination and Occam's Razor

Larry Laudan provides a helpful account of the various ways in which the underdetermination thesis has been used by critics of objectivist science, from Quine and Lakatos through Kuhn and Hesse to Derrida, and concludes that they all founder on the basic assumption that "the logically possible and the reasonable are co-extensive" (1996: 29), that "formal logic exhausts the realm of the 'rational,'" and so that "everything is either deductive logic or sociology" (50). A wonderful spoof from the satirical paper *The Onion* illustrates Laudan's point quite vividly.[18] Framed by a photo of an archeologist measuring a recently exhumed human skeleton, the headline reads, "Archaeological Dig Uncovers Ancient Race Of Skeleton People."

---

[18] *The Onion*, Dec. 8, 1999, issue 35.45. Reprinted with permission of *The Onion*. Copyright © 2007, by ONION, INC. (www.theonion.com).

AL JIZAH, EGYPT – A team of British and Egyptian archaeologists made a stunning discovery Monday, unearthing several intact specimens of "skeleton people" – skinless, organless humans who populated the Nile delta region an estimated 6,000 years ago. "This is an incredible find," said Dr. Christian Hutchins, Oxford University archaeologist and head of the dig team. "Imagine: At one time, this entire area was filled with spooky, bony, walking skeletons."

Various theories are advanced to explain how these spooky skeleton people might have lived; as "Dr. Hutchins" explains, "Although we found crude cooking utensils in the area, as well as evidence of crafts like pottery and weaving, we are inclined to believe that the skeletons' chief activity was jumping out at nearby humans and scaring them. And though we know little of their language and means of communication, it is likely that they said 'boogedy-boogedy' a lot." Attempts are made to explain away evidence that appears to contradict the "skeleton people" theory, and potential flaws internal to the theory itself are explored:

Approximately 200 yards west of the excavation site, the archaeologists also found evidence of farming.

"What's puzzling about this," Cambridge University archaeologist Sir Ian Edmund-White said, "is that skeletons would not benefit from harvested crops, as any food taken orally would immediately fall through the hole behind the jaw and down through the rib cage, eventually hitting the ground. Our best guess is that they scared away a group of human farmers, then remained behind to haunt the dwelling. Or perhaps they bartered goods in a nearby city to acquire skeleton accessories, such as chains, coffins and tattered, dirty clothing."

Continued Edmund-White: "The hole in that theory, however, is that a 1997 excavation of this area which yielded extensive records of local clans and merchants made no mention of even one animated mass of bones coming to town for the purpose of trade. But we are taking great pains to recover as much of the site as possible, while also being extremely careful not to fall victim to some kind of spooky skeleton curse."

Finally, as is often the case in archeological reports, the researchers conclude their more rigorous empirical discussion with a bit of theoretical speculation:

As for what led to the extinction of the skeletons, Edmund-White offered a theory.

"Perhaps an Egyptian priest or king broke the curse of the skeletons, either by defeating the head skeleton in combat or by discovering the magic words needed to send their spirits back to Hell," Edmund-White said. "In any case, there is strong evidence that the Power of Greyskull played a significant role in the defeat of the skeleton people."

It is important to note that – although they contradict everything we think we know about biology, history, and physics – there is nothing *formally* wrong with the sorts of hypotheses forwarded here: we cannot, a priori, block the deductive move from the discovery of a human like skeleton in the ground to the theory of the fearsome tribe of warrior-skeletons – nor, of course, can we ever conclusively rule out the possible influence of the Power of Greyskull. To take a more practically relevant, but no less fantastic, example, the extant fossil record suggests that the earth is quite old, and that species have changed gradually over time in a manner that is consistent with Darwinian evolution. However, the set of data represented by the fossil record is equally compatible with the theory that the earth and all of its species were created by God within the time frame suggested by the Bible, and that a deliberately misleading set of fossils was then created by God (or Lucifer) to test humankind's faith. There is no formal algorithm for deciding between these hypotheses – it is just that the latter seems pretty wacky to most people.

"Sounds wacky" does not seem like a particularly confidence-inspiring or rational basis for rejecting a hypothesis. As noted earlier, Larry Laudan observes, however, the lack of an airtight, formal procedure for deciding between potential hypotheses is a problem only if one believes that the "formal logic exhausts the realm of the 'rational.'" The humor of the *Onion* piece derives from its obvious absurdity, and what makes the absurdity "obvious" is common sense: our nonformal, intuitive *feeling* for where the boundaries of the reasonable lie. This feeling is sometimes wrong – most important scientific revolutions have required flouting it, and the development of post-Newtonian physics has required a sustained suspension of it. The degree to which it is shared, as well as its general shape, is also affected by the background beliefs and practices of one's social group – fundamentalist explanations for the fossil record apparently sound reasonable to some people. In its basic form, though, this sense appears to be widely shared, and for better or worse it sets strict boundaries on what we are willing to conceptually entertain.

Although common sense has no a priori warrant, does not guarantee us a God's-eye view of truth, and is to a certain extent the contingent product of social consensus, our very existence is testament to the fact that it has done a pretty good job of guiding our ancestors and ourselves through the world. Putnam provides a pragmatic defense of commonsense induction, logical flaws and all:

In general, and in the long run, true ideas are the ones that succeed – how do we know this? This statement too is a statement about the world; a statement we have come to from experience of the world; and we believe in the practice to which this idea corresponds, and in the idea as informing that kind of practice, on the basis that we believe in any good idea – it has proved successful! In this sense "induction is circular." But of course it is! Induction has no deductive justification; induction is not deduction . . . We do have a propensity – an *a priori* propensity, if you like – to reason "inductively," and the past success of "induction" increases that propensity. (1991 : 79)

Our continued belief in the reliability of ordinary induction – a belief "implanted in us by nature," as Hume puts it (1777/1975: 55) – and our resistance to entertaining the vast majority of the infinite logically possible hypotheses are nothing more than formally indefensible hunches, but ones that have served us well and continue to do so.

These sorts of hunches are sometimes given official names. "Occam's razor," for instance – the injunction to avoid needlessly multiplying entities – is often presented as if it were a logical necessity or natural law. Despite all attempts to formalize it,[19] however, it remains clear that Occam's famous razor is essentially a pragmatic heuristic: whether and how it is applied depends on unformalizable hunches about how many is "too many" and a probabilistic sense of what is reasonable. We see the context-dependent nature of Occam's razor clearly in the example of the discovery of Neptune discussed in Chapter 1: postulating the existence of a hypothetical, previously unknown planet to save Newton's mechanics seems like a classic example of unnecessarily multiplying entities – reminiscent of the epicycles and deferents that Ptolemaic astronomers needed to make their calculations work. However, the astronomic community at the time postulating this additional planet just *felt* right considering the solidity and massive explanatory power of Newtonian mechanics, and lack of any viable replacement for it.

To get a more visceral sense of how pragmatic intuitions play a crucial role in the formulation and acceptance of scientific theories, it might be helpful to consider a contemporary and – until quite recently, at least – controversial example. I am writing this paragraph in July 2006. I can remember a time, not very long ago, when there was deep disagreement in the scientific community about the reality of global warming – whether supposedly higher temperatures were anything more than noise, normal fluctuations unrelated to any kind of long-term, statistically significant trend. Something seems to have changed recently, and now the debate is not so much about whether or not global warming is a reality, but about how fast it is happening, what can be done about it, and what the likely consequences are. So what changed? Certainly this shift was not the result of one particular new observation or crucial experiment. It seems as if an accumulating "weight" of evidence in favor of global warming has caused the perceptible "shift" – and I use scare quotes in order to draw our attention to an important point: the fundamentally metaphorical, embodied nature of the process. We might be able to put our finger on something specific that finally converted any given global warming skeptic: the freakishly warm winter and lethally hot summer of 2006; the additional retreat of the Arctic ice cap; a highly publicized study on the slowdown of the Atlantic Gulf Stream; the damage caused by a new warm-weather pest invading Canadian pine forests; the international sovereignty posturing inspired by the increasingly real prospect of a commercially viable Northwest passage; or – as I suspect is often the case – simply a personal, local observation ("Damn, I remember sledding on that hill every winter, and it hasn't seen snow since my ten-year-old was born"). Whatever the "final straw" – and I will stop with the annoying scare quotes now, but please continue to notice how metaphorical all of this is – it is probably less a formal

---

[19] See, e.g., Jefferys & Berger 1992, who attempt to provide an objective, Bayesian formulation of Occam's razor.

process of Bayesian analysis or hypothetico-deductive reasoning and more a *feeling*
of weight and shifting, ultimately grounded in a bodily sense of balance,[20] that is
involved here. This does not make it any less true, in the species-specific, pragmatic
sense of "truth" that we are working with here. Our bodily sense of balance does a
very good job of allowing us to move effectively through the world as bipeds. The
metaphorical extension of this sense to more abstract considerations of evidence
in legal cases, scientific disputes, or the decision of what car to buy or what person
to marry is no less effective – and despite the relatively recent creation of formal
decision making or reasoning protocols, it is this prerational sense that still has
the final say. There is also some evidence that in many, if not most, situations, this
sense does a better job of guiding us through the world than formalized, drawn-out
deliberation.[21]

The slippery slide down the underdetermination slope is blocked, then, by a
collection of hunches, prejudices, and intellectual values that have evolved as part of
human cognitive architecture. It is these intuitions that organize our experience of
the world, play a major role in determining the sorts of hypotheses we can formulate,
and help us to decide between competing hypotheses. As Paul Churchland observes
in his evolutionary defense of "super-empirical values" such as those exemplified
by Occam's razor,

values such as ontological simplicity, coherence, and explanatory power are some of the
brain's most basic criteria for recognizing information, for distinguishing information
from noise. And I think they are even more fundamental values than is "empirical
adequacy," since collectively they can overthrow an entire conceptual framework for
representing empirical facts. Indeed, they even dictate how such a framework is constructed by the questing infant in the first place. (1985: 42)[22]

The theoretical commitments that emerge triumphant from our cognitive filters are
not guaranteed to be accurate, objective representations of a human-independent
reality, but we don't need that – and have never needed it. The fact that organisms
possessing such filters have survived for so many generations merely assures us
that the theories approved by our hunches are likely to help us cope with the world
effectively. As Quine has observed with regard to induction, "Creatures inveterately
wrong in their inductions have a pathetic but praise-worthy tendency to die before
reproducing their kind" (1969: 126).[23]

---

[20] See Johnson 1987: 72–100 on the inextricably embodied, gestalt nature of our abstract conception of
     balance, also discussed in Chapter 4.
[21] See Wilson & Schooler 1991, Wilson 2002, and Dijksterhuis et al. 2006.
[22] Cf. Michael Ruse's argument that the biological value of math, simplicity, causal inference, and
     consilience supports the conclusion that "scientific methodology is grounded in epigenetic rules,
     brought into existence by natural selection" (1998: 168).
[23] As noted in Chapter 1, Paul Churchland and Stephen Stich have argued that Quine's argument
     should not be taken as support for human beings' possessing an accurate *representation* of reality;
     it may very well be the case that our deductions and inductions result in models that are inaccurate

Preserving a Notion of Progress

Kuhn is most famous for arguing that the scientific community manufactures an illusion of progress by systematically stamping out traces of its own history. "The member of a mature scientific community is, like the typical character of Orwell's *1984*, the victim of a history rewritten by the powers that be" (1962/1970: 167). In place of the positivist model of science as the steady accumulation of more and more data, and a closer and closer approximation to reality, Kuhn proposed his notion of paradigm shifts: scientific change involves gestalt shifts between completely incommensurable frameworks. According to this notion, it makes no more sense to speak of any given paradigm as "more accurate" than it does to declare which is the "right" way of seeing the sort of visual illusion diagrams that switch between looking like a duck or a rabbit.

As I have already discussed in Chapter 1, Kuhn's observations are an important corrective to naïve, positivistic accounts of scientific methodology and theoretical progress. If we are willing to give up the objectivist dream of a complete, unified theory of everything, however, it is possible to preserve a pragmatic account of how current scientific theories are, in some important way, "better" than previous ones.[24] Larry Laudan, for instance, argues that the lack of strict cumulativity in scientific progress – the fact that Newtonian physics, for instance, is not encompassed in any straightforward way by Einsteinian physics – does not in any way invalidate the idea that we are getting better and better paradigms for dealing with the world.

Outside of science, when we are asking whether one thing is an improvement on another, we do not insist upon cumulativity. Thus, we do not hesitate to say that we humans are smarter than birds, even though birds know how to do certain things (e.g., navigate accurately over long distances) that humans have only recently mastered. We hold that modern medicine is an improvement on African tribal medicine, even though some witch doctors could evidently cure certain diseases whose analysis continues to elude modern medicine . . . If we can make these uncontroversial judgments of progress outside the sciences as such, even when there is a partial loss of problem-solving ability, why should we have any difficulty doing so within science? (1996: 22)

Philip Kitcher similarly argues for a "realist-rationalist" model of scientific progress (1998), based on a "naturalistic epistemology" that treats "the growth of science as a process in which cognitively limited biological entities combine their efforts in a social context" (1993: 9). He notes that a closer examination of some of Kuhn's prime examples of paradigm shift, such as the case of Lavoisier and the phlogiston controversy, reveals them to be fairly clear examples of how reasonable people can

---

but adaptive nonetheless – for instance, in cases where the danger of a false negative far outweighs that of a false positive, as in the detection of poisons. See Churchland 1985 and Stich 1990.

[24] Kuhn later explained that he did not intend to rule out this possibility; see Kuhn 1970 (I thank Mohammed Reza Memar-Sadeghi for this observation).

disagree for a very long time and yet ultimately find themselves compelled by the evidence to reach consensus (272–290).

A commonsense, pragmatic view of our contact with reality helps break us out of a theory-fetish view of science and scientific progress. Ian Hacking notes that it is often immediate observation that stimulates new theorizing; the story of the discovery of radio waves or the development of big bang theory is often spun into a "theory-centric" retelling, but the process itself seems basically to involve embodied human beings noticing things about the world that appear important to them (1983b: 157–160). As I argued earlier in my critique of the "bad" Kuhn, the very idea of "anomaly" is incoherent unless one assumes that human beings can notice things that do not match their theories, and thereby be motivated to change those theories accordingly.

Limited Realism Concerning Observables and Unobservables

There is a nontrivial sense in which Galileo created a new way of "seeing" with the invention of the telescope, a heavily mediated and novel technology. As Feyerabend has pointed out, no one at the time could give an adequate theoretical account of how the telescope functioned, and – considering the fairly widely accepted notion that the terrestrial and celestial spheres were entirely distinct ontological realms – why it should be expected to give an accurate picture of the heavens (1993: 77–105). Ian Hacking makes a similar point with regard to "observation" by means of complicated instruments such as optical or electron microscopes, which require both a host of theoretical assumptions and a fair degree of manipulation of the "observed" (1983b: 186–209). The fact that much of modern science is based on such extremely mediated ways of "seeing" has led Feyerabend, for one, to conclude that scientific observation statements are no different in kind from magical incantations or religious oracles.

What Feyerabend and other epistemological skeptics give inadequate weight to is the fact that, in the end, the only reason heavily mediated observations – whether through Galileo's telescope or a modern biochemist's electron microscope – are ever taken seriously is that they can (somehow, eventually, perhaps highly indirectly) be verified through more immediate means. One of the things that most power-fully and convincingly won over Galileo's doubters was practical demonstrations of the telescope that allowed for immediate verification: for instance, situating the telescope on a Tuscan hilltop so that viewers could read the small writing carved into the walls of a palace miles away.[25] Feyerabend argues that, according to the

---

[25] See the comments of Julius Caesar Lagalla, a professor of philosophy in Rome, who was present at one such demonstration of Galileo's device (Lagalla 1612: 8, quoted in Rosen 1947: pl. 54, in turn quoted in Feyerabend 1993: 84).

metaphysics of the time, there was no reason to think that the terrestrial triumph of the telescope should translate to the heavens, and therefore displays such as this were fundamentally no more than bits of "trickery" in service of Galileo's broader propaganda campaign.[26] Feyerabend is certainly getting at something important here: Galileo's various bits of evidence were *not* really theoretically justified, and therefore conversion to his view was, in a sense, irrational, if we take theoretical consistency to define rationality. If we, instead, rely on a pragmatic sense of reasonableness instead of demanding objectivist certainty, the triumph of Copernicanism can be attributed to the *felt weight* of the various demonstrations that Galileo was able to cobble together.[27] Its further entrenchment can be credited to the manner in which supporting observations – both direct and indirect – have continued to accumulate, and how successful the assumptions of Copernicanism have been in allowing us to *do* things in the world, like go to the moon and position satellites in geosynchronous orbit.

This is the central import behind William James's comment that "the hypothetical things that such men [as Galileo, Ampère, and Marconi] have invented, defined as they have defined them, are showing an extraordinary fertility in consequences verifiable by sense" (1907/1995: 72), as well as Nancy Cartwright and Ian Hacking's desire to replace objectivist scientific realism with what they refer to as "causalism." Hacking notes that otherwise nonobservable entities, such as electrons, can, in a predictable way, be used to cause changes at the macro level, such as altering the electronic charge of a niobium ball (1983b: 22–24, 36). "Reality has to do with causation and our notions of reality are formed from our abilities to change the world," Hacking observes. "We shall count as real what we can use to intervene in the world to affect something else, or what the world can use to affect us" (146). This leads to his famous dictum, "if you can spray them then they are real" (23): "The 'direct' proof of electrons and the like is our ability to manipulate them using well understood low-level causal properties," which means that "engineering, not theorizing, is the proof of scientific realism about entities" (1983a: 87). A great deal of ink has been spilled in the science studies literature on the indirectness of the evidence for such entities as DNA, which was originally "seen" only by means of quite difficult to interpret X-ray diffraction images. We have now reached the point, however, where improved imaging and manipulation techniques allow researchers to, for instance, attach a magnetic bead and a plastic "rotor bead" to a single strand of DNA in order to study the mechanisms of "negative DNA supercoiling" (Gore et al. 2006), which gives us an alternate version of Hacking's dictum: "if you can glue a plastic ball to it, it's real."

---

[26] Cf. Kuhn's discussion of scientific revolutions as ultimately rhetorical (1962/1970: esp. 92–95).

[27] See especially Chalmers 1985 and 1999: 161–163 for a pragmatic middle view of the Copernican revolution as involving a notion of evidence and proof somewhere in between objectivism and complete relativism.

SO WHAT'S SO GREAT ABOUT SCIENCE?

So what's so great about science? We like what it allows us to do. Why do we like what it allows us to do? Because evolution built us to like predicting and manipulating: potential ancestors who lacked these predictions simply didn't become *our* ancestors, or anyone's for that matter.

This side trip into theory of science and pragmatism can now be brought back to the main thrust of this book, which is that humanists need to pay more attention to the natural sciences. I cannot convince my fellow humanists that we need to attend more to empirical science unless there exist compelling reasons for thinking that empirical inquiry tells us something about the humanly meaningful world that armchair speculation does not. I hope that this outline of a pragmatic, embodied realist model of empirical inquiry has helped make the case that, even in our post-Kuhnian world, we can still come to the considered conclusion that some ideas just seem right and others wrong.

Why are the sorts of theories about the relation of thought to language outlined in Chapter 3 preferable to Whorf's or Durkheim's views? For one thing, they are based on large-scale behavioral and neuroimaging studies: to put it crudely, we have *pictures*. Yes, fMRI images are a highly mediated way of seeing, requiring a host of artificial skills and theoretical assumptions, and are potentially interpretable in a variety of ways.[28] As long as we maintain, though, that we are not looking for a single "true" description of reality, this should not fatally undermine our confidence in this sort of empirical inquiry. All that we need to accept is that these "pictures" allow us to make better predictions about what is going to happen if we do X – better than simply guessing, consulting our own intuitions, or relying on traditional cultural authorities. Taking them seriously puts us "in working touch" with the reality of human language and cognition so as "to handle it or something connected to it better than if we disagreed," to draw upon the formulation of William James, and they therefore demand our attention by virtue of this pragmatic utility.

We can argue, then, that the natural sciences get their immense prestige not through some conspiracy of white-coated powermongers, but because they demonstrably and reliably *work*. Even if we cannot literally see the laws of aerodynamics, we can see the performance of things built according to those principles – heavier-than-air metal tubes *fly* through the air, and cell phones transmit voices more or less reliably around the globe. This is the key to the natural sciences' current prestige, and it arises from an ancient human tendency: show me. As I will argue in Chapter 6, religion still plays, and will always continue to play, a crucial role in

---

[28] For a discussion of the reliability of the common practice of fMRI "reverse inference" – inferring engagement of a particular cognitive process as a result of observed activation of a particular region of the brain – see Christoff & Owen 2006 and Poldrack 2006; for the use of neuroimaging to localize psychological processes in social psychology, see Willingham & Dunn 2003.

answering inevitable questions about meaning (*Why* did Hurricane Katrina strike New Orleans?) – that is, inevitable for creatures like us, who appear incapable of refraining from projecting intentionality onto the world. The realm of these sorts of explanations is an area that natural scientific explanation will never encroach on, because these two sorts of explanation do not ultimately overlap. When it comes to practical decision making, however (Should we evacuate now? When is the hurricane likely to make landfall? Will the levees be able to handle it?), most of us listen to meteorologists and engineers, not Billy Graham. The same thing needs to happen in the humanities: if we want to figure out how a wink differs from a twitch, the old mysterian *Verstehen* story is simply not going to cut it any longer.

6

❧

Who's Afraid of Reductionism? Confronting Darwin's Dangerous Idea

*P*ERHAPS YOU ARE COMFORTABLE WITH THE IDEA THAT HUMAN BEINGS have an empirical prejudice, and that, because of the manner in which methods of empirical inquiry have been systematically developed in the natural sciences, natural scientific claims about a given phenomenon X are generally more reliable than guesses, intuitions, ungrounded assertions, or hearsay. Now, rate your comfort level with each of the following claims:

1. Life on earth originated through the algorithmic process of descent with variation combined with natural selection, as described by Darwin's theory of evolution.
2. Eagle eyeballs are the products of evolution.
3. Human eyeballs are the products of evolution.
4. Human bodies in general are the product of evolution; many physical differences between men and women (e.g., size, upper-body strength, ability to bear children and nurse them) are thus the product of evolution.
5. Human perceptual systems are the product of evolution; many details of the sensory organs and the mind's ability to perceive objects and direct the body to react to them are evolved traits.
6. The human mind in general is the product of evolution; many mental differences (e.g., general IQ, spatial-reasoning skills, emotional empathetic abilities) between individuals are therefore the products of evolution.
7. As products of a blind process of replication and selection, human beings as a whole – body and mind – differ only in degree of complexity from robots or machines: we, like everything in the world, are causally determined, purely physical systems.

If you are a fundamentalist Christian, I probably lost you at claim 1. If you are like the majority of my envisioned readers – university-educated humanists of some sort – you were probably fine following me up through claim 4, and perhaps into claim 5, but I would imagine most of you were reluctant to make the final step to claim 6. Claim 7 most likely seems downright bizarre: a nice premise for a dystopian science fiction novel, perhaps, but something that flies in the face of everything that we know about ourselves.

We generally have no problem with vertical integration when it comes to most parts of our bodies. Most of us cheerfully acknowledge that we cannot fly (at least not without modifying our bodies with mechanical aids) or teleport instantaneously, or that our blood and organs and our nervous system function in accordance with physiological principles that are in turn based on molecular biology, organic chemistry, and ultimately physics. Why is this? Why are most of us – "us" being well-educated academics or intellectuals, perhaps privately religious but with a deep commitment to the Western liberal separation of church and state – comfortable with evolutionary theory in a general sense, and confident that human bodies, like the bodies of other animals, are the products of evolution, but deeply troubled by the idea that anything we take to be fundamental about us as human beings – our ability to reason, to make decisions, to feel emotions, to make commitments – is part of our evolutionary design? Most of us feel comfortable acknowledging that women are generally shorter than men and have less upper-body strength, and we are all clear what a generic claim such as this entails: it is statistically true, and is not invalidated by the fact that there exist many women who are quite tall and many who are able to bench press more than most men. The suggestion dropped by Harvard president Lawrence Summers that women may, as a statistical group, be less adept at mathematics and engineering, however, was met with a firestorm of protest and ultimately cost him his job.[1]

As far as I am aware, there is no major protest movement aimed at improving the representation of women in the NFL or NBA: when it comes to sports we seem quite comfortable with segregating men and women into different leagues. When it comes to *mental* qualities, however, any type of generic claim involving gender-based differences makes us, as modern Western liberals, extremely uncomfortable, and seems on the face of it to be immoral. This sharp distinction we see when it comes to the physical versus the mental, in turn, gets to the heart of what makes us squirm when we contemplate claim 7. Evolutionary or natural scientific models of human behavior and cognition seem profoundly alien and implausible to most people, and this contributes significantly to our core resistance to a vertically integrated approach to the humanities. I would like to conclude my argument for integrating science and the humanities by confronting the question of why physicalist accounts of the self disturb us so much, why there do not currently appear to be any empirically viable alternatives to the physicalist position, and what all of this might mean for the humanities.

---

[1] Steven Pinker's *The Blank Slate* (2002) bears much of the blame for getting Summers into this mess; for a record of a resulting debate between Pinker and Elizabeth Spelke on the topic of potential gender differences in cognitive abilities, refer to the Web site http://www.edge.org/3rd_culture/debate05/debate05_index.html#s25. Also see Barres 2006 for a critique of Summers's and Pinker's position.

DARWIN'S DANGEROUS IDEA

Richard Dawkins and Daniel Dennett are two prominent intellectuals who have probably done the best job of working out the implications of a physicalist, Darwinist approach to the human being, and then presenting these implications in a vivid, unflinching manner – and this is no doubt why their work is so widely reviled.[2] Grappling with the issues they discuss is unavoidable if we are to understand the difficulties involved in adopting a vertically integrated approach to human-level realities, as well as what such an approach might look like.

Richard Dawkins's *The Selfish Gene* (1976/2006) is perhaps the most influential book on evolutionary theory in the past quarter century, a status celebrated in its recent thirtieth anniversary edition.[3] Dawkins's seminal book provided a coherent account of how inorganic molecules could conceivably acquire the ability to make copies of themselves, and how this mechanical ability to replicate, combined with limited errors in copying and the forces of natural selection, could give rise to all of the wildly complex forms of life that we currently see around us. Building on existing, but not yet widely appreciated, theoretical work by the likes of William Hamilton (1964), John Maynard Smith (1964, 1974), and Robert Trivers (1971, 1972, 1974), he also shepherded in the era of "neo-Darwinism" by making a devastatingly effective case for the position that the individual gene, or "replicator," must be the unit of natural selection – not the group or, as Darwin himself had thought, the individual organism. The gene-level approach to natural selection solved a variety of theoretical problems that had been plaguing Darwinist theory, from such broad issues as how altruism might have evolved or why sexual reproduction has become so widespread, to smaller but nagging questions such as the presence in organisms of large amounts of "surplus" DNA that does not code for proteins.

The gene-level account of natural selection is immensely theoretically satisfying, which is why it currently reigns as the orthodox version of neo-Darwinism, but it has some implications that are rather disturbing to most people. As Dawkins presents the history of evolution, the form of replicator that won the war for natural resources in the primordial soup was the precursor to DNA, which in turn began teaming up with other bits of DNA to form increasingly elaborate "survival machines" – from simple single-celled organisms all the way up to complex plant and animal bodies – to help garner more resources and spread copies of itself in the world. Animals and plants, according to this understanding, are thus essentially the creations of "teams" of replicating molecules, working together for reasons of

---

[2] Owen Flanagan notes that some prominent popularizers of the physicalist view of the self, such as Antonio Damasio, present a picture that is less overtly threatening to our traditional views of the self than Dennett's and Dawkins's, but this is because they are merely more circumspect, not because the picture that they are presenting really differs in any fundamental fashion (1992: 85–86).

[3] Grafen & Ridley 2006 presents a helpful collection of essays on Dawkins's model of neo-Darwinism and its intellectual impact.

convenience, and created solely to preserve these genes long enough to transmit them into the next generation. This means that all of the varieties of complex organisms that we see active in the world around us are fundamentally no more than "robot vehicles blindly programmed to preserve selfish molecules known as genes" (Dawkins 1976/2006: xxi). Dawkins's history ends with a vision of our present biological world as seen through a very strange new lens:

Now [the replicators] swarm in huge colonies, safe inside gigantic lumbering robots, sealed off from the outside world, communicating with it by tortuous indirect routes, manipulating it by remote control. They are in you and me; they created us, body and mind; and their preservation is the ultimate rationale for our existence. They have come a long way, those replicators. Now they go by the name of genes, and we are their survival machines. (19–20)

Darwin saw the struggle for survival and reproduction as occurring at the level of individual organisms, which makes intuitive sense to us: we certainly want to survive and flourish, and we have no trouble projecting this intentionality onto other living species. Neo-Darwinism turns this model upside down: individual plants or animals exist solely to further the "interests" of the genes contained inside them, not the other way around.

The gene-level perspective is disturbing enough in itself. Even more troubling is the fact that the entire process is entirely mechanical. The purposelessness of evolution is, of course, already a feature of classic Darwinism, but it emerges all the more starkly when we abandon the organism-level perspective: we cannot help but project meaning onto the struggle of an antelope to escape the clutches of a lion, or the lion to feed its offspring, but to think of both of these creatures as puppets merely carrying out the imperatives of their genes powerfully crystallizes the repulsive strangeness of a world without conscious design. The mindlessness of the evolutionary process is often obscured by the metaphors we – as possessors of theory of mind – inevitably fall back on in describing it, but it is important to keep in mind that talk of gene "interests" or "selfishness" is not meant literally. These mentalistic concepts are helpful heuristics, drawn from the domain of theory of mind to help us think about evolution, but the process itself is entirely mindless and purposeless. Why do genes *want* to be transmitted into the next generation? There is no "why" and no "wanting": reproduction is just what they do. Somewhere a long, long time ago a simple molecule began replicating itself, and the rest is evolutionary history: all of the beautiful complexity of the natural world, and the *Sturm und Drang* of human affairs, is merely the outcome of the descendents of this original replicator blindly repeating a purposeless, mechanical process. This is some dark stuff.

The application of this brand of neo-Darwinism to specific issues in comparative ethology is, as one would expect, no less disturbing. Parental altruism, for instance, is a widespread phenomenon in the natural world: we are not surprised when a bird, threatened by our approach to its nest, feigns injury and attempt to draw us away from its newly hatched offspring, at considerable risk to itself. We would do the same thing. The gene-level explanation for such behavior is that it is a special expression of the more general forces of "kin selection": parents in sexually reproducing species share a certain proportion of genes with their offspring, which means that – as gene survival machines – they should be designed to sacrifice themselves when the "math" dictates: that is, when such an action would result in a higher proportion of the survival machine's genes being transmitted into the next generation, based on such factors as degree of relatedness and actuarian considerations.[4] As the famous "Hamilton's Rule" (Hamilton 1964) dictates, a gene for a given type of altruistic behavior will be selected for when $b > c/r$, where "b" is the benefit received by the recipient of the type of altruistic act, "c" is the cost incurred by the actor, and "r" is the "co-efficient of relationship" between the actor and recipient. This "co-efficient," in turn, is determined by the genetic relatedness of the two individuals, being 0.5 for full siblings, 0.25 for grandparents and their grand-offspring, 0.125 for full cousins, and so on. If you are a well-designed survival machine, you will be inclined to leave two cousins behind as you flee the pursuing tiger, but two full siblings will make you pause.

Neo-Darwinist theory also makes very specific predictions with regard to such issues as mother-child conflict or sibling rivalry. For instance, from a neo-Darwinist perspective, weaning in mammalian species involves a conflict of interest between the genes housed in the mother and those in the child: the genes housed in the child want their survival machine to continue breast-feeding as long as possible, since breast milk is a low-cost (at least to the infant!) and extremely nourishing food. The genes housed in the mother have reproduced approximately 50 percent of themselves in the child, and so have an interest in allowing their survival machine to nourish its descendent as much as possible, but also would like to hedge their bets by producing some other descendent survival machines to carry versions of themselves. The genes in the infant are 100 percent related to themselves, and only 50 percent related to the genes in any sibling survival machine, and so it has an interest in favoring itself over any potential rivals who might divert resources. It wants to breast-feed as long as possible. The mother survival machine is 50 percent related to *all* of its offspring, and so has no reason not to spread its resources as equally as possible, which means that weaning should occur as quickly as is consistent with the likely survival of the first offspring. The work of Robert Trivers (1974) explores how this fundamental divergence of interest works itself out in the weaning strategies of many mammalian species, including humans, and does quite a good job of predicting both what these strategies should look like and what conflicts are likely to arise.

---

[4] Of course, neo-Darwinists do not think that organisms are actually doing such calculations consciously or in real time: "what really happens is that the gene pool becomes filled with genes that influence bodies in such a way that they behave as if they had made the calculations" (Dawkins 1976/2006: 97).

The fact that the ultimate reason for these various strategies (i.e., the genes' desire to most efficiently get copies of themselves into the next generation) do not necessarily resemble the proximate mechanisms that the genes design to make sure this happens (e.g., altruistic feelings, maternal love) means that such analyses are bound to appear profoundly alien to us. The neo-Darwinist model of the origin of human beings and other animals, and its formulation of the ultimate reasons for many of our abilities and behaviors, is thus theoretically powerful and satisfying while simultaneously appearing alien, and often repugnant, from any sort of normal human perspective.

The person who has perhaps done the most toward clearly spelling out the disturbing implications of neo-Darwinism for the humanities is the philosopher Daniel Dennett. His aptly titled *Darwin's Dangerous Idea* (1995) is a monumental survey of the current state of Darwinist theory, as well as an explicit exploration of what this theory means for our concept of the universe and of the person. This is an important project because, although most humanists have at least a fuzzy grasp of what Darwinism is all about, very few really grasp the challenge to traditional conceptions of the person that evolutionary theory represents. In this respect, Christian fundamentalist defenders of creationism, though typically derided by liberal intellectuals, are in fact a bit ahead of the curve: whatever one might feel about their standards of evidence or specific beliefs, creationists understand quite clearly, as Dennett notes, that Darwinism "cuts much deeper into the fabric of our most fundamental beliefs than many of its sophisticated apologists have yet admitted, even to themselves" (18). Unlike the majority of liberals, who see no tension between their championing of Darwinism in the classroom and their ideals of freedom and respect for human rights, fundamentalist Christians have no illusions about the "danger" of Darwin's conception of a mindless, designerless, mechanistic universe.

The dangerousness of Darwinism is captured quite nicely in Dennett's metaphor of Darwinism as a "universal acid": it "eats through just about every traditional concept, and leaves in its wake a revolutionized world-view, with most of the old landscape still recognizable, but transformed in fundamental ways" (63). Dennett notes that people have generally been resistant to working out the implications of Darwinism for human affairs, observing that "we" – that is, modern Western liberals – are content to endorse it as an explanation for the existence of plants and animals, and even for our own physical bodies, but draw the line when it comes to the realm of the *Geist*. The classic move made by those who wish to have their evolutionary cake and eat it too is to declare that science and religion are simply two different kinds of truth, focused on completely separate domains of human existence, and therefore do not come into conflict.[5] This is an argument based essentially on

---

[5] A prominent contemporary advocate of the position was Stephen Jay Gould, with his concept of "nonoverlapping magisteria" (1997); cf. Michael Ruse 2001. It is also the position advanced by the American Association for the Advancement of Science – the world's largest scientific society – in its recent and widely publicized book on the evolution-creationism debate, *The Evolution Dialogues: Science, Christianity, and the Quest for Understanding* (Baker 2006).

dualism: evolution describes how our *bodies* and the vast expanse of nonhuman reality came into existence, but our minds are a different matter (as it were). This is a comforting and convenient position, but the creationists are not buying it, and for good reason: the attempt to hold the mind-body line against the acid of Darwinism appears ultimately doomed to failure. As Dennett observes, "If we concede to Darwin our bodies, can we keep him from taking our minds as well?" (65).

Briefly reviewing Dennett's conception of the "Darwinized mind" is a helpful exercise, because formulating a coherent, physicalist conception of the mind is a crucial step in bridging the explanatory gap between physical and human phenomena. As Dennett explains, Darwin's great contribution to human inquiry was a framework for understanding how human-level phenomena such as consciousness and free will could have emerged from nonhuman, physical reality. The core Darwinian idea is that an utterly mindless, algorithmic process of descent with variation combined with natural selection can, given enough time, move us from Dawkins's primitive, selfish replicators competing for amino acids in the primordial soup to Immanuel Kant's *Critique of Pure Reason*. Like the Reverend William Paley coming across a pocket watch on the heath, human beings find it extremely difficult to get away from the idea that complex design requires an Intelligence to design it. Darwin's amazing insight was that such an original intelligence was not required, or rather – as Dennett puts it – that "Intelligence could be broken into bits so tiny and stupid that they didn't count as intelligence at all, and then distributed through space and time in a gigantic, connected network of algorithmic process" (133). The implication of Darwin's vision – again, infuriatingly clear to creationists and defenders of Intelligent Design, but rarely followed through to the end by defenders of Darwin in the classroom – is that "an impersonal, unreflective, robotic, mindless, little scrap of molecular machinery is the ultimate basis of all the agency, and hence meaning, and hence consciousness, in the universe" (203).

What this means is that the human mind is not a refuge of freedom and autonomy in an otherwise deterministic world, but rather "a huge, semi-designed, self-redesigning amalgam of smaller machines, each with its own design history, each playing its own role in the 'economy of the soul'" (206). One of Dennett's central organizing metaphors was inspired by observing a construction site where workers were using a small crane to construct a larger crane. This is a nice model for how evolution works: the functional power of a small machine representing the accumulation of billions of iterations of a blind, algorithmic design process – a single-celled organism, for instance – can be used by this process as a platform for an even more complex machine: the single-celled organism becoming a mitochondrion in a larger, more complex cell. The process of evolution is like a series of "cascading cranes" (75) performing the huge amount of design "lifting" that needs to get performed in order to take us from a chaotic primordial soup to human beings. We seem to be capable of imagining how this might work when it comes to retinas or spleens, but when it comes to the human mind, people have a powerful desire to look for "skyhooks" – magic cranes that descend from the sky, deus ex machina interventions from outside the chain of causation, exceptions to "the bleak vision of Darwin's algorithmic churning away" (75). If Darwin is right, however, we have no need for skyhooks to explain the world, no need for "mind-first" forces or powers. The human mind is a very complex crane built-up by billions of previous cranes, causally traceable back to the primitive neural circuits that allowed single-celled organisms to move toward light or away from toxins.

"Thinking" under this understanding, then, is not a ghostly, disembodied process, but rather a series of brain states – a series of physical configurations of matter – each causing the next in accordance with the deterministic laws that govern the interactions of physical objects. Ideas, as physical states of matter within our brains, can interact with one another, blend with one another, and transform themselves in predictable ways, but there is no superphysical soul or self, outside of the chain of physical causation, controlling or overseeing the process. This means that our thoughts and behavior are, at least in principle, as predetermined and predictable as any other physical process. It also means that the self as we ordinarily understand it – as a disembodied something, soul or spirit or mind, caused by nothing other than itself – is nothing more than an illusion created by the workings of our embodied brain. The picture of the human mind/self/soul that Dennett presents as the inevitable conclusion of Darwinism is summed up vividly and succinctly in a quotation from the Italian philosopher Giulio Giorello: "Yes, we have a soul, but it is made up of many tiny robots."[6]

The late Francis Crick, who spent the latter part of his career exploring the neuroscience of consciousness, called this idea that "*all* aspects of the brain's behavior are due to the activities of neurons" (1994: 259) – that is, that consciousness can ultimately be reduced to a physical chain of firing neurons – the "astonishing hypothesis." It is, in fact, more than astonishing: the physicalist view of the human self and the human mind is alien and profoundly disturbing. If you are not disturbed and somewhat repelled, then I have not done an adequate job of explaining this material, and refer you to the more eloquent and capable hands of Dennett and Dawkins. In any case, Dawkins 1976/2006 and Dennett 1995, in particular, seem to me required reading for any modern humanist. Whatever view one ultimately adopts vis-à-vis this thoroughly materialist view of the self (and I will suggest a slightly alternate view later), these ideas have to be grappled with because, strange as they are, it is difficult to see what choice we have once we take the decisive step of giving up our belief in a Cartesian ghost in the machine – of believing, to put a finer point on it, in magic. Unless we are prepared to invoke supernatural belief – Dennett's skyhooks – it is hard to avoid the conclusion we are "little robots" all the way down.

---

[6] Giorello 1997, quoted in Dennett 2003: 1.

At first blush this would seem to imply that we, as humanists, are now out of a job: what need is there for the *Geisteswissenschaften* if there is no more *Geist*? In the remainder of this chapter, I would like to discuss the issues of reductionism, levels of explanation, and innate human cognitive resistance to vertical integration, and finally draw on the work of Charles Taylor to sketch out a somewhat more finessed conception of "realism" than one tends to encounter among scholars with strong natural scientific bents. I hope to convince you that we do not need to retreat to some vaguely conceived form of dualism to do justice to both our sense of what is empirically plausible and our deep intuitions about the world – that we can acknowledge the reality of Darwin's dangerous idea while still living and working in an environment rich with human meaning.

THE BOGEYMAN OF REDUCTIONISM

One of the standard critiques of the physicalist view of the human being is that it is overly "reductionistic," an adjective that – like the equally damning charge of "realist" that one hears quite frequently in humanistic circles – functions nowadays primarily as a vague term of abuse. Daniel Dennett quite cogently argues that, "like most terms of abuse, 'reductionism' has no fixed meaning" (1995: 80). He observes that there are both "bland" and "preposterous" understandings of what it would mean to make a "reductionistic" claim, the former being essentially the sort of vertical integration being argued for here, and the latter being the sort of eliminative reductionism that serves as the great bogeyman of humanists. "Probably nobody is a reductionist in the preposterous sense," he declares, "and everybody should be a reductionist in the bland sense, so the 'charge' of reductionism is too vague to merit a response." (81) We can grant the thrust of Dennett's argument while still feeling that humanistic concerns about reductionism *do* merit a response, which will involve getting clearer about what it means to "reduce," what different species of reductionism look like, and what status human-level concepts would have in a vertically integrated chain of causation.

To begin with, it is important to realize that any truly interesting explanation of a given phenomenon is interesting precisely *because* it involves reduction of some sort – tracing causation from higher to lower levels or uncovering hidden correlations. As Steven Pinker puts it, the difference between reductive and nonreductive explanation is "the difference between stamp collecting and detective work, between slinging around jargon and offering insight, between saying something just is and explaining why it had to be that way as opposed to some other way it could have been" (2002: 72). He cites the wonderful Monty Python skit involving the brontosaurus "expert" Anne Elk – John Cleese in drag, if my recollection serves – presenting her radical new theory about the creatures: "All brontosauruses are thin at one end, much MUCH thicker in the middle, and then thin again at the far end." As Pinker observes, we find this "theory" absurd and amusing because

Ms. Elk "has not explained her subject in terms of deeper principles – she has not 'reduced' it, in the good sense. Even the word understand – literally, 'stand under' – alludes to descending to a deeper level of analysis" (72). We see this desire to dig into deeper levels of causation at work at the interpersonal level all the time. "Why did John do that?" one might ask. "Because he did" does not answer the question; we want deeper principles. "Because he wanted to." "Why?" "Because he was angry/ jealous / stood to gain financially." We are not satisfied with explanations unless they answer the "why" question by means of reduction: by linking the *explanandum* to some deeper, hidden, more basic *explanans*.

This is why the way that even traditional humanist scholars go about their work is already essentially reductionistic. My first monograph was a study of five early Chinese thinkers. I argued that these thinkers shared a common spiritual ideal, that there was a tension internal to this spiritual ideal that motivated much of their theorizing about human nature and self-cultivation, and that looking at these thinkers through the lens of this tension explained the development of early Chinese thought – and indeed the later trajectory of East Asian religious thought – in a uniquely satisfying and revealing way. I did not simply write my own version of an early Chinese philosophical text,[7] I *reduced*, trying to show how five apparently disparate texts could, in fact, be seen as motivated by a single, "deeper" shared goal and common conceptual tension. Now, some of my colleagues think that my book is a *bad* reduction – that it glosses over important distinctions, or distorts certain positions to make them fit this new narrative – but no one criticizes the project as "reductionistic" tout court. Reduction is what we do as scholars, humanistic or otherwise, and when someone fails to reduce we rightly dismiss their work as trivial, superficial, or uninformative.

When the deeper principles behind things are poorly understood – that is, when lower levels of causation underlying phenomena we are interested in explaining are not accessible to our prying – we are often forced to invent vague, placeholder entities to stand in for the missing information. Sometimes we are aware that this is what we are doing. For instance, Mendel could reason about the inheritance of traits without knowing how information about them was physically instantiated or transmitted, and Darwin could similarly map out the implications of natural selection without any clear conception of the substrate of inheritance. In such cases there is an implicit faith that the lower-level entities and processes will eventually be specified; if not, the theory may have to be abandoned. A discipline can find itself in a dead end, however, when it has postulated vague, placeholder entities without realizing that this is what it is doing – when it takes these unspecified and unknowable entities or faculties to have genuine explanatory force. Leibniz felt that

---

[7] Although if I *had* done this as an academic exercise, it would have to have been written as an imitation transparent enough (note the metaphor) to serve as a commentary on how such texts were structured.

this was the case with regard to the field of human psychology at his time, which relied heavily on such concepts as "the intellect" or "understanding." He notes that to invoke concepts like these is merely to save appearances

by fabricating faculties or occult qualities, . . . and fancying them to be like little demons or imps which can without ado perform whatever is wanted, as though pocket watches told the time by a certain horological faculty without needing wheels, or as though mills crushed grain by a fractive faculty without needing anything in the way of millstones (1768/1996: 68)

Nietzsche similarly mocked Kant for thinking that he was saying something substantive about the human capacity to create and feel the force of moral imperatives with his analysis of synthetic a priori judgments:

"How are synthetic judgments *a priori possible?*" Kant asked himself – and what really is his answer? *"By virtue of a faculty"* (*Vermöge eines Vermögens*)[8] – but unfortunately not in five words, but so circumstantially, venerably, and with such a display of German profundity and curlicues that people simply failed to note the comical *niaiserie allemande* involved in such an answer. People were actually beside themselves with delight over this new faculty . . . "By virtue of a faculty" – [Kant] had said, or at least meant. But is that – an answer? An explanation? Or is it not rather merely a repetition of the question? How does opium induce sleep? "By virtue of a faculty," namely the *virtus dormitiva*, replies the doctor in Molière,
  Because it contains a sleepy faculty
  Whose nature is to put the senses to sleep.[9]

"Such replies belong in comedy," Nietzsche concludes, and so should we.

  The force of the argument of cognitive scientists and evolutionary psychologists who are pushing for vertical integration between the humanities and the natural sciences – for embodying culture – is that the humanities have yet to genuinely free themselves from this sort of "Tartuffery,"[10] and continue to rely on impressive-sounding but explanatorily empty entities and faculties. For instance, Tooby and Cosmides note that the "Standard Social Scientific Model" is satisfied by the explanation that the blank slate of human nature gets filled up by means of "learning," which is about as helpful an explanation as that opium produces sleep by means of its "sleepy faculty":

"Learning" – like "culture," "rationality," and "intelligence" – is not an explanation for anything, but is rather a phenomenon that itself requires explanation. In fact, the concept of "learning" has, for the social sciences, served the same function that the concept of "protoplasm" did for so long in biology. (1992: 122–123)

[8] Lit.: "By means of a means."
[9] Translation from Kaufmann (Nietzsche 1886/1966: 18–19).
[10] Nietzsche's wonderful term for this sort of circular or nonsensical reasoning, after the Molière play from which the doctor's speech is cited.

Just as this mysterious "protoplasm" turned out to consist of a collection of distinct intricate structures with specific functions, so, Tooby and Cosmides argue, will words like "learning," "intelligence," and "rationality" turn out to be blanket terms for what are really a variety of specific, modular, evolved cognitive processes that allow human beings to selectively extract and process adaptively relevant information from the world. For instance, a proper answer to Ryle's question, considered in Chapter 3, of how we can tell a wink from a twitch is going to have to involve an account of the sort of facial recognition and theory of mind modules built into the human brain that we also discussed in that chapter. Following Ryle and Geertz and invoking mysterious words like *Verstehen* or "learning" to "explain" how we know that a wink is a wink in fact explains nothing and misses the point that recognition of the "semiotic meaning" of this gesture is grounded in a suite of functionally specialized and physically grounded cognitive mechanisms. The fact that any of these steps can be selectively knocked out by localized brain damage suggests that the empirical self plays more than just a placeholding role in the process of human understanding.

Of course, Ryle and Geertz can also be understood as making the more plausible point that the larger meaning of a particular wink – Why is *this person* winking at me? What should I do? – is embedded in a set of long, complex stories, and that for the unpacking and analysis of these stories we require the higher-level expertise of anthropologists, novelists, and historians. Such humanistic work, however, should not be seen as occurring in an explanatory cloud-cuckoo land, magically hovering above the mundane world of physical causation. Despite their variety and "disunity," the disciplines of the natural sciences have managed to arrange themselves in a rough explanatory hierarchy, with the lower levels of explanation (such as physics) setting limits on the sorts of explanations that can be entertained at the higher levels (such as biology). To move forward as a field of human inquiry, the humanities need to plug themselves into their proper place at the top of this explanatory hierarchy, because the lower levels have finally advanced to a point that they have something interesting to say to the higher levels.[11] Human-level meaning emerges organically out of the workings of the physical world, and we are being "reductive" in a good way when we seek to understand how these lower-level processes allow the higher-level processes to take place.

FROM PHYSICALISM TO THE HUMANITIES: LEVELS OF EXPLANATION

Having sent the bogeyman of reductionism back to its cave, it is now possible to talk about good and bad forms of reductionism – because, of course, it is really "greedy"

---

[11] As Barkow et al. complain, "To propose a psychological concept that is incompatible with evolutionary biology is as problematic as proposing a chemical reaction that violates the laws of physics. A social scientific theory that is incompatible with known psychology is as dubious as a neurophysiological theory that requires an impossible biochemistry. Nevertheless, theories in the behavioral and social sciences are rarely evaluated on the grounds of conceptual integration and multidisciplinary, multilevel compatibility" (1992: 4).

or "eliminative" reductionism that most humanists have in mind when they bandy about this charge. In order to distinguish productive, explanatory reductionism from crudely eliminative reductionism, it is important to get some clarity about the heuristic and ontological status of entities at various levels of explanation.

Levels of Explanation and Emergent Qualities

Although no evolutionary psychologist or cognitive scientist would purport to be an eliminative reductionist, and all give lip service to the idea that higher levels of explanation can feature emergent qualities not present at the lower levels, there is a common tendency nonetheless to privilege the material level of explanation: we are "really" just mindless robots or physical systems, no matter how things might appear to us phenomenologically. There are some very good reasons for this privileging of lower levels of explanation. To begin with, the physicalist stance has proven extremely productive, allowing such dramatic technological developments as supercomputers and pharmacological treatments for mental illnesses. Moreover, there is an a priori reason for giving precedence to the physical: the structure of the various upper levels of explanation emerges out of and depends on the lower levels, so the lower levels *are* causally privileged in this way. Molecules form and behave in accordance with more basic principles that govern both inorganic and organic substances, which means that a hypothesis in molecular biology that violates well-established physical chemistry principles is wrong, or else a reason for us to rethink our physical chemistry.

It is equally the case, however, that as we move up the explanatory chain we witness the emergence of what appear to be new entities, which possess their own novel and unpredictable organizational principles. As Patricia Churchland explains the concept of emergence, "If a property of one theory has causal powers that are not equaled or comprehended by any property in the second, more basic theory, then the property is considered to be emergent with respect to the second theory" (1986: 324). One of the clearest ways to get a grasp on how emergent properties emerge, as well as what their ontological status might be, is to turn to a model discussed in Dennett 1995, the "Game of Life" developed by the mathematician John Conway.[12] The game is played on a two-dimensional grid – originally a checkerboard – with each cell of the grid arbitrarily set to an initial "alive" (COUNTER) or "dead" (NO COUNTER) state. In the first round, the initial grid is then transformed in accordance with a simple set of rules:

Survivals. Every counter with two or three neighboring counters survives for the next generation.

[12] See Dennett 1995: 166–181. The "Game of Life" was first presented to a wide audience in Gardner 1970 and 1971, and since has become an Internet phenomenon, with innumerable sites dedicated to working out Life Worlds with various rules and initial states.

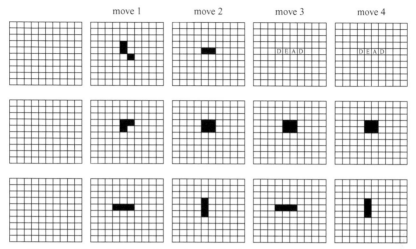

14. The fate of three initial configurations in the "Game of Life" (after Gardner 1970).

Deaths. Each counter with four or more neighbors dies (is removed) from overpopulation. Every counter with one neighbor or none dies from isolation.

Births. Each empty cell adjacent to exactly three neighbors – no more, no fewer – is a birth cell. A counter is placed on it at the next move. (Gardner 1970: 120)

There are two important things to note about the Game of Life. The first is that it is an obviously deterministic world: once the initial state is set, the manner in which this state will transform is determined algorithmically and is perfectly predictable. As Dennett puts it, "when we *adopt the physical stance* toward a configuration in the Life world, our powers of prediction are perfect: there is no noise, no uncertainty, no probability less than one" (1995: 169). The second feature of the Game is how quickly it gives rise to emergent phenomena: as counters are removed or placed on the board with each iteration of the algorithm, specific and coherent shapes begin to emerge, and these shapes often appear to begin "behaving" and "interacting" in novel ways. Although many initial configurations either "die out" quickly, or lead to stable configurations that cease to change (what Conway called "still lifes"), others are more dynamic. Figure 14 illustrates three of the sample initial states and their outcomes described by Gardner in his original article.

The first Life World quickly dies out, the second freezes into a static block, and the third results in a "blinker," which appears to perpetually flip back and forth between a horizontal and vertical orientation.

After being introduced by Gardner's articles in *Scientific American*, the Game of Life was quickly adapted to the computer, with digital grids blinking ON and OFF replacing the chess squares and counters. The massively greater computational power and speed of the digital computer allowed huge grids and an infinite number

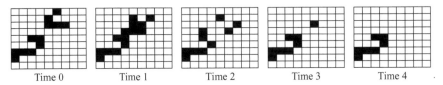

| Time 0 | Time 1 | Time 2 | Time 3 | Time 4 |

15. One glider consuming another (after Poundstone 1985: 40).

of randomly generated initial states to be "run," resulting in Life Worlds of greater and greater complexity, as well as a growing menagerie of Life World "entities." One of the most interesting and yet simplest is the "glider," an apparently self-propelled configuration that moves diagonally across the Life World grid, often colliding with and interacting with other emergent "entities." Figure 15 is a five-generation snapshot of a two gliders approaching each other from opposite corners of the Life World and colliding, with only one emerging "alive."

As William Poundstone observes concerning basic glider behavior in the simulations that he ran:

A glider can eat a glider in four generations. Whatever is being consumed, the basic process is the same. A bridge forms between the eater and its prey. In the next generation, the bridge region dies from overpopulation, taking a bite out of both eater and prey. The eater then repairs itself. The prey usually cannot. If the remainder of the prey dies out as with the glider, the prey is consumed.[13]

It is revealing how easily and quickly observers of the Life World begin to attribute both bounded identities and intentionality to what is, we have to remind ourselves, merely a pattern of squares turning on and off in accordance with a basic algorithm. It is also important to note how, once we become interested in emergent patterns such as "gliders," we begin to formulate new generalizations – completely unrelated to the simple, rigid algorithm that is the basis of the entire world – to describe and predict their "behavior." As Dennett observes, referring to this new level of description as the *design* level:

Notice that something curious happens to our "ontology" – our catalogue of what exists – as we move between levels. At the physical level there is no motion, just ON and OFF, and the only individual things that exist, cells, are defined by their fixed spatial locations. At the design level we suddenly have the motion of persisting objects . . . Notice, too, that whereas at the physical level there are absolutely no exceptions to the general law, at this level our generalizations have to be hedged: they require "usually" or "provided nothing encroaches" clauses. (1995: 171)

---

[13] Poundstone 1985: 38, quoted in Dennett 1995: 170–171.

The Life World thus provides us with a wonderfully simple model of how a completely deterministic, clearly algorithmic system can give rise to emergent, "higher" levels of reality – the design level of gliders and blinkers – that function in a manner not obviously predictable from basic, lower-level laws. There is no way, given an initial state and the guiding algorithm, that one could predict that entities called "gliders" will arise and will tend to "behave" in certain ways: you need to actually *run* the Life World simulation on a computer and see what happens. With the advent of the Internet, increasingly complex Life World computer simulations have become extremely popular, and entire menageries of wild entities – "glider guns" that shoot out steady streams of new gliders, logic gates, prime number generators – have been "discovered," none of which could have been predicted by Conway when he originally conceived of his simple checkerboard solitaire game. And yet we can readily acknowledge that none of these entities "really" exists: because we have been shown how the system is constructed, we are capable of pulling back from the drama of glider predator or the operations of logic gates to remind ourselves that all of this is merely the blinking ON and OFF of fixed, square cells.

To relate the Life World model and the lessons it teaches us to more obviously relevant concerns, we see a similar shift in ontology and variation in degrees of certainty as we move up through the levels of the reality studied by the natural sciences. The field of organic chemistry is based on principles that emerge at the level of organic molecules, and which cannot be fully predicted from the perspective of physical chemistry. Generalizations about the behavior of organic molecules also tend to be less precise, and more subject to ceteris paribus clauses, than the principles of physical chemistry. Similarly, no amount of intimacy with quantum mechanical principles will allow one to even begin to predict the behavior of macrolevel solid objects. As Hilary Putnam (1973) famously observed, there are entire fields of human knowledge, such as geometry, that emerge only once we reach the level of macro objects. The fact that a square peg 15/16 inch on a side will fit through a 1-inch by 1-inch square hole, but not through a 1-inch-diameter circular hole, is a function of the peg's geometric properties; referring to the properties of the molecules that make up the pegs or the materials from which the holes are drilled would be heuristically useless.

Even within what are sometimes assumed to be single fields, such as biology, there exist multiple levels of explanation, with structures at the higher levels being in no clear way predictable from or simply reducible to the levels below. As E. O. Wilson notes, the organization of social insect societies, such as termites and ants, is made possible only because of an unusual reproductive strategy, haplodiploidy, whereby fertilized eggs produce females and unfertilized eggs produce males. How or why this strategy may have evolved is open to speculation, but whatever its cause it led to the development of a unique form of social organization. This is because, with haplodiploidy reproduction, sisters are more closely related to each other than mothers are to daughters, which makes the strategy of females becoming a sterile slave caste dedicated to the rearing of sisters a potentially advantageous one. As Wilson observes,

The societies of wasps, bees, and ants have proved so successful that they dominate and alter most of the land habitats of the Earth. In the forests of Brazil, their assembled forces constitute more than 20 percent of the weight of all land animals, including nematode worms, toucans, and jaguars. Who could have guessed all this from a knowledge of haplodiploidy? (1978: 12–13)

When it comes to closely associated levels, causal predictive power can also move in either direction of the vertically integrated chain. Lindley Darden and Nancy Maull (1977), for instance, provide an illuminating account of the historical development in two closely related fields, cytology (cell biology) and genetics, noting that throughout this history "predictions went in both ways" (53), with discoveries at each level focusing attention in the other level in ways impossible to anticipate in advance.

This mutual dependence and interaction of levels of explanation is taken for granted in the natural sciences and is in fact one of the guiding principles driving natural scientific inquiry. The challenge for defenders of true vertical integration is hooking the various levels of explanation in the humanities into their proper place at the top of this causal explanatory chain. To oversimplify a bit by bringing this back to our Life World example, humanists are currently in the position of trying to explain emergent entity behavior as a mysterious, sui generis phenomenon, and react with hostility or disdain to the suggestion that, for instance, blinking squares have anything to do with the free and autonomous workings of the glider spirit. There *is*, as we have seen, something novel and heuristically useful about the principles of glider-level behavior. Moreover, real-life natural scientists, who have as yet only a partial understanding of a physical world inconceivably more complex than Conway's Life World, would no doubt find accounts of glider-level phenomena very helpful in their struggle to decipher these real world, lower-level mechanisms. These two sets of researchers need to begin comparing notes, though, with the recognition that both have something important to bring to the table. Long before the emergence of sociobiology and evolutionary psychology, John Dewey argued for a "principle of continuity" between the various fields of human inquiry and the natural sciences, noting that there was no reason to see a "breach in continuity between operations of inquiring and biological operations and physical operations" (1938/1991: 26). He also saw that continuity did not mean ignoring the existence of different levels of explanation, each with its own guiding principles. Continuity between such human-level phenomena as rationality and more basic-level phenomena as human biology means that "rational operations *grow out of* organic activities, without being identical with that from which they emerge" (26). Let us now turn to a discussion of how some human-level phenomena that seem extremely real and important to humanists could plausibly emerge from lower-level phenomena, as well as how precisely we should understand the ontological status of these various levels.

The Emergence of Free Will and Intentionality

How could free will emerge from a deterministic universe, without our having to postulate an entirely new type of entity? In the past decade or so a veritable cottage industry has sprung up dedicated to physicalist, neurobiological accounts of consciousness, free will, and human intentionality, and providing even a brief survey of this vast literature would require a book in itself.[14] For the sake of continuity, I will stick with my bad-boy, reductionist duo of Dawkins and Dennett, fleshing out their views with some observations from other researchers in the field.

Dawkins notes that it is important to realize that even though survival machines are made by genes, they are not *directly* controlled by them. Genes influence survival-machine behavior "not directly with their fingers on puppet strings, but indirectly like the computer programmer. All they can do is set it up beforehand; then the survival machine is on its own, and the genes can only sit passively inside" (1976/2006: 52). This is because of the problem of time lag: all that genes can actually *do* directly is code for the construction of proteins. Coding for protein synthesis is a very slow process, whereas behavior in the world – at least for any kind of reasonably complex survival machine – has to happen fast:

[Behavior] works on a time-scale not of months but of seconds and fractions of seconds. Something happens in the world, an owl flashes overhead, a rustle in the long grass betrays prey, and in milliseconds nervous systems crackle into action, muscles leap, and someone's life is saved – or lost. Genes don't have reaction times like that. (55)

Genes are thus, Dawkins notes, in the position of a group of computer programmers sending out designs for a robot to be built in the future, and by other people, but which needs to serve the interests of the programmers. Because of the uncertainties involved, the optimal program would probably be a mixture of basic desiderata and general strategies for satisfying those desiderata in various foreseeable circumstances. Such a program should also allow the robot to adapt these default strategies in response to the actual circumstances encountered – in other words, to *learn*:

One way for genes to solve the problem of making predictions in rather unpredictable environments is to build in a capacity for learning. Here the program may take the form of the following instructions to the survival machine: "Here is a list of things defined as rewarding: sweet taste in the mouth, orgasm, mild temperature, smiling child. And

---

[14] Readers wishing to get their feet wet are referred to Dennett 1991, 2003, and 2005; Flanagan 1992 and 2002; Humphrey 1992; Crick 1994; Chalmers 1996; Searle 1997 and 2004; Ramachandran & Blakeslee 1998; Wegner 2002; Koch 2004; and Ramachandran 2004.

here is a list of nasty things: various sorts of pain, nausea, empty stomach, screaming child. If you should happen to so something that is followed by one of the nasty things, don't do it again, but on the other hand repeat anything that is followed by one of the nice things." The advantage of this sort of programming is that it greatly cuts down the number of detailed rules that have to be built into the original program; and it is also capable of coping with changes in the environment that could not have been predicted in detail. (57)[15]

Of course, the disadvantage of such programming is that is has to rely on certain assumptions, and if the world changes in such a way that these no longer obtain, the robot's behavior may deviate from the original intentions of the programmers. As Dawkins notes, the genes that programmed us assumed that sugar and fat were unadulterated goods – an assumption that no longer holds when both are instantly and easily obtainable in large quantities from the local convenience store.

Another manner in which the genes' indirect planning may lead to – at least from their perspective – suboptimal results is explored by Dennett in his consideration of how unusually complex survival machines are, by their very nature, prone to gradually acquire their "own" goals and motivations. Dennett asks his reader to consider possible strategies available to someone keen on preserving himself or herself in a cryogenic chamber into the twenty-fifth century, faced by the need to plan for energy needs, safety from natural disaster, and so on, with really only a vague sense of what challenges this chamber will face over the next few centuries.[16] A fixed chamber well-supplied with what it could foreseeably need (the "plant" strategy) is one possibility, but a major drawback is that it cannot move if resources run out or destructive changes occur to its habitat. A mobile chamber option (the "animal" strategy) is more flexible: it can be designed to actively seek out resources to keep itself running, and also to perceive and avoid potential dangers. One catch is that you are unlikely to be the only person to have thought of this strategy, so a major danger facing your cryogenic chamber is no doubt going to be other cryogenic chambers, all competing for the same resources and possibly cannibalizing each other for parts and fuel. Basically, the best strategy in the face of these design constraints is to program your cryogenic machine with a set of basic desiderata, basic capacities for acquiring and processing information from the world that will be relevant to its mission, and then let it go. This robot will by necessity be

capable of exhibiting self-control of a high order. Since you must cede fine-grained real-time control to it once you put yourself to sleep, you will be as "remote" as [engineers designing an autonomous space probe]. As an autonomous agent, it will be capable of

---

[15] Cf. Andy Clark's observation that "robots intended to explore distant worlds cannot rely on constant communication with earth-based scientists – the time lags would soon lead to disaster" (1997: 11), and his discussion of the need in the field of AI to develop robots able to pursue general goals and deal with unexpected and unpredictable difficulties. The R&D project faced by programmers sending out space probes is essentially the same as the one that genes faced when they decided to start building mobile organisms to carry them around and get them into the next generation.

[16] Originally presented in Dennett 1987: 295–298; a revised form is found in Dennett 1995: 422–427.

deriving *its own* subsidiary goals from its assessment of its current state and the import of that state for its ultimate goal (which is to preserve you till 2401). These secondary goals, which will respond to circumstances you cannot predict in detail (if you could, you could hard-wire the best responses to them), may take the robot far afield on century-long projects, some of which may be ill advised, in spite of your best efforts. Your robot may embark on actions antithetical to your purposes, even suicidal, having been convinced by another robot, perhaps, to subordinate its own life mission to some other . . . All the preference it will ever have will be offspring of the preferences you initially endowed it with, in hopes that they will carry you into the twenty-fifth century, but that is no guarantee that actions taken in light of the robot's descendent preferences will continue to be responsive, directly, to your best interests. (1995: 424–425)

The robot, of course, is a Dawkinsesque survival machine, and the planner of this robot is the genes. This thought-experiment makes two important points. One is that, although the basic motivational and behavioral profile of a survival machine should be roughly comprehensible in terms of its original programmed operating instructions, there is no guarantee that its actual motivations or behavior will not deviate from these instructions in unpredictable ways. Consider, for instance, our discussion of cognitive fluidity in Chapter 4. The ability to draw connections between schemas from different domains is a powerful feature of the variety of survival machine known as *Homo sapiens*, and the genes that included it in their design have done fairly well. They could never have predicted, however, that the quite reasonable factory-installed desire for cleanliness or physical purity – an excellent mechanism for assuring that your survival machines avoid taking in fuel that will harm their operating systems – could be drawn on and projected onto the realm of sexual relations. Throughout human history, this mapping has independently and repeatedly resulted in certain survival machines deciding that *sex*, their very raison d'être, is unclean and should be avoided by those machines desiring to remain "spiritually" clean. Although this is obviously a bad outcome for the particular genes residing in those survival machines, the payoff of cognitive fluidity must be high enough that their terrible fate has been historically outweighed by the success of copies of them residing in other individual survival machines fortunate enough not to have embraced this particular metaphor.

The second important point of the cryogenic robot scenario is that it is not at all surprising that robots built by genes to get them into the next generation could possess extremely broad degrees of behavioral freedom and unpredictability as basic design features. In other words, "freedom evolves" (Dennett 2003): behavioral self-control and the ability to reassess motivations and goals emerge gradually as the complexity of survival machines increases, in a manner that we can perceive quite clearly from surveying the varying degrees of self-awareness and intelligence among the profusion of species that have made it this far in our world. Our intuitive sense that we possess free will, deliberate over choices, are torn in different directions, and ultimately make decisions that could have gone either way is not at all mistaken. We just need to recognize that this free will is not some magical, inexplicable quality existing completely outside the chain of causation and possessed only by human souls. It is, rather, an emergent quality that is helpful for understanding the behavior of *any* survival machine functioning at a sufficient level of complexity.

Weak Versus Strong Emergence: Blocking the Move to Mysterianism

We are familiar with how the process of evolution and natural selection has produced more and more complex feeding and fleeing machines, working at many different layers in the food chain, as well as wildly diverse strategies of hunting, mating, parenting, and social organization (Dawkins 1976/2006). Very crude survival machines are built to sense temperature and inorganic nutrient gradients and adapt their movements and simple feeding behaviors accordingly. More complex ones are then built to take advantage of the work already done by these simple machines in concentrating diffused inorganic nutrients in one valuable package: they are the first predators, and require more complicated sensory and behavioral programming to track down and capture their prey. The prey, in turn, become more complex in response to this pressure, acquiring the ability to detect and evade predators. At a certain point in this process of exponentially increasing complexity, it became more efficient for survival machines to have built into them the set of heuristics Dennett refers to as the "intentional stance" (1987) to predict and respond to the behavior of other complex survival machines – trying to rely on the physical stance, still helpful for dealing with simple rocks and trees and coconuts, simply was not fast enough. Thus theory of mind developed: survival machines began viewing other survival machines as "fearing," "wanting," and "liking." Especially in the mental repertoire of the most complex of these survival machines, whose adaptive environment consists primarily of other conspecifics rather the dumb world of things, the concepts of behavioral "choice" and "freedom" became very useful heuristics.

This is the story of the emergence of human free will presented by "weak" emergentists: freedom as an emergent quality of very complex machines, with there being no point in this chain of increasing complexity where something magic happens.[17] Like the category of "glider," we can have new "kinds" emerging at each new level of explanation – kinds that are heuristically indispensable, that present themselves irresistibly to the human mind as crucial features of causal explanation, and yet that are not composed of novel stuff. As Michael Arbib puts it, referring to folk psychology concepts or "person-talk," they "are useful for encapsulating

---

[17]   Also cf. the example of the electrical generator "virtual governor" from Dewan 1976 (described in Hooker 1981: 509 and in Patricia Churchland 1986: 365–366) where several individual generators linked together in network begin to function as if they were a single, larger generator with increased frequency reliability.

meaningful patterns of what our brains can do, but not as describing a distinct reality" (1985: 115).[18]

Opposing the "weak emergence" stance are the advocates of various forms of "strong" or "ontological" emergence. These include, of course, old-fashioned substance dualists, who claim that mind and matter are two independent ontological realms. Descartes is the classic exponent of this position, and – despite the ill repute into which Cartesianism has fallen in recent decades – full-blown substance dualists are still fairly thick on the ground. Those who adhere to traditional religious models of the self are obviously and explicitly dualistic in this sense, but even many otherwise committed secular physicalists appear to continue to hear the siren call of substance dualism.[19]

A more updated, but – to my mind, at least – indistinguishable position is so-called property dualism, which argues that things like human "qualia" are ineffable and possess strongly emergent properties. "Qualia" is a technical-sounding philosophical term for what is, in fact, a quite folksy idea: there is a "what-it-is-like-ness" to my conscious experience that is immediately and exclusively accessible only to myself, and this special qualitativeness is what would be left out of any third-person description of my experience. Thomas Nagel provided the classic statement of this position in his famous 1974 essay, "What Is It Like to Be a Bat?" where he argued that, essentially, we can never answer that question: we are not bats, and no matter how much third-person descriptive knowledge we accumulate about bat behavior and physiology, we can never have access to the first-person (first-mammal?) qualia of bat consciousness.

The qualia "argument," as intuitively appealing as it is, has always seemed to me more an item of faith or bald assertion than an argument per se, and both Daniel Dennett and Hilary Putnam – to take just two examples – have formulated eloquent and convincing critiques of the concept.[20] To begin with, despite its initial intuitiveness, it is hard to know exactly what it is that qualia might be. Dennett notes that the distinctive "richness" of qualia is linked in most people's minds to our experiential *je ne sais quoi* – the fact that the lived details of our experience seem to defy adequate verbal description. In "Quining Qualia" (1988), he asks us to consider a Jell-O box that has been torn in half, with one half forming a complexly contoured shape we will label "M." Providing a full and adequate description of M is virtually impossible, and for practical purposes the only way

[18] Cf. Francis Crick's comment that much of the brain's behavior is emergent, but not in any mystical sense: it can, at least in principle, be predicted from the nature of the parts involved combined with an account of how these parts interact (1994: 11).

[19] See, for instance, David Chalmers's comment that conscious experience is "a fundamental feature of the world, alongside mass, charge, and space-time" (1995).

[20] Dennett's original position is laid out in Dennett 1988; also see his debunking of Frank Jackson's (1982) qualia-based "Mary the color scientist" thought experiment (2005: Ch. 5). For a full account of Putnam's criticism of the general qualia argument, see Putnam 1999, esp. 151–175.

to identify M is to rely on the unique "M-detector" – that is, the other half of the box. The shape of M, Dennett notes, "may *defy description* but it is not literally ineffable or unanalyzable; it is just extremely rich in information. It is a mistake to inflate practical indescribability into something metaphysically more portentous" (2005: 111).

Hilary Putnam makes a related point in his discussion of the so-called zombie problem in philosophy of consciousness, which in its contemporary form can be traced back to Descartes' apparently quite unhealthy obsession with automatons[21] and William James's musings about an "automatic sweetheart" indistinguishable from a flesh-and-blood woman.[22] What are we to make of a machine/creature that looks exactly like a normal human being, talks exactly like a normal human being – in short, is indistinguishable from a normal human being on the surface – but, in fact, completely lacks consciousness, and therefore the experience of qualia? Putnam argues forcefully that the zombie scenario is in fact a nonproblem, caused by unexamined and ultimately untenable dualist assumptions. "In the absence of soul talk," he notes, "the very idea that our mental properties might be 'subtracted' from us without disrupting our bodies or altering our environments" is basically "unintelligible" (1999: 98). Unintelligible, that is, in light of the physicalist assumptions that guide our interactions with the rest of nonhuman reality, which – in light of their success to date – we have no principled reason to avoid extending to human consciousness. Qualia are supposedly something above and beyond the functioning of our embodied minds as it goes about its work, but we have no reason to believe that what we experience as consciousness *is* anything other than the embodied mind going about its work.

Furthermore, the privilege given to the first-person perspective is a natural human prejudice, but a built-in bias – no matter how powerful – is not, in and of itself, adequate evidence for the existence of an ontologically distinct realm. At a crucial point in his 1974 article, Nagel asks rhetorically, "Does it make sense . . . to ask what my experiences are *really* like, as opposed to how they appear to me?" (448), and this is really the key to his "argument." Our bad argument radar should go off when a philosopher's core position is expressed as a rhetorical question, and we can defang the rhetorical bite of Nagel's query by answering it in the affirmative. Of course it makes sense to ask what my experiences are "really" like as opposed to how they seem to me: the idea that third-person accounts can never get to the essence of first-person phenomenology is nothing more than a feeling that we have – an expression of the illusion of self-unity and complete self-transparency that is created by our fragmented and multilevel mind. In Chapter 1 we saw how work coming out of cognitive and social psychology is calling into question our folk intuition that we possess a unified locus of consciousness: a fully self-aware

---

[21] See Bloom 2004: xii–xiii.
[22] See the discussion in Dennett 1991: Chs. 10–12 and Putnam 1999: 73–91.

homunculus supposedly pulling the levers and running the show. The research surveyed there – for instance, Nisbett and Wilson's findings concerning the opacity of people's own motivations or Gazzaniga's work on the left-brain "spin doctor" – appears to contradict the Cartesian assumption that the knowing, verbal subject has privileged and infallible access to the content of its own consciousness. Similarly, Jonathan Schooler and Charles Schreiber's (2004) survey of experimental work on introspection and "meta-consciousness" suggests that first-person accounts of one's own mental imagery, thought processes, or hedonic states can be highly inaccurate.[23] To answer Nagel's supposedly unanswerable question, then, we can say that a measure of the difference between what one's experiences are "really like" and how they appear introspectively can, as Schooler and Schreiber put it, be derived from "the degree to which self-reports systematically co-vary with the environmental, behavioral, and physiological concomitants of experience" (2004: 17). We can acknowledge the important role that "qualia" play in the experienced economy of the human psyche without attributing to them mysterious powers or special ontological status.

Perhaps the most prominent and prolific critic of a thoroughgoing materialist view of human consciousness is John Searle, who argues that no third-person, purely physicalist account can capture the "original intentionality" or "ontological subjectivity" that is an essential characteristic of human consciousness (1983, 1992, 2004).[24] Searle's argument at times seems structurally identical to the "qualia" argument, although it is somewhat difficult to get a real handle on his position. To begin with, in his more recent work he is an outspoken critic of substance dualism and more explicitly "mysterian" positions such as the one espoused by Nagel. He now characterizes himself as a "biological naturalist" (2004: 113), and purports to be a physicalist in the sense that he does not believe that there is any substance in the universe over and above physical things: conscious states have "absolutely no life of their own, independent of the neurobiology" (113). His position sometimes sounds like what we would characterize as weak emergence: "roughly speaking, consciousness is to neurons as the solidity of pistons is to the metal molecules" (131). On the other hand, he still wants to maintain that conscious states are in some way "ontologically irreducible" to physical states: the emergent property of piston solidity is both causally and ontologically reducible to the characteristics of metal molecules, whereas consciousness is causally, but not ontologically, reducible to neuron activity. Why is this? Because we "just know" that conscious states exist, in that we experience them all the time. Searle is relying here on Descartes' basic

---

[23] Cf. the work of Daniel Kahneman and his colleagues on people's systematic distortions of experienced pleasure and pain (Fredrickson & Kahneman 1993, Kahneman et al. 1993, Redelmeier & Kahneman 1996, Schreiber & Kahneman 2000).

[24] Daniel Dennett has been the most dogged and vociferous critic of Searle's position; see especially Dennett 1991 and 1995: 397–400.

cogito argument: "If it consciously seems to be that I am conscious, then I am conscious. I can make all sorts of mistakes about the contents of my conscious states, but not in that way about their very existence" (122). He thus concludes that there is something special about consciousness that warrants us postulating the existence of a unique "first-person ontology" alongside the ordinary "third-person ontology" that is adequate for characterizing the rest of the physical world.

Unless Searle is using the word "ontology" in a radically idiosyncratic sense, however, he seems to be falling back here into precisely the sort of substance dualist position that he elsewhere argues has outlived its usefulness. To get a sense of how "original intentionality" or "ontological subjectivity" requires a strong sense of emergence, let us return to the Life World example. As we get increasing levels of complexity, new heuristics for predicting what patterns of squares are going to appear in the next generations become available to us: blinkers will switch from a horizontal to vertical orientation, gliders will "try" to eat other gliders when they collide, and so forth. Bringing this back home to the biological world, life began when some molecules managed to begin replicating themselves. Soon collections of these molecules began manufacturing membranes to more effectively seal themselves off as a unit from other molecules in the world, and eventually collections of these proto-cells came together to form multicellular organisms, developing specialized sensory organs, motor organs, and so on. Presumably no one would deny that physicalism effectively captures everything that is happening in this world. At some point, the conglomerations of molecules start moving around the Life World in ways that are most efficiently characterized by adopting the intentional stance. We can get a snapshot of the phylogenic unfolding of this process by looking around at degrees of complexity in our current natural world. A protozoan senses nutrients and moves up the nutrient gradient because, we are tempted to say, it "wants" to eat. Schools of sardines swim tightly together for safety and initiate evasive action when presented with a predator-like stimulus. Small packs of savanna carnivores coordinate their movements in order to flush their prey out into the open where it can be more easily brought down. Chimpanzees engage in social deception, multistage planning for the future, and culturally transmitted tool use. Human beings read and write books about consciousness. Where and when in this chain of increasing complexity does ontological subjectivity pop into existence? Where does it *come* from?

Searle of course rejects mystical substance dualism, and he has no patience for those who dogmatically declare that only humans have consciousness: when he comes home from work and observes his dog jumping about, wagging its tail, Searle is fairly confident that his dog is conscious, and indeed conscious of the specific emotional state of happiness. This confidence is based not simply on behavioral clues, but because his dog is phylogenically closely related to himself, and therefore the "causal underpinnings of [its] behavior are relatively similar to mine" (2004: 38). Searle is similarly confident that other close relatives of humans, such as chimpanzees, possess consciousness, and notes that the presence or lack of consciousness in other animal species is an empirical issue, a matter of whether or not a given species has "a rich enough neurobiological capacity" to support consciousness (39). "Rich enough," however, does not seem like a particularly sharp distinguishing characteristic, whereas possession or lack of original intentionality apparently is. This gets to the heart of the problem with this concept from an evolutionary perspective: whatever you call it – "substance," "property," "X ontology" – marking consciousness or intentionality off as a special something makes you a strong emergentist, and therefore essentially a dualist, whether you are comfortable with those labels or not.

Back in the 1980s, Searle tried to get across his sense that intentionality is something special, as well as his conviction that the "strong AI" project was essentially doomed, with his famous Chinese Room thought experiment (1980). Imagine a person in a room with all the Chinese characters in the language at his disposal in the form of chits, as well as an incredibly detailed rule book that tells him, when a certain set of chits with characters is given to him through a window (i.e., when he is given an input), what set of characters to take down from the wall and slide back out in return (what to give as an output). As Searle accurately predicts, our intuitive folk psychology tells us that this person does not really "understand" Chinese: he is merely carrying out a mindless algorithm. Searle takes this to "prove" that there is something special about intentionality that cannot be captured by a mechanistic algorithm. Michael Arbib, however, draws the opposite and, I think, more appropriate conclusion:

[Upon considering Searle's Chinese Room argument] I am reminded of a classic story about Norbert Wiener, the "father" of cybernetics . . . Wiener believed he had resolved a famous nineteenth-century mathematical conjecture – the Riemann hypothesis – and mathematicians flocked from Harvard and MIT to see him present his proof. He soon filled blackboard after blackboard with Fourier series and Dirichlet integrals. But as time went by, he spent less and less time writing, and more and more time pacing up and down, puffing at a black cheroot, until finally he stopped and said, "It's no good, it's no good, I've proved too much. I've proved there are no prime numbers." And this is my reaction to Searle. "It's no good, it's no good, he's proved too much. He's proved that even *we* cannot exhibit intelligence." (1985: 30)

In other words, what the Chinese Room thought experiment helps us get a handle on is that, since there is no little person inside the Chinese Room that is our brains, even *we* don't understand Chinese or English or anything – in the strong sense of "understand" as *Verstehen*, or the unexplainable, mystical workings of original or ontological Intentionality with a capital "I."

Substance and property dualists aside, the final group of resisters to the idea that mere physical processes can account for human consciousness are what Patricia Churchland refers to as "boggled skeptics" (1986: 315): the idea just seems so damn hard to believe. John Locke expresses the boggled skeptics' position quite clearly: "For it is as impossible to conceive that ever bare incogitative Matter should produce a thinking intelligent Being, as that nothing should of itself produce Matter" (1690/1975: 623). As I mentioned briefly in the Introduction, this was, at one time, quite a powerful argument, despite its apparent simplicity: conscious beings seem to be able to do things that completely fly in the face of what we know about the behavior of inert matter. The conclusion that there has to be something else involved is therefore hard to avoid. As Dennett puts it, "Until fairly recently, [the] idea of a rather magical extra ingredient was the only candidate for an explanation of consciousness that even seemed to make sense" (2005: 3). He goes on, however, to argue that the last few decades have seen the development of a crucial bit of evidence tipping things in favor of the physicalist view of consciousness: the development of Artificial Intelligence, which finally put to rest the "boggled" argument that no amount of physical complexity could produce consciousness-like phenomena. We have now built machines, which we know are just machines, that are capable of defeating Grand Masters at chess, plausibly holding up their end of a free-form conversation, and demonstrating many of the powers that were previously seen as the exclusive province of conscious, intentional agents. Dennett observes that "the sheer existence of computers has provided an existence proof of undeniable influence: there are mechanisms – brute, unmysterious mechanisms operating according to routinely well-understood physical principles – that have many of the competences heretofore assigned only to minds" (7). As Hilary Putnam concludes, the overwhelming success of the physicalist model puts the folk model of dualism in an empirically untenable position, despite its intuitive appeal:

We learn the so-called mental predicates by learning to use them in explanatory practices that involve embodied creatures. The idea that they refer to "entities" that might be present or absent independently of what goes on in our bodies and behavior has a long history and a powerful . . . appeal. Yet to say that the idea "might be true" is to suppose that a clear possibility has been described, even though no way of using the picture to describe an actual case has really been proposed. (Putnam 1999: 148)

To say that soul-dependent theories "might be true" is thus a little generous; it is more accurate to say that they "appear to be false."

   AI systems are still quite crude, and they are extraordinarily inept at many tasks that are accomplished with ease by a five-year-old human. Similarly, there is still only a very rudimentary understanding of how the body-brain subserves even quite basic functions as memory, emotion, and self-consciousness. Our current blind spots, however, should not be taken as proof that a useful and empirically rigorous science of human consciousness is a priori impossible. As Owen Flanagan notes, the current imperfect state of the field of the human mind sciences often prompts a jump to mysterianism, and it is important to see how unnecessary and unjustified this jump is:

Although everyone thinks that cars and bodies obey the principles of causation – that for every event that happens there are causes operating at every junction – no one thinks that it is a deficiency that we don't know, nor can we teach, strict laws of auto-mechanics or anatomy... [so,] when an auto mechanic or a physician says that he just can't figure out what is causing some problem, he never says, "perhaps a miracle occurred." (2002: 65)

We might make a similar observation concerning the unpredictability of human thought and behavior, which is often cited as a sign of human beings' essential ineffability. It is exceedingly likely that, no matter how far the neuroscience of consciousness advances, it will remain impossible – because of sheer computational intractability, quantum randomness, whatever – to accurately predict the future behavior of even a single human being, let alone groups of human beings interacting with one another and with a constantly changing physical environment. It is equally likely that, no matter what advances we make in hydrology and meteorology, it will never be possible to pick out a single molecule of H_2O from the ocean inlet outside my window and predict where that molecule will be one year from now. We never for a minute, though, doubt that molecule's future movements will be fully determined by the laws of physics. By extension, we have no more reason to believe that the cascades of neural impulses in our brains are any less determined and governed by physical causation than the water molecule.

Why should we want to block the move to ontological emergence, especially if it comes so naturally to us, and takes so much work to get away from? Contrary to some doctrinaire physicalists, there is nothing about physicalism per se that makes it uniquely scientific. If we had an accumulation of a critical mass of replicable evidence for the existence of some nonphysical, causally efficacious, intention-bearing substance, it would be unscientific *not* to be a dualist – and of course we cannot rule out the possibility that such a point will ever be reached.[25] A pragmatic conception of scientific "truth" requires that our ideas of what could count as a viable explanation remain constantly open to revision. It just seems that physicalism is currently our best, most productive stance toward the world.

In the Game of Life example discussed earlier, we know that "blinkers" and "gliders" are not "real," because we have been shown how the system works: it is just a very large collection of squares turning ON and OFF. Despite what dogmatic materialists might say, we do not know with the same kind of certainty that there is

---

[25] I here take issue with Searle's claim that physicalism functions as a modern religious dogma, accepted "without question" and with "quasi-religious faith" (2004: 48). No doubt some physicalists are dogmatists as well, but dogmatism is not intrinsic to the position. Searle's assertion that physicalism leaves out "some *essential* mental feature of the universe, which *we know*, independently of our philosophical commitments, *to exist*" – that it denies "the *obvious fact* that we all *intrinsically have* conscious states and intentional states" (49, emphases added) – seems to me much more faithlike than the claim defended by the likes of Dennett that physicalism just seems to be the best explanation that we have right now.

no such thing as a soul. We don't know *anything* about our world for sure, because – unlike the artificial Life World – we were not invited to observe its creation. What we *can* say, though, is that the best evidence for the existence of a soul has been undermined by AI, which is, in essence, an exceedingly crude, Life World–like simulation of a person. In addition, everything that we know about how the world in general works suggests that there is no place for nonphysical causation. No one has come up with a story that would explain how something like a soul could exist in the world as we currently understand it, although we are, qua human beings, highly motivated to come up with and to believe such stories. Given the explanatory track record of physicalist accounts of the universe, as well as the failure thus far of highly motivated humans to come up with an empirically viable alternative to it,[26] it would thus seem that a strong emergentist view of mental or intentional properties can only be defended as an article of religious faith. In the absence of an empirically defensible account of dualism, the explanation of reality that best enables us to get a grip on the world does not involve ghosts, souls, miracles, or original intentionality: human beings, like all of the other entities that we know about, appear to be robots or zombies all the way down, whether we like that idea or not.

The Limits of Physicalism: Why We Will Always Be Humanists

Having, I hope, blocked the move to mysterianism or ontological emergentism, I would here like to address in more detail the issue of why these intellectual moves are so compelling to us, as well as what this compulsion *does* reveal about the special status of human-level concepts. I argued earlier that John Searle is engaging in a bit of philosophical sleight of hand when he purports to be a biological materialist but then continues to insist on a special ontological status for human subjectivity. Searle is a brilliant philosopher with a quite detailed grasp of the state of the field in the cognitive and neurosciences: why this refusal to relinquish the idea of two

---

[26] For instance, many recent attempts to escape the conclusions of physicalism focus on the phenomenon of indeterminacy at the quantum level, which seems to break us out of a deterministic universe. Certain prominent scientists, such as Roger Penrose (1989), argue that quantum indeterminacy is the locus of human free will. This seems, however, to be a fundamentally flawed and desperate strategy. To begin with, it is based on a distant and thin similarity between what we think human free will must be like and a completely unrelated phenomenon that shares one of the desired characteristics: indeterminancy. There is also the inconvenient fact that the wondrous quality of indeterminacy is present only at the quantum level: once we get up into levels that are humanly relevant, such as that of neurons or hormones, LaPlacian determinism reexerts its iron grip. The most basic and fatal flaw in this argument, however, is that indeterminacy is nothing more than randomness, which is not really what defenders of strong free will are after (Searle 2004: 24–25). The human conception of free will requires that this will be determined by *something* – reasons, desires, spontaneous impulses, etc. Free will as utter randomness is as horrific a concept at a human level as the deterministic absence of free will. See Dennett 1995: 428–451 and Flanagan 2002: 127–132 for cogent discussions of Penrose's position.

distinct ontologies? And why two, we might ask, and not three, or ten? In this section I would like to explore the intuition that I think motivates the defenders of dualism in all of its various forms: the recognition that human-level reality is real for humans, and that it is so deeply entrenched that no third-person description can ever completely dislodge it. In other words, we apparently cannot help but at some level see a *Geist* in the machine, which means there will always be something importantly different about the *Geisteswissenschaften.*

Why Physicalism Does Not Matter

Hard-core physicalists such as Dennett are inclined to dismiss positions such as Searle's or Nagel's as a mere statement of religious belief or personal sentiment. Dennett and some other advocates of vertical integration argue that, since intentionality and consciousness are like gliders in the Game of Life – helpful for certain heuristic purposes but with no underlying reality – the rigorous study of human affairs will eventually be able to dispense with them entirely. Owen Flanagan, for instance, urges us to get beyond such concepts as the "soul" or "free will": "Since these concepts don't refer to anything real, we are best off without them" (2002: xiii). He compares such dualistic concepts to shadows on the wall of Plato's cave – the result of mistaking Appearance for Reality (20). Flanagan also suggests that our belief in the soul is the result of our particular cultural tradition, traceable back to the Judeo-Christian worldview, and is therefore best seen as a passing "fashion" (9–10).

A common analogy drawn by those who believe dualism will soon go the way of bell-bottoms and disco balls is the shift in human sensibilities that occurred with the Copernican revolution. Copernicanism presented a view of the solar system that contradicted not only scriptural authority but also the evidence of our senses: the Bible states quite clearly that the sun moves around the earth, and this also happens to accord with our everyday sensory experience. Yet the accumulation of empirical evidence eventually resulted in Copernicanism's winning the day – trumping both religion and common sense – and nowadays every educated person takes the heliocentric solar system for granted. Dennett argues that the current physicalism versus dualism controversy is analogous to the early days of Copernicanism: we are resistant to physicalism because it goes against our religious beliefs and our common sense, but the weight of the empirical evidence is on its side. Eventually – after all of the controversy has played itself out – we will learn to accept the materialist account of the self with as much equanimity as the fact that the earth goes around the sun (1995: 19).[27] Dennett illustrates our tendency to

---

[27] Cf. Dennett's comment regarding the "zombie hunch" (the feeling that it makes sense to speak of consciousness as something over and above the functioning of the embodied mind): "If you are patient and open minded, it will pass" (2005: 23).

seek Intelligence with a capital "I" in the universe with a song he learned as a child, entitled "Tell Me Why":

> Tell my why the stars do shine,
> Tell me why the ivy twines
> Tell me why the sky's so blue
> Then I will tell you just why I love you
> Because God made the stars to shine.
> Because God made the ivy twine.
> Because God made the sky so blue.
> Because God made you, that's why I love you. (1995: 17)

Just as children come eventually to realize that there is no such thing as Santa Claus or the tooth fairy, so will dualistic adults eventually grow up intellectually, realize the truth of physicalism, and come to see such songs and sentiments as childish wishful thinking – beautiful and once quite comforting, but not a proper component of a mature worldview.

Even if one accepted the argument that we must dispense intellectually with mentalistic terms, one might still maintain that mentalistic entities will continue to persist for us perceptually – we will continue to see them in the world, even though we know they are not real. This sort of argument grows out of the observation that those of us who accept a heliocentric solar system generally continue to live our everyday lives in a phenomenologically Ptolemaic universe: the sun appears to rise and set, and the earth appears to stand still. Paul Churchland wishes to dispute even this weaker argument, believing that even the mere perception of mental qualities will eventually be overcome. He argues that perceptual Ptolemaicism is the result of human beings' having not yet sufficiently integrated the heliocentric worldview into their quotidian perception of the world, and he claims that it is possible for human beings to train themselves out of perceptual geocentrism. He even provides his readers with some strategies for experiencing the perceptual shift themselves (1979: 30–34), which will allow them to directly see the solar system as it really is, and "feel at home in [the] solar system for the first time" (34). Churchland then draws the analogy to dualism and materialism: just as we can train ourselves to correctly perceive the solar system, so we can also train ourselves to correctly perceive ourselves, which will involve weaning ourselves off mentalistic, folk psychological concepts and learning to experience ourselves and others as purely physical systems.

Churchland may be right about our ability to change our immediate perception of the solar system – I gave his instructions a try and remained unable to free myself from Ptolemy, but it is possible that I simply did not try hard enough. A basic problem with the positions of both Churchland and Dennett, however, is that there is a profound disanalogy between the Copernican revolution and the revolution represented by physicalist models of the mind. The Ptolemaic model of the solar system falls quite naturally out of the functioning of our built-in perceptual systems, but it is not itself part of that system: we do not appear to possess an innate Ptolemaic solar system module. Switching to a post-Copernicus model, at least intellectually, requires us to suspend our commonsense perceptions, but it does not involve a direct violation of any fundamental, innate human ideas. Physicalism as applied to mind *does* require such a violation, and this has a very important bearing on how realistic it is to think that we can dispense with mentalistic talk once and for all. Owen Flanagan characterizes dualism as something that has troubled us "for centuries" (2002: 8), but seeing agents as something special goes back for at least as long as people have had theory of mind – perhaps a hundred thousand years.[28] This is the psychological fact behind the argument put forward by Searle and others that consciousness is special: it is inescapably real for us.

We Are Robots Designed Not to Believe That We Are Robots

The idea of human beings as ultimately mindless robots, blindly "designed" by a consortium of genes to propagate themselves, has so much difficulty gaining a foothold in human brains because it dramatically contradicts other factory-issued and firmly entrenched ideas, such as the belief in *soul, freedom, choice, responsibility* – in short, all of the qualities that seem to us to distinguish human beings from mere things. The dualism advocated by Plato and Descartes was not a historical or philosophical accident, but rather a development of an intuition that comes naturally to us, as bearers of theory of mind: agents are different from things. Agents actively think, choose, and move themselves; things can only be passively moved. The locus of agents' ability to think and choose is the mind, and because of its special powers the mind has to be a fundamentally different sort of entity than the body. Even cultures that did not develop a doctrine of strong mind-body substance dualism – such as the early Chinese – nonetheless believed that there was something special about the mind. As the fourth-century B.C.E. Chinese thinker Mencius put it, what distinguishes the heart/mind (*xin*) – the locus of agency in human beings – from other organs of the body is that it issues commands, whereas the other parts of the body merely follow them (Lau 1970: 168).

The idea that human beings, like all other animals on the planet, are physical systems produced by a mindless, purposeless process of differential reproduction combined with natural selection is fundamentally troubling to us because it denies that we have souls. Many, if not most, modern Western secular intellectuals would

---

[28] Archaic modern humans have been burying their dead for at least 92,000 years (Bar-Yosef 2006). Elaborate, ritualized burial is as good a litmus test as any of the presence of theory of mind. When an implement breaks, you throw it away, and the remains of living prey are disposed of as quickly and conveniently as possible. Special treatment of the human corpse indicates that a shift has occurred, and the human body is now being viewed as linked to something fundamentally distinct from objects.

perhaps protest that they do not believe in a "soul," but I would argue that *all* of us – stone psychopaths and perhaps severe autistics excepted – cannot get away from the powerful intuition that there is something special about people that makes them different from mere things.[29] The precise characterization of what this special something might be differs slightly from person to person, but it usually centers on the human possession of free will, as well as the dignity and responsibility that goes along with such autonomy. Most of us also have a powerful sense, whether we would be willing to defend it or not, that this something special about a person is not identical to the mere collection of their cells: the feeling that the most important part of a person – especially ourselves and the people whom we love – might somehow subsist after death presents itself spontaneously and quite powerfully to human beings, appears to be universal, and takes quite a bit of cognitive work to overcome. In other words, although we are obviously capable of entertaining nondualist ideas at some abstract level,[30] we seem to have evolved in such as way as to be ultimately invulnerable to the idea of thoroughgoing materialism.

The cognitive module producing this fundamental intuition, our "theory of mind" (ToM), was discussed in some detail in Chapter 3. There the focus was on how theory of mind governs our interactions with other people – causing us to "paint" mental properties onto what, when we take a step back, we can acknowledge is really just a sequence of physical states: pupils dilating, limbs moving, jaw and lip muscles contracting in a certain sequence. We also discussed how easily we extend theory of mind to pretty much *anything* moving in a particular kind of way: geometric shapes in a short animation or single dots moving around on a screen appear irresistibly to us to be involved in goal-directed, mentalistic behavior, and for this reason engage our sympathy. It is hard, for instance, not to root for the plucky little circle trying to climb the hill in Kuhlmeier et al.'s (2003) experiment. In his 1993 book *Faces in the Clouds: A New Theory of Religion*, Stewart Guthrie argues that our tendency to overproject agency onto the world is what gives rise to religion – in his definition, the belief in supernatural beings (7). He portrays this universal tendency to see faces in the clouds and to see rocks as bears as the evolutionary equivalent of Pascal's wager. Pascal, of course, famously argued that we can never be sure that God does not exist; considering that the cost of believing in God is finite, whereas the consequence of not believing in God if God does exist is infinite (eternal damnation), it would be irrational not to be a theist. Guthrie argues that overprojection of agency is the result of a similar, evolutionary wager:

We animate and anthropomorphize because, when we see something as alive or human-like, we can take precautions. If we see it as alive we can, for example, stalk it or flee. If we see it as humanlike, we can try to establish a social relationship. If it turns out not to

---

[29] For a very readable and extended introduction to this line of argument, see Bloom 2004.
[30] Purely materialist and mechanical models of the self and the universe go back at least as far Lucretius's (ca. 99–ca. 55 B.C.E.) *De Rerum Natura* (On the nature of the Universe).

be alive or humanlike, we usually lose little by having thought it was. This practice thus yields more in occasional big successes than it costs in frequent little failures. In short, animism and anthropomorphism stem from the principle, "better safe than sorry." (5)

Although Guthrie's book makes no reference to the innate cognitive modules dedicated to theory of mind and animate objects discussed in Chapter 3, it is easy to see how the phenomena he discusses can be understood as the result of the over-application of these modules – their projection onto domains for which, strictly speaking, they were not originally designed.

Guthrie does an exhaustive job of documenting the long history and pervasive presence of anthromorphism and animism in human perception, art, philosophy, science, and religion. It is clear that human beings, no matter how professionally or intellectually committed they are to physicalism, feel a constant compulsion to project agency onto the inanimate. A representative example comes from a *Los Angeles Times* article from a few years back entitled "Stalwart Galileo Is Vaporized Near Jupiter" (McFarling 2003). The piece discussed the deliberate crashing of the space probe Galileo into the planet Jupiter at the end of the probe's fourteen-year mission – necessary because Galileo's fuel tank was finally about to run dry, and scientists wanted to prevent it from inadvertently crashing into and contaminating one of Jupiter's moons. Galileo had far outperformed its design specifications and continued transmitting data until the last fiery minutes of its descent into Jupiter. The main photo accompanying the article shows engineers at Pasadena's Jet Propulsion Laboratory, the creators of Galileo, standing and applauding the space probe "as it performed a dramatic suicide plunge into the giant planet," their faces full of emotion and many with tears in their eyes. The project manager, Claudia Alexander, is quoted as saying that the space probe was "like the little engine that could. Galileo the man, with the force of his personality, changed a lot of opinions. Galileo the spacecraft, by sheer cussedness, did the same thing." Of course, these JPL engineers would never have gotten that probe into space if they were not capable of at least *partially* or temporarily withdrawing their projections and treating Galileo the space probe instrumentally and objectively. As we have discovered with particular rapidity over the past few centuries, this disengaged stance gives us a great deal of leverage over ourselves and the world. Nonetheless, even though the creators of Galileo should know better than anyone that it was nothing more than a collection of physical parts, they appeared incapable of resisting the temptation to invest it with such human qualities as "cussedness" and "stalwartness," and became as emotionally attached to it as if it were an old friend.

We all know this experience, having to deal daily with stubborn, diabolical computers bent on erasing our data, crotchety old cars that refuse to start, and beloved old pairs of pants that finally have to be laid to rest – or, as in my case, that have to be carefully kept hidden from one's wife to avoid their being forcibly put out of their misery. The anthropomorphic drive seems to be universal and appears quite early in development. Deborah Kelemen (1999a, 1999b, 2003, 2004) has documented the widespread projection of invisible or supernatural agency onto the world – what she refers to as "promiscuous teleology" – in children of various ages and education levels and argues that agent-centered, teleological explanations for phenomena seem to be the human cognitive default position, only gradually, with difficulty, and incompletely dislodged by mechanistic explanation.[31] We are obviously capable of withdrawing our projections when we have to – recognizing that the beloved pants are just pieces of fabric, or that our computer is not really out to get us – but it takes cognitive effort, which suggests that it does not come naturally and is not easily sustainable. As Steven Pinker notes, this is why even researchers in the cognitive and neurosciences – of all people, the ones who should be clearest about the absolutely physical nature of the human mind – usually end up smuggling some form of dualism back into their picture of the human being by means of what he calls the "Pronoun in the Machine": a vague seat of free will and human dignity, stripped of metaphysical overtones but essentially fulfilling the same function as Descartes' ghost. "As men of scientific acumen," Pinker observes, "they cannot but endorse the claims of biology, yet as political men they cannot accept the discouraging rider to those claims, namely that human nature differs only in degree of complexity from clockwork" (2002: 126).

The power of human cognitive defaults should not be underestimated. In my own field of religious studies, we see the power of folk theories manifest itself in the gap between certain religious doctrines and the way people process these doctrines and apply them to their lives. The Buddhist doctrine of *anatman* ("no-self"),[32] for instance, is about as counterintuitive as the modern neuroscientific model of the mind – indeed, as many scholars have argued, there seems to be a fair amount of overlap between the two.[33] Perusal of the Pali Canon – the earliest records of the Buddha's teachings – reveals the immense difficulty that the historical Buddha, Siddhartha Gautama, apparently had in trying to get his disciples to grasp the concept of no-self.[34] It is also very revealing that, not long after the death of the historical Buddha, the various descendent strands of Buddhism that eventually labeled themselves as the "Great Vehicle" (Mahayana) essentially snuck the self back in through such doctrines as "Buddha nature," and that once Buddhism spread to East Asia this understanding of Buddha nature took on an obviously substantial form. Although to this day there are Buddhists who advocate and defend the orthodox "no-self" doctrine, and despite the centrality of "no-self" to Buddhist

---

[31] Cf. Jesse Bering's work on the attribution of supernatutal agency by adults and children to explain otherwise mysterious, causeless events (Bering 2002, Bering & Parker 2006).

[32] The doctrine of *anatman* argues that our experience of a unitary and substantial self is an illusion, and that "the" self is in fact merely a temporary, constantly recycled collection of metaphysical "aggregates."

[33] See, for instance, Varela et al. 1991.

[34] For a representative sampling, see Embry 1988: 103–108.

teachings, the vast majority of Buddhists throughout history seem to have been unable or unwilling to seriously entertain it.[35]

The pervasive, subtle power of innate modules appears to contaminate every attempt to break away from ordinary human thought. Consider the example from Chapter 3 of Camus and his vision of *l'homme absurde*, who supposedly sees the world as it appears through the lens of Darwinism: mechanistic, unfeeling, and meaningless. Much of this book has been dedicated to arguing that both Darwin and Camus are right about this much: we *do* live in a mechanistic, meaningless universe. Yet we are mistaken if we think that insight into lower levels of causation can, in any existential sense, completely free us from the higher-level structures of meaning in which we are innately entwined. Despite its surface bleakness, Camus' vision strikes many people – including myself – as powerful and beautiful. Why is this? It is because, despite Camus' conceit that he has freed himself from false consciousness, works like *The Myth of Sisyphus* are inextricably permeated with human-level values such as clarity, freedom, and strength, and the fundamental motivation of such work is the wonderful feeling of control and understanding that we acquire when we have seen through surface appearances to the very "truth" of things.

It is thus a mistake to say that we will ever completely dispense with mentalistic concepts or ever entirely succeed in withdrawing our projections from the world. My disagreement in this regard with, for instance, Dennett, is best illustrated by the respective songs we would choose to illustrate the human tendency to project theory of mind onto the world. Dennett's choice is a children's song, one that we now look back at with affection, but also with a hint of indulgent superiority – it was a comforting thought, but we know better now. I think that a much more representative choice would be the song "Feeling Good,"[36] as performed by Nina Simone (*I Put A Spell On You*, 1965), where the singer sees her ebullient sense of freedom and joy echoed in the natural world around her – in high-flying birds, free-running rivers, a contentedly lazy breeze, dancing butterflies, and shining stars. It is a rare cognitively intact person who can listen to Simone without feeling in his or her bones the emotional and mental contagion that is constantly taking place between human beings and their world. A slowly drifting breeze can make us feel calm, and a feeling of calmness can color our perception of the breeze. Rivers really do seem to run free, and the play of butterflies cannot help but seem fun to us – even though, qua scientists, we know at some level that nothing is really going on except water molecules being drawn downward by gravity and some large insects engaged in a random feeding pattern. Most important of all, feeling this kind of resonance between our own concerns and the functioning of the universe makes us feel really, really *good*.

---

[35] Cf. the concept of "theological incorrectness," discussed in Chapter 3.

[36] By Leslie Bricusse and Anthony Newley, originally composed for the musical *The Roar of the Greasepaint – The Smell of the Crowd* (1964).

This feeling is, I think, why Guthrie's "Pascal's wager" theory of agency over-projection is incomplete, as well as why Dennett is wrong about our potential to completely leave dualism behind. Our promiscuous teleology and overactive theory of mind play a less accidental and peripheral role in the economy of the human psyche than the simple "better safe than sorry" explanation would have it. As the basis of perceiving meaning in the world, theory of mind would appear to be the foundation of any kind of long-term, large-scale motivation. I can be moved to engage in short-term, limited acts – consuming a cheeseburger when hungry or seeking out sleep when tired – without inquiring into the "meaning" of what I am doing, but the universal and pervasive tendency of human beings to tell and hear stories answering the question *why* suggests that long-term planning and motivation require such a sense. The feeling that our work or our life has a purpose involves embedding it in an at least implicit narrative, and the agent-centered nature of such narratives suggests to me that the human ability to remain motivated over the course of long-term, multistep, delayed-gratification tasks involves the evolutionary hijacking of reward centers in the brain whose original or proper domain is interpersonal approval and acceptance. In cognitively fluid humans, reward expectancy over long-term tasks may be maintained at least in part by the feeling that some metaphorical conspecific "up there" is watching and approving or disapproving of our actions, or (in its modern iteration) a more diffuse, nontheistic sense that what we are doing "matters" – a conceit that makes no sense unless we project some sort of abstract, metaphorical agency onto the universe. I would also suggest that in suicidal depressives we see a breakdown of this system: severely depressed individuals are actual realizations of Camus' *homme absurde*, and genuinely *do* seem to perceive the world as unfeeling, mechanistic, and mean-ingless all the way down. The result is not a feeling of clarity or power, however, but profound behavioral paralysis and overwhelming suicidal tendencies.[37] Evo-lution is a tinkerer, and when faced with the task of getting live-in-the-moment social animals to start thinking in more complex and indirect ways about the long term, I believe that it simply coopted a previously existing and very big carrot and stick. Prehuman social animals are powerfully motivated to shape their behavior in such a way as to win the approval and avoid the disapprobation of their literal social group. The great cognitive innovation that led to us – cognitive fluidity, the ability to project from one domain to another – perhaps also enabled literal social approval and disapproval to be projected onto a much larger scale: not just our immediate tribe, but the cosmos itself.

As the reader has probably gathered by now, I am an atheist: I think that evolution is the best explanation for how people and everything else in the universe got here, and I don't believe in supernatural beings or souls. And yet, at some level, I cannot help but feel that, for instance, I was "meant" to meet my wife, and in fact that we

---

[37] A chilling literary portrait of such a state is provided by William Styron in his 1992 *Darkness Visible*.

were meant to meet when we did: if we hadn't each gone through our respective life experiences, we would not have been so well suited for each other when we finally did meet. We now have a wonderful life with a beautiful daughter and rewarding jobs in a city that we love, and when I reflect on how it all "worked out," I cannot avoid that metaphor: it *does* seem like things "worked out," although I would be hard-pressed to tell you who the worker was or why the work should have involved me. I don't believe in an afterlife or a nonmaterial soul, and yet, if you press me, I would have to admit to a sneaking feeling that my favorite grandmother is somehow watching me: she was a gardener and I am comforted by the fact that she would love what I have done with the yard, and I am also sometimes deterred from engaging in actions of which I imagine she'd disapprove. When my daughter asks me about where people go after they die, I'll probably resort to the usual secular humanist explanation for this sort of phenomenon: the people we love live on in our memories, they become a part of us, and so on. And yet when we talk about people "living on" in our memories, the metaphor is not innocuous – it insinuates, at some level, the existence of the self as an enduring, nonmaterial entity.

We will apparently always see meaning in our actions – populating our world with "angry" seas, "welcoming" harbors – and other human beings as unique agents worthy of respect and dignity, and distinct from objects in some way that is hard to explain in the absence of soul-talk, but nonetheless very real for us. We will continue to perceive our work, families, and lives as being "meaningful" at some inchoate level, and to be strongly motivated to make the appropriate changes whenever we begin to lose this sense. Qua scientists, we can acknowledge that this feeling is, in some sense, an illusion. For better or worse, though, we are apparently designed to be irresistibly vulnerable to this illusion – in this respect, Appearance *is* Reality for us human beings. This is where, in fact, we see the limits of a thoroughly "scientific" approach to human culture and need to finesse a bit our understanding of what counts as a "fact" for beings like us.

Human Reality Is Real

Humanists and natural scientists concerned with the issue of levels of explanation and emergent properties have much to learn from the work of the Canadian philosopher Charles Taylor. Taylor is a humanist who has grappled with vertical integration and come away unimpressed, and he sees his work as a defense of humanism against the reductionistic threat posed specifically by sociobiology, and more generally by the broader "naturalistic" bent of the modern world. We do not have to follow Taylor to his conclusion, which is essentially to reaffirm the Cartesian gulf between the *Geistes-* and *Naturwissenschaften*, to feel the power of his basic position. His conception of human-level reality provides us with a nuanced, sophisticated model for understanding the place of the person in the great physicalist chain of causation.

One of Taylor's most important points is that human beings, by their very nature, can operate only within the context of a normative space defined by a framework of empirically unverifiable beliefs (1989). The Enlightenment conceit that one can dispense with belief or faith entirely, and make one's way through life guided solely by the dictates of objective reason, is nothing more than that: a conceit, itself a type of faith in the power of a mysterious faculty, "reason," to reveal incorrigible truth. In addition to the panoply of "weak evaluations" – such as a preference for chocolate over vanilla ice cream – that we are familiar with, humans are also inevitably moved to assert "strong" or normative evaluations. This latter type of evaluation is based on one or more explicit or implicit ontological claims and therefore is perceived as having objective force rather than being a merely subjective whim. For instance, I don't particularly like chocolate ice cream, and believe that the flavor of vanilla ice cream is superior. I don't, however, expect everyone to share my preference, and am certainly not moved to condemn my wife for preferring chocolate. I am also not inclined to sexually abuse small children, but this feels like a different sort of preference to me: abusing small children seems *wrong*, and I would condemn and be moved to punish anyone who acted in a manner that violated this feeling. If I were pressed on the matter, this condemnation would be framed, moreover, in terms of beliefs about the value of undamaged human personhood, and the need to prevent suffering and safeguard innocence.

All of the classic Enlightenment values that we continue to embrace as modern liberals – the belief in human rights, the valuation of freedom and creativity, the condemnation of inflicting suffering on innocents – are strong evaluations of this sort, dependent on an implicit set of beliefs about human beings historically derived from Christianity, but reflecting common human normative judgments. Although the Enlightenment *philosophes* began disengaging these beliefs from their explicitly religious context, and we in the last century have more or less completed this process, this does not change their status as beliefs. The "self-evident truths" enshrined in such classic liberal documents as the Declaration of Independence of the United States and the UN Universal Declaration of Human Rights are not revealed to us by the objective functioning of our a priori reason, but are rather items of faith.

Taylor argues that metaphysically grounded normative reactions such as these are inevitable for human beings. The fact that we cannot coherently account for our own or others' behavior without making reference to metaphysical beliefs, as well as the fact that they irresistibly present themselves to us as objective despite our lack of proof for them, says something important about what it means for something to be "real" for human beings. Although values are not part of the world as studied by natural science, the fact that value terms such as "freedom" and "dignity" are "ineradicable in first-person, non-explanatory uses" (1989: 57) means that they are, in a nontrivial sense, real. "[Human] reality is, of course, dependent upon us, in the sense that a condition for its existence is our existence," Taylor concedes. "But once granted that we exist, it is no more a subjective projection than what physics deals with" (59). For the peculiar type of animal that we are, moral space is as much a part of reality as physical space, in that we cannot avoid having to orient ourselves with respect to it.

To reformulate Taylor's insights into the naturalistic framework I have been arguing for throughout this book, we can say, qua naturalist, that our overactive theory of mind causes us to inevitably project intentionality onto the world – to see our moral emotions and desires writ large in the cosmos. It would be empirically unjustified to take this projection as "real." Nonetheless, the very inevitability of this projection means that, whatever we may assert qua naturalists, we cannot escape from the lived reality of moral space. As neuroscientists, we might believe that the brain is a deterministic, physical system, like everything else in the universe, and recognize that the weight of empirical evidence suggests that free will is a cognitive illusion (Wegner 2002). Nonetheless, no cognitively undamaged human being can help *acting* like and at some level really *feeling* that he or she is free.[38] There may well be individuals who lack this sense, and who can quite easily and thoroughly conceive of themselves and other people in purely instrumental, mechanistic terms, but we label such people "psychopaths," and quite rightly try to identify them and put them away somewhere to protect the rest of us (Blair 1995, 2001). Similarly, from the perspective of evolutionary psychology, I can believe that the love that I feel toward my child and my relatives is an emotion installed in me by my genes in accordance with Hamilton's rule. This does not, however, make my experience of the emotion, nor my sense of its normative reality, any less real to me. Indeed, this is precisely what I would expect from the third-person perspective: the gene-level, ultimate causation would not *work* unless we were thoroughly sincere at the proximate level. The whole purpose of the evolution of social emotions is to make sure that these "false" feelings seem inescapably real to us, and this lived reality will never change unless we turn into completely different types of organisms. As Steven Pinker puts it,

Whatever its ontological status may be, a moral sense is part of the standard equipment of the human mind. It's the only mind we've got, and we have no choice but to take its intuitions seriously. If we are so constituted that we cannot help but think in moral terms (at least some of the time and toward some people), then morality is as real for us as if it were decreed by the Almighty or written into the cosmos. (2002: 193)[39]

---

38 Cf. Dennett's characterization of free will as "an evolved creation of human activity and beliefs," and therefore "just as real as such other human creations as music and money" (2003: 13). Also see John Searle's (1995) discussion of the inescapability of humanly created reality, the features of which appear "as natural to us as stones and water and trees" (4).

39 Cf. Michael Ruse's comment that, "as a function of our biology, our moral ideas are thrust upon us, rather than being things needing or allowing decision at an individual level" (1998: 259).

This principle is not confined to natural scientific explanations of human phenomena: it holds with regard to *any* sort of "objective," "reductive," third-person explanation, even those coming from within the humanities, such as Taylor's genealogy of the construction of the modern Western self. For instance, qua historian, I believe that my sense that human rights ought to be defended is a contingent item of faith, a product of the Enlightenment that I happen to have inherited because of the age and place in which I was born. This abstract insight is potentially quite helpful in facilitating communication with people from other moral traditions, but such interactions are unlikely to shake my faith in the importance of, say, women's rights – unless this faith is, perhaps through conversion to a fundamentalist strand of traditional religion, replaced by an opposing belief. Completely extracting ourselves from moral space is as impossible as stopping our visual systems from processing information when we open our eyes, or our stomach from registering distress when our blood sugar level drops below a certain point. In this sense, then, human-level truth is inescapably "real."

THE IMPORTANCE OF PHYSICALISM: WHY PHYSICALISM BOTH DOES AND DOES NOT MATTER

To the extent that human-level reality will always have a hold on us, then, we are entitled to say that physicalism does not matter. This leads Taylor to conclude that the unavoidability of human-level concepts is not merely a phenomenological observation, but rather a clue as to the "transcendental conditions" (32) of "undamaged human personhood" (26), and thereby a refutation of any sort of third-person, naturalistic account of the humanities.[40] If human reality is indeed real for us, why *not* follow Taylor and say that it is just as real as anything studied by the natural sciences?

Why Physicalism Does *Matter*

The short response to Taylor is that, at least for anyone even casually familiar with the current state of the art in the cognitive sciences, human reality is simply *not* as real as physical reality. Or, to put this more accurately, our innate empirical prejudice appears to be so constituted that, once we have *explained* something – that is, reduced a higher-level phenomenon to lower-level causes – the higher-level phenomenon inevitably loses some of its hold on us.[41] Despite what Stephen Jay Gould and the AAAS say, there is an important difference between believing that God literally created the world in seven days and thinking that this is a beautiful

---

[40] This is essentially the same insight behind Searle's granting of special ontological status to human consciousness.

[41] See Preston & Epley 2005 for a recent study illustrating this phenomenon.

story that can mean something to us on Sundays, but must be put aside when we go about our daily work. Evolution is such a relatively new idea, and its message is so fundamentally alien to us, that its real implications for our picture of human reality have yet to fully sink in, which is why most liberal intellectuals continue to believe that Darwinism does not seriously threaten traditional religious beliefs or conceptions of the self. It clearly *does*, however, and once we have begun down the physicalist path we cannot go back to the old certainties. This is not merely because it would be illogical to do so – although it would – but because we just seem to be built in such a way that we want to deal with and picture the world as it "really" is, no matter how unpleasant.

We can get a sense of this human "truth" prejudice – really, a preference for lower-level over higher-level explanation – by thinking about a typical reaction to a science-fiction movie that was very popular some years back called *The Matrix* (1999). For those unfamiliar with the plot, the protagonist, "Neo," begins to uncover puzzling clues that his everyday world is an illusion. He eventually discovers that his body and those of others in his apparently real world of "the Matrix" are, in fact, being maintained in sinister life-support tanks housed in a vast factory. Their brain activity is being farmed as a source of energy by the evil machines who created the Matrix – an elaborate virtual world, projected onto the brains of the bodies in the tanks – in order to fool their prisoners into thinking that they are free. Neo eventually gets in touch with a doughty band of humans who have liberated themselves from the life-support tanks and who live crude, uncomfortable, but "free" lives in an underground refuge called (rather heavy-handedly) Zion.

One of the more interesting points in the movie is when a cowardly informant is induced to betray the inhabitants of Zion and return to the tanks in exchange for a particularly pleasant illusory lifestyle: in the virtual world of the Matrix, he is to be a rich and powerful man, with every sensory pleasure one could desire. Most importantly, he will not *remember* that this is all an illusion: his fine steak and excellent red wine will taste just as good as the "real" things would, and the pleasure he will derive from his new virtual life will be – to him, at least – inescapably true and powerfully felt. Especially when compared to the threadbare and uncomfortable life in the bleak underground burrow of Zion, this seems like a pretty good deal: if you don't know the Matrix is not real, what difference does it make? If the steak tastes like steak, why should you care that you are "really" pickled in a tank and being farmed by evil machines? If your memories are to be perfectly erased, why would it matter that you had betrayed your comrades and your former cause?

It probably *would not* matter. The important thing, though, is that we, as human beings, feel that it *would* – we feel anger with this traitor, as well as revulsion at the idea of returning voluntarily to the Matrix. Why? Because, as Aristotle said, we are constituted in such as way as to desire the Good, and the Good for human beings involves being properly situated with regard to what we feel to be the "truth." Promised future rewards that we know to be illusory seem less valuable to us, even if we are assured that they will *seem* real when we get them. The same inchoate instinct that makes life in the Matrix abhorrent to us makes it impossible to continue to embrace, at least in precisely the same way, traditional religious ideals that appear to be in conflict with what we are convinced we now know about the world. And – at least as long as physicalism remains our current best explanation of the world – any religious or philosophical belief based on dualism is going to be in this sort of conflict.

A strikingly beautiful recent novel by Audrey Niffenegger called *The Time Traveler's Wife* (2003) concerns itself with a man who, as a result of a mysterious neurological disorder, find himself involuntarily and unpredictably traveling through time – sans clothes or any other artifacts, which often proves extremely inconvenient, to say the least. He quite wisely keeps the existence of this disorder mostly to himself, because, of course, no one would believe him: time travel goes against everything that we know about how the universe works. Some people, however – including his future (former? present?) wife and doctor – need to be let in on the secret, and they are predictably dubious until they are given Othello's ocular proof and personally witness the time traveler appear and disappear into thin air. This visual evidence is supplemented by other sorts of proof – he provides really good stock tips, for instance – but the real turning point is, as always with humans, the "show-me" moment. The premise of Niffenegger's portrayal of time travel is that human consciousness is real and somehow outside of the bounds of space and time, and the fact that this is a deeply intuitively appealing idea has much to do with the power and beauty of the book. But this is ultimately a work of fiction, and none of us would be any more inclined than the characters in the novel to accept the reality of time travel without *seeing* it happen, right in front of our eyes. This is why physicalism reigns supreme as our current best explanatory framework, and why it will not be dislodged from this place without some really impressive new evidence. The soul was a pretty good hypothesis for a while, because it certainly is hard to see how mind could come from matter. But it apparently *can* and *does*, and once the implications of this fact work their way through our innate resistance we will no longer be able to embrace dualism in quite the same manner as we once did.

This is where the Copernican analogy *is* helpful. We quite happily live our everyday lives in a geocentric solar system, seeing the sun rise and set and enjoying the felt stability of the earth under our feet. We acknowledge, though, that this appearance is an illusion, and that the earth is really racing through space around the sun at 108,000 kilometers per hour. Why does it matter what is "really" the case, if it makes no difference to the way we see things? It matters because making important, practical decisions based on what is really the case, as opposed to what seems to be the case, works better. Launching satellites or sending off space probes simply would not work very well unless we suspended our intuitive geocentric worldview when engaged in this sort of work. The same is true of human-level realities. The realization that the body-mind is an integrated system is counterintuitive, but treatments based on this insight appear to be massively more effective than dualism-based treatments – pharmaceutical interventions, for instance, have done more for the treatment of mental illness in a few decades than millennia of spiritual interventions, from exorcisms to Freudian analysis. Recognizing that there is no point at which the ghost enters the machine allows us to go ahead with stem cell research, and understanding that personhood is not an all-or-nothing affair helps us get a better grip on what is going on with severe dementia in the elderly. Physicalism matters because it simply works better than dualism, and – once the reality of this superiority is fully grasped – this pragmatic consideration is an irresistibly powerful argument for creatures like us.

Dual Consciousness: Walking the Two Paths

How can physicalism both matter and not matter? We can answer this question by returning to Nietzsche's wonderful critique of Kant and seeing how *both* Niezsche and Kant were right. To take moral intuitions as an example, we can follow Nietzsche – somewhat updated and put into the role of an evolutionary psychologist – and see why it is important and revealing to ask about the adaptive forces that cause us to feel the force of synthetic a priori claims, rather than simply experiencing them as unquestioned intuitions. Answering the question of origins – uncovering the lower-level, ultimate explanations for our moral intuitions – has important practical implications, but most of all we just simply want to *know*. We also need to follow Kant, however, in recognizing that, no matter what the origins of these intuitions, they are the spontaneous product of a very powerful, built-in faculty, the output of which seem inescapably right to us. This means that, as empirically responsible humanists – or even as humans tout court, living in the modern world of pharmaceuticals and behavioral neuroscience – we need to pull off the trick of simultaneously seeing the world as Nietzsche and as Kant, holding *both* perspectives in mind and employing each when appropriate. Those who have allowed the acid of Darwinism to finally breach the mind-body barrier thus end up living with a kind of dual consciousness, cultivating the ability to view human beings simultaneously under two descriptions: as physical systems and as persons. On the one hand, we are convinced that Darwinism is the best account we have for explaining the world around us, and therefore that human beings are physical systems and the idea that there is a "ghost in the machine" should be abandoned. On the other hand, cognitively intact humans apparently cannot help but feel the strong pull of human-level truth.

Taking consilience or vertical integration seriously thus involves a balancing act that serves as a testament to our human ability to hold multiple, mutually contradictory perspectives in our minds at once. This ability, of course, derives from our capacity to form mental spaces, as discussed in Chapter 4. Most likely the adaptive function of mental spaces – which must have an adaptive function, as neurologically expensive as they are – was originally, and continues to be, the ability to hold multiple *social* perspectives at once. This is a crucial talent for functioning successfully in even a moderately sized social group. Among other things, it is crucial for social deception: when you lie, you need to keep at least two different models of the world in your mind at once, and we humans are remarkably good at this exceedingly difficult task. This ability to simultaneously hold different perspectives in mind, though originally evolved for the purpose of social deception, can apparently be exapted and applied to explanations of the world. It forms the basis of our ability to entertain alternative perspectives, to see anything in the world "qua" some role – "qua" physicialist or "qua" everyday person reading a novel.

We should also recognize that mental spaces, by their very nature, are not all created equal – otherwise they would be indistinguishable from each other. One of the most difficult things about lying, for instance, is that we appear to be unable to maintain as detailed and vivid a model of the "lie world" as of our real world. This leads to certain problems – we can be "tripped up" by our lies in a way that is impossible if we are telling the truth – but it is probably a crucial design feature: if both spaces were equally powerfully realized, we would lose track of the lie, which would defeat the very purpose of lying. The same principle holds with mentally visualized imagery versus real-time perception: an imagined object or scene is always less vivid than the "real" thing, and it is extremely important that this be so, lest we become confused about whether we were really being chased by a tiger or just worrying about the possibility.

I would speculate that, when it comes to dual consciousness regarding physical and human levels of explanation, the human level will always be much more vivid and real to us – evolution would have done a poor job if it were otherwise, and evolution does not do poor jobs. This means that taking the physicalist stance will require the same sort of effort and training that any counterintuitive ability requires, and our ability to remain in the physicalist mental space will always be somewhat limited. Francis Crick, at one point in his discussion of the "astonishing hypothesis" that the mind is nothing other than the brain, observes somewhat bemusedly: "I myself find it difficult at times to avoid the idea of a homunculus. One slips into it so easily" (1994: 258). Crick was not alone. The interpretive space involving the perception of agency and consciousness, in ourselves as well as in others, is a product of one of the most basic of human cognitive modules, and we will never escape its gravitational pull for long. The fact that Richard Dawkins and Daniel Dennett remain at large, simultaneously espousing thoroughgoing physicalism in their professional work while – at least to the best of my knowledge – continuing to participate in and derive pleasure from normal human relationships and goal-directed activities, says more about the robustness and automaticity of our theory of mind space than the plausibility of fully and continuously embracing a mechanistic view of the universe.

We can mine the world's religious traditions for helpful metaphors for what this kind of dual stance toward the world might be like. Jesus famously advised his followers to be "in the world but not of it" (John 17: 14–15), and the figure of the Bodhisattva in the Mahayana Buddhist tradition dwells simultaneously in two realms: that of "ultimate" truth, where there are no distinctions and no suffering and therefore no need for compassion or Buddhism, and that of "conventional" truth, where suffering is real and the Bodhisattva is called on to exercise finely tuned and deeply felt compassion. My favorite analogy comes from the fourth-century B.C.E. Chinese thinker Zhuangzi, who describes his ideal person as "walking the two paths" – that of the "Heavenly"/Natural (*tian*) and the human. From the Heavenly/ natural perspective, there are no distinctions, no right and wrong, no feelings, no truth. From the human perspective, all of these things are acutely real. The key to moving successfully through the world, Zhuangzi believes, is simultaneously keeping both perspectives in mind, seeing the human "in the light of the Heavenly," and thus seeing through to its contingent nature, while at the same time acting in accordance with the constraints of being a human in the world of humans (Watson 2003: 40–41). This kind of dual consciousness is also perhaps what Kant was getting at in a curious passage from the *Groundwork* when he declares that we must "lend" the idea of freedom to rational beings:

Now I assert that every being who cannot act except under the Idea of freedom is by this alone – from a practical point of view – really free; that is to say, for him all the laws inseparably bound up with freedom are valid just as much as if his will could be pronounced free in itself on grounds valid for theoretical philosophy. And I maintain that to every rational being possessed of a will we must also lend (*leihen*) the Idea of freedom as the only one under which he can act. (1785/1964: 115–116)

We know, qua physicalist, that we are not free, but in our everyday lives we cannot help acting as if we are free, lest we find ourselves exiled from the Kingdom of Ends – that is, no longer recognizable as undamaged human agents.

EMBRACING VERTICAL INTEGRATION

To conclude, then, we should not allow our distaste for physicalist explanations of the human to turn us into reactionaries. The subject of humanist inquiry is not the workings of some Cartesian *Geist* in the machine, but rather the wonderfully complex set of emergent realities that constitute the lived human world in all of its cultural and historical diversity. The realization of the thoroughly physical nature of this reality does not condemn us, however, to live forever after in an ugly world of things. For undamaged humans, other humans can never be a existentially grasped as mere things,[42] and our promiscuous projection of teleology onto the

---

[42] Of course, what counts as "human" is up for grabs, and the idea that every member of the biological species *Homo sapiens* is "human" is a relatively recent idea – the category has historically tended to encompass only one's own tribe. The recurrent reality of genocide, even in our modern world, serves as a chilling reminder of how quickly and easily groups formerly seen as humans can be reclassified as "things."

world assures that we will continue to find the whole materialist universe a rather beautiful place once it is properly understood. The fact that even the most resolutely physicalist conception of the world cannot help but continue to inspire awe and an implicit sense of meaning in human beings is captured quite well in the character of Henry Perowne, a neurosurgeon and committed materialist, in Ian McEwan's recent novel *Saturday*. Prompted by a poem to imagine being "called in" to create a new religion, Perowne declares that he would base his on evolution:

What better creation myth? An unimaginable sweep of time, numberless generations spawning by infinitesimal steps complex living beauty out of inert matter, driven on by the blind furies of random mutation, natural selection and environmental change, with the tragedy of forms continually dying, and lately the wonder of minds emerging and with them morality, love, art, cities – and the unprecedented bonus of this story happening to be demonstrably true. (2005: 56)

Our innate cognitive mechanisms ensure that the modern scientific model of human beings as essentially very complicated things will not lead to nihilism or despair. In the end, acknowledging our inescapable embodiment not only possesses the excellent advantage of being "demonstrably true," but also cannot help but enrich our sense of wonder at the dependent and tragic human condition, detracting nothing from the felt beauty and nobility of it all.

Conclusion

I WILL NOW ASK YOU TO FORGET ALL ABOUT REPLICATORS AND LUMBERING robots, algorithmic processes and the unfeeling universe. Discussing these issues was important in order to see how human-level reality can survive even the starkest version of physicalism as a global explanation for our universe, but there are at least a couple of reasons why physicalism will usually play no immediate role in our work.

First of all, it is entirely possible that, at some point in the future, we will find ourselves having to modify or even abandon strong physicalism. A colleague of mine, a renowned social psychologist, is currently devoting a significant portion of his lab resources to proving that human consciousness constitutes a full-blown fifth dimension of reality, a claim he intends to substantiate in part by demonstrating the reality of precognition (ESP). Although they are not yet published or widely peer reviewed, he claims to have replicated results where events that have not yet happened are exerting a priming effect on subjects: that is, the subjects are apparently showing signs of being primed by stimuli that they *will* see in the future. He anticipates a great deal of resistance to his theory – which, incidentally, is one reason he did not begin pursuing it until he had a secure day job – and for good reason: it goes against everything else we know about how the universe works. So did quantum theory, though, so if he and his colleagues can accumulate a massive enough quantity of replicable data we might have to recognize some form of dualism as more than just a deeply ingrained intuition.

More important, even if the fifth dimension fails to pan out, the robustness and automaticity of our theory of mind module(s) will assure that the world as seen by *l'homme absurde* will recede into an abstract intellectual commitment the minute we put down our dog-eared copy of *The Selfish Gene* and begin going about our normal human business again – appearing to us perhaps only from time to time in the form of momentary glimpses. We all live our daily lives in the rich world of emergent human meaning, and those of us who are humanists also earn our keep by studying it: unlike natural scientists, we do not necessarily have to withdraw our projections in order to perform our day jobs.

This leads to an important question, however. Given that the levels of explanation studied by the natural sciences are often not directly relevant to humanistic inquiry, why should we care about them? Concretely speaking, what do we stand to gain from adopting a vertically integrated approach? I would like to conclude this book by reviewing some of the current barriers to vertical integration, arguing that humanists are going to have to bear a large part of the burden in overcoming those barriers, and finally trying to suggest why making the effort to do so would be worthwhile.

MOVING FROM A BIVERSITY TO A TRUE UNIVERSITY

As I have argued at some length, Western institutions of higher learning are currently "biversities," with scholars in such humanistic disciplines as anthropology, art history, comparative and national literatures, philosophy, and religious studies going about their business in complete ignorance of what their colleagues in those nice new buildings on the other side of campus are up to. This ignorance is not only complete but also principled. Not only do humanists know very little or nothing about the natural sciences, but their at least implicit metaphysical dualism allows them to feel intellectually justified about it. The power of ideology to prevent genuine engagement with new perspectives is clear from the plight of anthropology departments throughout Western academia, where the inability of traditional cultural anthropologists and those with a more naturalist bent to see eye to eye has led to institutional splits and endless acrimony. The level of acrimony seems to be highest in anthropology because, of all the core humanities disciplines, it most clearly straddles the *Geist* versus *Natur* divide: the objects studied by physical anthropologists come permeated with cultural meaning, while militant social constructivists are constantly being presented with inconveniently robust artifacts and other sorts of physical evidence. The reason that we have not seen similar bloodletting in other core humanities departments is because they tend to be comfortably and uniformly committed to either objectivism or postmodernism, and challenges to these frameworks have so far been quickly squashed or marginalized.

This is a shame for many reasons, not least of which is the missed opportunity to fill the burning need for humanistic expertise in those disciplines that most directly border on the demilitarized zone between the humanities and sciences: behavioral neuroscience, the various branches of psychology, cognitive linguistics, and AI research. Even within the natural sciences, most breakthroughs happen through mutual fertilization of disciplines dealing with adjacent levels of explanation. The integrating of human-level frameworks into the chain of explanation promises an even greater degree of cross-fertilization, and there are many areas where precisely this sort of integration is required to break borderland disciplines out of conceptual dead ends or unfortunate detours. Cognitive scientists exploring human-level realities need a great deal of help in framing their research questions and interpreting their data and are often hampered by an ignorance of even the most basic history or "thick" cultural background of the topics they are investigating. An entire subfield of cross-cultural psychology, for instance, is based on a model of East Asian thought as "holistic," as opposed to the "analytic" West (Nisbett 2003, Nisbett et al. 2001). As I suggested in Chapter 4, the empirical data being gathered by these

East-West psychologists is extremely interesting, but when it comes to *interpreting* this data – telling a coherent historical narrative that will explain it – they often fall back on unhelpful and essentialistic stereotypes. Eastern "holism," for instance, is traced back to such foundational texts of Chinese thought as the *Classic of Changes* (*Yi Jing*, or *I Ching*) or the *Daodejing* (*Tao Te Ching*), but without any clear sense of when or how these texts were composed, how representative they are of "Eastern" thought, or how they have historically been used and interpreted in East Asia.

Researchers in the various branches of the cognitive sciences thus have much to learn from humanists, and the cognitive sciences absolutely require the higher-level expertise of anthropologists, literary scholars, and historians if they are to avoid reinventing the wheel or committing egregious interpretative errors. The expertise humanists bring to the table, however, should not be seen as descending from some explanatory cloud-cuckoo land, magically hovering above the mundane world of physical causation. Despite their variety and "disunity," the various disciplines of the natural sciences have managed to arrange themselves in a rough explanatory hierarchy, with the lower levels of explanation (such as physics) setting limits on the sorts of explanations that can be entertained at the higher levels (such as biology). To move forward as a field of human inquiry, the humanities need to plug themselves into their proper place at the top of this explanatory hierarchy, because the lower levels have finally advanced to a point that they both need to hear from us and have many interesting things to say in return.

WHY HUMANISTS NEED TO WORK HARDER

Some of my humanities colleagues have complained that I put too much emphasis on how *they* need to change and to learn from natural sciences, instead of the other way around. Of course, becoming a member of a true university requires work on both sides, but unfortunately humanists are going to have to bear much of the burden. There are a couple of reasons for this. To begin with, natural scientists have the advantage of incidentally being *humans*, and therefore having both intuitive access to human-level structures of meaning and a natural interest in them. Behavioral neuroscientists, for instance, are likely to also be interested in literature, classical music, or art. Although it is conceivable that their appreciation of such areas might be relatively untutored or unreflective, a musicologist or an art historian trying to explain his or her work to a neuroscientist has a lot less built-in cognitive resistance to overcome than vice versa. As a result, natural scientists seem much more excited about the prospect of cross-disciplinary collaboration than do humanists, as well as more proactive in initiating contact and dialogue.[1]

---

[1] For instance, at a conference I recently attended in Switzerland called the "World Knowledge Dialogue," dedicated to trying to bridge the humanities–natural science divide, humanists made up only a small proportion of the participants, although the conference was widely publicized to Faculty of Arts departments.

A more significant factor, however, is that the place of the humanities in the larger world of human knowledge is a bit like that of present-day North Korea: having lived in jealously guarded isolation for so long, it is going to be much more difficult for North Koreans to adapt to and learn about the modern, globalized world than it will be for this world to accommodate the North Koreans, although such accommodation seems both inevitable and desirable. Among humanists, basic ignorance of how science works and what is currently going on in relevant scientific disciplines is mixed with a degree of envy, resentment, and hostility vis-à-vis the natural sciences because of resource allocation and social prestige. In humanist circles, the higher salaries and funding levels that accrue to the natural sciences tend to be viewed with a mixture of envy and disdain for the manner in which the study of mere things is valued over the study of human meaning. Behind the standard High Humanist sanctimony concerning the ineffable essence of the human spirit can be discerned a quite poisonous sort of *ressentiment*, and this remains a major stumbling block to constructive dialogue.

Consider, for example, the piece by Louis Menand (2005) discussed in the Introduction, which concludes that the way out of the malaise currently afflicting the humanities has to lie in an aggressive "colonization" by the humanities of more and more areas of human inquiry. This will involve humanists standing by their guns and refusing, for instance, to submit their esoteric postmodern analyses to standards of intelligibility set by noninitiates. Commenting on a newspaper article describing some of the more counterintuitive and mysterious implications of string theory, such as that "space and time are illusions" or that the universe is two-dimensional, Menand observes:

My first thought was that if someone in a French department had written this, the *New York Times* would have held the person up for ridicule on the front page, and so, soon after, would the *New Criterion*, the *New Republic*, the *New York Review of Books*, *Commentary*, the *National Review*, the *Nation*, and *Dissent*... It really is a little hard to understand. If you say that the meaning of a poem is indeterminate, you are accused of posing a threat to Western values – often by people who have never read poetry. But if you say that the universe is like an ATM card, you get the Nobel Prize. (2005: 10)[2]

Menand's analogy between string theory and deconstruction is, of course, entirely fatuous, and the reason that postmodernist gobblygook is taken less seriously than scientific gobblygook is not at all hard to understand. As we discussed in Chapter 5, the only reason scientists get away with crazy counterintuitive constructs such as waves that are simultaneously particles or string theory is that, at some point, these weird ideas pay off in terms that satisfy our common sense and pragmatically *do*

---

[2] Cf. Clifford Geertz's comment that the natural sciences should be subsumed by the humanities, a task that is to be spearheaded by bold new humanists "unwilling to stop at the borders of disciplinary authority or to cower before the solemnities of Nobel laureates" (1997/2000: 164). This petulance regarding the Nobel Prize is a recurring motif in High Humanist writing.

things for us. As a classic High Humanist, Menand contemptuously dismisses the need for humanistic work to do anything or to make sense to ordinary people and those scientific philistines who never read poetry. He appears to miss the point that, since the humanities' raison d'être is human-level reality, they damn well better make sense to people. The humanities are not concerned with helping us build a better mousetrap, but they should edify and move us, and teach us something about ourselves that we did not already know. This, of course, does not mean that we do not try to force young people to think in new ways, to linger over texts in a manner quite alien to the MTV age, or to genuinely grapple with ideas from another age or place instead of simply subsuming them under their own preconceived notions of the Good. Trying to justify shoving Theory down people's throats because some intellectual Brahmins have decided it is for their own good, though, is a counterproductive stance to take, and Menand's comment is typical of the sort of envy-driven rigidity that continues to stand in the way of vertical integration.

This *ressentiment* is probably intensified by humanists' realization, at some level, that they are all constantly taking advantage of and benefiting from the advances made possible by the natural sciences, as they check into their state-of-the-art university hospitals, fly on airplanes, and type their antiscience rants on slick laptops and send them over wireless servers to their compatriots on another continent. Humanists are often wont to dismiss the inordinate valuing of the sciences over the humanities as part of some fascist plot to subdue the human spirit, or the latest stage of the capitalist dehumanization of the globe. In fact, this growing imbalance in value ascribed to the humanities and natural sciences is a direct consequence of perhaps the most basic human quality of all: the desire to know how things work, so that we can move through the world more effectively. We as a society are much more inclined to financially reward someone for achievements that will help cure cancer or build a better mousetrap because both of these things seem obviously *useful*, and not just to capitalists or fascists or non–poetry-readers, but to your average person trying to get through life.

I will go out on a limb and predict that we will never have a multibillion-dollar center dedicated to semiotic cultural anthropology or deconstructive unpacking of Elizabethan sonnets, simply because such activities seem so patently self-indulgent and pointless to most people. Money is pouring into the sciences because they are achieving results and discovering exciting new things about who we are and the nature of the world in which we live. In this environment, humanistic inquiry – at least as carried on in most core humanities departments – seems to me like a stagnant lagoon cut off from a great fertile ocean of scientific innovation and progress. Breaking down the dike and opening the humanities up to what lower-levels disciplines have to say to them would represent a sorely needed injection of intellectual nutrients and help to jolt the humanities out of the stagnation that is obvious to even their most ardent defenders. This is a necessary step because, despite the High Humanists' contemptuous dismissal of practical concerns, progress is what we rightly demand of our elites, no matter what field they are working in.

IN WHAT SENSE DOES VERTICAL INTEGRATION REPRESENT PROGRESS?

It is immediately obvious how the principles of organic chemistry shape the sort of questions that molecular biologists can ask, and strongly constrain the sorts of answers that can be provided. It is perhaps less obvious what behavioral neuroscience has to tell us about analyzing an Elizabethan sonnet or explaining the interplay of patronage and literary forms in medieval Japan. Even if the relevance could be defended, we must go on to ask how applying neuroscience or evolutionary theory to, say, literary studies can be seen as representing progress.

To my mind, the single most important implication of the vertically integrated approach to culture is at the meta-level of general theories of human cognition and culture. Once we require humanistic levels of explanation to be constrained by the principles of lower levels of explanation, a host of pervasive and foundational theories about the human mind have to be abandoned as empirically untenable. At the very least, the evidence presented in Chapters 1 through 4 calls seriously into question such deeply entrenched dogmas as the "blank slate" theory of human nature, strong versions of social constructivism and linguistic determinism, and the ideal of disembodied reason. This has immediate and obvious global implications for humanistic inquiry, and it represents an important step forward.

Consider the figure-ground shift that occurs when we abandon social constructivism. Most humanistic work these days begins from the assumption of extreme cultural incommensurability and strangeness: humanities scholars tend to view cultures as coherent units and adopt radical difference as their basic interpretative starting point. This makes good sense if humans are blank slates and cultures autonomous entities that irresistibly impress their arbitrary uniqueness on this pliable medium.

In my field, early Chinese thought, this default assumption of radical difference has led to absurd claims becoming established as commonplaces. For instance, a slim book published by Herbert Fingarette in 1972 famously argued that "Western" concepts such as interiority or free choice were completely lacking in early Confucian thought, and that the early Chinese view of the self and the mind was radically different from anything that would be recognizable to a modern Westerner. Even decades later, the idea that the early Chinese lack anything corresponding to the modern Western conception of "the self" is still a surprisingly widespread and resilient view (Jochim 1998, Chaibong 2001).[3] Another prominent scholar of early

---

[3] Fingarette's book remains a mainstay in Chinese thought survey classes and has recently been reissued in a French translation by the University of Montréal (2004).

Chinese thought, Chad Hansen, continues to argue that the classical Chinese language possesses only mass nouns (such as "water" in English), as opposed to "count nouns" that pick out distinct objects. As a result, he claims, early Chinese is based on a "mereological" ontology aimed at drawing boundaries in the otherwise continuous "stuff" of reality, as opposed to the entity-based ontology that "we" in the West have inherited from the Greeks (Hansen 1983, 1992; cf. Lloyd and Sivin 2003). Scholars of China working from an explicitly postmodernist perspective, such as Lydia Liu (2004), have portrayed even something as mundane as the application of Western grammatical categories to the classical Chinese language as a colonialist imposition, a violent forcing of a pristine and amorphous "native" language into the Procrustean bed of Indo-European thought. A surprising number of recent treatments of early Chinese thought continue to portray it as radically "other" (Geaney 2002, Fox 2005, Yuan 2006) and present the comparison of modern Western and early Chinese thought as, for instance, an endless "rhythmic and dialectical interplay between difference and complementarity, continuity and discontinuity" (Shen 2003) or a sort of vague interpenetration of otherwise incommensurable "landscapes" of *culturéalité* (Botz-Bornstein 2006).

Again, the only way claims like these could gain credence is against the background assumption of social constructivism and radical difference. This theoretical stance causes real but minor differences to be seized on and magnified, while whole swaths of contradictory evidence are swept under the rug or simply ignored. As I have conceded at several points in this book, the postmodern celebration of difference was an important corrective to naïve Enlightenment universalism, and of course, as humanists the exploration of cultural nuance is our particular métier. When I teach early Chinese thought to North American undergraduates, I spend a lot of my time emphasizing to them how different some of these conceptions of the self are. My goal is to thereby encourage them to question their unreflective and historically myopic assumption that, for instance, modern Western liberalism is the only framework for conceptualizing the self and its relationship to society, or to undermine their Romantic conceit of themselves as bearers of wild, Promethean individual creativity. Indeed, this is arguably one of the primary reasons that we study other cultures in the first place: to learn how they are different, why they are different, and what this difference might teach us about ourselves. None of this questioning makes sense, however, unless it is performed against a background assumption of deep and pervasive commonality. This is where postmodernism has gone too far, turning the celebration of difference into a bizarre fetish, and undermining the very idea that we can learn anything about anyone. The evidence that we have reviewed in this book strongly suggests that human culture is created by, transmitted between, and continuously subjected to the filtering of human minds that share a rich and robust universal structure, which is why we can even begin to understand the products of other human minds. High Humanist posturing notwithstanding, the theoretical assumptions and methodological techniques that emerge from vertical integration therefore represent our best hope for pulling the humanities out of its current relativist quagmire.

Consider, for instance, the promise of metaphor and metaphoric blend analysis as a tool for humanities scholars. The basic humanistic problem seems to me to be: how do we know the insides of other people? If we do, in fact, conceptualize such abstract subjects as the world, ourselves, our place in the world, and our normative relationships to others by means of bodily based metaphors, situationalist reconstructions, and metaphoric blends, this gives us a concrete way to answer this question. If we want to study what people think about, say, religion, and how this differs from other ways of thinking, we should be looking at the level of image schemas, conceptual blends, and conceptual metaphors in addition to individual words or abstract philosophical theories. The structure of image schemas is more general than any individual linguistic sign but also more basic than a theory, and it seems that it is on this intermediate level of conceptualization that most of our reasoning patterns are based. In other words, then, if we want to know what people think about concept X, we need to look at the metaphors and blends they use when discussing the concept. This means that, despite differences between, say, traditional Confucian and modern Western liberal theories of morality or the self, both of these theoretical conceptions grow out of and make use of a deeper metaphysical grammar that has its roots in common human embodied experience. When we process these metaphors and metaphoric blends – whether from fourth-century B.C.E. China or from our friend making an argument for why we should stop investing in technology stocks – we can draw on our embodied minds to serve as a universal human decoding pad.

Of course, we should expect this approach to uncover both similarities and differences. Because of the pan-species commonalities mapped out in Chapters 1 through 4, one would expect to find a high degree of similarity with regard to conceptual metaphors and blends across human cultures and languages, especially with regard to primary metaphors. Human beings have to physically move in order to get something that they want, and they obtain most of their information about the world through their sense of sight (the experiential basis of the common primary metaphor, KNOWING AS SEEING). Arguably the basic overall repertoire of motions and physical interactions possessed by a modern American is not terribly different from that possessed by, say, a Chinese person in the fifth-century B.C.E. However, since these image patterns arise through the interactions of our embodied minds with our environment – which, in the case of *Homo sapiens sapiens*, involves the "made" social-cultural environment – we would also expect that changes in this environment would be reflected in the creation of novel conceptual metaphors, or in the way basic metaphors are interpreted.

We see this happen constantly with the creation of new technologies – for instance, the advent of widespread computer use in the 1970s and 1980s gave rise to a new metaphor for the mind in first-generation cognitive science, the MIND AS COMPUTER. Social structures and modes of production are also implicated: it would be interesting to examine, for instance, whether or not the now quite common metaphor TIME AS RESOURCE ("you are *wasting* my time"; "I need to *save* time") was at all widespread before the industrial revolution and institution of hourly wages. Even such basic metaphors as KNOWING AS SEEING are mediated by technology and culture: the image of a departing lover arguably functions rather differently for a medieval Japanese poet than for a modern American equipped with digital photography, e-mail, and live Web cams. In addition, different cultures draw on different domains to structure given abstract domains. For instance, the metaphor MORALITY AS ACCOUNTING features prominently in modern Western discourse, as well as in East Asian Buddhist accounts of the functioning of *karma*, but plays less of a role in pre-Buddhist China, where morality is primarily conceptualized in terms of being properly centered in a bounded space. This has a subtle but pervasive effect on the manner in which people in these various cultures think about ethics and the individual's relationship to society. To take another example, human beings share an aversion to uncleanliness, but it is a contingent metaphoric innovation to develop a blend whereby uncleanliness becomes a characteristic of a certain class of people (although classing people into groups seems to be a cognitive universal). Similarly, parental affection for children is a common mammalian trait, but the blend whereby all human beings become children of God is the product of a specific religious and social culture.

The embodied approach to culture thus allows us to talk in a responsible way about specieswide conceptual and affective norms, while at the same time enabling us to remain sensitive to differences and focused on cultural nuance. Recognizing basic human cognitive tendencies as well as our ability to creatively transform these realities allows us to account for Kierkegaard's celebration of the "sickness unto death," or the compilers of the Daoist *Daodejing's* recommendation of the yielding path of weakness, while still seeing how the power of these religious visions is derived precisely from a universal human aversion to sickness and weakness. The approach to culture sketched out in this book offers, then, a way for humanists to steer between the Scylla of objectivist intellectual imperialism and the Charybdis of the postmodern "prison house of language," and have access to both a powerful and concrete methodology for cultural studies and a coherent theoretical grounding for this methodology.

As I have argued in Chapter 5, human beings are willing to listen to all sorts of claims and speculations, but in the end the proof is in the pudding. Space limitations make it impossible for me to provide the reader with a genuinely satisfying amount of pudding, but I can at least point him or her in the direction of the kitchen. Let me begin with two brief sketches suggesting how the embodied approach to culture might change the way we study ethics and aesthetics, freeing the former from narrow and empirically inaccurate objectivist assumptions and the latter from the debilitating effects of postmodern relativism.

Beyond Objectivism: Embodying Ethics

Normative judgments are part of the emergent world of human-level meaning, and by their very nature would seem immune to the influence of empirical evidence. David Hume (1739/1978), of course, famously gave expression to this sentiment with his claim that what "is" can never lead to conclusions about what normatively "ought" to be. Ethics would therefore seem a perfect example of an area of inquiry that should remain untouched by vertical integration. *Pace* Hume, however, it is hard to see how we can remain unmoved by the fact that the empirical evidence emerging from cognitive science, cognitive linguistics, social psychology, and primatology that I have already reviewed calls seriously into question the objectivist model of the self on which the two dominant approaches to ethics in the post-Enlightenment West, deontology and utilitarianism, rely.

To simplify somewhat for the sake of discussion, deontological ethical theories are rule-based: moral action is understood as involving adherence to certain rules or maxims, such as "It is wrong to lie." When presented with a situation, we can consult our definition of a "lie" to determine whether act X in a given situation was or was not an instance of lying, and then once this is determined we can decide whether it was right or wrong depending on where this particular maxim is located in a hierarchy of maxims – for example, perhaps it is trumped by the maxim that we should strive to preserve life. Utilitarianism, on the other hand, judges the goodness of an action on the basis of its consequences or outcomes. If we are utilitarians, in any situation we should be able to unproblematically tally up the costs and benefits of proposed courses of actions, do the math, and thereby figure out which course of action maximizes whatever good our brand of utilitarianism deems important (happiness, justice, gross national product, etc.). In either case, the entire process of moral reasoning is rational and algorithmic, transparent and under our conscious control, and has nothing to do with emotions, implicit skills, or unconscious habits.

If the work on human cognition that we explored in Chapter 1 is at all accurate, neither of these models of moral reasoning seems adequate as either descriptive accounts or normative ideals. If, for instance, the objectivist subject is not master of its own house – that is, if there is no little homunculus collecting data and running a central command post in the brain – this problematizes the very ideal of rule following or rational calculation: who is the rule follower and enforcer, who does the calculating? Similarly, the literature reviewed on the actual psychology of human categorization suggests that people class novel situations in terms of learned prototypes, a process that in turn involves a kind of intuitive pattern matching rather than explicit definitions or conscious rule following. Mark Johnson notes that work on prototype semantics has found that English words such as "lie" demonstrate radial category structure:[4] there are better and worse instances of what constitutes a "lie," and subjects' judgment of whether or not a given act constitutes a lie depends on a set of implicit criterion that are contextually weighted, as well as on what Eve Sweetser refers to as "idealized cognitive models" of knowledge and communication.[5] Applying these models to novel situations involves the reactivation of previous sensory-motor experiences, the identification of relevant features in the novel situation, and the recruitment of both implicit and explicit social knowledge.

This process cannot be captured in an algorithmic maxim-following or cost-benefit analysis. What this means is that moral education will involve training individuals – explicitly or implicitly – to develop more and more sophisticated imagistic models, as well as the ability to extend them in a consistent manner. As Johnson explains, in any kind of reasonably complex situation "moral reasoning cannot consist merely in the rational unpacking of a determinate concept. Instead, it requires imaginative extensions to nonprototypical cases" (Johnson 1993: 100). Such extension often involves the use of metaphors or analogies, and thus both internal moral reasoning and public moral debate will often take the form of battling metaphors – which metaphor or analogy best captures the current situation? Is the current U.S. position in Iraq a "quagmire" like Vietnam, or is it like the difficulties encountered in the early period of implementing the Marshall Plan? When a senator vetoes an aid bill to help Sudanese famine victims, is he or she snatching food out of the mouths of hungry children, or is the senator helping the Sudanese to learn to stand on their own two feet? Are people seen leaving a ruined supermarket in flooded New Orleans "looters," or are they scrappy "survivors" making the best of a bad situation? How we choose to metaphorically frame a situation is probably the single most crucial element in how we will morally reason and morally *feel* about it, which leads us to a second point.

A growing number of cognitive scientists and philosophers have come to agree with Hume and the Greek Stoics that, contrary to what either deontology or utilitarianism would countenance, normative judgments are ultimately derived from human emotional reactions. A classic study by Jonathan Haidt et al. (1993), for instance, found that, when people are presented with verbal scenarios, their affective reactions to them were better predictors of their moral judgments than their claims about harmful consequences, and that people who have a strong negative affective reaction to a scenario often have to struggle to provide a rational justification, with sometimes rather silly results.[6] This has led Joshua Greene (in press)

---

[4] Coleman & Kay 1981, refined by Sweetser 1987.
[5] See Johnson 1993: 91–98 for a discussion of this work.
[6] Cf. Wheatley & Haidt (2005) for a study that employs hypnotically induced disgust reactions to support the idea that moral judgments are grounded in affectively laden, somatically based intuitions.

to conclude that deontological moral maxims, for instance, are best understood as ex post facto rationalizations of what are fundamentally emotional reactions.

This should not surprise us when we consider the work of behavioral neuroscientists such as Antonio Damasio. Damasio's prefrontal cortex patients, discussed in Chapter 1, provide a perfect controlled experiment for rationalist models of ethics: they possess all of the cognitive faculties that, for instance, Kant or Bentham would require of a moral agent, and yet in fact they are completely incapable of acting morally, or even competently, in everyday life. This strongly suggests that there is something to moral reasoning in particular, and human reasoning in general, that objectivist "high-reason" approaches to ethics fail to capture. I do not see how we can avoid concluding that, after millennia of disagreement over the relative importance of algorithmic reason and emotional dispositions in moral education and decision making, fields such as behavioral neuroscience are now in a position to weigh in on at least certain aspects of the debate in a substantive and decisive manner. By combining the refined question asking that has been cultivated in philosophy and religious studies with the tools of cognitive science, we can begin making breakthroughs on issues, such as the nature of moral reasoning or the ethical content of untutored human nature, that have been debated around and around in circles for millennia on the basis of armchair speculation, and at the very least rule out certain venerable positions.

Much more could be said about how cognitive science is poised to make a major impact on philosophical inquiry, and the reader is referred to the Appendix for selected references. Hume's concerns notwithstanding, it is hard to deny that psychological feasibility is an important desideratum for any ethical theory. If deontology and utilitarianism require us to think or behave in manners that are simply not possible or sustainable in quotidian life, this should temper our enthusiasm for adopting them as moral ideals. Evidence about how real human beings actually engage in moral reasoning (a descriptive claim) can therefore provide us with a framework for formulating a psychologically realistic model of moral reasoning and moral education (a normative claim).[7] This is progress.

Accounting for Taste: The Embodied Approach to Aesthetics

For a quick suggestion of what taking embodiment seriously might mean for the study of the arts, let us consider Pierre Bourdieu's account of taste. For Bourdieu, taste is a socially constructed and socially defined signifier: "what is commonly called distinction, that is, a certain quality of bearing and manners, most often considered innate (one speaks of *distinction naturelle*, "natural refinement"), is nothing other than *difference*, a gap, a distinctive feature, in short, a relational

---

[7] See especially Flanagan 1991 for an early argument along these lines, as well as Greene 2003 for a more recent discussion.

property existing only in and through its relation with other properties" (1994: 6). Like any good postmodernist, he is celebrating radical difference and taking aim at the Enlightenment; Bourdieu's particular *bête noire* here is Kant, with his notion of transcendental aesthetic standards. Bourdieu does a brilliant job of showing how the ideal of "natural taste" has been used to legitimize and reinforce class distinctions, and how aesthetic judgments and lifestyle decisions in superficially unrelated "fields" in fact cohere in proclaiming to the world and to oneself a particular class identity: the preponderance of sleek new Volvo wagons in the Ikea parking lot is not purely fortuitous, nor is the fact that the owners of these cars also tend to buy their clothes at Banana Republic, read the *New Yorker*, and profess a passion for Pan-Asian fusion cuisine paired with a nice Gewürztztraminer.[8]

We have here, though, a classic example of postmodern "slippage" in my sense of the term: the slide from a perfectly reasonable claim that questions overly naïve objectivist models into unjustified cultural relativism. Many things typically or formerly viewed as natural are, in fact, not; however, it does not necessarily follow from this fact that *nothing* is natural. Bourdieu's style of analysis works best at picking out fine and arbitrary distinctions, the sort that matter especially when one is considering, say, postmodern art. The idea of invoking transcendental Kantian judgments is patently absurd when we want to explain why a shark floating in formaldehyde is merely a specimen in a naturalist's lab, but is "art" – and quite expensive art at that – when Damien Hirst places it in an imposing temple of postmodern aesthetics.[9]

However, there is considerable evidence that human taste is *not* a completely contingent social construct, but is grounded in a set of fairly robust innate dispositional propensities and perceptual capacities. The works cited in the Appendix marshal a fairly impressive body of evidence for the position that there are important commonalities underlying human taste – both literal and metaphorical. We appear to have evolved preferences for particular types of sights, tastes, sounds, and sensations, and even the strangest manifestations of postmodern art work precisely because they plug into the power of these preferences – if only to negate them. An "evolutionary Kantian" approach to taste would want to go deeper than Bourdieu's analyses, asking what, if any, constraints on taste formation there might be, or why people might want to mark class distinctions in the first place. Bourdieu defines *habitus* at one point as "embodied history," an unconscious but nonetheless "active presence of the whole past of which it is the product" (1990b: 56). Perhaps one way of understanding his limitations – and the limitations of the entire social

---

[8] I think a case could be made, however, that once a culture has acquired Pan-Asian fusion cuisine and nice Gewürztztraminers, pairing the two is an inevitably emergent "Good Trick."

[9] Hirst's work (entitled *The Physical Impossibility of Death in the Mind of Someone Living*) was purchased in 2005 by an American collector for £7 million; a similarly preserved sheep is thought to have netted him £2.1 million.

constructivist paradigm within which he is working – is to see him as not going *far enough back* in his conception of history. The deposited layers of history that form our schemas of perception and motivation go much deeper than the reaction against L'École des Beaux-Arts or the rise of the salon: they go back into *evolutionary* time, into the history of interactions between creatures more and more like us trying to make their way through a complex world. So, in an important sense we might say that the problem with postmodernism is not that it is overly historicist, but that it has an overly superficial and myopic conception of what history *is*. Why should Baudelaire's proclamation of the absolute distinction between art and morality count as a historical incident capable of contributing to *habitus*, and not the mutation in some nameless mammalian ancestor's genes that caused it to value symmetrical faces over others?

Obviously we still need the sort of high-level, subtle analysis Bourdieu is able to provide in order to fully understand the functioning of "fields" such as artistic production: no amount of theorizing by a team of cognitive scientists and evolutionary psychologists is *alone* sufficient to explain the appeal of, say, Manet's *The Absinthe Drinker*. But Bourdieu's account of the symbolic revolution brought about by the Impressionists' break with the academic system makes sense only when understood against the background of evolved human preferences and motivations. Similarly, his attack on the myth of the "fresh eye" in art appreciation is predicated on the claim that "there is no perception which does not involve an unconscious code" (1993: 217), and this is no doubt true. But again he is too shallow in his history: it has to be realized that the sort of culturally constructed code that he focuses on is merely a rather superficial manifestation of a deep and complex perceptual system that comes as standardized equipment in creatures like us. Against Bourdieu, then, it seems that to fully understand human culture and cognition we *do* need something like a naturalistic version of Kant's a priori categories of understanding and judgment. The tools of vertical integration tell a plausible story about how the sorts of novel, idiosyncratic, high-level cultural- or class-specific distinctions analyzed and catalogued with such nuance by Bourdieu and his students could be seen as grounded in basic and universal human capacities and dispositions.

Other Applications

As I mentioned in the Introduction, my previous work in the field of early Chinese thought has tried to show how adopting the methodologies of an "embodied realist" might change the way we view the development of Chinese thought or our approach to comparative religion,[10] and a follow-up volume to this book is planned as a detailed case study of what a vertically integrated approach to early Chinese thought

---

[10] For applications to early Chinese thought, see Slingerland 2003, 2004b, and 2005; for a more general discussion regarding comparative religion, see Slingerland 2004a.

might look like. For much more extensive and detailed applications of vertical integration to humanistic disciplines, the reader is referred to the Appendix, where I provide a selected bibliography of embodied approaches to culture in general, aesthetics, literature, philosophy, and religious studies. The process of genuinely integrating the natural sciences and the humanities is still in its initial stages, but I believe the works cited in the Appendix will provide the reader with confirmation that integrating science and the humanties is both possible and desirable.

There remains an entire book to be written about "what the humanities offer science." As the various disciplines of the natural sciences begin to encroach on traditionally humanistic subject areas, such as religious belief or moral reasoning, they cannot even begin to frame intelligent research questions or methodologies without the sort of deep expertise that comes only with extensive training in the humanistic disciplines. I recently sat on the dissertation defense of a Ph.D. student in psychology, a specialist in the psychology of religion, who was operating in almost complete ignorance of everything that has been written about religion for the past couple of hundred years – his total knowledge of the academic study of religion was apparently gleaned from an undergraduate survey class taken about a decade earlier. My horror at this was not simply the reaction of a specialist defending his turf: the candidate's lack of knowledge about even the rudiments of how religions have traditionally operated outside the confines of twenty-first-century North American university dormitories fundamentally undermined the validity of his "findings" and, in my experience, he is not at all an anomaly. With some notable exceptions, psychologists and cognitive scientists interested in religion have very little training in the humanistic, academic study of their subject matter, and the result is often a shocking degree of historical myopia and cultural naïveté.

This said, I still find that scientists are more open to the idea that they have something to learn from humanists than the other way around. The psychology of religion student's advisor plans to spend a considerable chunk of his upcoming sabbatical boning up on his religious studies training, and I have rarely met a psychologist or cognitive scientist who was not interested in what humanists might have to contribute to their research, or in what we might offer in the way of alternative hypotheses for their experimental data. If I have perhaps erred on the side of pushing humanists more to engage with the institutional "Other," it is because the biggest barrier to truly interdisciplinary dialogue and collaboration is not the supposed arrogance of Nobel laureates or white-coated custodians of scientific truth. The primary roadblock is the rigid, outdated, ideologically based resistance to empirical enquiry and to even mild forms of realism that continue to dominate the humanities. It is time to move on.

This book's cover image, "The Grandmother Tree," appealed to me because it seems a perfect graphic representation of vertical integration: the two intersecting spheres corresponding to science and the humanities, with the wildly diverse branches of the tree of human culture rooted in the deep common earth of our evolved cognitive capacities. It is my hope that in the decades ahead the humanities can begin to move in a direction where their subject of inquiry becomes the human figure depicted in the center of this image, composed of both the biological and the cultural, amenable to both scientific and humanistic analysis, and able to bestride the simultaneously separate and coterminous paths of the human and the natural.

Appendix: Embodying Culture: Selected Bibliography and Other Resources

The selected list of resources provided here is, by its very nature, guaranteed to be obsolete by the time this book is published, and is already no doubt marred by important omissions. It is my hope, however, that it can serve as a helpful starting point, and the Web-based resources should prove useful in bringing the reader up to date.

GENERAL RESOURCES FOR EMBODIED APPROACHES TO CULTURE

Programs and Centers

This is merely a selection, ranging from centers dedicated to lecture series and occasional conferences to full-blown degree-granting programs.

NORTH AMERICA
Brain and Creativity Institute, University of Southern California (www.usc.edu/schools/college/bci/index.html)
Center for Behavior, Evolution, and Culture (BEC), University of California, Los Angeles (www.bec.ucla.edu)
Center for Cognition and Culture, Case Western Reserve University (http://case.edu/artsci/cogs/CenterforCognitionandCulture.html)
Centre for the Study of Human Evolution, Cognition and Culture (HECC), The University of British Columbia (www.hecc.ubc.ca)
Culture and Cognition Program, University of Michigan (www.lsa.umich.edu/psych/grad/program/affiliations/cultcog)
Department of Cognitive Science, University of California, San Diego (http://www.cogsci.ucsd.edu/)
Evolution, Mind, and Behavior Program, University of California, Santa Barbara (www.psych.ucsb.edu/research/cep/emb.htm)
Evolutionary Studies Program, Binghamton University, State University of New York (bingweb.binghamton.edu/~evos/)
IGERT Program in Evolutionary Modeling, Washington State University and University of Washington (depts.washington.edu/ipem/)

313

Program in Culture, Language, and Cognition, Northwestern University (www.northwestern.edu/culture)

AHRC Centre for the Evolution of Cultural Diversity, University College London (www.cecd.ucl.ac.uk/home/)

Centre for Anthropology and Mind, Oxford University (www.iceq.ox.ac.uk)

Institute of Cognition and Culture, Queen's University, Belfast (www.qub.ac.uk/schools/InstituteofCognitionCulture)

Institute Nicod, Ecole Normale Superieure and the Ecole des Hautes Etudes en Sciences Sociales in Paris (www.institutnicod.org)

Books

Arbib, Michael. 1985. *In search of the person: Philosophical explorations in cognitive science.* Amherst: University of Massachusetts Press.

Barkow, Jerome, Leda Cosmides & John Tooby (eds.). 1992. *The adapted mind: Evolutionary psychology and the generation of culture.* New York: Oxford University Press.

Buss, David. 1998. *Evolutionary psychology: The new science of the mind.* Boston: Allyn & Bacon.

(ed.). 2005. *The handbook of evolutionary psychology.* Hoboken, NJ: John Wiley & Sons.

Carruthers, Peter & Andrew Chamberlain (eds.). 2000. *Evolution and the human mind: Modularity, language and meta-cognition.* Cambridge: Cambridge University Press.

Carruthers, Peter, Stephen Laurence & Stephen Stich (eds.). 2005. *The innate mind: Structure and content.* New York: Oxford University Press.

2006. *The innate mind: Culture and cognition.* New York: Oxford University Press.

Clark, Andy. 1997. *Being there: Putting brain, body and world together again.* Cambridge, MA: MIT Press.

Gallagher, Shaun. 2005. *How the body shapes the mind.* New York: Oxford University Press.

Gibbs, Raymond. 2006. *Embodiment and cognitive science.* Cambridge: Cambridge University Press.

Hirschfeld, Lawrence & Susan Gelman (eds.). 1994. *Mapping the mind: Domain specificity in cognition and culture.* New York: Cambridge University Press.

Hogan, Patrick. 2003. *Cognitive science, literature, and the arts: A guide for humanists.* New York: Routledge.

Johnson, Mark. 1987. *The body in the mind: The bodily basis of meaning, imagination and reason.* Chicago: University of Chicago Press.

Pecher, Diane & Rolf Zwaan (eds.). 2005. *Grounding cognition: The role of perception and action in memory, language and thinking.* Cambridge: Cambridge University Press.

Pinker, Steven. 2002. *The blank slate: The modern denial of human nature.* New York: Viking.

Thompson, Evan. 2007. *Mind in life: Biology, phenomenology, and the sciences of mind.* Cambridge, MA: Harvard University Press.

Varela, Francisco, Evan Thompson & Eleanor Rosch. 1991. *The embodied mind: Cognitive science and human experience.* Cambridge, MA: MIT Press.

EMBODIED APPROACHES TO SPECIFIC DISCIPLINES

Aesthetics

Aiken, Nancy. 1998. *The biological origins of art.* Westport, CT: Praeger.

Dissanayake, Ellen. 1992. *Homo aestheticus: Where art comes from and why.* Seattle: University of Washington Press.

Etcoff, Nancy. 1999. *The Survival of the prettiest: The science of beauty.* New York: Doubleday.

Gombrich, Ernst. 1982. *The sense of order: A study in the psychology of decorative art.* London: Phaidon Press (2nd ed., 1995).

Journal of Consciousness Studies: Special Feature on Art and the Brain. 1999. Vol. 6, no. 6/7 (June/July).

Kaplan, Stephen. 1992. Environmental preference in a knowledge-seeking, knowledge-using organism. In Barkow et al. 1992, 581–598.

Komar, Vitaly, Aleksandr Malamid & Joann Wypijewski. 1997. *Painting by numbers: Komar and Melamid's scientific guide to art.* New York: Farrar, Straus & Giroux.

Langlois, Judith & Lori Roggman. 1990. Attractive faces are only average. *Psychological Science* 1: 115–121.

McDermott, Josh & Marc Hauser. 2004. Are consonant intervals music to their ears? Spontaneous acoustic preferences in a nonhuman primate. *Cognition* 94: B11–B21.

Miller, Geoffrey. 2001. Aesthetic fitness: How sexual selection shaped artistic virtuosity as a fitness indicator and aesthetic preferences as mate choice criteria. *Bulletin of Psychology and the Arts* 2: 20–25.

Orians, Gordon & Judith Heerwagen. 1992. Evolved responses to landscapes. In Barkow et al. (1992), 555–580.

Solso, Robert. 2004. *The psychology of art and the evolution of the conscious brain.* Cambridge, MA: MIT Press.

Sugiyama, Lawrence. 2005. Physical attractiveness in adaptationist perspective. In Buss 2005, 292–343.

Thornhill, Randy. 1998. Darwinian aesthetics. In Charles Crawford & Dennis Krebs (eds.), *Handbook of evolutionary psychology: Ideas, issues, and applications,* 542–572. Mahwah, NJ: Lawrence Erlbaum Associates.

Tooby, John & Leda Cosmides. 2001. Does beauty build adapted minds? Toward an evolutionary theory of aesthetics, fiction, and the arts. *SubStance* 30: 6–27.

Turner, Mark. 2002. The cognitive study of art, language, and literature. *Poetics Today* 23: 9–20.

   (ed.). 2006. *The artful mind: Cognitive science and the riddle of human creativity.* New York: Oxford University Press.

Literature

The Web site "Literature, Cognition and the Brain," maintained by Alan Richardson and Mary Crane, Boston College (http://www2.bc.edu/%7Ericharad/lcb/home.html), is a helpful resource.

Barash, David & Nanelle Barash. 2005. *Madame Bovary's ovaries: A Darwinian look at literature.* New York: Delacorte Press.

Boyd, Brian. 1998. Jane, meet Charles: Literature, evolution, and human nature. *Philosophy and Literature* 22: 1–30.

2005. Literature and evolution: A biocultural approach. *Philosophy and Literature* 29: 1–23.

2006. Getting it all wrong: Bioculture critiques cultural critique. *American Scholar* 75: 18–30.

Forthcoming. *On the origin of stories.*

Carroll, Joseph. 1995. *Evolution and literary theory.* Columbia: University of Missouri Press.

2004. *Literary Darwinism: Literature and the human animal.* New York: Routledge.

Crane, Mary. 2001. *Shakespeare's brain: Reading with cognitive theory.* Princeton, NJ: Princeton University Press.

Freeman, Donald. 1995. "Catch[ing] the nearest way": *Macbeth* and cognitive metaphor. *Journal of Pragmatics* 24: 689–708.

Freeman, Margaret. 1995. Metaphor making meaning: Dickinson's conceptual universe. *Journal of Pragmatics* 24: 643–666.

Gottschall, Jonathan. 2007. *The rape of Troy: Evolution, violence, and the world of Homer.* New York: Cambridge University Press.

Gottschall, Jonathan & David Sloan Wilson (eds.). 2005. *The literary animal: Evolution and the nature of narrative.* Evanston, IL: Northwestern University Press.

Hogan, Patrick. 2003. *The mind and its stories: Narrative universals and human emotions.* New York: Cambridge University Press.

Nordlund, Marcus. 2007. *Shakespeare and the nature of love: Literature, culture, evolution.* Evanston, IL: Northwestern University Press.

Oatley, Keith. 1999. Why fiction may be twice as true as fact: Fiction as cognitive and emotional stimulation. *Review of General Psychology* 3.2: 101–117.

Richardson, Alan. 1999. Cognitive science and the future of literary studies. *Philosophy and Literature* 23: 157–173.

Scarry, Elaine. 1999. *Dreaming by the book.* New York: Farrar, Straus & Giroux.

Spolsky, Ellen. 1993. *Gaps in nature: Literary interpretation and the modular mind.* Albany, NY: SUNY Press.

2002. Darwin and Derrida: Cognitive literary theory as a species of post-structuralism. *Poetics Today* 23: 43–62.

Storey, Robert. 1996. *Mimesis and the human animal: On the biogenetic foundations of literary representation.* Evanston, IL: Northwestern University Press.

Turner, Frederick. 1985. *Natural classicism: Essays on literature and science.* New York: Paragon.

Turner, Mark. 1991. *Reading minds: The study of English in the age of cognitive science.* Princeton, NJ: Princeton University Press.

1996. *The literary mind.* New York: Oxford University Press.

Whitfield, John. 2006. Textual selection: Can reading the classics through Charles Darwin's spectacles reawaken literary study? *Nature* 439: 388–389.

Morality and Ethics

Helpful online resources include the "experimental philosophy" blog at http://experimentalphilosophy.typepad.com and the entry in the *Stanford Encyclopedia of Philosophy* on "Moral Psychology: Empirical Approaches," by John Doris and Stephen Stich (http://plato.stanford.edu/entries/moral-psych-emp/).

Alexander, Richard. 1987. *The biology of moral systems.* Hawthorne, NY: Aldine de Gruyter.

Axelrod, Robert. 1984. *The evolution of cooperation.* New York: Basic Books.

Brosnan, Sarah & Frans de Waal. 2003. Monkeys reject unequal pay. *Nature* 425: 297–299.

Casebeer, William. 2005. *Natural ethical facts: Evolution, connectionism, and moral cognition.* Cambridge, MA: MIT Press.

Churchland, Patricia. 1986. *Neurophilosophy: Toward a unified science of the mind-brain.* Cambridge, MA: Bradford Books/MIT Press.

Churchland, Paul. 1998. Toward a cognitive neurobiology of the moral virtues. *Topoi* 17: 83–96.

Cosmides, Leda & John Tooby. 2004. Knowing thyself: The evolutionary psychology of moral reasoning and moral sentiments. In Edward Freeman & Patricia Werhane (eds.), *Business, science, and ethics,* the Ruffin Series in Business Ethics no. 4, 93–128. Charlottesville, VA: Society for Business Ethics.

De Quervain, Dominique, Urs Fischbacher, Valerie Treyer, Melanie Schellhammer, Ulrich Schnyder, Alfred Buck & Ernst Fehr. 2004. The neural basis of altruistic punishment. *Science* 305: 1254–1258.

De Waal, Frans. 1996. *Good natured: The origins of right and wrong in humans and other animals.* Cambridge, MA: Harvard University Press.

2006. *Primates and philosophers: How morality evolved.* Princeton, NJ: Princeton University Press.

Doris, John & Stephen Stich. 2005. As a matter of fact: Empirical perspectives on ethics. In Frank Jackson & Michael Smith (eds.), *The Oxford handbook of contemporary analytic philosophy,* 114–152. Oxford: Oxford University Press.

Fehr, Ernst & Simon Gächter. 2000. Fairness and retaliation: The economics of reciprocity. *Journal of Economic Perspectives* 14: 159–181.

2002. Altruistic punishment in humans. *Nature* 415: 137–140.

Flanagan, Owen. 1991. *Varieties of moral personality: Ethics and psychological realism.* Cambridge, MA: Harvard University Press.

(ed.). 1996. *Self-expressions: Mind, morals, and the meaning of life.* New York: Oxford University Press.

Flanagan, Owen & Amélie O. Rorty (eds.). 1990. *Identity, character, and morality: Essays in moral psychology.* Cambridge, MA: MIT Press.

Joyce, Richard. 2006. *The evolution of morality.* Cambridge, MA: MIT Press.

Krebs, Dennis. 2005. The evolution of morality. In Buss 2005, 747–775.

Gazzaniga, Michael. 2005. *The ethical brain.* Washington, DC: Dana Press.

Goldman, Alvin (ed.). 1993. *Readings in philosophy and cognitive science.* Cambridge, MA: MIT Press.

Greene, Joshua. 2003. From neural "is" to moral "ought": What are the moral implications of neuroscientific moral psychology? *Nature Reviews Neuroscience* 4: 847–850.

Greene, Joshua & Jonathan Haidt. 2002. How (and where) does moral judgment work? *Trends in Cognitive Science* 6: 517–523.

Greene, Joshua, Leigh Nystrom, Andrew Engell, John Darley & Johnathan Cohen. 2004. The neural bases of cognitive conflict and control in moral judgment. *Neuron* 44: 389–400.

Greene, Joshua, Brian Sommerville, Leigh Nystrom, John Darley & Jonathan Cohen. 2001. An fMRI investigation of emotional engagement in moral judgment. *Science* 293: 2105–2108.

Haidt, Jonathan. 2001. The emotional dog and its rational tail: A social intuitionist approach to moral judgment. *Psychological Review* 108: 813–834.

Haidt, Jonathan & Joseph Craig. 2004. Intuitive ethics: How innately prepared intuitions generate culturally variable virtues. *Daedalus* 133: 55–66.

Haidt, Jonathan, Silvia Koller & Maria Dias. 1993. Affect, culture, and morality, or is it wrong to eat your dog? *Journal of Personality and Social Psychology* 65: 613–628.

Haidt, Jonathan, Paul Rozin, Clark McCauley & Sumio Imada. 1997. Body, psyche, and culture: The relationship between disgust and morality. *Psychology and Developing Societies* 9: 107–131.

Hauser, Marc. 2006. *Moral minds: How nature designed our universal sense of right and wrong.* New York: Ecco Press.

Johnson, Mark. 1993. *Moral imagination: Implications of cognitive science for ethics.* Chicago: University of Chicago Press.

Katz, Leonard (ed.). 2000. *Evolutionary origins of morality: Cross-disciplinary perspectives.* Exeter, UK: Imprint Academic.

Kitcher, Philip. 1993. The evolution of human altruism. *Journal of Philosophy* 90: 497–516.

Lakoff, George. 1996. *Moral politics: What conservatives know that liberals don't.* Chicago: University of Chicago Press.

Lakoff, George & Mark Johnson. 1999. *Philosophy in the flesh: The embodied mind and its challenge to Western thought.* New York: Basic Books.

MacIntyre, Alasdair. 1998. What can moral philosophers learn from the study of the brain? *Philosophy and Phenomenological Research* 58: 865–869.

May, Larry, Marilyn Friedman & Andy Clark (eds.). 1996. *Mind and morals: Essays on ethics and cognitive science.* Cambridge, MA: MIT Press.

Moll, Jorge, Ricardo de Oliveira-Souza, Paul Eslinger, Ivanei Bramati, Janaina Mouro-Miranda, Pedro Andreiuolo & Luiz Pessoa. 2002. The neural correlates of moral sensitivity: A functional magnetic resonance imaging investigation of basic moral emotions. *Journal of Neuroscience* 22: 2730–2737.

Munro, Donald. 2005. *A Chinese ethics for the new century: The Ch'ien Mu lectures in history and culture, and other essays on science and Confucian ethics.* Hong Kong: The Chinese University of Hong Kong.

Nesse, Randolph (ed.). 2001. *Evolution and the capacity for commitment.* New York: Russell Sage.

Nichols, Shaun. 2004. *Sentimental rules: On the natural foundations of moral judgment.* New York: Oxford University Press.

Preston, Stephanie & Frans de Waal. 2002. Empathy: Its ultimate and proximate bases. *Behavioral and Brain Sciences* 25: 1–72.

Price, Michael. 2005. Punitive sentiment among the Shuar and in industrialized societies: Cross-cultural similarities. *Evolution and Human Behavior* 26: 279–287.

Prinz, Jesse. 2006. *The emotional construction of morals.* New York: Oxford University Press.

Rozin, Paul. 1996. Towards a psychology of food and eating: From motivation to module to model to marker, morality, meaning, and metaphor. *Current Directions in Psychological Science* 5: 18–24.

Rozin, Paul, Michael Markwith & Caryn Stoess. 1997. Moralization and becoming a vegetarian: The transformation of preferences into values and the recruitment of disgust. *Psychological Science* 8: 67–73.

Sanfrey, Alan, James Riling, Jessica Aronson, Leigh Nystrom & Jonathan Cohen. 2003. The neural basis of economic decision-making in the ultimatum game. *Science* 300: 1755–1758.

Skyrms, Brian. 1996. *Evolution of the social contract.* New York: Cambridge University Press.

Sober, Elliott & David Sloan Wilson. 1998. *Unto others: The evolution and psychology of unselfish behavior.* Cambridge, MA: Harvard University Press.

Stich, Stephen. 2006. Is morality an elegant machine or a kludge? *Journal of Cognition and Culture* 6: 181–189.

Tancredi, Laurence. 2005. *Hardwired behavior: What neuroscience reveals about morality.* Cambridge: Cambridge University Press.

Thompson, Paul (ed.). 1995. *Issues in evolutionary ethics.* Albany, NY: SUNY Press.

Trivers, Robert. 1971. The evolution of reciprocal altruism. *Quarterly Review of Biology* 46: 35–57.

Religion

The International Association for the Cognition Science of Religion (IACSR) maintains a helpful Web site (www.iacsr.com/); also see István Czachesz's religion and cognition Web site (www.religionandcognition.com/) hosted by the University of Groningen.

Andresen, Jensine & Robert Forman (eds.). 2000. *Religion in mind: Cognitive perspectives on religious belief, ritual and experience.* Cambridge: Cambridge University Press.

Atran, Scott. 2002. *In gods we trust: The evolutionary landscape of religion.* New York: Oxford University Press.

Barrett, Justin. 2004. *Why would anyone believe in God?* Walnut Creek, CA: AltaMira Press.

Boyer, Pascal. 1994. *The naturalness of religious ideas: A cognitive theory of religion.* Berkeley and Los Angeles: University of California Press.

2001. *Religion explained: The evolutionary origins of religious thought.* New York: Basic Books.

Cohen, Emma. 2007. *The mind possessed: The cognition of spirit possession in an Afro-Brazilian religious tradition.* New York: Oxford University Press.

Kelemen, Deborah. 1999. Function, goals, and intention: Children's teleological reasoning about objects. *Trends in Cognitive Sciences* 3: 461–468.

Kirkpatrick, Lee. 2004. *Attachment, evolution and the psychology of religion.* New York: Guilford Press.

Lawson, E. Thomas & Robert McCauley. 1990. *Rethinking religion: Connecting cognition and culture.* Cambridge: Cambridge University Press.

Malley, Brian. 1996. The emerging cognitive psychology of religion: A review article. *Method and Theory in the Study of Religion* 8: 109–141.

McCauley, Robert & Thomas Lawson. 2002. *Bringing ritual to mind: Psychological foundations of cultural forms.* Cambridge: Cambridge University Press.

Pyysiainen, Ilkka. 2001. *How religion works: Towards a new cognitive science of religion.* Leiden: Brill.

Pyysiainen, Ilkka & Veikko Anttonen (eds.). 2002. *Current approaches in the cognitive science of religion.* New York: Continuum.

Slone, D. Jason. 2004. *Theological incorrectness: Why religious people believe what they shouldn't.* New York: Oxford University Press.

(ed.). 2006. *Religion and cognition: A reader.* London: Equinox.

Tremlin, Todd. *Minds and gods: The cognitive foundations of religion.* New York: Oxford University Press.

Whitehouse, Harvey. 2000. *Arguments and icons: The cognitive, social, and historical implications of divergent modes of religiosity.* Oxford: Oxford University Press.

2004. *Modes of religiosity: A cognitive theory of religious transmission.* Walnut Creek, CA: AltaMira Press.

Whitehouse, Harvey & Luther Martin (eds.). 2005. *The cognitive science of religion.* Special issue of *Method and Theory in the Study of Religion.* Vol. 16, no. 3.

Whitehouse, Harvey & Robert N. McCauley (eds.). 2005. *Mind and religion: Psychological and cognitive foundations of religiosity.* Walnut Creek, CA: AltaMira Press.

Wilson, David Sloan. *Darwin's cathedral: Evolution, religion, and the nature of society.* Chicago: University of Chicago Press.

References

Abdulmoneim, Mohamed Shokr. 2006. The metaphorical concept "Life is a Journey" in the Qur'an: A cognitive-semantic analysis. *Metaphorik* 10: 94–132.

Abler, William. 2005. Evidence of group learning does not add up to culture. *Nature* 438: 422.

Abutalebi, Jubin, Antonio Miozzo & Stefano Cappa. 2000. Do subcortical structures control "language selection" in polyglots? Evidence from pathological language mixing. *Neurocase* 6: 51–56.

Adams, Fred & Kenneth Campbell. 1999. Modality and abstract concepts (response to Barsalou 1999a). *Behavioral and Brain Sciences* 22: 610.

Aglioti, Salvatore, Joseph DeSouza & Melvyn Goodale. 1995. Size contrast illusions deceive the eye but not the hand. *Current Biology* 5: 679–685.

Aguiar, André & Renée Baillargeon. 1999. 2.5-month-old infants' reasoning about when objects should and should not be occluded. *Cognitive Psychology* 39: 116–157.

Aiello, Leslie & Robin Dunbar. 1993. Neocortex size, group size and the evolution of language. *Current Anthropology* 34: 184–193.

Aiello, Leslie & Peter Wheeler. 1995. The expensive tissue hypothesis. *Current Anthropology* 36: 199–211.

Alexander, Richard. 1979. *Darwinism and human affairs.* Seattle: University of Washington Press.

Anthony, Herbert Douglas. 1948. *Science and its background.* London: Macmillan.

Arbib, Michael. 1972. *The metaphorical brain: An introduction to cybernetics as artificial intelligence and brain theory.* New York: John Wiley & Sons.

   1985. *In search of the person: Philosophical explorations in cognitive science.* Amherst: University of Massachusetts Press.

   1989. *The metaphorical brain 2: Neural networks and beyond.* New York: John Wiley & Sons.

Arbib, Michael, E. Jeffrey Conklin & Jane Hill. 1987. *From schema theory to language.* New York: Oxford University Press.

Arbib, Michael & Giacomo Rizzolatti. 1996. Neural expectations: A possible evolutionary path from manual skills to language. *Communication and Cognition* 29: 393–424.

Arnheim, Rudolf. 1969. *Visual thinking.* Berkeley: University of California Press.

Atran, Scott. 1987. Ordinary constraints on the semantics of living kinds. *Mind & Language* 2: 27–63.

   1990. *Cognitive foundations of natural history: Toward an anthropology of science.* Cambridge: Cambridge University Press.

   1995. Causal constraints on categories and categorical constraints on biological reasoning across cultures. In Sperber et al. 1995, 205–233.

1998. Folk biology and the anthropology of science: Cognitive universals and cultural particulars. *Behavioral and Brain Sciences* 21: 547–609.

Aunger, Robert (ed.). 2000. *Darwinizing culture: The status of memetics as a science.* New York: Oxford University Press.

2006. What's the matter with memes? In Grafen & Ridley 2006, 176–190.

Avis, Jeremy & Paul Harris. 1991. Belief-desire reasoning among Baka children: Evidence for a universal conception of mind. *Child Development* 62: 460–467.

Axelrod, Robert. 1984. *The evolution of cooperation.* New York: Basic Books.

Bacon, Francis. 1620/1999. *Selected philosophical works* (ed. Rose-Mary Sargent). Cambridge, MA: Hackett Publishing Company.

Baier, Annette. 1994. *Moral prejudices: Essays on ethics.* Cambridge, MA: Harvard University Press.

Bailenson, Jeremy, Michael Shum, Scott Atran, Douglas Medin & John Coley. 2002. A bird's-eye view: Biological categorization and reasoning within and across cultures. *Cognition* 84: 1–53.

Baillargeon, Renée. 1986. Representing the existence and the location of hidden objects: Object permanence in 6- and 8-month-old infants. *Cognition* 23: 21–41.

1991. The object concept revisited: New directions in the investigation of infants' physical knowledge. In Carl Granrud (ed.), *Visual perception and cognition in infancy*, 265–315. Hillsdale, NJ: Lawrence Erlbaum Associates.

Baillargeon, Renée, Laura Kotovsky & Amy Needham. 1995. The acquisition of physical knowledge in infancy. In Sperber et al. 1995, 79–116.

Baillargeon, Renée, Elizabeth Spelke & Stanley Wasserman. 1985. Object permanence in five-month-old infants. *Cognition* 20: 191–208.

Baillargeon, Renée, & Su-hua Wang. 2002. Event categorization in infancy. *Trends in Cognitive Sciences* 6: 85–93.

Baker, Catherine (ed. by James Miller). 2006. *The evolution dialogues: Science, Christianity, and the quest for understanding.* Washington, DC: The American Association for the Advancement of Science.

Balaban, Victor. 1999. Self and agency in religious discourse: Perceptual metaphors for knowledge at a Marian apparition site. In Gibbs & Steen 1999, 125–144.

Ballard, Dana. 1991. Animate vision. *Artificial Intelligence* 48: 57–86.

2002. On the function of visual representation. In Noë & Thompson 2002, 459–479.

Balter, Michael. 2006. First jewelry? Old shell beads suggest early use of symbols. *Science* 23: 1731.

Bargh, John & Tanya Chartrand. 1999. The unbearable automaticity of being. *American Psychologist* 54: 462–479.

Barkow, Jerome. 1989. *Darwin, sex, and status: Biological approaches to mind and culture.* Toronto: University of Toronto Press.

Barkow, Jerome, Leda Cosmides & John Tooby (eds.). 1992. *The adapted mind: Evolutionary psychology and the generation of culture.* New York: Oxford University Press.

Barnes, Barry & David Bloor. 1982. Relativism, rationalism and the sociology of knowledge. In Martin Hollis & Steven Lukes (eds.), *Rationality and relativism*, 21–47. Cambridge, MA: MIT Press.

Baron-Cohen, Simon. 1995. *Mindblindness: An essay on autism and theory of mind.* Cambridge, MA: MIT Press.

Baron-Cohen, Simon & John Harrison (eds.). 1997. *Synaesthesia: Classic and contemporary readings.* Oxford: Blackwell.

Baron-Cohen, Simon, Alan Leslie & Christopher Frith. 1985. Does the autistic child have a "theory of mind"? *Cognition* 21: 37–46.

Barres, Ben. 2006. Does gender matter? *Nature* 442: 133–136.

Barrett, H. Clark, Peter Todd, Geoffrey Miller & Philip Blythe. 2005. Accurate judgments of intention from motion cues alone: A cross-cultural study. *Evolution and Human Behavior* 26: 313–331.

Barrett, Justin. 1999. Theological correctness: Cognitive constraint and the study of religion. *Method and Theory in the Study of Religion* 11: 325–339.

2000. Exploring the natural foundations of religion. *Trends in Cognitive Sciences* 4: 29–34.

Barrett, Justin & Melanie Nyhof. 2001. Spreading non-natural concepts: The role of intuitive conceptual structures in memory and transmission of cultural materials. *Journal of Cognition and Culture* 1: 69–100.

Barsalou, Lawrence. 1999a. Perceptual symbol systems. *Behavioral and Brain Sciences* 22: 577–609.

1999b. Perceptions of perceptual symbols (author's response to commentary). *Behavioral and Brain Sciences* 22: 633–660.

Barsalou, Lawrence, Kyle Simmons, Aron Barbey & Christine Wilson. 2003, Grounding conceptual knowledge in modality-specific systems. *Trends in Cognitive Sciences* 7: 84–91.

Barsalou, Lawrence & Katja Wiemer-Hastings. 2005. Situating abstract concepts. In Pecher & Zwaan 2005, 129–163.

Barth, Hilary, Kristen La Mont, Jennifer Lipton, Stanislas Deheane, Nancy Kanwisher & Elizabeth Spelke. 2006. Non-symbolic arithmetic in adults and young children. *Cognition* 98: 199–222.

Barthes, Roland. 1967. *Writing degree zero* (trans. Annette Lavers & Colin Smith). New York: Hill & Wang.

1968. *Elements of semiology* (trans. Annette Lavers & Colin Smith). New York: Hill & Wang.

1972. To write: An intransitive verb? In Richard Macksey & Eugenio Donato (eds.), *The languages of criticism and the science of man: The structuralist controversy*, 134–144. Baltimore: Johns Hopkins University Press.

1982. *The empire of signs* (trans. Richard Howard). New York: Hill & Wang.

Bar-Yosef, Ofer. 2006. Human migrations in prehistory: The cultural record. Presentation at World Knowledge Dialogue, Crans-Montana, Switzerland, September 15.

Baudrillard, Jean. 1994. *Simulacra and simulation* (trans. Sheila Faria Glaser). Ann Arbor: University of Michigan Press.

1995. *The Gulf War did not take place* (trans. Paul Patton). Bloomington and Indianapolis: Indiana University Press.

Baumeister, Roy. 1984. Choking under pressure: Self-consciousness and paradoxical effects of incentives on skillful performance. *Journal of Personality and Social Psychology* 46: 610–620.

Baumeister, Roy, Ellen Bratslavsky, Mark Muraven & Dianne Tice. 1998. Ego depletion: Is the active self a limited resource? *Journal of Personality and Social Psychology* 74: 1252–1265.

Bechara, Antoine, Antonio Damasio, Hannah Damasio & Steven Anderson. 1994. Insensitivity to future consequences following damage to human prefrontal cortex. *Cognition* 50: 7–15.

Bechara, Antoine, Hannah Damasio & Antonio Damasio. 2000. Emotion, decision making, and the orbitofrontal cortex. *Cerebral Cortex* 10: 295–307.

Bechara, Antoine, Hannah Damasio, Daniel Tranel & Antonio Damasio. 1997. Deciding advantageously before knowing the advantageous strategy. *Science* 275: 1293–1295.

Beer, Francis & Christ'l de Landtsheer (eds.). 2004. *Metaphorical world politics*. East Lansing: Michigan State University Press.

Behl-Chadha, Gundeep. 1996. Basic-level and superordinate-like categorical representations in early infancy. *Cognition* 60: 105–141.

Bekoff, Marc & John Alexander Byers (eds.). 1998. *Animal play: Evolutionary, comparative, and ecological perspectives*. Cambridge: Cambridge University Press.

Berger, Peter & Thomas Luckmann. 1966. *The social construction of reality: A treatise in the sociology of knowledge*. New York: Anchor Books.

Bering, Jesse. 2002. The existential theory of mind. *Review of General Psychology* 6: 3–24.

Bering, Jesse & Becky Parker. 2006. Children's attributions of intentions to an invisible agent. *Developmental Psychology* 42: 253–262.

Berkson, Mark. 1996. Language: The guest of reality – Zhuangzi and Derrida on language, reality, and skillfulness. In Paul Kjellberg & Philip J. Ivanhoe (eds.), *Essays on skepticism, relativism and ethics in the* Zhuangzi, 97–126. Albany, NY: SUNY Press.

Berlin, Brent, Dennis Breedlove & Peter Raven. 1973. General principles of classification and nomenclature in folk biology. *American Anthropologist* 75: 214–242.

Berlin, Brent & Paul Kay. 1969. *Basic color terms: Their universality and growth*. Berkeley: University of California Press.

Bernstein, Richard. 1983. *Beyond objectivism and relativism: Science, hermeneutics, and praxis*. Philadelphia: University of Pennsylvania Press.

Black, Max. 1954–1955. Metaphor. *Proceedings of the Aristotelian Society* 55: 273–294.

Blackmore, Susan, Gavin Brelstaff, Kay Nelson & Tom Troscianko. 1995. Is the richness of our visual world an illusion? Transsaccadic memory for complex scenes. *Perception* 24: 1075–1081.

Blair, R. James. 1995. A cognitive developmental approach to morality: Investigating the psychopath. *Cognition* 57: 1–29.

    2001. Neurocognitive models of aggression, the antisocial personality disorders, and psychopathy. *Journal of Neurology, Neurosurgery, and Psychiatry* 71: 727–731.

Blaisdell, Aaron, Kosuke Sawa, Kenneth Leising & Michael Waldmann. 2006. Causal reasoning in rats. *Science* 311: 1020–1022.

Blakemore, Sarah-Jayne & Jean Decety. 2001. From the perception of action to the understanding of intention. *Nature Neuroscience* 2: 561–567.

Block, Ned. 1983. Mental pictures and cognitive science. *Philosophical Review* 93: 499–542.

Bloom, Paul. 2004. *Descartes' baby: How the science of child development explains what makes us human*. New York: Basic Books.

Boas, Franz. 1962. *Anthropology and modern life*. New York: Norton.

Boden, Margaret. 1990. *The creative mind: Myths and mechanisms*. London: Weidenfeld & Nicholson.

    1994. Précis of *The creative mind: Myths and mechanisms*. *Behavioral and Brain Sciences* 17: 519–570.

Boghossian, Paul. 2000. What the Sokal hoax ought to teach us, and selected responses. In The Editors of *Lingua Franca* 2000, 172–186.

Borges, Bernhard, Daniel Goldstein, Andreas Ortmann & Gerd Gigerenzer. 1999. Can ignorance beat the stock market? In Gigerenzer et al. 1999, 59–74.

Borghi, Anna. 2004. Objects, concepts, and actions: Extracting affordances from objects' parts. *Acta Psychologia* 115: 69–96.

2005. Objects, concepts, and actions. In Pecher & Zwaan 2005, 8–34.

Bornstein, Marc. 1985. Habituation as a measure of visual information processing in human infants: Summary, systemization, and synthesis. In Gilbert Gottlieb & Norman Krasnegor (eds.), *Measurement of audition and vision in the first year of postnatal life*, 253–295. Norwood, NJ: Ablex.

Boroditsky, Lera. 2001. Does language shape thought? English and Mandarin speakers' conceptions of time. *Cognitive Psychology* 43: 1–22.

Botz-Bornstein, Thorsten. 2006. Ethnophilosophy, comparative philosophy, and pragmatism: Toward a philosophy of ethnoscapes. *Philosophy East and West* 56: 153–171.

Bouchard, Thomas. 1994. Genes, environment, and personality. *Science* 264: 1700–1701.

1998. Genetic and environmental influences of intelligence and special mental abilities. *Human Biology* 70: 257–259.

Bourdieu, Pierre. 1977. *Outline of a theory of practice* (trans. Richard Nice). Cambridge: Cambridge University Press.

1984. *Distinction: A social critique of the judgment of taste* (trans. Richard Nice). Cambridge, MA: Harvard University Press.

1990a. *In other words: Essays toward a reflexive sociology* (trans. Matthew Adamson). Stanford: Stanford University Press.

1990b. *The logic of practice* (trans. Richard Nice). Stanford: Stanford University Press.

1993. *The field of cultural production*. New York: Columbia University Press.

Boyd, Brian. 2006. Getting it all wrong: Bioculture critiques cultural critique. *American Scholar* 75: 18–30.

Boyd, Robert & Peter Richerson. 1992. Punishment allows the evolution of cooperation (or anything else) in sizable groups. *Ethology and Sociobiology* 13: 171–195.

2005. *Not by genes alone: How culture transformed human evolution*. Chicago: University of Chicago Press.

Boyer, Pascal. 1994. Cognitive constraints on cultural representations: Natural ontologies and religious ideas. In Hirschfeld & Gelman 1994a, 391–411.

2001. *Religion explained: The evolutionary origins of religious thought*. New York: Basic Books.

2005. Domain specificity and intuitive ontology. In Buss 2005, 96–118.

Boyer, Pascal & H. Clark Barrett. 2005. Domain specificity and intuitive ontology. In Buss 2005, 96–118.

Bregman, Albert & Steven Pinker. 1978. Auditory streaming and the building of timbre. *Canadian Journal of Psychology* 32: 19–31.

Brooks, E. Bruce & Taeko Brooks. 1998. *The original Analects*. New York: Columbia University Press.

Brooks, Rodney. 1991. Intelligence without representation. *Artificial Intelligence* 47: 139–159.

Brosnan, Sarah & Frans de Waal. 2003. Monkeys reject unequal pay. *Nature* 425: 297–299.

Brown, Donald. 1991. *Human universals*. New York: McGraw-Hill.

2000. Human universals and their implications. In Neil Roughley (ed.), *Being humans: Anthropological universality and particularity in transdisciplinary perspectives*, 156–174. New York: Walter de Gruyter

Brown, Theodore. 2003. *Making truth: Metaphor in science.* Urbana: University of Illinois Press.

Bruner, J. S. & Leo Postman. 1949. On the perception of incongruity: A paradigm. *Journal of Personality* 18: 206–223.

Buonomano, Dean & Michael Merzenich. 1998. Cortical plasticity: From synapses to maps. *Annual Review of Neuroscience* 21: 149–186.

Burgess, Curt & Christine Chiarello. 1996. Neurocognitive mechanisms underlying metaphor comprehension and other figurative language. *Metaphor and Symbolic Activity* 11: 67–84.

Burnyeat, Myles. 1980. Aristotle on learning to be good. In Amélie O. Rorty (ed.), *Essays on Aristotle's ethics,* 69–92. Berkeley: University of California Press.

Buss, David (ed.). 2005. *The handbook of evolutionary psychology.* Hoboken, NJ: John Wiley & Sons.

Butler, Judith. 1997. Further reflections on the conversations of our time. *Diacritics* 27: 13–15.
2004. *Undoing gender.* New York: Routledge.

Butterworth, George. 1991. The ontogeny and phylogeny of joint visual attention. In Andrew Whiten (ed.), *Natural theories of mind: Evolution, development, and simulation of everyday mind reading,* 223–232. Oxford: Basil Blackwell.

Byrne, Richard & Andrew Whiten (eds.). 1988. *Machiavellian intelligence: Social expertise and the evolution of intellect in monkeys, apes, and humans.* Oxford: Oxford University Press.

Camus, Albert. 1942. *Le mythe de sisyphe.* Paris: Gallimard.
1947. *La peste.* Paris: Gallimard.

Caramazza, Alfonso, Argye Hillis, Elwyn Lee & Michele Miozzo. 1994. The organization of lexical knowledge in the brain: Evidence from category- and modality-specific deficits. In Hirschfeld & Gelman 1994a, 68–84.

Carey, Susan. 1985. *Conceptual change in childhood.* Cambridge, MA: MIT Press.
1991. Knowledge acquistion: Enrichment or conceptual change? In Carey & Spelke, 1994, 257–291.
1995. On the origin of causal understanding. In Sperber et al. 1995, 268–302.

Carey, Susan & Rochel Gelman (eds.). 1991. *The epigenesis of mind: Essays on biology and cognition.* Hillsdale, NJ: Lawrence Erlbaum Associates.

Carey, Susan & Elizabeth Spelke. 1994. Domain-specific knowledge and conceptual change. In Hirschfeld & Gelman 1994a, 169–200.

Carruthers, Peter. 2005. The case for massively modular models of mind. In Robert Stainton (ed.), *Contemporary debates in cognitive science,* 205–225. Oxford Basil: Blackwell.

Carruthers, Peter & Jill Boucher (eds.). 1998. *Language and thought: Interdisciplinary themes.* Cambridge: Cambridge University Press.

Carruthers, Peter & Andrew Chamberlain (eds.). 2000. *Evolution and the human mind: Modularity, language and meta-cognition.* Cambridge: Cambridge University Press.

Carruthers, Peter, Stephen Laurence & Stephen Stich (eds.). 2005. *The innate mind: Structure and content.* New York: Oxford University Press.
2006. *The innate mind: Culture and cognition.* New York: Oxford University Press.

Carruthers, Peter & Peter Smith (eds.). 1996. *Theories of theories of mind.* Cambridge: Cambridge University Press.

Cartwright, Nancy. 1983. *How the laws of physics lie.* New York: Oxford University Press.
1999. *The dappled world: A study of the boundaries of science.* Cambridge: Cambridge University Press.

Casasola, Marianella, Leslie Cohen & Elizabeth Chiarello. 2003. Six-month-old infants' categorization of containment spatial relations. *Child Development* 74: 679–693.

Cavell, Stanley. 1979. *The claim of reason.* New York: Oxford University Press.

Chaibong, Hahm. 2001. Confucian rituals and the technology of the self: A Foucaultian interpretation. *Philosophy East and West* 51: 315–324.

Chalmers, Alan. 1985. Galileo's telescopic observations of Venus and Mars. *British Journal for the Philosophy of Science* 36: 175–191.

1999. *What is this thing called science?* 3rd ed. Indianapolis: Hackett Publishing Company.

Chalmers, David. 1995. Facing up to the problem of consciousness. *Journal of Consciousness Studies* 2: 200–219.

1996. *The conscious mind: In search of a fundamental theory.* New York: Oxford University Press.

Cheney, Dorothy & Robert Seyfarth. 1990. *How monkeys see the world: Inside the mind of another species.* Chicago: University of Chicago Press.

Cheng Shude. 1990. *Lunyu Jijie.* Beijing: Zhonghua Shuju.

Chilton, Paul. 1996. *Security metaphors: Cold War discourse from containment to common house.* New York: Peter Lang.

Choi, Hoon & Brian Scholl. 2006. Perceiving causality after the fact: Postdiction in the temporal dynamics of causal perception. *Perception* 35: 385–399.

Chomsky, Noam. 1965. *Aspects of the theory of syntax.* Cambridge, MA: MIT Press.

Christoff, Kalina & Adrian Owen. 2006. Improving reverse neuroimaging inference: Cognitive domain versus cognitive complexity. *Trends in Cognitive Science* 10: 352–353.

Churchland, Patricia. 1986. *Neurophilosophy: Toward a unified science of the mind-brain.* Cambridge, MA: Bradford Books/MIT Press.

Churchland, Patricia, V. S. Ramachandran & Terrence Sejnowski. 1994. A critique of pure vision. In Christof Koch & Joel Davis (eds.), *Large-scale neuronal theories of the brain,* 23–60. Cambridge, MA: MIT Press.

Churchland, Paul. 1979. *Scientific realism and the plasticity of the mind.* Cambridge: Cambridge University Press.

1985. The ontological status of observables: In praise of the superempirical virtues. In Paul Churchland & Clifford Hooker (eds.), *Images of science: Essays on realism and empiricism,* 35–47. Chicago: University of Chicago Press.

Churchland, Paul & Terrence Sejnowski. 1992. *The computational brain.* Cambridge, MA: MIT Press.

Cienki, Alan. 2005. Image schemas and gesture. In Hampe 2005, 421–442.

Clark, Andy. 1997. *Being there: Putting brain, body and world together again.* Cambridge, MA: MIT Press.

1999. Visual awareness and visuomotor action. In Núñez & Freeman 1999, 1–18.

Clements, Wendy & Josef Perner. 1994. Implicit understanding of belief. *Cognitive Development* 9: 377–397.

Coleman, Linda & Paul Kay. 1981. Prototype semantics: The English word lie. *Language* 57: 26–44.

Connor, Steven (ed.). 2004. *The Cambridge companion to postmodernism.* Cambridge: Cambridge University Press.

Coppola, Marie & Elissa Newport. 2005. Grammatical subjects in home sign: Abstract linguistic structure in adult primary gesture systems without linguistic input. *Proceedings of the National Academy of Sciences* 102: 19249–19253.

Corbey, Raymond. 2005. *The metaphysics of apes: Negotiating the animal–human boundary*. New York: Cambridge University Press.

Cosmides, Leda. 1989. The logic of social exchange: Has natural selection shaped how humans reason? Studies with the Wason selection task. *Cognition* 31: 187–276.

Cosmides, Leda & John Tooby. 1992. Cognitive adaptations for social exchange. In Barkow et al. 1992, 163–228.

—— 1994. Origins of domain specificity: The evolution of functional organization. In Hirschfeld & Gelman 1994a, 85–116.

—— 2000. The cognitive neuroscience of social reasoning. In Michael Gazzaniga (ed.), *The new cognitive neurosciences*, 2nd ed., 1259–1270. Cambridge, MA: MIT Press.

—— 2005. Neurocognitive adaptations designed for social exchange. In Buss 2005, 584–627.

Coulson, Seana. 2001. *Semantic leaps: Frame-shifting and conceptual blending in meaning construction*. Cambridge: Cambridge University Press.

Creem-Regehr, Sarah & James Lee. 2005. Neural representations of graspable objects: Are tools special? *Cognitive Brain Research* 22: 457–469.

Crick, Francis. 1994. *The astonishing hypothesis: The scientific search for the soul*. New York: Simon & Schuster.

Crinion, Jenny, R. Turner, A. Grogan, T. Hanakawa, U. Noppeney, J. T. Devlin, T. Aso, S. Urayama, H. Fukuyama, K. Stockton, K. Usui, D. W. Green & C. J. Price. 2006. Language control in the bilingual brain. *Science* 312: 1537–1540.

Crutch, Sebastian & Elizabeth Warrington. 2005. Abstract and concrete concepts have structurally different representational frameworks. *Brain* 128: 615–627.

Dally, Joanna, Nathan Emery & Nicola Clayton. 2006. Food-caching Western scrub-jays keep track of who was watching when. *Science* 312: 1662–1665.

Damasio, Antonio. 1985. Disorders of Complex visual processing: Agnosias, achromatopsia, Balint's syndrome, and related difficulties of orientation and construction. In M. M. Mesulam (ed.), *Principles of behavioural neurology*, 259–288. Philadelphia: Davis.

—— 1989. The brain binds entities and events by multiregional activation from convergence zones. *Neural Computation* 1: 123–132.

—— 1994. *Descartes' error: Emotion, reason, and the human brain*. New York: G. P. Putnam's Sons.

—— 2000. *The feeling of things: Body and emotion in the making of consciousness*. New York: Harvest.

—— 2003. *In search of Spinoza: Joy, sorrow, and the feeling brain*. New York: Harvest.

Damasio, Antonio & Hannah Damasio. 1994. Cortical systems for retrieval of concrete knowledge: The convergence zone framework. In Christof Koch & Joel Davis (eds.), *Large-scale neuronal theories of the brain*, 61–74. Cambridge, MA: MIT Press.

Dancygier, Barbara. 2006. What can blending do for you? *Language and Literature* 15: 5–15.

Dancygier, Barbara & Eve Sweetser. 2005. *Mental spaces in grammar: Conditional structures*. New York: Cambridge University Press.

Darden, Lindley & Nancy Maull. 1977. Interfield theories. *Philosophy of Science* 44: 43–64.

Darwin, Charles. 1872. *The expression of emotions in man and animals*. New York: New York Philosophical Library.

Darwin, Charles & Paul Ekman. 1998. *The expression of emotions in man and animals* (collated and edited, with introduction and afterword, by Paul Ekman). New York: Oxford University Press.

Davidson, Donald. 1974. On the very idea of a conceptual scheme. *Proceedings and Addresses of the American Philosophical Association* 47: 5–20.

1978/1981. What metaphors mean. *Critical Inquiry* 5: 31–47. [Reprinted in Johnson 1981a, 200–220].

Dawkins, Richard. 1976/2006. *The selfish gene*. New York: Oxford University Press.

De Gelder, Beatrice. 2006. Towards the neurobiology of emotional body language. *Nature Reviews Neuroscience* 7: 242–249.

Dehaene, Stanislas. 1997. *The number sense: How the mind creates mathematics*. New York: Oxford University Press.

Dehaene, Stanislas, Veronique Izard, Pierre Pica & Elizabeth Spelke. 2006. Core knowledge of geometry in an Amazonian indigene group. *Science* 311: 381–384.

Dehaene, Stanislas, Elizabeth Spelke, Philippe Pinel, Ruxandra Stanescu & Sanna Tsivkin. 1999. Sources of mathematical thinking: behavioral and brain-imaging evidence. *Science* 284: 970–974.

De Man, Paul. 1978. The epistemology of metaphor. *Critical Inquiry* 5: 31–47.

Dennett, Daniel. 1978. Beliefs about beliefs. *Behavior and Brain Science* 4: 568–570.

1984a. Cognitive wheels: The frame problem of artificial intelligence. In Christopher Hookway (ed.), *Minds, machines, and evolution*, 129–151. Cambridge: Cambridge University Press.

1984b. *Elbow room: The varieties of free will worth wanting*. Cambridge, MA: MIT Press.

1987. *The intentional stance*. Cambridge, MA: MIT Press.

1988. Quining qualia. In Anthony Marcel & Edoardo Bisiach (eds.), *Consciousness in contemporary science*. 42–77. New York: Oxford University Press.

1991. *Consciousness explained*. Boston: Little Brown.

1995. *Darwin's dangerous idea: Evolution and the meaning of life*. New York: Simon & Schuster.

2003. *Freedom evolves*. New York: Viking.

2005. *Sweet dreams: Philosophical obstacles to a science of consciousness*. Cambridge, MA: MIT Press.

De Quervain, Dominique, Urs Fischbacher, Valerie Treyer, Melanie Schellhammer, Ulrich Schnyder, Alfred Buck & Ernst Fehr. 2004. The neural basis of altruistic punishment. *Science* 305: 1254–1258.

Derrida, Jacques. 1978. *Of grammatology* (trans. Gayatri Spivak). Baltimore: Johns Hopkins University Press.

1979. Living on: Borderlines. In Harold Bloom et al. (eds.), *Deconstruction and criticism*, 75–176. New York: Seabury Press.

1981. *Positions* (trans. Alan Bass). Chicago: University of Chicago Press.

1984. Interview with Richard Kearney in Kearney (ed.), *Dialogues with contemporary thinkers*, 83–105. Manchester, UK: Manchester University Press.

De Sousa, Ronald. 1987. *The rationality of emotion*. Cambridge, MA: Cambridge University Press.

Devlin, Joseph, Richard Russell, Matthew Davis, Cathy Price, Helen Moss, M. Jalal Fadili & Lorraine Tyler. 2002. Is there an anatomical basis for category-specificity? Semantic memory studies in PET and fMRI. *Neuropsychologia* 40: 54–75.

De Waal, Frans. 1983/1998. *Chimpanzee politics: Power and sex among apes*. 2nd ed. Baltimore: Johns Hopkins University Press.

1996. *Good natured: The origins of right and wrong in humans and other animals*. Cambridge, MA: Harvard University Press.

2001. *The ape and the sushi master: Cultural reflections of a primatologist*. New York: Basic Books.

Dewan, Edmond. 1976. Consciousness as an emergent causal agent in the context of control system theory. In Gordon Globus, Grover Maxwell, Irwin Savodnik & Edmond Dewan (eds.), *Consciousness and the brain*, 181–198. New York: Plenum.

Dewey, John. 1938/1991. *John Dewey, The later works, 1925–1953*. Vol. 12: *Logic: The theory of inquiry*. Carbondale: Southern Illinois University Press.

      1981. *Experience and nature*. In Jo Ann Boydston (ed.), *John Dewey: The later works, 1925–1953*. Vol. 1. Carbondale: Southern Illinois University Press.

Diamond, Jared. 1997. *Guns, germs, and steel: The fates of human societies*. New York: Norton.

Dickinson, Anthony & David Shanks. 1995. Instrumental action and causal representation. In Sperber et al. 1995, 5–25.

Dijksterhuis, Ap, Maarten Bos, Loran Nordgren & Rick van Baaren. 2006. On making the right choice: The deliberation-without-attention effect. *Science* 311: 1005–1008.

Donald, Merlin. 1991. *Origins of the modern mind: Three stages in the evolution of culture and cognition*. Cambridge, MA: Harvard University Press.

Duhem, Pierre. 1906/1954. *The aim and structure of physical theory*. Princeton, NJ: Princeton University Press.

Dunbar, Kevin. 1999. The scientist in vivo: How scientists think and reason in the laboratory. In Lorenzo Magnani, Nancy Nersessian & Paul Thagard (eds.), *Model-based reasoning in scientific discovery*, 89–98. New York: Plenum.

      2001. The analogical paradox: Why analogy is so easy in naturalistic settings yet so difficult in the psychological laboratory. In Gentner et al. 2001, 313–334.

Dunbar, Robin. 1992. Neocortex size as a constraint on group size in primates. *Journal of Human Evolution* 20: 469–493.

      1993. Co-evolution of neocortical size, group size and language in humans. *Behavioral and Brain Sciences* 16: 681–735.

      1995. *The trouble with science*. Cambridge, MA: Harvard University Press.

      1996. *Gossip, grooming, and the evolution of language*. Cambridge, MA: Harvard University Press.

      2004. Gossip in evolutionary perspective. *Review of General Psychology* 8: 100–110.

Dunbar, Robin, Chris Knight & Camilla Power (eds.). 1999. *The evolution of culture: An interdisciplinary view*. New Brunswick, NJ: Rutgers University Press.

Dupré, John. 1993. *The disorder of things: Metaphysical foundations of the disunity of science*. Cambridge, MA: Harvard University Press.

Durkheim, Emile. 1895/1962. *The rules of the sociological method*. Glencoe, IL: Free Press.

      1915/1966. *The elementary forms of the religious life* (trans. Joseph Swain). New York: Free Press.

Eagleton, Terry. 1983. *Literary theory: An introduction*. Minneapolis: University of Minnesota Press.

      2003. *After theory*. New York: Penguin.

Edelman, Gerald. 1992. *Bright air, brilliant fire: On the matter of the mind*. New York: Basic Books.

Egge, James. 2004. Comparative analysis of religious metaphor: Appreciating similarity as well as difference. Presented at the American Academy of Religion Annual Meeting, San Antonio, TX, November 22.

Ekman, Paul. 1972/1982. *Emotion in the human face.* 2nd ed. Cambridge: Cambridge University Press.

1980. Biological and cultural contributions to body and facial movement in the expression of emotions. In A. Rorty 1980b, 73–102.

1999. Basic emotions. In Tim Dalgleish and Mick Power (eds.), *Handbook of cognition and emotion*, 45–60. Sussex, UK: John Wiley & Sons.

2003. *Emotions revealed: Recognizing faces and feelings to improve communication and emotional life.* New York: Owl Books.

Ekman, Paul & Richard Davidson. 1994. *The nature of emotion.* New York: Oxford University Press.

Elbert, Thomas et al. 1995. Increased cortical representation of the fingers of the left hand in string players. *Science* 270: 305–307.

Elvee, Richard (ed.). 1992. *The end of science? Attack and defense/ Nobel Conference XXV.* Lanham, MD: University Press of America.

Embry, Ainslie (ed.). 1988. *Sources of Indian tradition.* 2nd ed. Vol. 1. New York: Columbia University Press.

Emery, Nathan & Nicola Clayton. 2001. Effects of experience and social context on prospective caching strategies by scrub jays. *Nature* 414: 443.

2004. The mentality of crows: Convergent evolution of intelligence in corvids and apes. *Science* 306: 1903–1907.

Fadiga, Luciano, Laila Craighero & Etienne Olivier. 2005. Human motor cortex excitability during the perception of others' actions. *Current Opinion in Neurobiology* 15: 213–218.

Fauconnier, Gilles. 1996. Analogical counterfactuals. In Fauconnier & Sweetser 1996, 57–90.

1997. *Mappings in thought and language.* Cambridge: Cambridge University Press.

1999. Creativity, simulation, and conceptualization (response to Barsalou 1999a). *Behavioral and Brain Sciences* 22: 615.

Fauconnier, Gilles & Eve Sweetser (eds.). 1996. *Spaces, worlds and grammar.* Chicago: University of Chicago Press.

Fauconnier, Gilles & Mark Turner. 2002. *The way we think: Conceptual blending and the mind's hidden complexities.* New York: Basic Books.

Fehr, Ernst, Urs Fischbacher & Simon Gächter. 2002. Strong reciprocity, human cooperation and the enforcement of social norms. *Human Nature* 13: 1–25.

Fehr, Ernst & Simon Gächter. 2002. Altruistic punishment in humans. *Nature* 415: 137–140.

Feigenson, Lisa & Susan Carey. 2003. Tracking individuals via object-files: Evidence from infants' manual search. *Developmental Science* 6: 568–584.

2005. On the limits of infants' quantification of small object arrays. *Cognition* 97: 292–313.

Fernandez, James (ed.). 1991. *Beyond metaphor: The theory of tropes in anthropology.* Stanford: Stanford University Press.

Fesmire, Steven. 1994. What is "cognitive" about cognitive linguistics? *Metaphor and Symbolic Activity* 9: 149–154.

Feyerabend, Paul. 1993. *Against method.* 3rd ed. New York: Verso.

Figueredo, Aurelio, Jon Sefcek, Geneva Vasquez, Barbara Brumbach, James King & W. Jake Jacobs. 2005. Evolutionary personality psychology. In Buss 2005, 851–877.

Fingarette, Herbert. 1972. *Confucius: Secular as sacred.* New York: Harper Torchbooks.

2004. *Confucius: Du profane au sacré* (trans. Charles Le Blanc). Montréal: Les Presses de l'Université de Montréal.

Finocchiaro, Maurice (ed.). 1989. *The Galileo affair: A documentary history*. Berkeley: University of California Press.

Flanagan, Owen. 1991. *Varieties of moral personality: Ethics and psychological realism*. Cambridge, MA: Harvard University Press.

1992. *Consciousness reconsidered*. Cambridge, MA: MIT Press.

2002. *The problem of the soul: Two visions of mind and how to reconcile them*. New York: Basic Books.

Flanagan, Owen & Amélie O. Rorty (eds.). 1990. *Identity, character, and morality: Essays in moral psychology*. Cambridge, MA: MIT Press.

Flinn, Mark, David Geary & Carol Ward. 2005. Ecological dominance, social competition, and coalitionary arms races: Why humans evolved extraordinary intelligence. *Evolution and Human Behavior* 26: 10–46.

Flombaum, Jonathan, Justin Junge & Mark Hauser. 2005. Rhesus monkeys (*macaca mulatta*) spontaneously compute addition operations over large numbers. *Cognition* 97: 315–325.

Fodor, Jerry. 1983. *The modularity of the mind*. Cambridge, MA: MIT Press.

1987. Modules, frames, fridgeons, sleeping dogs, and the music of the spheres. In Jay Garfield (ed.), *Modularity in knowledge representation and natural-language understanding*, 26–36. Cambridge, MA: MIT Press.

Foucault, Michel. 1971. *The order of things: An archaeology of the human sciences*. New York: Pantheon.

1972. *The archaeology of knowledge* (trans. A. M. Sheridan Smith). New York: Pantheon.

1977. Nietzsche, genealogy, and history. In Donald Bouchard (ed.), *Language, countermemory, practice: Selected essays and interviews* (trans. Donald Bouchard & Sherry Simon), 139–164. Ithaca, NY: Cornell University Press.

1978. *The history of sexuality*. Vol. 1: *An introduction* (trans. Robert Hurley). New York: Random House.

Fox, Alan. 2005. Process ecology and the "ideal" Dao. *Journal of Chinese Philosophy* 32.1: 47–57.

Fraser, Mariam & Monica Greco (eds.). 2005. *The body: A reader*. New York: Routledge.

Frazer, Sir James George. 1922/1963. *The golden bough*. New York: Macmillan Publishing Company.

Fredrickson, Barbara & Daniel Kahneman. 1993. Duration neglect in retrospective evaluations of affective episodes. *Journal of Personality and Social Psychology* 65: 45–55.

Freeman, Derek. 1983. *Margaret Mead and Samoa: The making and unmaking of an anthropological myth*. Cambridge, MA: Harvard University Press.

Friedman, Thomas. 1999. *The lexus and the olive tree*. New York: Farrar, Straus & Giroux.

Frisina, Warren. 2002. *The unity of knowledge and action: Toward a nonrepresentational theory of knowledge*. Albany, NY: SUNY Press.

Gadamer, Hans-Georg. 1975. *Truth and method*. New York: Continuum.

1976a. Man and language. In David Linge (trans. and ed.), *Philosophical Hermeneutics*, 59–68. Berkeley: University of California Press.

1976b. On the problem of self-understanding. In Linge 1976a, 44–58.

1976c. The universality of the hermeneutical problem. In Linge 1976a, 3–17.

Galef, Bennett. 1987. Social influences on the identification of toxic foods by Norway rats. *Animal Learning and Behavior* 15: 327–332.

Gallagher, Helen & Christopher Frith. 2003. Functional imaging of "theory of mind." *Trends in Cognitive Sciences* 7: 77–83.

Gallagher, Shaun. 2005. *How the body shapes the mind.* New York: Oxford University Press.

Gallese, Vittorio, Luciano Fadiga, Leonardo Fogassi & Giacomo Rizzolatti. 1996. Action recognition in the premotor cortex. *Brain* 119: 593–609.

Gallese, Vittorio & Alvin Goldman. 1998. Mirror neurons and the simulation theory of mind-reading. *Trends in Cognitive Sciences* 2: 493–501.

Gallese, Vittorio & George Lakoff. 2005. The brain's concepts: The role of the sensory-motor system in conceptual knowledge. *Cognitive Neuropsychology* 22: 455–479.

Galton, Francis. 1880. Statistics of mental imagery. *Mind* 5: 301–318.

Garcia, John & Robert Koelling. 1966. Relation of cue to consequence in avoidance learning. *Psychonomics Science* 4: 123–124.

Gardner, Martin. 1970. Mathematical games. *Scientific American* 223: 120–123.

    1971. Mathematical games. *Scientific American* 224: 112–117.

Gazzaniga, Michael. 1998. *The mind's past.* Berkeley: University of California Press.

    2001. *The cognitive neurosciences.* 2nd ed. Cambridge, MA: MIT Press

Gazzaniga, Michael & Joseph LeDoux. 1978. *The integrated mind.* New York: Plenum.

Geaney, Jane. 2002. *On the epistemology of the senses in early Chinese thought.* Honolulu: University of Hawaii Press.

Geertz, Clifford. 1973. *The interpretation of cultures: Selected essays.* New York: Basic Books.

    1984/2000. Anti anti-relativism. *The American Anthropologist* 86: 263–278. (Reprinted in Geertz 2000.)

    1997/2000. The legacy of Thomas Kuhn: The right text at the right time. *Common Knowledge* 6: 1–5. (Reprinted in Geertz 2000, 160–166.)

    2000. *Available light: Anthropological reflections on philosophical topics.* Princeton, NJ: Princeton University Press.

Gelman, Rochel. 1990. First principles organize attention to and learning about relevant data: Number and the animate-inanimate distinction as examples. *Cognitive Science* 14: 79–106.

    1991. Epigenetic foundation of knowledge structures: Initial and transcendent constructions. In Carey & Gelman 1991, 293–322.

Gelman, Rochel & Gallistel, Randy. 2004. Language and the origin of numerical concepts. *Science* 306: 441–443.

Gelman, Susan. 2003. *The essential child.* New York: Oxford University Press.

    2004. Psychological essentialism in children. *Trends in Cognitive Science* 8: 404–409.

Gelman, Susan, John Coley & Gail Gottfried. 1994. Essentialist beliefs in children: The acquisition of concepts and theories. In Hirschfeld & Gelman 1994a, 341–365.

Gelman, Susan & Gail Gottfried. 1996. Children's causal explanations of animate and inanimate motion. *Child Development* 67: 1970–1987.

Gelman, Susan & Henry Wellman. 1991. Insides and essences: Early understandings of the nonobvious. *Cognition* 38: 213–244.

Gentner, Dedre & Donald Gentner. 1983. Flowing water or teeming crowds: Mental models of electricity. In Dedre Gentner & Albert Stevens (eds.), *Mental models,* 99–129. Hillsdale, NJ: Lawrence Erlbaum Associates.

Gentner, Dedre, Keith Holyoak & Boicho Kokinov (eds.). 2001. *The analogical mind: Perspectives from cognitive science.* Cambridge, MA: MIT Press.

Gentner, Dedre, Mutsumi Imai & Lera Boroditsky. 2002. As time goes by: Evidence for two systems in processing space-time metaphors. *Language and Cognitive Processes* 17: 537–565.

Gentner, Timothy, Kimberly Fenn, Daniel Margoliash & Howard Nusbaum. 2006. Recursive syntactic pattern learning by songbirds. *Nature* 440: 1204–1207.

Gergely, György, Zoltán Nádasdy, Gergely Csibra & Szilvia Bíró. 1995. Taking the intentional stance at 12 months of age. *Cognition* 56: 165–193.

Gerstmann, Josef. 1940. Syndrome of finger agnosia, disorientation for right and left, agraphia, acalculia. *Archives of Neurology and Psychology* 44: 398–408.

Geurts, Kathryn. 2003. *Culture and the senses: Bodily ways of knowing in an African community.* Berkeley: University of California Press.

Gibbons, Euell. 1962. *Stalking the wild asparagus.* New York: David McKay Company.

Gibbs, Raymond. 1994. *The poetics of mind: Figurative thought, language, and understanding.* Cambridge: Cambridge University Press.

    1999. Taking metaphor out of our heads and putting it into the cultural world. In Gibbs & Steen 1999, 145–166.

    2003. Embodied experience and linguistic meaning. *Brain and Language* 84: 1–15.

    2005. Embodiment in metaphorical imagination. In Pecher & Zwaan 2005, 65–92.

    2006. *Embodiment and cognitive science.* Cambridge: Cambridge University Press.

Gibbs, Raymond & Eric Berg. 1999. Embodied metaphor in perceptual symbols (response to Barsalou 1999a). *Behavioral and Brain Sciences* 22: 617–618.

Gibbs, Raymond & Herbert Colston. 1995. The cognitive psychological reality of image schemas and their transformations. *Cognitive Linguistics* 6: 347–378.

Gibbs, Raymond & Gerard Steen (eds.). 1999. *Metaphor in cognitive linguistics.* Philadelphia: John Benjamins.

Gibson, James. 1979. *The ecological approach to visual perception.* Boston: Houghton Mifflin.

Gifford, Julie. 2004. The art of seeing the invisible: An interpretation of the terraces atop Barabudur. Presented at the American Academy of Religion Annual Meeting, San Antonio, TX, November 22.

Gigerenzer, Gerd. 2000. *Adaptive thinking: Rationality in the real world.* Oxford: Oxford University Press.

Gigerenzer, Gerd & Daniel Goldstein. 1996. Reasoning the fast and frugal way: Models of bounded rationality. *Psychological Review* 103: 650–669.

Gigerenzer, Gerd, & Reinhard Selten (eds.). 2001. *Bounded rationality: The adaptive toolbox.* Cambridge, MA: MIT Press.

Gigerenzer, Gerd, Peter Todd & the ABC Research Group (eds.). 1999. *Simple heuristics that make us smart.* New York: Oxford University Press.

Gintis, Herbert. 2000. Strong reciprocity and human sociality. *Journal of Theoretical Biology* 206: 169–179.

Giorello, Giulio. 1997. Sì, abbiamo un anima. Ma è fatta di tanti piccoli robot (interview with Daniel Dennett). *Corriere della Sera* (Milan), April 28.

Glenberg, Arthur, David Havas, Raymond Becker & Mike Rinck. 2005. Grounding language in bodily states. In Pecher & Zwaan 2005, 115–28.

Glenberg, Arthur & Michael Kaschak. 2002. Grounding language in action. *Psychonomic Bulletin and Review* 9: 558–565.

Goldstein, Daniel & Gerd Gigerenzer. 2002. Models of ecological rationality: The recognition heuristic. *Psychological Review* 109: 75–90.

Gonzalez-Marquez, Monica & Michael Spivey. 2004. Mapping from real to abstract locations: Experimental evidence from the Spanish verb ESTAR. Unpublished manuscript.

Goodale Melvyn, A. David Milner, Lorna Jakobson & David Carey. 1991. A neurological dissociation between perceiving objects and grasping them. *Nature* 349: 154–156.

Goodall, Jane. 1979. Life and death at Gombe. *National Geographic* 155: 592–621.

Goodman, Nelson. 1954/1983. *Fact, fiction and forecast.* 4th ed. Cambridge, MA: Harvard University Press.

Gopnik, Alison & Henry Wellman. 1994. The theory theory. In Hirschfeld & Gelman 1994a, 257–293.

Gordon, Peter. 2004. Numerical cognition without words: Evidence from Amazonia. *Science* 306: 496–499.

Gordon, Robert. 1986. Folk psychology as simulation. *Mind and Language* 1: 158–171.

Gore, Jeff, Zev Bryant, Michael Stone, Marcelo Nöllman, Nicholas Cozzarelli & Carlos Bustamante. 2006. Mechanochemical analysis of DNA gyrase using rotor bead tracking. *Nature Reviews* 439: 100–104.

Gore, Rick. 2000. The dawn of humans: People like us. *National Geographic* 198: 90–117.

Gould, Stephen Jay. 1997. Nonoverlapping magisteria. *Natural History* 106: 16–22.
    2000. More things in heaven and earth. In Rose & Rose 2000, 101–125.

Grady, Joseph. 1997. Foundations of meaning: Primary metaphors and primary scenes. Ph.D. diss. University of California, Berkeley.

Grady, Joseph, Todd Oakley & Seana Coulson. 1999. Blending and metaphor. In Gibbs & Steen 1999, 101–124.

Grafen, Alan & Mark Ridley (eds.). 2006. *Richard Dawkins: How a scientist changed the way we think.* New York: Oxford University Press.

Greene, Joshua. 2003. From neural "is" to moral "ought": What are the moral implications of neuroscientific moral psychology? *Nature Reviews Neuroscience* 4: 847–850.
    (in press). The secret joke of Kant's soul. In W. Sinnott-Armstrong (ed.), *Moral psychology.* Vol. 3: *The neuroscience of morality: Emotion, disease, and development.* Cambridge, MA: MIT Press.

Greene, Joshua & Jonathan Haidt. 2002. How (and where) does moral judgment work? *Trends in Cognitive Science* 6: 517–523.

Grewel, F. 1952. Acalculia. *Brain* 75: 397–427.

Griffin, Donald. 1984. *Animal thinking.* Cambridge, MA: Harvard University Press.

Gross, Paul & Norman Levitt. 1994. *Higher superstition: The academic left and its quarrels with science.* Baltimore: Johns Hopkins University Press.

Gross, Paul, Norman Levitt & Martin Lewis. 1996. *The flight from science and reason.* Baltimore: Johns Hopkins University Press.

Gumperz, John & Stephen Levinson (eds). 1996. *Rethinking linguistic relativity.* Cambridge: Cambridge University Press.

Guthrie, Stewart. 1993. *Faces in the clouds: A new theory of religion.* Oxford: Oxford University Press.

Haack, Susan. 2003. *Defending science within reason: Between scientism and cynicism.* Amherst, NY: Prometheus Books.

Hacking, Ian (ed.). 1981. *Scientific revolutions.* New York: Oxford University Press.
    1983a. Experimentation and scientific realism. *Philosophical Topics* 13: 71–87.
    1983b. *Representing and intervening: Introductory topics in the philosophy of natural science.* Cambridge: Cambridge University Press.

1999. *The social construction of what.* Cambridge, MA: Harvard University Press.

Haidt, Jonathan. 2001. The emotional dog and its rational tail: A social intuitionist approach to moral judgment. *Psychological Review* 108: 813–834.

Haidt, Jonathan, Silvia Koller & Maria Dias. 1993. Affect, culture, and morality, or is it wrong to eat your dog? *Journal of Personality and Social Psychology* 65: 613–628.

Hamilton, William. 1964. The genetical evolution of social behaviour (I and II). *Journal of Theoretical Biology* 7: 1–16, 17–52.

Hampe, Beate (ed.). 2005. *From perception to meaning: Image schemas in cognitive linguistics.* Berlin: Mouton de Gruyter.

Hansen, Chad. 1983. *Language and logic in early China.* Ann Arbor: University of Michigan Press.

1992. *A Daoist theory of Chinese thought.*New York: Oxford University Press.

Haraway, Donna. 1991. *Simians, cyborgs, and women: The reinvention of nature.* New York: Routledge.

Harding, Sandra. 1992. Why physics is a bad model of physics. In Richard Elvee (ed.), *The end of science? Attack and defense*, 1–21. Lanham, MD: University Press of America.

1996. Science is "good to think with." *Social Text* 46/47: 15–26.

Hare, Brian, Josep Call, Brian Agnetta & Michael Tomasello. 2000. Chimpanzees know what conspecifics do and do not see. *Animal Behavior* 59: 771–785.

2001. Do chimpanzees know what conspecifics know? *Animal Behavior* 61: 139–151.

Hare, Brian, Josep Call & Michael Tomasello. 2006. Chimpanzees deceive a human competitor by hiding. *Cognition* 101: 495–514.

Harris, Judith. 1998. *The nurture assumption: Why children turn out the way they do.* New York: Free Press.

Hauser, Marc. 2005. Our chimpanzee mind. *Nature* 437: 60–63.

Heidegger, Martin. 1962. *Being and Time* (trans. John Macquarrie & Edward Robinson). New York: Harper & Row.

1971. *Poetry, language, thought* (trans. Albert Hofstadter). New York: Harper & Row.

1993a. Building, dwelling, thinking. In David Krell, *Martin Heidegger: Basic writings*, 2nd ed., 344–363. New York: Harper & Row.

1993b. Letter on humanism. In Krell 1993, 217–265.

1993c. On the essence of truth. In Krell 1993, 115–138.

1993d. The origin of the work of art. In Krell 1993, 143–212.

1993e. The way to language. In Krell 1993, 397–426.

Heider, Fritz & Mary-Ann Simmel. 1944. An experimental study of apparent behavior. *American Journal of Psychology* 57: 243–259.

Heise, Ursula. 2004. Science, technology, and postmodernism. In Connor 2004, 136–167.

Hempel, Carl. 1966. *Philosophy of natural science.* Englewood Cliffs, NJ: Prentice-Hall.

Henrich, Joseph & Robert Boyd. 2001. Why people punish defectors: Weak conformist transmission can stabilize costly enforcement of norms in cooperative dilemmas. *Journal of Theoretical Biology* 208: 79–89.

Henrich, Joseph, Richard McElreath, Abigail Barr, Jean Ensminger, Clark Barrett, Alexander Bolyanatz, Juan Camilo Cardenas, Michael Gurven, Edwins Gwako, Natalie Henrich, Carolyn Lesorogol, Frank Marlowe, David Tracer & John Ziker. 2006. Costly punishment across human societies. *Nature* 312: 1767–1770.

Hespos, Susan & Renée Baillargeon. 2006. Décalage in infants' knowledge about occlusion and containment events: Converging evidence from action tasks. *Cognition* 99: B31–B41.

Hesse, Mary. 1966. *Models and analogies in science*. Notre Dame, IN: University of Notre Dame Press.

Hiraga, Masako. 1995. *Literary pragmatics: Cognitive metaphor and the structure of the poetic text*. New York: Elsevier.

1999. DEFERENCE as DISTANCE: Metaphorical base of honorific verb construction in Japanese. In Masako Hiraga, Chris Sinha & Sherman Wilcox (eds.), *Cultural, psychological and typological issues in cognitive linguistics: Selected papers of the biannual ICLA meeting in Albuquerque, July 1995*, 47–68. Amsterdam/Philadelphia: John Benjamins.

Hirschfeld, Lawrence & Susan Gelman (eds.). 1994a. *Mapping the mind: Domain specificity in cognition and culture*. New York: Cambridge University Press.

1994b. Toward a topography of mind: An introduction to domain specificity. In Hirschfeld & Gelman 1994a, 3–35.

Hirschkop, Ken. 2000. Cultural studies and its discontents: A comment on the Sokal affair. *In The Editors of Lingua Franca* 2000, 230–233.

Hogan, Patrick. 2003. *Cognitive science, literature, and the arts: A guide for humanists*. New York: Routledge.

Holton, Gerald. 1993. *Science and anti-science*. Cambridge, MA: Harvard University Press.

Holyoak, Keith & Paul Thagard. 1995. *Mental leaps: Analogy in creative thought*. Cambridge, MA: MIT Press.

Hooker, Clifford. 1981. Towards a general theory of reduction. Part I: Historical and scientific setting. Part II: Identity in reduction. Part III: Cross-categorical reduction. *Dialogue* 20: 38–59, 201–236, and 496–529.

Horton, Robin. 1993. *Patterns of thought in Africa and the West: Essays on magic, religion and science*. Cambridge: Cambridge University Press.

Hubbard, Edward, A. Cyrus Arman, V. S. Ramachandran & Geoffrey Boynton. 2005. Individual differences among grapheme-color synesthetes: Brain-behavior correlations. *Neuron* 45: 975–985.

Hubbard, Edward & V. S. Ramachandran. 2001. Cross wiring and the neural basis of synasthesia. *Investigative Opthamology and Visual Science* 42: S712.

2005. Neurocognitive mechanisms of synesthesia. *Neuron* 48: 509–520.

Hubbard, Timothy. 1996. Synesthesia-like mappings of lightness, pitch and melodic interval. *American Journal of Psychology* 109: 219–238.

Hume, David. 1739/1978. *A treatise of human nature*. 2nd ed. (ed. L. A. Selby-Bigge). Oxford: Clarendon Press.

1777/1975. *Enquiries concerning human understanding and concerning the principles of morals*. 3rd ed. (ed. L. A. Selby-Bigge). Oxford: Clarendon Press.

Humphrey, Nicholas. 1976. The social function of intellect. In Bateson, P. P. G. & R. A. Hinde (eds.), *Growing points in ethology*, 303–318. Cambridge: Cambridge University Press.

1984. *Consciousness regained*. Oxford: Oxford University Press.

1986. *The inner eye*. London: Faber and Faber.

1992. *A history of the mind: Evolution and the birth of consciousness*. London: Chatto & Windus.

Ibarretxe-Antuñano, Iraide. 1999. Metaphorical mappings in the sense of smell. In Gibbs & Steen 1999, 29–46.

Inagaki, Kayako & Giyoo Hatano. 1993. Young children's understanding of the mind-body distinction. *Child Development* 64: 1534–1549.

2004. Vitalistic causality in young children's naïve biology. *Trends in Cognitive Science* 8: 356–362.

Irwin, Terence (trans.). 1985. *Aristotle: Nichomachean ethics.* Indianapolis: Hackett Publishing Company.

Jackendoff, Ray. 1996. How language helps us think. *Pragmatics and Cognition* 4: 1–34.

Jackson, Frank. 1982. Epiphenomenal qualia. *Philosophical Quarterly* 32: 127–136.

Jäkel, Olaf. 2003. Hypotheses revisited: The cognitive theory of metaphor applied to religious texts. *Metaphorik* 2: 20–41.

James, William. 1907/1995. *Pragmatism.* New York: Dover.

Jammer, Max. 1961. *Concepts of mass.* Cambridge, MA: Harvard University Press.

Jefferys, William & James Berger. 1992. Ockham's razor and Bayesian analysis. *American Scientist* 89: 64–72.

Jinmenshi bowuguan. 1998. *Guodian Chumu Zhujian.* Beijing: Wenwu.

Jochim, Chris. 1998. Just say "no" to no-self in Zhuangzi. In Roger Ames (ed.), *Wandering at ease in the* Zhuangzi, 35–74. Albany, NY: SUNY Press.

Johnson, Mark. 1981a (ed.). *Philosophical perspectives on metaphor.* Minneapolis: University of Minnesota Press.

1981b. Metaphor in the philosophical tradition. In Johnson 1981a, 3–47.

1987. *The body in the mind: The bodily basis of meaning, imagination and reason.* Chicago: University of Chicago Press.

1993. *Moral imagination: Implications of cognitive science for ethics.* Chicago: University of Chicago Press.

2005. The philosophical significance of image schemas. In Hampe 2005, 15–34.

Johnson-Laird, Phillip. 1989. Analogy and the exercise of creativity. In Stella Vosniadou & Andrew Ortony (eds.), *Similarity and analogical reasoning*, 313–331. New York: Cambridge University Press.

Joseph, George Gheverghese. 1991. *The crest of the peacock.* London: Penguin.

Kahneman, Daniel, Paul Slovic & Amos Tversky (eds.). 1982. *Judgement under uncertainty: Heuristics and biases.* Cambridge: Cambridge University Press.

Kahneman, Daniel & Amos Tversky. 2000. *Choices, values, and frames.* Cambridge: Cambridge University Press.

Kahneman, Daniel, Barbara Fredrickson, Charles Schreiber & Donald Redelmeier. 1993. When more pain is preferred to less: Adding a better end. *Psychological Science* 4: 401–405.

Kahneman, Daniel, David Schkade & Cass Sunstein. 1998. Shared outrage and erratic rewards: The psychology of punitive damages. *Journal of Risk and Uncertainty* 16: 49–86.

Kant, Immanuel. 1785/1964. *Groundwork of the metaphysic of morals* (trans. H. J. Paton). New York: Harper Torchbooks.

Kanwisher, Nancy. 2006. What's in a face? *Science* 311: 617–618.

Kaschak, Michael & Arthur Glenberg. 2000. Constructing meaning: The role of affordances and grammatical constructions in sentence comprehension. *Journal of Memory and Language* 43: 508–529.

Kaschak, Michael, Carol Madden, David Therriault, Richard Yaxley, Mark Aveyard, Adrienne Blanchard & Rolf Zwaan. 2005. Perception of motion affects language processing. *Cognition* 94: B79–B89.

Katz, Albert, Cristina Cacciari, Raymond Gibbs & Mark Turner. 1998. New York: Oxford University Press.

Katz, Steven. 1978. Language, epistemology, and mysticism. In Steven Katz (ed.), *Mysticism and Philosophical Analysis*, 22–74. New York: Oxford University Press.

Kay, Paul & Willett Kempton. 1984. What is the Sapir-Whorf hypothesis? *American Anthropologist* 86: 65–79.

Kay, Paul & Terry Regier. 2006. Language, thought and color: Recent developments. *Trends in Cognitive Sciences* 10: 51–54.

———. 2007. Color naming universals: The case of Berinmo. *Cognition* 102: 289–298.

Keil, Frank. 1989. *Concepts, kinds, and cognitive development*. Cambridge, MA: MIT Press.

———. 1994. The birth and nurturance of concepts by domains: The origins of concepts of living things. In Hirschfeld & Gelman 1994a, 234–254.

Kelemen, Deborah. 1999a. Function, goals, and intention: Children's teleological reasoning about objects. *Trends in Cognitive Sciences* 3: 461–468.

———. 1999b. Why are rocks pointy? Children's preference for teleological explanations of the natural world. *Developmental Psychology* 35: 1440–1452.

———. 2003. British and American children's preferences for teleo-functional explanations. *Cognition* 88: 201–221.

———. 2004. Are children "intuitive theists"? Reasoning and purpose and design in nature. *Psychological Science* 15: 295–301.

Kenshur, Oscar. 1996. The allure of the hybrid: Bruno Latour and the search for a new grand theory. *Annals of the New York Academy of Sciences* 775: 288–297.

Kenward, Ben, Alex Weir, Christian Rutz & Alex Kacelnik. 2005. Tool manufacture by naïve juvenile crows. *Nature* 433: 121.

Kimmel, Michael. 2005. Culture regained: Situated and compound image schemas. In Hampe 2005, 285–311.

Kitayama, Shinobu, Sean Duffy, Tadashi Kawamura & Jeff Larsen. 2003. Perceiving an object and its context in different cultures: A cultural look at new look. *Psychological Science* 14: 201–206.

Kitcher, Philip. 1985. *Vaulting ambition: Sociobiology and the quest for human nature*. Cambridge, MA: MIT Press.

———. 1993. *The advancement of science: Science without legend, objectivity without illusions*. New York: Oxford University Press.

———. 1998. A plea for science studies. In Koertge 1998, 32–56.

Knight, Chris, Robin Dunbar, Robin Power & Camilla Power. 1999. An evolutionary approach to human culture. In Dunbar et al. 1999, 1–11.

Knight, Nicola, Paulo Sousa, Justin Barrett & Scott Atran. 2004. Children's attributions of beliefs to humans and God: Cross-cultural evidence. *Cognitive Science* 28: 117–126.

Knoblock, John (trans.). 1994. *Xunzi: A translation and study of the complete works*. Vol. 3. Stanford: Stanford University Press.

Kobayashi, Tessei, Kazuo Hiraki, Ryoko Mugitani & Toshikazu Hasegawa. 2004. Baby arithmetic: One object plus one tone. *Cognition* 91: B23–B34.

Koch, Christof. 2004. *The quest for consciousness: A neurobiological approach*. Englewood, CO: Roberts & Company.

Koertge, Noretta (ed.). 1998. *A house built on sand: Exposing postmodernist myths about science*. New York: Oxford University Press.

Koestler, Arthur. 1975. *The act of creation*. London: Picador.

Köhler, Wolfgang. 1929. *Gestalt psychology*. New York: Liveright.

Kokinov, Boicho & Alexander Petrov. 2001. Integrating memory and reasoning in analogy-making: The AMBR model. In Gentner et al. 2001, 59–124.

Kosslyn, Stephen. 1994. *Image and brain: The resolution of the imagery debate.* Camrbidge, MA: MIT Press.

2005. Mental images and the brain. *Cognitive Neuropsychology* 22: 333–347.

Kosslyn, Stephen, Carolyn Backer Cave, David Provost & Susanne von Gierke. 1998. Sequential processing in image generation. *Cognitive Psychology* 20: 319–343.

Kövecses, Zoltán. 1986. *Metaphors of anger, pride and love: A lexical approach to the structure of concepts.* Philadelphia: John Benjamins.

1990. *Emotional concepts.* New York: Springer-Verlag.

2002. *Metaphor: A practical introduction.* Oxford: Oxford University Press.

Kuhlmeier, Valerie, Karen Wynn & Paul Bloom. 2003. Attribution of dispositional states by 12-month-old infants. *Psychological Science* 14: 402–408.

Kuhn, Thomas. 1962/1970. *The structure of scientific revolutions.* Chicago: University of Chicago Press (2nd ed., 1970).

1970. Reflections on my critics. In Imre Lakatos and Alan Musgrave (eds.), *Criticism and the growth of knowledge*, 231–278. Cambridge: Cambridge University Press.

Kummer, Hans. 1995. Causal knowledge in animals. In Sperber et al. 1995, 26–36.

Kunst-Wilson, William & Robert Zajonc. 1980. Affective discrimination of stimuli that cannot be recognized. *Science* 207: 557–558.

Lagalla, Julius Caesar. 1612. *De phaenomenis in orbe lunae novi telescopii use a D. Galileo Galilei nunc iterum suscitatis physica disputatio.* Venice.

Lakoff, George. 1987. *Women, fire and dangerous things: What categories reveal about the mind.* Chicago: University of Chicago Press.

1990. The invariance hypothesis: Is abstract reasoning based upon image schemas? *Cognitive Linguistics* 1: 39–74.

1993. The contemporary theory of metaphor. In Ortony 1993a, 202–251.

1996. *Moral politics: What conservatives know that liberals don't.* Chicago: University of Chicago Press.

2004. *Don't think of an elephant! Know your values and frame the debate.* White River Junction, VT: Chelsea Green.

Lakoff, George & Mark Johnson. 1980. *Metaphors we live by.* Chicago: University of Chicago Press.

1999. *Philosophy in the flesh: The embodied mind and its challenge to Western thought.* New York: Basic Books.

Lakoff, George & Raphael Núñez. 2000. *Where mathematics comes from: How the embodied mind brings mathematics into being.* New York: Basic Books.

Lakoff, George & Mark Turner. 1989. *More than cool reason: A field guide to poetic metaphor.* Chicago: University of Chicago Press.

Langacker, Ronald. 1987. *Foundations of cognitive grammar.* Vol. 1: *Theoretical prerequisites.* Stanford: Stanford University Press.

1991. *Foundations of cognitive grammar.* Vol. 2: *Descriptive application.* Stanford: Stanford University Press.

1999. A view from cognitive linguistics (response to Barsalou 1999a). *Behavioral and Brain Sciences* 22: 625.

2005. Dynamicity, ficticity, and scanning: The imaginative basis of logic and linguistic meaning. In Pecher & Zwaan 2005, 164–197.

Latour, Bruno. 1993. *We have never been modern* (trans. Catherine Porter). Cambridge, MA: Harvard University Press.

2004. Why has critique run out of steam? From matters of fact to matters of concern. *Critical Inquiry* 30: 225–248.

Latour, Bruno & Steven Woolgar. 1979/1986. *Laboratory life: The construction of scientific facts*. Princeton, NJ: Princeton University Press (2nd ed., 1986).

Lau, D. C. (trans.). 1970. *Mencius*. London: Penguin.

Laudan, Larry. 1990. Demystifying underdetermination. In C. Wage Savage (ed.), *Minnesota studies in the philosophy of science*. Vol. 14, 267–297. Minneapolis: University of Minnesota Press.

1996. *Beyond positivism and relativism: Theory, method, and evidence*. Boulder, CO: Westview Press.

LeDoux, Joseph. 1996. *The emotional brain: The mysterious underpinnings of emotional life*. New York: Simon & Schuster.

Leibniz, Gottfried Wilhelm. 1768/1996. *New essays on human understanding* (trans. and ed. Peter Remnant & Jonathan Bennett). New York: Cambridge University Press.

Leslie, Alan. 1982. The perception of causality in infants. *Perception* 11: 173–186.

1987. Pretence and representation in infancy: The origins of "theory of mind." *Psychological Review* 94: 412–426.

1988. The necessity of illusion: Perception and thought in infancy. In Lawrence Weiskrantz (ed.), *Thought without language*, 85–210. Oxford: Oxford Science Publications.

1994. ToMM, ToBy, and agency: Core architecture and domain specificity. In Hirschfeld & Gelman 1994a, 119–148.

1995. Pretending and believing: Issues in the theory of ToMM. *Cognition* 50: 193–220.

Leslie, Alan & Stephanie Keeble. 1987. Do six-month-old infants perceive causality? *Cognition* 25: 265–288.

Lewis, Michael & Jeanette Haviland-Jones (eds.). 2000. *Handbook of emotions*. 2nd ed. New York: Guilford Press.

Lewontin, Richard. 1991. *Biology as ideology: The doctrine of DNA*. Concord, Ontario: Anansi Press.

Lewontin, Richard, Steven Rose & Leon Kamin. 1984. *Not in our genes*. New York: Pantheon.

Lipton, Jennifer & Elizabeth Spelke. 2003. Origins of number sense: Large-number discrimination in human infants. *Psychological Science* 14: 396–401.

Liu, Lydia. 2004. *The clash of empires: The invention of China in modern world making*. Cambridge, MA: Harvard University Press.

Lloyd. Elisabeth. 1996. Science and anti-science: Objectivity and its real enemies. In Lynn Hankinson Nelson & Jack Nelson (eds.), *Feminism, science, and the philosophy of science*, 217–259. New York: Kluwer.

Lloyd, G. E. R. & Nathan Sivin. 2003. *The Way and the word: Science and medicine in early China and Greece*. New Haven, CT: Yale University Press.

Locke, John. 1690/1975. *An essay concerning human understanding*. Oxford: Clarendon Press.

Lodge, David. 1975. *Changing places*. London: Penguin Books.

1984. *Small world: An academic romance*. New York: Warner Books.

1988. *Nice work*. New York: Penguin Books.

2001. *Thinks . . . A novel*. London: Secker & Warburg.

Loehlin, John & Robert Nichols. 1976. *Heredity, environment, and personality: A study of 850 sets of twins*. Austin: University of Texas Press.

Loewenstein, George, Elke Weber, Christopher Hsee & Ned Welch. 2001. Risk as feelings. *Psychological Bulletin* 127: 267–286.

Loy, David. 1987. The cloture of deconstruction: A Mahayana critique of Derrida. *International Philosophical Quarterly* 27: 59–80.

Lupfer, Michael, Donna Tolliver & Mark Jackson. 1996. Explaining life-altering occurrences: A test of the "god-of-the-gaps" hypothesis. *Journal for the Scientific Study of Religion* 35: 379–391.

Lyotard, Jean-François. 1984. *The postmodern condition: A report on knowledge* (trans. Geoff Bennington & Brian Massumi). Minneapolis: University of Minnesota Press.

MacCormac, Earl. 1976. *Metaphor and myth in science and religion.* Durham, NC: Duke University Press.

Mandler, Jean. 1992. How to build a baby, II: Conceptual primitives. *Psychological Review* 99: 587–604.

    2004a. *The foundations of mind: Origins of conceptual thought.* New York: Oxford University Press.

    2004b. Thought before language. *Trends in Cognitive Sciences* 8: 508–513.

Mann, Charles. 2005. *1491: New revelations of the Americas before Columbus.* New York: Knopf.

Marcus, Gary. 2006. Language: Startling starlings. *Nature* 440: 1117–1118.

Marglin, Frederique. 1990. Smallpox in two systems of knowledge. In Marglin & Marglin 1990, 102–144.

Marglin, Frederique & Stephen Marglin (eds.). 1990. *Dominating knowledge: Development, culture and resistance.* Oxford: Clarendon Press.

Markman, Ellen. 1989. *Categorization and naming in children: Problems of induction.* Cambridge, MA: MIT Press.

Marks, Lawrence. 1975. On colored hearing synesthesia: Cross-modal translations of sensory dimensions. *Psychological Bulletin* 82: 303–331.

Marr, David. 1982. *Vision.* San Francisco: W. H. Freeman.

Martin, Alex & Linda Chao. 2001. Semantic memory and the brain: Structure and processes. *Current Opinion in Neurobiology* 11: 194–201.

Martin, Alex, Leslie Ungerleider & James Haxby. 1996. Neural correlates of category-specific knowledge. *Nature* 379: 649–652.

    2001. Category specificity and the brain: The sensory-motor model of semantic representations of objects. In Gazzaniga 2001, 1023–1036.

Masuda, Takahiko & Richard Nisbett. 2001. Attending holistically vs. analytically: Comparing the context sensitivity of Japanese and Americans. *Journal of Personality and Social Psychology* 81: 922–934.

Matsuzawa, Tetsuro. 1985. Colour naming and classification in a chimpanzee (*pan troglodytes*). *Journal of Human Evolution* 14: 283–291.

Maynard Smith, John. 1964. Group selection and kin selection. *Nature* 201: 1145–1147.

    1974. The theory of games and the evolution of animal conflicts. *Journal of Theoretical Biology* 47: 209–221.

McCarthy, Rosaleen & Elizabeth Warrington. 1988. Evidence for modality specific meaning systems in the brain. *Nature* 88: 428–429.

McCrink, Koleen & Karen Wynn. 2004. Large-number addition and substraction by 9-month-old infants. *Psychological Science* 15: 776–791.

McCutcheon, Russell. 2006a. "It's a lie. There's no truth to it! It's a sin!": On the limits of the humanistic study of religion and the costs of saving others from themselves. *Journal of the American Academy of Religion* 74: 720–750.

2006b. A response to Courtright. *Journal of the American Academy of Religion* 74: 755–756.

McEwan, Ian. 2005. *Saturday*. Toronto: Alfred A. Knopf.

McFarling, Usha. 2003. Stalwart Galileo is vaporized near Jupiter. *Los Angeles Times*, September 22.

McNeill, David. 1992. *Hand and mind: What gestures reveal about thought*. Chicago: University of Chicago Press.

Mead, Margaret. 1928. *Coming of age in Samoa: A psychological study of primitive youth for Western civilisation*. New York: Blue Ribbon Books.

Medin, Douglas. 1989. Concept and conceptual structure. *American Psychologist* 44: 1469–1481

Medin, Douglas & Scott Atran (eds.). 1999. *Folkbiology*. Cambridge, MA: MIT Press.

Medin, Douglas, Norbert Ross, Scott Atran, Douglas Cox, Hilary J. Waukau, John Coley, Julia Proffitt & Sergey Blok. 2006. Folkbiology of freshwater fish. *Cognition* 99: 237–273.

Megill, Allan. 1985. *Prophets of extremity: Nietzsche, Heidegger, Foucault, Derrida*. Berkeley: University of California Press.

Meltzoff, Andrew & Keith Moore. 1977. Imitation of facial and manual gestures by human neonates. *Science* 198: 74–78.

1994. Imitation, memory, and the representation of persons. *Infant behavior and development* 17: 83–99.

Melville, Stephen. 2004. Postmodernism and art. In Connor 2004, 82–96.

Menand, Louis. 2005. Dangers within and without. *Modern Language Association, Profession 2005*: 10–17.

Mercader, Julio, Huw Barton, Jason Gillespie, Jack Harris, Steven Kuhn, Robert Tyler & Christophe Boesch. 2007. 4,300-year-old chimpanzee sites and the origins of percussive stone technology. *Proceedings of the National Academy of Sciences* 104: 3043–3048.

Merquoir, J. G. 1985. *Foucault*. Berkeley: University of California Press.

Michotte, Albert & Georges Thinès. 1963. La causalité perceptive. *Journal de Psychologie Normale et Pathologique* 60: 9–36.

Miller, George. 1979/1993. Images and models, similes and metaphors. In Orton 1979/1993a, 357–400.

Milner, A. David & Melvyn Goodale. 1995. *The visual brain in action*. Oxford: Oxford University Press.

Mithen, Stephen. 1996. *The prehistory of the mind: The cognitive origins of art and science*. London: Thames & Hudson.

1999. Symbolism and the supernatural. In Dunbar et al. 1999, 147–169.

Miyamoto Yuri, Richard Nisbett & Takahiko Masuda. 2006. Culture and the physical environment: Holistic versus analytic perceptual affordances. *Psychological Science* 17: 113–119.

Moura, Antonio & Phyllis Lee. 2004. Capuchin stone tool use in Caatinga dry forest. *Science* 306: 1909.

Mulvenna, Catherine, Edward Hubbard, V. S. Ramachandran & Frank Pollick. 2004. The relationship between synaesthesia and creativity. *Journal of Cognitive Neuroscience Suppl.* 16: 188.

Muraven, Mark, Dianne Tice & Roy Baumeister. 1998. Self-control as a limited resource: Regulatory depletion patterns. *Journal of Personality and Social Psychology* 74: 774–789.

Nagel, Thomas. 1974. What is it like to be a bat? *Philosophical Review* 83: 435–450.

Nanda, Meera. 1998. The epistemic charity of the social constructivist critics of science and why the Third World should refuse the offer. In Koertge 1998, 286–311.

     2000. The science wars in India. *In The Editors of Lingua Franca*, 205–213.

Neisser, Ulric. 1976. *Cognition and reality: Principles and implications of cognitive psychology.* San Francisco: W. H. Freeman.

Nersessian, Nancy. 1992. In the theoretician's laboratory: Thought experimenting as mental modeling. *Proceedings of the Philosophical Association of America* 2: 291–301.

Nichols, Shaun & Stephen Stich. 2003. *Mindreading: An integrated account of pretence, self-awareness, and understanding other minds.* New York: Oxford University Press.

Nieder, Andreas, Ilka Diester & Oana Tudusciuc. 2006. Temporal and spatial enumeration processes in the primate parietal cortex. *Science* 313: 1431–1436.

Nietzsche, Friedrich. 1886/1966. *Beyond good and evil* (trans. Walter Kaufmann). New York: Vintage.

Niffenegger, Audrey. 2003. *The time traveler's wife.* New York: Harvest Books.

Nisbett, Richard. 2003. *The geography of thought: How Asians and Westerners think differently – and why.* London: Nicholas Brealey.

Nisbett, Richard, Kaiping Peng, Incheol Choi & Ara Norenzayan. 2001. Culture and systems of thought: Holistic versus analytic cognition. *Psychological Review* 108: 291–310.

Nisbett, Richard & Timithy Wilson. 1977. Telling more than we can know: Verbal reports on mental processes. *Psychological Review* 84: 231–259.

Nishida, Tomomi. 1987. Local traditions and cultural transmission. In Barbara Smuts, Dorothy Cheney, Robert Seyfarth & Richard Wrangham (eds.), *Primate Societies*, 462–474. Chicago: University of Chicago Press.

Noë, Alva. 2004. *Action in perception.* Cambridge, MA: MIT Press.

Noë, Alva & Evan Thompson (eds.). 2002. *Vision and mind: Selected readings in the philosophy of perception.* Cambridge, MA: MIT Press.

Norenzayan, Ara & Scott Atran. 2004. Cognitive and emotional processes in the cultural transmission of natural and nonnatural beliefs. In Mark Schaller & Christian Crandall (eds.), *The psychological foundations of culture*, 149–169. Mahwah, NJ: Lawrence Erlbaum Associates.

Norenzayan, Ara, Scott Atran, Jason Faulkner & Mark Schaller. 2006. Memory and mystery: The cultural selection of minimally counterintuitive narratives. *Cognitive Science* 30: 531–553.

Norris, Christopher. 1992. *Uncritical theory: Postmodernism, intellectuals and the Gulf War.* Amherst: University of Massachusetts Press.

Núñez, Rafael & Walter J. Freeman (eds.). 1999. *Reclaiming cognition: The primacy of action, intention and emotion.* Bowling Green, OH: Imprint Academic.

Nussbaum, Martha. 1988. Non-relative virtues: An Aristotelian account. In Peter French (ed.), *Midwest studies in philosophy.* Vol. 13: *Ethical theory: Character and virtue*, 32–53. Notre Dame, IN: University of Notre Dame Press.

     2001. *Upheavals of thought: The intelligence of the emotions.* Cambridge: Cambridge University Press.

Oakley, Todd. 2005. Force-dynamical dimensions of rhetorical effect. In Hampe 2005, 443–473.

Oden, David, Roger Thompson & David Premack. 2001. Can an ape reason analogically? Comprehension and production of analogical problems by Sarah, a chimpanzee (*Pan troglodytes*). In Gentner et al. 2001, 471–497.

O'Gorman, Rick, David Wilson & Ralph Miller. 2005. Altruistic punishment and helping differ in sensitivity to relatedness, friendship, and future interactions. *Evolution and Human Behavior* 26: 375–387.

Olds, Linda. 1991. Chinese metaphors of interrelatedness: Re-imagining body, nature, and the feminine. *Contemporary Philosophy* 13: 16–22.

Onishi, Kristine & Renée Baillargeon. 2005. Do 15-month-old infants understand false belief? *Science* 308: 255–258.

Orlov, Tanya, Daniel Amit, Volodya Yakovlev, Ehud Zohary & Shaul Hochstein. 2006. Memory of ordinal number categories in macaque monkeys. *Journal of Cognitive Neuroscience* 18: 399–417.

Ortman, Scott. 2000. Conceptual metaphor in the archaeological record: Methods and an example from the American Southwest. *American Antiquity* 65: 613–645.

Ortony, Andrew (ed.). 1979/1993a. *Metaphor and thought.* 2nd ed. Cambridge: Cambridge University Press.

   1979/1993b. The role of similarity in similes and metaphors. In Ortony 1979/1993a, 342–356.

Ortony, Andrew, Gerlad Clore & Allan Collins. 1990. *The cognitive structure of emotion.* Cambridge: Cambridge University Press.

Pascual-Leone, Alvaro & Fernando Torres. 1993. Plasticity in the sensorimotor cortex representation of the reading finger in Braille readers. *Brain* 116: 39–52.

Paul, Elizabeth, Emma Harding & Michael Mendl. 2005. Measuring emotional processes in animals: The utility of a cognitive approach. *Neuroscience and Behavioral Reviews* 29: 469–491.

Pecher, Diane, René Zeelenberg & Lawrence Barsalou. 2003. Verifying different-modality properties for concepts produces switching costs. *Psychological Science* 14: 119–124.

Pecher, Diane & Rolf Zwaan (eds.). 2005. *Grounding cognition: The role of perception and action in memory, language and thinking.* Cambridge: Cambridge University Press.

Peirce, Charles Sanders. 1868/1992. Some consequences of four incapacities. In Nathan Houser & Christian Kloesel (eds.), *The essential Peirce: Selected philosophical writings.* Vol. 1, 28–55. Bloomington: Indiana University Press. (Originally published in *Journal of Speculative Philosophy* 2: 140–157.)

   1905/1992. What pragmatism is. In Nathan Houser & Christian Kloesel (eds.), *The essential Peirce: Selected philosophical writings.* Vol. 2, 331–345. Bloomington: Indiana University Press. (Originally published in *The Monist* 15: 161–181.)

Pennisi, Elizabeth. 2006. Social animals prove their smarts. *Science* 312: 1734–1738.

Penrose, Roger. 1989. *The emperor's new mind: Concerning computers, minds, and the laws of physics.* New York: Oxford University Press.

Perani, Daniela & Jubin Abutalebi. 2005. The neural basis of first and second language processing. *Current Opinion in Neurobiology* 15: 202–206.

Perner, Josef & Ted Ruffman. 2005. Infants' insight into the mind: How deep? *Science* 308: 214–216.

Pessoa, Luiz. 2005. To what extent are emotional visual stimuli processed without attention and awareness? *Current Opinion in Neurobiology* 15: 188–196.

Phillips, Ann & Henry Wellman. 2005. Infants' understanding of object-directed action. *Cognition* 98: 137–155.

Piaget, Jean. 1954. *The construction of reality in the child* (trans. Margaret Cook). New York: Basic Books.

Pica, Pierre, Cathy Lemer, Véronique Izard & Stanislas Dehaene. 2004. Exact and approximate arithmetic in an Amazonian Indigene group. *Science* 306: 499–503.

Pinker, Steven. 1994. *The language instinct.* New York: HarperCollins.

1997. *How the mind works.* New York: Norton.

2002. *The blank slate: The modern denial of human nature.* New York: Viking.

Pinker, Steven & Paul Bloom. 1992. Natural language and natural selection. In Barkow et al. 1992, 451–494.

Polanyi, Michael. 1967. *The tacit dimension.* Garden City, NY: Doubleday.

Poldrack, Russell. 2006. Can cognitive processes be inferred from neuroimaging data? *Trends in Cognitive Sciences* 10: 59–63.

Pollitt, Katha. 2000. Pomolotov cocktail and selected responses. In The Editors of *Lingua Franca* 2000, 96–100.

Popper, Karl. 1934/1959. *The logic of scientific discovery.* London: Hutchinson.

Poundstone, William. 1985. *The recursive universe: Cosmic complexity and the limits of scientific knowledge.* New York: Morrow.

Povinelli, Daniel. 2000. *Folk physics for apes.* New York: Oxford University Press.

Povinelli, Daniel & Jennifer Vonk. 2003. Chimpanzee minds: Suspiciously human? *Trends in Cognitive Science* 7: 157–160.

Pratt, Chris & Paula Bryant. 1990. Young children understand that looking leads to knowing. *Child Development* 61: 973–983.

Premack, David & Ann Premack. 1983. *The mind of an ape.* New York: Norton.

1995. Origins of human social competence. In Michael Gazzaniga (ed.), *The Cognitive neuroscience,* 205–218. Cambridge, MA: MIT Press.

2003. *Original intelligence: Unlocking the mysteries of who we are.* New York: McGraw Hill.

Preston, Jesse & Nicholas Epley. 2005. Explanations versus applications: The explanatory power of valuable beliefs. *Psychological Science* 16: 826–832.

Preston, Stephanie & Frans de Waal. 2002. Empathy: Its ultimate and proximate bases. *Behavioral and Brain Sciences* 25: 1–72.

Price, Michael. 2005. Punitive sentiment among the Shuar and in industrialized societies: Cross-cultural similarities. *Evolution and Human Behavior* 26: 279–287.

Prinz, Jesse. 2005. Passionate thoughts: The emotional embodiment of moral concepts. In Pecher & Zwaan 2005, 93–114.

2006. *Gut reactions: A perceptual theory of emotion.* New York: Oxford University Press.

Pulvermüller, Friedemann. 1999. Words in the brain's language. *Behavioral and Brain Sciences* 22: 253–336.

Putnam, Hilary. 1973. Reductionism and the nature of psychology. *Cognition* 2: 131–146.

1981. The "corroboration" of theories. In Hacking 1981, 60–79.

1990. *Realism with a human face* (ed. James Conant). Cambridge, MA: Harvard University Press.

1999. *The threefold cord: Mind, body, and world.* New York: Columbia University Press.

Pylyshyn, Zenon. 1980. Computation and cognition: Issues in the foundation of cognitive science. *Behavioral and Brain Sciences* 3: 111–134.

1981. The imagery debate: Analogue media vs. tacit knowledge. *Psychological Review* 88: 16–45.

2003. Mental imagery: In search of a theory. *Behavioral and Brain Sciences* 25: 157–237.

Quine, Willard Van Orman. 1951. Two dogmas of empiricism. *The Philosophical Review* 60: 20–43.

1960. *Word and object*. Cambridge, MA: MIT Press.

1969. Epistemology naturalized. In W. V. O. Quine (ed.), *Ontological relativity and other essays*, 69–90. New York: Columbia University Press.

Quinn, Naomi. 1991. The cultural basis of metaphor. In Fernandez 1991, 56–93.

Rakison, David & Diane Poulin-Dubois. 2001. Developmental origin of the animate–inanimate distinction. *Psychological Bulletin* 127: 209–228.

Ramachandran, V. S. 2004. *A brief tour of human consciousness: From imposter poodles to purple numbers*. New York: PI Press.

Ramachandran, V. S. & Sandra Blakeslee. 1998. *Phantoms in the brain*. New York: Quill.

Ramachandran, V. S. & Edward Hubbard. 2001a. Psychophysical investigations into the neural basis of synaesthesia. *Proceedings of the Royal Society of London B: Biological Sciences* 268: 979–983.

2001b. Synaesthesia: A window into perception, thought and language. *Journal of Consciousness Studies* 8: 3–34.

2003. Hearing colors, tasting shapes. *Scientific American* (May): 53–59.

Rauschecker, Josef. 1995. Compensatory plasticity and sensory substitution in a cerebral cortex. *Trends in Neurosciences* 18: 36–43.

Redelmeier, Donald & Daniel Kahneman. 1996. Patients' memories of painful medical treatments: Real-time and retrospective evaluations of two minimally invasive procedures. *Pain* 66: 3–8.

Redelmeier, Donald, Joel Katz & Daniel Kahneman. 2003. Memories of colonoscopy: A randomized trial. *Pain* 104: 187–194.

Regier, Terry. 1996. *The human semantic potential: Spatial language and constrained connectionism*. Cambridge, MA: MIT Press.

Rensink, Ron, J. O'Regan & J. Clark. 1997. To see or not to see: The need for attention to perceive changes in scenes. *Psychological Science* 8: 368–373.

Richards, I. A. 1936. *The philosophy of rhetoric*. New York: Oxford University Press.

Richards, Janet Radcliffe. 1996. Why feminist epistemology isn't. In Paul Gross et al. 1996, 385–412.

Richardson, Daniel, Michael Spivey, Lawrence Barsalou & Ken McRae. 2003. Spatial representations activated during real-time comprehension of verbs. *Cognitive Science* 27: 767–780.

Richardson, Daniel, Michael Spivey, Shimon Edelman & Adam Naples. 2001. Language is spatial: Experimental evidence for image schemas of concrete and abstract verbs. *Proceedings of the Twenty-third Annual Meeting of the Cognitive Science Society*, 873–878. Mahwah, NJ: Lawrence Erlbaum Associates.

Richerson, Peter & Robert Boyd. 2004. *Not by genes alone: How culture transformed human evolution*. Chicago: University of Chicago Press.

Ricoeur, Paul. 1977. *The rule of metaphor* (trans. Robert Czerny). Toronto: University of Toronto Press.

1981. Creativity in language: Word, polysemy, and metaphor. In Charles Reagan & David Stewart (eds.), *The philosophy of Paul Ricoeur: An anthology of his work*, 120–133. Boston: Beacon Press.

Rizzolatti, Giacomo & Michael Arbib. 1998. Language within our grasp. *Trends in Neuroscience* 21: 188–194.

Rizzolatti, Giacomo & Laila Craighero. 2004. The mirror neuron system. *Annual Review of Neuroscience* 27: 169–192.

Rizzolatti, Giacomo, Luciano Fadiga, Vittorio Gallese & Leonardo Fogassi. 1996. Premotor cortex and the recognition of motor actions. *Cognitive Brain Research* 3: 131–141.

Rizzolatti, Giacomo, Leonardo Fogassi & Vittorio Gallese. 2001. Neurophysiological mechanisms underlying the understanding and imitation of action. *Nature Reviews Neuroscience* 2: 661–670.

Robbins, Bruce & Andrew Ross. 2000. Response: Mystery Science Theater. In The Editors of *Lingua Franca* 2000, 54–58.

Robertson, Lynn & Noam Sagiv (eds.). 2005. *Synaesthesia: Perspectives from cognitive neuroscience*. New York: Oxford University Press.

Röder, Brigitte, Wolfgang Teder-Sälejärvi, Anette Sterr, Frank Rösler, Steven Hillyard & Helen J. Neville. 1999. Improved auditory special tuning in blind humans. *Nature* 400: 162–166.

Rohrer, Tim. 1995. The metaphorical logic of (political) rape: George Bush and the new world order. *Metaphor and Symbolic Activity* 10: 113–131.

2001. Pragmatism, ideology and embodiment: William James and the philosophical foundations of cognitive linguistics. In Rene Dirven (ed.), *Language and ideology: Cognitive theoretical approaches*. Vol. 1, 49–81. Amsterdam: John Benjamins.

2005. Image schemata in the brain. In Hampe 2005, 165–196.

Rorty, Amélie Oksenberg (ed.). 1980a. *Essays on Aristotle's ethics*. Berkeley: University of California Press.

1980b. *Explaining emotions*. Berkeley: University of California Press.

Rorty, Richard. 1970. In defense of eliminative materialism. *Review of Metaphysics* 24: 112–121.

1979. *Philosophy and the mirror of nature*. Princeton: Princeton University Press.

1980. Pragmatism, relativism, and irrationalism. *Proceedings and Addresses of the American Philosophical Association* 53: 717, 719–738.

1991. *Objectivity, relativism, and truth*. Cambridge: Cambridge University Press.

Rosch, Eleanor. 1973. Natural categories. *Cognitive Psychology* 4: 328–350.

1975. Cognitive representations of semantic categories. *Journal of Experimental Psychology* 104: 192–233.

Rosch, Eleanor, Carolyn Mervis, Wayne Gray, David Johnson & Penny Boyes-Braem. 1976. Basic objects in natural categories. *Cognitive Psychology* 8: 382–439.

Rose, Hilary & Steven Rose. (eds.) 2000. *Alas, poor Darwin! Arguments against evolutionary psychology*. New York: Harmony Books.

Rosen, Edward. 1947. *The naming of the telescope*. New York: Henry Schuman.

Rosenzweig, Mark, S. Marc Breedlove & Neil Watson. 2005. *Biological psychology: An introduction to behavioral and cognitive neuroscience*. 4th ed. Sunderland, MA: Sinauer Associates.

Rozin, Paul & Carol Nemeroff. 1990. The laws of sympathetic magic. In James Stigler, Richard Schweder & Gilbert Herdt (eds.), *Cultural Psychology: The Chicago symposia on human development*, 205–232. Cambridge: Cambridge University Press.

Ruffman, Ted, Wendy Garnham, Arlina Import & Dan Connolly. 2001. Does eye gaze indicate knowledge of false belief? Charting transitions in knowledge. *Journal of Experimental Child Psychology* 80: 201–224.

Ruffman, Ted, Lance Slade & Jessica Redman. 2005. Young infants' expectations about hidden objects. *Cognition* 97: 35–43.

Rumbaugh, Duane & David Washburn. 2003. *Intelligence of apes and other rational beings.* New Haven, CT: Yale University Press.

Ruse, Michael. 1998. *Taking Darwin seriously: A naturalistic approach to philosophy.* 2nd ed. Oxford: Basil Blackwell.

   2001. *Can a Darwinian be a Christian? The relationship between science and religion.* New York: Cambridge University Press.

Ryle, Gilbert. 1949. *The concept of mind.* London: Hutchinson.

   1971. "The thinking of thoughts: What is 'le penseur' doing?" In *Collected papers.* Vol. 2, 480–496. London: Hutchinson.

Sacks, Oliver. 1995. *An anthropologist on Mars: Seven paradoxical tales.* New York: Alfred Knopf.

Sandler, Wendy, Irit Meir, Carol Padden & Mark Aronoff. 2005. The emergence of grammar: Systematic structure in a new language. *Proceedings of the National Academy of Sciences* 102: 2661–2665.

Sanz, Crickette, Dave Morgan & Steve Gulick. 2004. New insights into chimpanzees, tools, and termites from the Congo basin. *The American Naturalist* 164: 567–581.

Schick, Theodore (ed.). 2000. *Readings in the philosophy of science: From positivism to postmodernism.* London: Mayfield.

Schmid, D. Neil. 2002. Yuanqi: Medieval Buddhist narratives from Dunhuang. Ph.D. diss., University of Pennsylvania.

Schooler, Jonathan & Tanya Engstler-Schooler. 1990. Verbal overshadowing of visual memories: Some things are better left unsaid. *Cognitive Psychology* 22: 36–71.

Schooler, Jonathan & Charles Schreiber. 2004. Experience, meta-consciousness, and the paradox of introspection. *Journal of Consciousness Studies* 11: 17–39.

Schreiber, Charles & Daniel Kahneman. 2000. Determinants of the remembered utility of aversive sounds. *Journal of Experimental Psychology: General* 129: 27–42.

Searle, John. 1980. Minds, brains, and programs. *Behavioral and Brain Sciences* 3: 417–457.

   1983. *Intentionality.* Cambridge: Cambridge University Press.

   1992. *The rediscovery of the mind.* Cambridge, MA: MIT Press.

   1995. *The construction of social reality.* New York: Free Press.

   1997. *The mystery of consciousness.* New York: New York Review of Books.

   2004. *Mind: A brief introduction.* New York: Oxford University Press.

Sebanz, Natalie, Harold Bekkering & Günther Knoblich. 2006. Joint action: Bodies and minds moving together. *Trends in Cognitive Sciences* 10: 70–76.

Segerstråle, Ullica. 2000. *Defenders of the truth: The battle for sociobiology and beyond.* New York: Oxford University Press.

Sellars, Wilfrid. 1963. *Science, perception, and reality.* London: Routledge & Kegan Paul.

Senghas, Ann, Sotaro Kita & Asli Özyürek. 2004. Children creating core properties of language: Evidence from an emerging sign language in Nicaragua. *Science* 305: 1779–1782.

Shapere, Dudley. 1981. Meaning and scientific change. In Hacking 1981, 28–59.

Shen, Vincent. 2003. Some thoughts on intercultural philosophy and Chinese philosophy. *Journal of Chinese Philosophy* 30: 357–372.

Shepard, Roger & Lynn Cooper. 1982. *Mental images and their transformations.* Cambridge, MA: MIT Press.

Silverman, Irwin & Jean Choi. 2005. Locating places. In Buss 2005, 177–199.

Simmons, Kyle & Lawrence Barsalou. 2003. The similarity-in-topography principle: Reconciling theories of conceptual deficits. *Cognitive Neuropsychology* 20: 451–486.

Simmons, W. Kyle, Diane Pecher, Stephan Hamann, René Zeelenberg & Lawrence Barsalou. 2003. fMRI evidence for modality-specific processing of conceptual knowledge on six modalities. *Meeting for the Society of Cognitive Neuroscience*. New York.

Simon, Herbert. 1956. Rational choice and the structure of the environment. *Psychological Review* 63: 129–138.

Simons, Daniel & Christopher Chabris. 1999. Gorillas in our midst: Sustained inattentional blindness for dynamic events. *Perception* 28: 1059–1074.

Simons, Daniel & Daniel Levin. 1997. Change blindness. *Trends in Cognitive Science* 1: 261–267.

Sinha, Chris & Kristine Jensen de Lopez. 2000. Language, culture and the embodiment of spatial cognition. *Cognitive Linguistics* 11: 17–41.

Slingerland, Edward. 2000. Why philosophy is not 'extra' in understanding the *Analects*, a review of Brooks and Brooks, *The original Analects*. *Philosophy East and West* 50.1: 137–141, 146–147.

  2003. *Effortless action: Wu-wei as conceptual metaphor and spiritual ideal in early China.* New York: Oxford University Press.

  2004a. Conceptions of the self in the *Zhuangzi*: Conceptual metaphor analysis and comparative thought. *Philosophy East and West* 54: 322–342.

  2004b. Conceptual metaphor theory as methodology for comparative religion. *Journal of the American Academy of Religion* 72: 1–31.

  2005. Conceptual blending, somatic marking, and normativity: A case example from ancient Chinese. *Cognitive Linguistics* 16: 557–584.

Slingerland, Edward, Eric Blanchard & Lyn Boyd-Judson. 2007. Collision with China: Conceptual metaphor analysis, somatic marking, and the EP-3 incident. *International Studies Quarterly* 51: 53–77.

Slone, D. Jason. 2004. *Theological incorrectness: Why religious people believe what they shouldn't.* New York: Oxford University Press.

Smilek, Daniel, Mike Dixon, Cera Cudahy & Philip Merikle. 2001. Synaesthetic photisms influence visual perception. *Journal of Cognitive Neuroscience* 13: 930–936.

Smith, Carol, Joseph Snir & Lorraine Grosslight. 1992. Using conceptual models to facilitate conceptual change: The case of weight/density differentiation. *Cognition and Instruction* 9: 221–283.

Smith, William Cantwell. 1959. The comparative study of religion – Whither and why? In Mircea Eliade & Joseph Kitagawa (eds.), *The history of religions: Essays in methodology*, 31–58. Chicago: University of Chicago Press.

Sokal, Alan. 1996. Transgressing the boundaries: Toward a transformative hermeneutics of quantum gravity. *Social Text* 46/47: 217–252.

  2000a. Revelation: A physicist experiments with cultural studies. In The Editors of *Lingua Franca*, 49–53.

  2000b. Why I wrote my parody. In The Editors of *Lingua Franca*, 127–129.

Sokal, Alan & Bricmont, Jean. 1998. *Fashionable nonsense: Postmodern intellectuals' abuse of science.* New York: Picador.

Solomon, Robert (ed.). 2003. *What is an emotion? Classic and contemporary readings.* New York: Oxford University Press.

2004. *Thinking about feeling: Contemporary philosophers on emotion.* New York: Oxford University Press.

Song, Hyun-joo, Renée Baillargeon & Cynthia Fisher. 2005. Can infants attribute to an agent a disposition to perform a particular action? *Cognition* 98: B45–B55.

Spelke, Elizabeth. 1985. Preferential looking methods as tools for the study of cognition in infancy. In Gilbert Gottlieb & Norman Krasnegor (eds.), *Measurement of audition and vision in the first year of postnatal life,* 323–363. Norwood, NJ: Ablex.

1991. Physical knowledge in infancy: Reflections on Piaget's theory. In Carey & Gelman 1991, 133–169.

1994. Initial knowledge: Six suggestions. *Cognition* 50: 433–447.

Spelke, Elizabeth, Ann Phillips & Amanda Woodward. 1995. Infants' knowledge of object motion and human action. In Sperber et al. 1995, 44–78.

Sperber, Daniel 1985. Anthropology and psychology: Towards an epidemiology of representations. *Man* 20: 73–89.

1994. The modularity of thought and the epidemiology of representations. In Hirschfeld & Gelman 1994a, 39–67.

1996. *Explaining culture: A naturalistic approach.* Oxford: Basil Blackwell.

Sperber, Daniel & Lawrence Hirschfeld. 2004. The cognitive foundations of cultural stability and diversity. *Trends in Cognitive Sciences* 8: 40–46.

Sperber, Daniel, David Premack & Ann Premack (eds.). 1995. *Causal cognition: A multidisciplinary debate.* New York: Oxford University Press.

Spivey, Michael & Joy Geng. 2001. Oculomotor mechanisms activated by imagery and memory: Eye movements to absent images. *Psychological Research* 65: 235–241.

Spivey, Michael, Daniel Richardson & Monica Gozalez-Marquez. 2005. On the perceptual-motor and image-schematic infrastructure of language. In Pecher & Zwaan 2005, 246–281.

Stanfield, Robert & Rolf Zwaan. 2001. The effect of implied orientation derived from verbal context on picture recognition. *Psychological Science* 121: 153–156.

Steen, Francis & Stephanie Owens. 2001. Evolution's pedagogy: An adaptationist model of pretense and entertainment. *Journal of Cognition and Culture* 1: 289–321.

Sternberg, Robert (ed.). 1988. *The nature of creativity: Contemporary psychological perspectives.* Cambridge: Cambridge University Press

1999. *Handbook of creativity.* Cambridge: Cambridge University Press.

Stich, Stephen. 1990. *The fragmentation of reason.* Cambridge, MA: MIT Press.

Styron, William. 1992. *Darkness visible.* New York: Random House.

Sugiyama, Lawrence, John Tooby & Leda Cosmides. 2002. Cross-cultural evidence of cognitive adaptations for social exchange among the Shiwiar of Ecuadorian Amazonia. *Proceedings of the National Academy of Sciences* 99: 11537–11542.

Sweetser, Eve. 1987. The definition of "lie." In Dorothy Holland & Naomi Quinn (eds.), *Cultural models in language and thought,* 43–66. Cambridge: Cambridge University Press.

1990. *From etymology to pragmatics: Metaphorical and cultural aspects of semantic structure.* Cambridge: Cambridge University Press.

Sweetser, Eve & Barbara Dancygier. 2005. *Mental spaces in grammar: Conditional constructions.* New York: Cambridge University Press.

Swindale, Nicholas. 2001. Cortical cartography: What's in a map? *Current Biology* 11: R764–767.

Talmy, Leonard. 1988. Force dynamics in language and cognition. *Cognitive Science* 12: 49–100.

   2000. *Towards a cognitive semantics.* (2 vols.) Cambridge, MA: MIT Press.

Tanel, Daniel, Hannah Damasio & Antonio Damasio. 1997. A neural basis for the retrieval of conceptual knowledge. *Neuropsychologia* 35: 1319–1327.

Taub, Sarah. 2001. *Language from the body: Iconicity and metaphor in American Sign Language.* Cambridge: Cambridge University Press.

Taylor, Charles. 1989. *Sources of the self: The makings of modern identity.* Cambridge, MA: Harvard University Press.

   1992. *The ethics of authenticity.* Cambridge, MA: Harvard University Press.

Terranova, Tiziana. 2004. Communication beyond meaning: On the cultural politics of information. *Social Text* 22: 51–73.

Thach, W. Thomas, Howard Goodkin & James Keating. 1992. The cerebellum and the adaptive coordination of movement. *Annual Review of Neuroscience* 15: 403–442.

The Editors of *Lingua Franca* (eds.). 2000. *The Sokal hoax: The sham that shook the Academy.* Lincoln: University of Nebraksha Press.

Thompson, Evan. 2007. *Mind in life: Biology, phenomenology, and the sciences of mind.* Cambridge, MA: Harvard University Press.

Thornhill, Randy & Craig Palmer. 2000. *A natural history of rape: Biological bases of sexual coercion.* Cambridge, MA: MIT Press.

Tillich, Paul. 1957. *The dynamics of faith.* New York: Harper.

Tomasello, Michael, Josep Call & Brian Hare. 2003. Chimpanzees understand psychological states – The question is which ones and to what extent. *Trends in Cognitive Science* 7: 153–156.

Tooby, John & Leda Cosmides. 1990. The past explains the present: Emotional adaptations and the structure of ancestral environments. *Ethology and Sociobiology* 11: 375–424.

   1992. Psychological foundations of culture. In Barkow et al. 1992, 19–136.

   2005. Conceptual foundations of evolutionary psychology. In Buss 2005, 5–67.

Tranel, Daniel & Antonio Damasio. 1993. The covert learning of affective valence does not require structures in hippocampal system or amygdala. *Journal of Cognitive Neuroscience* 5: 79–88.

Tranel, Daniel, Hannah Damasio & Antonio Damasio. 1997. A neural basis for the retrieval of conceptual knowledge. *Neuropsychologia* 35: 1319–1327.

Trivers, Robert. 1971. The evolution of reciprocal altruism. *Quarterly Review of Biology* 46: 35–57.

   1972. Parental investment and sexual selection. In Bernard Campbell (ed.), *Sexual selection and the descent of man,* 136–179. Chicago: Aldine Atherton.

   1974. Parent-offspring conflict. *American Zoologist* 14: 249–264.

Tsao, Doris, Winrich Freiwald, Roger Tootell & Margaret Livingstone. 2006. A cortical region consisting entirely of face-selective cells. *Science* 311: 670–674.

Turnbull, Oliver, Cathryn Evans, Alys Bunce, Barbara Carzolio & Jane O'Connor. 2005. Emotion-based learning and central executive resources: An investigation of intuition and the Iowa Gambling Task. *Brain and Cognition* 57: 244–247.

Turnbull, Oliver & Cathryn Evans. 2006. Preserved complex emotion-based learning in amnesia. *Neuropsychologia* 44: 300–306.

Tversky, Amos. 1977. Features of similarity. *Psychological Review* 84: 327–352.

Tversky, Amos & Daniel Kahneman. 1974. Judgment under uncertainty: Heuristics and biases. *Science* 185: 1124–1131.

Umiltà, Alessandra, Evelyne Kohler, Vittorio Gallese, Leonardo Fogassi, Luciano Fadiga, Christian Keysers & Giacomo Rizzolatti. 2001. I know what you are doing: A neurophysiological study. *Neuron* 31: 155–165.

Ungerleider, Leslie & Mortimer Mishkin. 1982. Two cortical visual systems. In D. J. Ingle, M. A. Goodale & R. J. W. Mansfield (eds.), *Analysis of visual behavior*, 549–586. Cambridge, MA: MIT Press.

Van Fraassen, Bas. 1980. *The scientific image.* Oxford: Oxford University Press.

Vanhaeren, Marian, Francesco d'Errico, Chris Stringer, Sarah James, Jonathan Todd & Henk Mienis. 2006. Middle Paleolithic shell beads in Israel and Algeria. *Science* 23: 1785–1788.

Varela, Francisco, Evan Thompson & Eleanor Rosch. 1991. *The embodied mind: Cognitive science and human experience.* Cambridge, MA: MIT Press.

Vonnegut, Kurt, Jr. 1982. *Palm Sunday.* New York: Dell.

Vosniadou, Stella. 1994. Universal and culture-specific properties of children's mental models of the earth. In Hirshfeld & Gelman 1994, 412–430.

Wang, Su-Hua, Renée Baillargeon & Sarah Paterson. 2005. Detecting continuity violations in infancy: A new account and new evidence from covering and tube events. *Cognition* 95: 129–173.

Ward, Jamie, Brett Huckstep & Elias Tsakanikos. 2006. Sound-colour synaesthesia: To what extent does it use cross-modal mechanisms common to us all? *Cortex* 42: 264–280.

Warrington, Elizabeth & Rosaleen McCarthy. 1983. Category-specific access dysphasia. *Brain* 106: 859–878.

Warrington, Elizabeth & Tim Shallice. 1984. Category-specific semantic impairments. *Brain* 107: 829–854.

Watson, Burton (trans.). 2003. *Zhuangzi: Basic writings.* New York: Columbia University Press.

Wegner, Daniel. 2002. *The illusion of conscious will.* Cambridge, MA: MIT Press.

Weiskrantz, Lawrence (ed.). 1988. *Thought without language.* New York: Oxford University Press.

Weiss, Gail & Honi Fern Haber (eds.). 1999. *Perspectives on embodiment: The intersections of nature and culture.* New York: Routledge.

Weld, Susan. 1999. Chu law in action: Legal documents from tomb 2 at Baoshan. In Constance Cook & John Major (eds.), *Defining Chu: Image and reality in early China*, 77–97. Honolulu: University of Hawaii Press.

Wellman, Henry. 1990. *The child's theory of mind.* Cambridge, MA: MIT Press.

Wellman, Henry, David Cross & Julanne Watson. 2001. Meta-analysis of theory-of-mind development: The truth about false belief. *Child Development* 72: 655–684.

Wexler, Mark, Stephen Kosslyn & Alain Berthoz. 1998. Motor processes in mental rotation. *Cognition* 68: 77–94.

Wheatley, Thalia & Jonathan Haidt. 2005. Hypnoptic disgust makes moral judgments more severe. *Psychological Science* 16: 780–784.

Whiten, Andrew. 2005a. The second inheritance system of chimpanzees and humans. *Nature* 437: 52–55.

2005b. Animal culture is real but needs to be clearly defined. *Nature* 438: 1078.

Whiten, Andrew, Victoria Horner & Frans de Waal. 2005. Conformity to cultural norms of tool use in chimpanzees. *Nature* 439: 1–4.

Whorf, Benjamin Lee. 1956. *Language, thought, and reality: Selected writings of Benjamin Lee Whorf.* Cambridge, MA: MIT Press.

Wiemer-Hastings, Katja & Xu Xu. 2005. Content differences for abstract and concrete concepts. *Cognitive Science* 29: 719–736.

Wiggins, David. 1980. Deliberation and practical reason. In A. Rorty 1989a, 221–240.

Wilcox, Phyllis. 2001. *Metaphor in American Sign Language.* Washington, DC: Gallaudet University Press.

Williams, Bernard. 1985. *Ethics and the limits of philosophy.* Cambridge MA: Harvard University Press.

Willingham, Daniel & Elizabeth Dunn. 2003. What neuroimaging and brain localization can do, cannot do, and should not do for social psychology. *Journal of Personality and Social Psychology* 85: 662–671.

Wilson, Edward O. 1975/2000. *Sociobiology: The new synthesis* (25th anniversary ed., 2000). Cambridge, MA: Harvard University Press.

    1978. *On human nature.* Cambridge, MA: Harvard University Press.

    1998. *Consilience: The unity of knowledge.* New York: Alfred Knopf.

Wilson, Margaret. 2002. Six views of embodied cognition. *Psychonomic Bulletin and Review* 9: 625–636.

Wilson, Timothy. 2002. *Strangers to ourselves: Discovering the adaptive unconscious.* Cambridge, MA: Harvard University Press.

Wilson, Timothy, Dolores Kraft & Dana Dunn. 1989. The disruptive effects of explaining attitudes: The moderating effect of knowledge about the attitude object. *Journal of Experimental Social Psychology* 25: 379–400.

Wilson, Timothy & Richard Nisbett. 1978. The accuracy of verbal reports about the effects of stimuli on evaluations and behavior. *Social Psychology* 41: 118–131.

Wilson, Timothy & Jonathan Schooler. 1991. Thinking too much: Introspection can reduce the quality of preferences and decisions. *Journal of Personality and Social Psychology* 60: 181–192.

Wilson, William, Graeme Halford, Brett Gray & Steven Phillips. 2001. The STAR-2 model for mapping hierarchically structured analogs. In Gentner et al. 2001, 125–159.

Winawer, Jonthan, Nathan Witthoft, Alex Huk & Lera Boroditsky. 2005. Common mechanisms for processing of perceived, inferred, and imagined visual motion. *Journal of Vision* 5: 491.

Winter, Steven. 2001. *A clearing in the forest: Law, life, and mind.* Chicago: University of Chicago Press.

Wolf, Hans-Georg. 1994. *Folk model of the "internal self" in light of the contemporary view of metaphor: The self as subject and object.* Frankfurt: Peter Lang Publishing.

Wynn, Karen. 1992. Addition and subtraction by human infants. *Nature* 358: 768.

Xu, Fei & Elizabeth Spelke. 2000. Large number discrimination in 6-month-old infants. *Cognition* 74: B1–B11.

Yazdi, Amir, Tim German, Margaret Anne Defeyter & Michael Siegal. 2006. Competence and performance in belief-desire reasoning across two cultures: The truth, the whole truth and nothing but the truth about false belief? *Cognition* 100: 343–368.

Yuan, Jinmei. 2006. The role of time in the structure of Chinese logic. *Philosophy East and West* 56.1: 136–152.

Yu Ning. 1998. *The contemporary theory of metaphor: A perspective from Chinese*. Amsterdam: John Benjamins.

2003. Chinese metaphors of thinking. *Cognitive Linguistics* 14: 141–165.

Zajonc, Robert. 1980. Feeling and thinking: Preferences need no inferences. *American Psychologist* 35: 151–175.

1984. On the primacy of affect. *American Psychologist* 39: 117–123.

Zimbardo, Philip, Stephen Laberge & Lisa Butler. 1993. Psychophysiological consequences of unexplained arousal: A posthypnotic suggestion paradigm. *Journal of Abnormal Psychology* 102: 466–473.

Zwaan, Rolf. 2004. The immersed experiencer: Toward an embodied theory of language comprehension. In Brian Ross (ed.), *The psychology of learning and motivation*. Vol. 44, 35–62. New York: Academic Press.

Zwaan, Rolf & Carol Madden. 2005. Embodied sentence comprehension. In Pecher & Zwaan 2005, 224–245.

Zwaan, Rolf, Robert Stanfield & Richard Yaxley. 2002. Language comprehenders mentally represent the shapes of objects. *Psychological Science* 13: 168–171.

Index

Made in the USA
San Bernardino, CA
05 March 2014